# Russian
# Postmodernist
# Fiction

MARK LIPOVETSKY (pen name of Mark Leiderman) specializes in literary theory and contemporary Russian culture. He is the author of two books, *Poetics of the Literary Fairy-Tale* and *The Hard Work of Freedom: Articles on Contemporary Russian Literature* (both in Russian), and of numerous articles and critical essays published in the most popular Russian literary journals and newspapers. In the United States, his essays on Russian postmodernism have been published in the journal *Russian Studies in Literature* and in several collections of articles on contemporary Russian culture. He teaches Russian at Illinois Wesleyan University.

ELIOT BORENSTEIN specializes in twentieth-century Russian literature and culture. He has published articles on the fiction of the 1920s, Russian sexual discourse, and post-Soviet religious cults, and he is currently completing a book, *Men Without Women: Masculinity and Revolution in Russian Literature, 1917–1929.* Professor Borenstein received his doctorate from the University of Wisconsin–Madison. He teaches Russian and Slavic studies at New York University.

# Russian Postmodernist Fiction

## Dialogue with Chaos

Mark Lipovetsky

Edited by
Eliot Borenstein

*M.E. Sharpe*
Armonk, New York
London, England

**Library of Congress Cataloging-in-Publication Data**

Lipovetskiĭ, M.N. (Mark Naumovich)
Russian postmodernist fiction : dialogue with chaos / by Mark Lipovetsky;
edited by Eliot Borenstein.
p. cm.
Includes bibliographical references and index.
ISBN 0-7656-0176-1 (c : alk. paper).—ISBN 0-7656-0177-X (p : alk. paper)
1. Russian fiction—20th century—History and criticism.
2. Postmodernism (Literature)—Soviet Union.
3. Postmodernism (Literature)—Russia (Federation).
I. Borenstein, Eliot, 1966– . II. Title.
PG3098.4.L475    1998
891.73′4409113—dc21
98-7649
CIP

Printed in the United States of America

The paper used in this publication meets the minimum requirements of
American National Standard for Information Sciences—
Permanence of Paper for Printed Library Materials,
ANSI Z 39.48-1984.

MV (c)   10   9   8   7   6   5   4   3   2   1
MV (p)   10   9   8   7   6   5   4   3   2   1

*In Loving Memory of Valentina Andreevna Mikhailova*

# Contents

## I. Introduction

## II. Culture as Chaos

## III. The Poetics of Chaosmos

## IV. Conclusion

# Guide to Appendix: Biographical and Bibliographical Notes

# Acknowledgments

The genre of acknowledgments is not a standard part of Russian publishing etiquette, so I am happy to take advantage of this Western tradition and thank those who inspired and assisted me while I was working on this project. Any book, even a scholarly one, reflects the life of the author; at the very least, it represents a significant part of his or her life. This one is the product of my own post-Soviet "five-year plan," which covered the years between 1992 and 1997. And most of the people to whom I owe a debt of gratitude are not only my colleagues but my close and beloved friends.

First and foremost, I want to thank Eliot Borenstein for his cheerful support, hard work, and friendly advice as both editor and cotranslator of this book. He has made the whole process a rewarding experience for me. Eliot provided the introduction and translated chapters 1 (the section on "Postmodernism Plus/Minus Modernism"), 2, 3, 5, 10, and 11 and thoroughly edited the other chapters as well. The remainder of Chapter 1 was translated by Alexey Panchenko of the University of Oregon, a consummate professional who is also my old and trusted friend. Dianne Sattinger Goldstaub translated the articles that served as the basis for parts of Chapter 7 (the section on Rubinshtein), Chapter 8 (the section on Sokolov's *Astrophobia*), and all of Chapter 9. I am very thankful to Karen Rice McDowell for her translation of Chapter 4; to Maryll Hallet for translating Chapter 6, the Tolstaya and Sokolov sections of Chapter 7, and the Pietsukh and Erofeyev sections of Chapter 8; and to Mirande Bissel for translating part of Chapter 2. I would like gratefully to acknowledge the valuable contributions made by all these people. Without their generous help, this book would never have been completed.

I started this project with the support of the Fulbright program of the United States Information Agency, which sponsored my research and teaching at the University of Pittsburgh's Department of Slavic Languages and Literatures in 1994. I am especially grateful to Laurie Calhoun, the Fulbright program officer at the Council for International Exchange of Scholars, who was a true guardian angel for me and my family. My research on the final chapter was supported by a short-term grant from the Kennan Institute for Advanced Russian Studies in 1995.

Some sections of the book were published earlier as articles; all have been revised, and some of them have been substantially rewritten in part or entirely. Chapter 3 appeared as an essay in the collection *Venedikt Erofeev's Moskva–Petushki: Critical Perspectives,* edited by Karen L. Ryan-Hayes (New York: Peter Lang, 1997), 79–100. Parts of Chapter 7 (on Rubinshtein), Chapter 8 (on *Astrophobia*), and Chapter 9 (on Popov) derive from my essay "Self-Portrait on a Timeless Background: Autobiographical Mode in Russian Literature," published in the journal *a/b: Auto/Biography Studies* 11, no. 2 (Fall 1996): 142–65 (special editor: Marina Balina of Illinois Wesleyan University; editors: Rebecca and Joseph Hogan of University of Wisconsin–Whitewater). I would like to express my gratitude to the aforementioned publishers for permission to reprint the essays that first appeared on their pages. I would also like to thank Lev Rubinshtein for his permission to quote from his poem *Eto—ia (That's Me)*, originally published in *Novyi mir* 1 (1996): 69–76.

I am enormously indebted to Helena Goscilo, my beloved friend, whose intellectual energy has always inspired me. She was (and still is) my wise and wonderful guide in the realm of American scholarship and American life in general, and this book would never have been written without the driving force of her friendship.

My most profound thanks to Marina Balina, my dearest colleague and my true friend, from whose constant professional and personal support I have benefited in ways it is hardly possible to acknowledge.

This book gives me a rare chance to express my love and gratitude to the colleagues whose generous help and continuous encouragement have enabled me to complete my work—Alexander Arkhangelsky, Galina Belaia, Dmitrii Bak, Valentina Brougher, Nancy Condee, Sergei Chuprinin, Evgeny Dobrenko, Mikhail Epstein, Thomas Lahusen, Vladimir Novikov, Vladimir Padunov, the late Aleksandr Pankov, Karen Ryan-Hayes, Yevgeny Shklovsky, Natan Tamarchenko, and many others. I would also like to thank my friends and colleagues from Ural State University and Ural State Pedagogical University.

According to the laws of narratology, the most important is saved for last. My greatest and most personal debts are to:

- My parents: Lilia Vasserman, for her unconditional support and for always being on my side, and Naum Leiderman, who shaped my mind, and always set me an example of genuine professionalism; many of this book's ideas came out of my conversations with him; and
- Tanya Mikhailova, my wife and friend; without her love, emotional inspiration, energetic support, and, most of all, her sharp sense of humor that never let me take myself too seriously, this book would never have seen the light of day.

# Technical Note

The Library of Congress system of transliteration is used in this book whenever unfamiliar Russian words are introduced. It is also used in bibliographical references. For the sake of easier reading, however, when Russian authors are named in the body of the text, we have chosen the most familiar spelling for English readers, although in one case this meant spelling a shared surname in two different ways: the author of *Moscow to the End of the Line* is "Venedikt Erofeev," but the author of "The Parakeet" is "Viktor Erofeyev." When citing primary sources, we have used existing translations when possible, and we refer to the characters' names using whatever spelling was chosen by the translator.

# Editor's Introduction: Postmodernism, Duty-Free

## Eliot Borenstein

Recently one of my colleagues, a professor of French literature, was leafing through my copy of the program for a national conference on Slavic literatures when he stumbled on a panel devoted to Russian postmodernism. He raised his eyebrows, looked up, and asked, "When did postmodernism come to Russia?" The question reveals as much about my colleague's preconceptions about Russia as it does about postmodernism: any cultural development in the former Soviet Union clearly was brought in from the West and would therefore be a late arrival. Postmodernism, it seems, must have been smuggled across the border in a crate full of Snickers or an industrial-sized container of Marlboros; otherwise, how could such a patently subversive cultural import have overcome the obstacle of Russian customs?

Yet my colleague's question is posed repeatedly in Russia itself by representatives of all of the country's diverse ideological camps. The debate has evolved over the years and continues to do so. The question very often takes on the tone of moral imperative: "Should there be postmodernism in Russia?" If nothing else, the term itself has definitely arrived and can even be seen on the pages of respected national newspapers in 24-point headlines. Inevitably, the pendulum of fashion has begun to swing the other way; another of my colleagues, this time a Russian Slavist steeped in French critical theory, recently told me that if he heard the term one more time he could not be held accountable for his actions.

What, then, is the place of postmodernism in Russia? Is it another in a long line of Western cultural imports, the latest concession to cosmopolitanism? Or is it a natural outgrowth of Russian (Soviet) reality, the legitimate counterpart to similar phenomena in North America and Europe? And if Russian postmodernism is *sui generis,* can theoretical models developed in the West be applied to Russian cultural production—and if they can, should they?

Mark Lipovetsky's ambitious and thorough study, *Russian Postmodernist Fiction: Dialogue with Chaos,* is the most comprehensive attempt at addressing these questions to date. This is not to slight the impressive work that has been published on Russian postmodernism in recent years, such as Mikhail Epstein's *After the Future*. But where Epstein's collection of essays focuses on discrete postmodern phenomena (in particular, the works of the conceptualists and late Soviet deformations of language), Lipovetsky develops a model broad enough to encompass most of the trends in Russian postmodernism, a model that has significant ramifications for Western postmodernism as well.

For Lipovetsky, Russian postmodernism is both an integral part of a worldwide phenomenon and a product of the Russian cultural reality. Lipovetsky firmly links postmodernism to the modernist tradition, tracing such key postmodern features as self-referentiality to their roots in the Russian metafiction of the 1920s, which addresses two issues at once, one "global," the other "local": Lipovetsky is implicitly arguing for a model of at least limited continuity between modernism and postmodernism, a question that is debated by theorists the world over; by the same token, his demonstration of postmodernism's Russian modernist roots disarms nationalist critics who claim that postmodernism is merely an ill-suited Western import. Of course, in the first decades of the twentieth century, Russian modernism was also seen by many in Russia as an inappropriate imitation of European models, but the movement's repression by the Soviet regime has surrounded high modernism with an impenetrable aura of martyrdom: thanks to the passage of time and the backlash against official Socialist Realism, modernism has become what Lipovetsky calls a "native context."

Lipovetsky's approach to postmodernism incorporates the best of Western theory without attempting to apply it to Russia whole-cloth. Certainly, Lyotard's emphasis on postmodernism's "profound distrust of metanarratives" and Baudrillard's notion of simulation play a crucial role, while discussions of postmodernism as a phenomenon of "late capitalism" do not. Here again, Lipovetsky strikes a balance between the foreign and the domestic; in order to explain Russian postmodernism, he appeals to two of the most intriguing conceptual models in academia today: chaos theory (a "Western import") and the dialogism of Mikhail Bakhtin (a "Russian export"). Applying a model formulated in another discipline always has its risks, but Lipovetsky manages to avoid all the potential pitfalls as he develops his idea of a postmodern "dialogue with chaos": his explanations of chaos theory are remarkably lucid, and its application to Russian literature does not reduce verbal art to mathematical formulae. Rather, Lipovetsky uses chaos theory as a philosophical paradigm, a lens through which to view phenomena that are often distorted. Lipovetsky's approach is inspired by that of Ilya Prigogine (himself something of a cultural hybrid, born in

Russia but working in France); for Prigogine, chaos is a condition in which "all actualized possibilities coexist and interact, and the system turns out to be everything it can be simultaneously" (1989: 11). Chaos is not mere disorder but rather a state of heightened productive potential; rather than fighting chaos, the postmodern artist embraces it.

At the same time that Lipovetsky's work introduces chaos theory to the problematics of Russian postmodernism, it reintroduces postmodernism to the works of Mikhail Bakhtin. Thanks to time lags in translation and the vagaries of critical fashion, Bakhtin's ideas began to have an impact on Western criticism at roughly the same time that structuralism was giving way to poststructuralism. Bakhtin's emphasis on "multivoicedness" and the open-endedness" of the text had an innate appeal to the poststructuralist mindset, and as a result, Western poststructuralists display the unfortunate tendency to claim Bakhtin as one of their own. Given the professed hostility of poststructuralists to all forms of "hegemonic discourse," the irony involved in such an appropriation of Bakhtin is almost palpable. Bakhtin firmly rejected the Saussurian linguistics that lies at the heart of both structuralism and poststructuralism, and Lipovetsky knows all of these movements well enough to recognize the importance of this fact. At the same time, he does not share the knee-jerk defensiveness of some Russian critics regarding Bakhtin: Lipovetsky is more than willing to bring poststructuralism and Bakhtin into dialogue, but not at the expense of simply translating one into the language of the other.

In Part I, Lipovetsky sets forth the basis for his model: Where the modernist creative artist attempted to create order out of surrounding chaos, the postmodern writer recognizes the illusory nature of order itself. The author no longer abdicates his or her role as the text's external, god-like creator and is instead subject to the same destabilizing disorientation as the text's characters. This is not the total surrender to chaos but rather the recognition of chaos's vast creative potential. Indeed, Lipovetsky's conception of the Russian postmodernist approach to the world might best be characterized as "guardedly optimistic"; his analysis of the major works of recent Russian fiction shows that many of Russia's best writers manage to turn otherwise daunting, or even horrifying, phenomena into a source of wonder and inspiration. This is particularly apparent in Part II of *Russian Postmodernist Fiction,* which examines the role of the cultural heritage in three Russian postmodern "classics" (Bitov, Erofeev, and Sokolov). The near impossibility of any meaningful contact with the culture of the past is one of the central themes of Russian modernism, but the postmodernists take the problem one step further: Lipovetsky's writers see the culture of the past as irrevocably dead. Even this, however, does not discourage them; instead, the authors of *Pushkin House, Moscow to the End of the Line,* and *A School for Fools* create characters who live in the "afterlife of culture," playfully calling attention to the illusory nature of their posthumous existence. Part III continues Lipovetsky's examination of the postmodern response to the dead themes of modernism: utopianism, artistic creativity, and historical coherence are all subjected to the poetics of postmodern playfulness—not even the absurd, a phenomenon that would appear to parody itself, escapes the authors' deconstructive impulse.

Finally, and perhaps most important, *Russian Postmodernist Fiction* provides the English-speaking reader with the opportunity to become acquainted with some of the most significant works of Russian fiction of the past three decades, most of which exist in translation. From the playful fictional scholarship of Andrei Bitov to the drunken ramblings of Venichka Erofeev, from the arch whimsy of Tatyana Tolstaya to the absurdity of Yevgeny Popov, the novels and stories discussed in Lipovetsky's book are contemporary classics. For those who have long enjoyed these works, Lipovetsky's readings will provide a radically new perspective, and for those learning of these texts for the first time, *Russian Postmodernist Fiction* will serve as a worthy introduction to a bizarre but familiar world.

# I.
# Introduction

# 1

# Chaos as a System

## The Russian Oxymoron

Marjorie Perloff, a prominent American scholar of postmodernism, calls Russian postmodernism an oxymoron (1993). In a sense, she is correct, since her conclusions are based on conceptions of postmodernism that took shape in West European and North American cultures. There, the development of postmodernism was not hampered by such extraliterary factors as Socialist Realism, propaganda campaigns against "formalism," and the physical elimination of the foremost representatives of modernist culture. Widespread attempts to explain postmodernity as a phenomenon of "late capitalism" (Jameson 1991), or as the result of an information revolution leading to a computerized, media-saturated civilization (Baudrillard 1983), or even as a sign of "the end of history" (Fukuyama 1992) obviously fail to address Soviet and post-Soviet cultural realities. Popular interpretations of the postmodern condition based on Western, culture-specific concepts also leave much to be desired. For example, Leslie Fiedler suggests in his 1968 article-*cum*-manifesto "Cross the Border—Close That Gap" that postmodernism emerges from the synthesis of elitist high modernism and mass culture (Fiedler 1975), yet such an idea would appear alien to Russian literary postmodernism, which is still elitist to the core. Yet to some extent, Fiedler's approach can do much to explain the nature of one particular Russian postmodernist movement, Sots-Art (see Chapter 9). In the art of Vitaly Komar, Alexander Melamid, Ilya Kabakov, Erik Bulatov, and Grisha Bruskin, as well as in the literary works of Dmitri Prigov and Vladimir Sorokin, Socialist Realist models are reinterpreted; here one might say that Socialist Realism serves the same function for Russian postmodernism that "mass culture" does for its Western counterparts.

Andreas Huyssen (1984) sees postmodernism as a continuation of the counterculture of the sixties, the rebellion of youth against the modernist establishment. One might be tempted to establish similar connections between the postmodernism of Venedikt Erofeev, Andrei Bitov, Joseph Brodsky, and Sasha Sokolov and the culture of the Soviet version of the "rebellious youth of the sixties": the culture of the Thaw, the culture of the "*shestidesiatniki*" (the sixties generation).[1] Such connections are only reinforced when we consider such authors as Vasily Aksyonov and Yuz Aleshkovsky, "mediators" whose work blends the critical realism of the Thaw period with some elements of postmodernist discourse (see Chapter 6). Moreover, the ideological liberalization of the sixties often manifested itself through experiments with artistic form: The artist's inner freedom is reflected in the very poetics of literary texts.

Yet Huyssen's approach cannot be borrowed whole-cloth, since new spiritual freedom found its expression in many other Russian literary movements from the sixties through the eighties: from the traditionalist "prophecies" of Alexander Solzhenitsyn and the authors of "Village Prose" (Vasily Shukshin, Vasily Belov, Viktor Astafiev, Valentin Rasputin) to the grotesque realism of Abram Tertz, Aleksandr Galich, Fazil Iskander, and Vladimir Voinovich; from the rebelliousness of Vladimir Vysotsky to the peculiar existentialism of "war fiction" (Vasil Bykov, Grigory Baklanov, Konstantin Vorobiev, Vyacheslav Kondratiev); from the fiction of the so-called "fortysomething" writers (*sorokaletnie*) (Vladimir Makanin, Anatoly Kurchatkin, Anatoly Kim, Ruslan Kireev), with their emphasis on "private life," to the neo–avant-garde (itself a motley crew that encompasses such widely diverse authors as Vladimir Kazakov, Gennady Aigi, Vsevolod Nekrasov, Andrei Voznesensky, and Eduard Limonov).

On the other hand, the inability to apply Western concepts of postmodernity to Soviet and post-Soviet culture hardly means that there is no such thing as the Russian postmodern condition; rather, as Nancy Condee and Vladimir Padunov argue, Russia simply has a different teleology. In their view, the postmodernist vocabulary changes little in its post-Soviet transcription; instead, it is reminiscent of a language that is closely related to one's native tongue but that uses a different alphabet. Central to both Russian and Western postmodernism are the death of myth, the end of ideology and uniformity of thought, the emergence of multiple and diverse patterns of thought, a critical approach to institutions and institutionalized values, a movement from a single Culture to multiple cultures, the desecration of the canon, and the rejection of metanarratives (Condee and Padunov 1994).

"Contemporary progress threatens to be transformed into *its opposite,* as two world wars, Stalin's gulag, and the Nazis' mass murders clearly demonstrate," writes theologian Hans Küng. "Convictions based on a faith in Reason, so typical of the modernist era, have been shaken, especially *faith in the supreme divinity of modernism*—in the eternal, omnipotent and omniscient, wise and all-seeing, virtuous Progress. The crisis of progressive thought is essentially a *crisis of the modernist understanding of reason*" (Küng 1990: 225–26; emphasis in the original). Küng believes that the crisis of the ideas of Progress and Rationality is the primary factor defining the postmodernist cultural paradigm. Without a doubt, it was the rise of totalitarian regimes tracing their roots to absolutized modernist utopianism that dealt the decisive blow to the whole ideological edifice of modernity. It was totalitarianism that caused what Jean-Francois Lyotard calls "delegitimation," the collapse of all cultural and ideological discourses that structured this historic model of civilization from within: "The grand narrative has lost its credibility, regardless of what mode of unification it uses, regardless of whether it is a speculative narrative or a narrative of emancipation." (1984: 37) Like Lyotard, Charles Newman links postmodernity to the total inflation of all discourses as a result of permanent crises in the history and culture of the twentieth century. "The Post-Modern era," Newman writes, "represents only the last phase in a century of inflation—when it becomes structurally permanent" (1985: 5).

All of these features are quite applicable to the Soviet sociocultural reality of the 1960s–80s, when the metanarratives of Soviet utopianism undergo a process of deligitimation. What was called "Soviet ideology" is certainly nothing but a system of metanarratives, a system that used the machinery of the state to deal harshly and aggressively with any deviation. A number of recent studies have isolated connections between socialist culture and the aesthetics and philosophy of the avant-garde, and, more broadly, between communist utopianism and the utopian project of modernity,[2] suggesting that Soviet civilization is a particular—hypertrophied and pathological—version of the legitimation of the period of modernity. The years from 1965 to 1968 marked the failure of the Thaw to modernize the communist regime (not only in the USSR but in Eastern Europe as well). Such attempts were by their very nature paradoxical, since after thirty years a society that had been predicated on the slogans of "emancipation of labor," "freedom of the people," and "the free development of everybody" as a requirement for the "free development of all" discovered that liberalization (albeit inconsistent and half-hearted) was necessary for its survival. However, the dramatic story of the Thaw (1956–68) unambiguously demonstrated that the established societal structures could not accept even such timid attempts at greater freedom. No less dramatically, the period of "perestroika" showed that, under the pressures of a more consistent effort at liberalization, the only thing such structures can do is simply collapse.[3] Certainly, this qualifies as a crisis of legitimacy. But at the same time, unlike in the West, the values of emancipation and liberalization have not been subject to inflation; on the contrary, they have become crucial not only for the liberalism of the sixties generation but more generally for the cultural and, in particular, literary developments of the seventies and eighties, including the evolution of postmodernism.

It is no accident that the beginning of the seventies witnessed the almost simultaneous completion of such works as, on the one hand, Solzhenitsyn's *Gulag Archipelago* (1968–70)—which marks the total delegitimation of the entire Soviet mythology of history—and, on the other hand, such exemplary works of Russian postmodernism as Venedikt Erofeev's *Moscow to the End of the Line* (1970) and Andrei Bitov's *Pushkin House* (completed in 1971). It would seem that there is no connection between Solzhenitsyn's documentary epic and Erofeev's unruly ramblings. Yet both contribute to the process of delegitimation, whether in the realm of history (Solzhenitsyn) or culture and philosophy (postmodernism).

In the realm of aesthetics, the crisis of legitimacy is primarily related to the crisis of the axiological center of any culture, from antiquity to avant-garde: the category of the aesthetic ideal. Traditional art has always aspired to create an ideal representation of both historical and contemporary worlds and has always examined reality in the light of this ideal, whether through praise or condemnation, through questions or curses, through blissful distraction or appeals to conscience. Even the avant-garde, with all its irreverence toward tradition, reinforced rather than subverted this myth-making function of culture. However, it was the same avant-garde that turned a cultural myth into a political utopia by erasing the boundaries between art and life. The fiasco of political utopianism, which would lead inevitably to the gulag or the Holocaust, dealt a hard blow to the possibility of modeling life after an ideal. In other words, it deprived culture of its right to create a myth capable of affecting life. But can culture exist without such a right? Can culture still be treated as such, if there is no place in it for an aesthetic ideal? This is probably what was meant by Theodor Adorno's famous question about poetry after Auschwitz, as well as by Varlam Shalamov's words (1989: 60) that "aestheticism" is impossible after the horrors of the gulag (the writer spent seventeen years in Stalin's labor camps). This is the source of postmodernist aesthetics.

"The collapse of the modernist system in every sphere became clear in 1968," writes Dubravka Oraić. "This year can be considered the cutoff between modernism and postmodernism as megacultures" (1994: 111). On the whole, her thesis is quite applicable to the Russian cultural model, which usually lags behind the West.

## Postmodernism Plus/Minus Modernism?

"In Soviet and Russian terms, 'post-modernism,' as it is currently applied, can be viewed as a misnomer. Modernism in Russia is a thing of the distant past. It goes back to the beginning of the century. Today Russian postmodernism is not a reaction to modernism but rather a reflex towards Soviet social, ideological, and aesthetic values, and a reaction against socialist realism"—N.N. Shneidman's harsh diagnosis (1995: 173) is actually a softened version of a widespread objection to the idea of Russian postmodernism: Postmodernism cannot exist where modernism was never fully developed. According to Shneidman's logic, Russian modernism is restricted to the so-called Silver Age, the period directly preceding the revolution (1890–1917), a time that saw a veritable explosion of modernist movements, including Symbolism, Acmeism, Futurism, and Imaginism.

However, such scholars as Aleksander Flaker, Nils Ake Nilsson, Jan van Baak, Iurii Levin, Vladimir Toporov, Igor Smirnov, and Renata Dering have argued on the pages of the Dutch journal *Russian Literature* that the evolution of Russian modernism continued not only after the October Revolution but even after the establishment of the Socialist Realist monopoly on culture. In Russia, such writers as Andrei Bely, Yevgeny Zamyatin, Osip Mandelstam, Anna Akhmatova, and Daniil Kharms, along with émigrés such as Vladimir Nabokov, Marina Tsvetaeva, and Vladislav Khodasevich, continued to develop modernist traditions in the twenties and thirties (although this hardly means that none of them tried to find a compromise with Socialist Realism or "renounce" modernism; we are concerned with the general trend). The fact that these authors were not "canonized," that they worked on the periphery of official "Soviet literature," only increases their authority with new generations.

It is very important that the traditions of both the Silver Age and late Russian modernism were reborn during the Thaw, when such "decadent" writers as Blok, Akhmatova, and Khlebnikov were first republished, along with the works of "émigré" writers such as Bunin and Tsvetaeva and such *personae non grata* as Babel, Platonov, Olesha, Kharms (his children's works), and, later, Mandelstam. The living presence of Anna Akhmatova, around whom a group of young poets including Joseph Brodsky formed, made the link between the new generation and Russian modernism tangible. The year 1967 saw the first publication of Bulgakov's *Master and Margarita* (1940), which had an enormous, almost cult-like effect on the Russian culture of the seventies, eighties, and nineties. At the same time, thanks to *samizdat* and smuggled copies of émigré publications, other forbidden works were being discovered by the Russian readership: Mandelstam, the later work of Kharms, Vvedensky, the early Zabolotsky, Oleinkov, Nabokov, Bulgakov, Platonov, Zamyatin, and Pasternak (*Doctor Zhivago*). For the generations of the sixties and seventies, Russian modernism was not a "thing of the past" but rather the hottest "new" works, whose appeal was perhaps only increased by the fact that reading them was a criminal offense.

In this atmosphere, Russian postmodernism came into being as the simultaneous expression of two contradictory tendencies. On the one hand, there was the need to return to modernism, to use the aesthetic arsenal of the classics; this is why the works of Russian postmodernists display so many features that are characteristic of modernist aesthetics. On the other hand, there was the gradual recognition of the impossibility of "restoring" modernism after decades of totalitarian aesthetics. We find this recognition in the search for an ironic contact with or distancing from the modernist classics (a strategy that finds its clearest embodiment in the poetry of Joseph Brodsky), as well as in the arrangement of a paradoxical dialogue between Soviet mass culture and high esoteric culture (from Venedikt Erofeev's *Moscow to the End of the Line* to the Sots-Art paintings and installations of Ilya Kabakov, Komar and Melamid, and Erik Bulatov). The resolution of this conflict is the subject of the second part of the present study (especially Chapter 2, on Bitov's *Pushkin House*). Here one must also stress that the early postmodernists' heightened sensitivity to the traditions of Russian modernism led to the further development of certain tendencies that were present in the Russian modernism of the twenties and thirties, which contained the seeds of many subsequent *postmodernist* discoveries.

The "postmodernist" potential of Russian modernism is easily demonstrated by the evolution of Vladimir Nabokov, who, in his youth, immersed himself in the cultural atmosphere of the Silver Age. As an émigré in the twenties and thirties, he created such exemplary works of Russian modernism as the metafictional *The Gift* and *Invitation to a Beheading;* subsequently, after moving to America, he wrote the novel that is now considered a classic of the American postmodernist canon: *Lolita* (1955).[4]

In a fascinating study of the relationship between American postmodernists and Nabokov, Maurice Couturier argues that the boundary between Nabokov's modernist and postmodernist works "corresponds exactly with World War II, which not only showed the fragility of the old values and of the real, but also constituted a universal liturgy of the ultimate real, death" (Couturier 1993: 257). Hence Nabokov's postmodern aesthetics is formed as a result of his discovery of "the unreality of the real and the arbitrariness of language in a more private and also more tragic fashion" (ibid.). Thus Couturier calls *The Gift* a truly modernist novel, comparable to Proust's *A la Recherche de temps perdu,* Joyce's *Ulysses,* and Faulkner's *The Sound and the Fury,* while he argues that *Bend Sinister* and *Invitation to a Beheading* represent "the militant stage of the late-modernism or of the 'pre-postmodernism' " (ibid.). Finally, Couturier considers *Lolita, Pale Fire,* and *Ada* to be "archetypal postmodernist novels" (ibid., 258): The protagonists of all three works "resort to art to recoup their losses in life. Their tragic desires could not be matched by real objects; it is the very elusiveness of the objects that makes their desires tragic. Hence, their demented effort, before death or sheer madness, to write a text that, while bearing witness to their failure to satisfy their desires, fulfills a more exalted form of desire, the artistic one, and gives birth to something intensely real, a work of art" (ibid.).

Even if we accept this typology in principle, we cannot ignore the fact that the "unreality of reality" is a fundamental part of Nabokov's metafiction in his Russian, thoroughly modernist period. Scholars of Nabokov's Russian period pay particular attention to such constant features as the author's playful attitude toward his text, which is expressed, on the one hand, by constantly exposing the author's role in the constriction of the work, the thematicization of the process of literary creation, and, on the other hand, by drawing the reader into the creative game, constantly undermining what little sense of reality and mimesis the novel has (see Medarić 1991 and Levin 1990).

Only Nabokov managed to realize the philosophical and aesthetic potential of Russian modernist metafiction, an important trend in the twenties and thirties. Patricia Waugh defines metafiction as "fictional writing which self-consciously and systematically draws attention to its status as an artifact in order to pose a question about the relationship between fiction and reality. In providing a critique of their own methods of construction, such writings not only examine the fundamental structures of narrative fiction, they also explore the possible fictionality of the world outside the literary fictional text" (1984: 2). The question of twentieth-century Russian metafiction was first raised by Dmitri Segal in an essay entitled "Literature as Safe Conduct" (1981). Although Segal never once uses the term "metafiction," his analysis of such works as Vasily Rozanov's *Fallen Leaves,* Osip Mandelstam's "The Egyptian Stamp," the novels of Konstantin Vaginov, Mikhail Bulgakov's *The Master and Margarita,* Nabokov's *The Gift* and *Pale Fire,* and Boris Pasternak's *Doctor Zhivago* emphasizes the truly metafictional features of these texts: *"[T]hey are about the creative process,"* Segal writes," and they interpret the theme of *the writer and writing;* some of them include—either as citations or through description—the very texts whose creation is the subject of the narrative" (ibid., 151).[5]

The strategies of metafiction correspond so precisely to the aesthetics of modernist discourse that these very strategies led to the point where modernism started to go beyond its own boundaries, somehow prefiguring postmodernism. David Shepherd finds the "Soviet metafiction of the 1920s and 1930s, chronologically much closer to modernism, to be somehow, mysteriously postmodernist *avant la lettre*" (1992: 174). But despite his cautious phrasing, he nonetheless draws parallels between the artistic conceptions of the metafiction of this period and postmodern aesthetics: "[T]he metafiction of Kaverin, Vaginov, and Shaginian do invite, even compel, us to make the conceptual leap between their fictional presentations of writers and artists and both contemporary and later theoretical approaches, for example, the consonance between the presentation in *The Troublemaker* or *Artist Unknown* [novels of the twenties by Veniamin Kaverin—M.L.] of the creative artist's status as a figure always already fictionally mediated, constructed, and Foucault's author as ideological product" (ibid., 162–63). Indeed, one can make the parallels more specific. Thus, Vaginov and Sigizmund Krzhizhanovsky are compared to Borges, while Dubravka Ugrešić finds that Vaginov's novels have much in common with the works of the contemporary conceptual artist Ilya Kabakov. Graham Roberts argues that Daniil Kharms's fiction reveals interesting parallels with the philosophical works of Wittgenstein and Foucault (1992), while Ronald Sukenick places Viktor Shklovsky's *Sentimental Journey* alongside the metafiction of André Gide, Samuel Beckett, and Vladimir Nabokov (1975: 41).

It is important to note a tendency in the Russian metafiction of the twenties and thirties to explore what Foucault calls the "kinship between writing and death." The "conception of a spoken or written narrative as a protection against death has been transformed by our culture," argues Foucault. "Writing is now linked to sacrifice and to the sacrifice of life itself. . . . Where a work had the duty of creating immortality, it now attains the right to kill, to become the murderer of its author" (1977: 116). Foucault wrote these words in 1969, in a work that has become one of the theoretical manifestos of postmodernism ("What Is an Author?"). But it is this very transformation of art and writing into death and the author's self-destruction that is at the heart of the metafiction of Vasily Rozanov, Viktor Shklovsky, and Sizigmund Krzhizhanovsky; it is particularly crucial to any understanding of such seminal works of metafiction as Mandelstam's "Egyptian Stamp" (1928), Vaginov's *Days and Works of Svistonov* (1929), and Daniil Kharms's *Cases* (1933–39).

In all these works, the theme of death is directly linked to various motifs of revolutionary-utopian attacks on culture and humanism. Death proves to be an integral image of the dark, unrecognizable, and horrifying chaos from which even the creative act is no protection. Vaginov's writer-protagonist identifies the world of creativity with the "hell" in which he puts the prototypes of his heroes; in the novel's end, he finds himself trapped within the "hereafter" of his novel, which has engulfed reality. Mandelstam describes the creative process during the catastrophic death of culture and civilization. By contrast, Kharms deliberately exaggerates the kinship of culture and chaos, transforming the artistic text into a machine for the (self-)destruction of cultural values; but in so doing, he accords the text the status of the only possible reality—the reality of death. In Kharms's work, the constant metafictional deconstruction of art equates writing with death, with nonexistence, which, according to the author's logic, is the only "real reality": only through self-negation can literature attain an ontological status, the status of a "self-sufficient thing."

In addition to the internal laws of modernist evolution, its self-reflective critique, one must also recognize that hints of postmodernism began to appear in Russian metafiction rather early, due to specific Russian cultural traditions. The power of the word and the belief in the truth expressed by the word are a tradition rooted in the Russian medieval period and reinforced by the moral authority of the Russian classics of the nineteenth century, yet they lead to a grotesque paradox in the twentieth century. The power of the word expands to become the power of a totalitarian ideology, one that requires a religious faith in the idea that reality is that which corresponds to the Word (of the Party, the Leader, the State); that which does not correspond to the Word is erased from reality and declared nonexistent.

This paradox inevitably leads us to another concept that is fundamental to the philosophy of postmodernism: Jean Baudrillard's theory of simulacra and simulation, which reflects the semiotic nature of postmodern reality. After attesting to the erosion of the boundary between signs and their real referents, Baudrillard asserts that reality in the postmodern era is replaced by a web of "simulacra"—self-sufficient semiotic systems that have no correspondence to the real world. Thus, Baudrillard argues, reality gives way to a "hyperreality of simulacra." As language expands, it turns into a system of signifiers without signifieds. Simulacra govern the behavior of people, their perceptions, and even their consciousness, which in turn leads to the "death of the subject": the self is also nothing more than an aggregate of simulacra (see Baudrillard 1993: 342–75), and human beings really do appear to be a "system of phrases," as Gorky's Klim Samgin would say.

The concept of "simulacra and simulation" lies at the core of Mikhail Epstein's study "The Origins and Meaning of Russian Postmodernism" (1995a: 188–212). This work contains a number of cogent observations on simulation in Socialist Realist culture, a culture that completely identified reality with ideological mythologies. Epstein argues that even in post-Soviet culture, simulation "devours" reality. In his opinion, Russian postmodernism lays bare the device of a lingering socialist simulation; it discovers the *emptiness* underlying any system of signs. Russian conceptualism and Sots-Art in particular provide persuasive confirmation of Epstein's thesis. Yet it would appear that for Epstein the range of Russian postmodernism is limited to these movements alone.

Epstein proposes that, broadly speaking, the perpetual production of simulacra has characterized Russian culture almost since the time of the forced Christianization of ancient Rus' by Prince Vladimir and that Socialist Realism represents "the first stage of the transition from modernism to Postmodernism. Socialist realism is postmodernism with a modernist face that continues to wear an expression of absolute seriousness" (ibid.: 207). But the difference between Socialist Realism and postmodernism can scarcely be reduced to the fact that one is serious while the other is ironic. If we do not depart from Epstein's schema, then postmodernism is linked first and foremost with the recognition of simulacra as such, whereas Socialist Realism is oriented toward a religious faith in the absolute reality of these sets of signifiers. At this point we must ask: From what is this notion of the simulative consciousness of Socialist Realism derived? Naturally, from today's—postmodern—experience. *Within* Socialist Realist discourse the category of the simulacrum simply does not function.

But the Russian metafiction of the twenties and thirties, as well as the works of Nabokov, did not belong to the realm of Socialist Realism, although it certainly reacted to the same cultural transformations that were taking place under the pressure of totalitarian simulation. The identification of writing and death is probably also a reaction to the culture's increased production of simulacra. Without a doubt, Socialist Realism has had an influence on the postmodern condition in Russia, but as a simulative context rather than a direct source, stimulating the cultural need for postmodern deconstruction. As a result, in the late sixties, when the crisis of the entire system of totalitarian legitimation and total simulation began, the insights of such modernists as Vaginov, Mandelstam, Kharms, and Nabokov began to register in the consciousness of a new generation of writers who were trying to return to modernism. The paradox of Russian postmodernism is that, in the attempt by authors such as Andrei Bitov, Venedikt Erofeev, Sasha Sokolov, and Joseph Brodsky to revive modernism, the authors respond to the unrealized "prepostmodernist" potential buried in the literature of the early twentieth century rather than actually restore the Silver Age. Another parallel line in Russian postmodernism is formed as a result of the historical "re-reading" of Socialist Realism from the modernist perspective in order to reveal the internal mechanisms behind the disappearance of reality and the subject and to deconstruct the very process of the production of simulacra. Of course, this is only a general outline of the historical dynamics of Russian postmodernism. Analysis of specific texts shows the complexity and variety of its development.

But before we proceed to the analysis of individual, primarily fictional, texts of the 1960s–90s that represent a rather idiosyncratic version of postmodern culture, a provisional sketch of the postmodernist artistic paradigm is in order. It will then be easier to demonstrate precisely why Russian postmodernism, for all its peculiarities, is still postmodernism, rather than some kind of latter-day modernism; it will also become clear precisely how Russian postmodernism differs from its Western counterparts.

The numerous theories, interpretations, and definitions that have accumulated around literary postmodernism sometimes give the impression that postmodernism was actually invented by literary critics for their own enjoyment and that it will disappear as soon as they come to an agreement on the exact meaning of the term and find a more interesting game to play. The most common arguments used to refute the existence of postmodernism in literature consist of the assertion that all the features of postmodernist poetics can be found in works considerably predating those by Borges, Nabokov, Cortazar, Pynchon, Eco, and other postmodern heavyweights. Edmund Smyth, for instance, after finding each and every essential trait of postmodernism in Rabelais, Cervantez, and Stern, comes to the conclusion that "postmodernism is a condition of reading" (1991: 11) and nothing more. In other words, the classification of a given work as "postmodern" depends entirely on the reader's willingness to define it as such. All the same, we should try to determine the characteristics of the postmodernist consciousness that are acceptable to the majority of scholars, as well as the corresponding features of the postmodernist fiction. This determination will serve as the point of departure in our search for the postmodernist artistic paradigm.

## Intertextual Play

> *The intertextuality in which any text is apprehended, since it is itself the intertext of another text, cannot be identified with some origin of the text: to seek out the "sources," the "influences" of a work is to satisfy the myth of filiation; the quotations a text is made of are anonymous, irrecoverable, and yet already read; they are quotations without quotation marks.*

> —Roland Barthes (1989: 60; emphasis in the original).

One might well argue whether or not this description can be universally applied to the literatures of other periods, and whether such a broad interpretation is nothing but a typical extrapolation of new artistic ideas *to* previous periods. However, in either case, such an understanding of intertextuality is directly related to postmodernism, in which this feature is used consciously as an artistic device.

One might call this idea, which erodes the traditional boundaries between art and reality, "the world as text"; in essence, the very category of
mimesis is abolished.[6] Yet postmodernism, unlike naturalism, does not recognize the priority of life over aesthetics; on the contrary, it understands all
existence as the realization of universal semiotic processes. And unlike
Romanticism and various neo-Romantic movements in the twentieth century
(such as aestheticism and Symbolism), postmodernism even rejects the inverted hierarchy of "poetry over art," replacing it with a picture of the world
in which a polylogue of cultural languages insistently comes to the fore; and
here the languages express themselves in high poetry and the crude prose of
reality, in the ideal and the earthly, in flights of fancy and the shuddering
of the flesh.

A particular sticking point is the boundary between modernist and
postmodernist intertextualities. Alexander Zholkovsky (1994), for example,
considers the frequent recourse to intertexts to be a feature specifically
characterizing the modernist style, supporting his thesis through observations drawn from intertexts by Akhmatova, Mandelstam, Zoshchenko,
Olesha, Bulgakov, and Brodsky. Postmodernism has undoubtedly inherited
intertextuality from modernism. But is this inheritance accepted as given, or
do the ungrateful heirs find it necessary to make changes of their own?

Dubravka Oraić (1988), in her theoretical exploration of the phenomenon of
quotation in Russian "high" modernism and the avant-garde, emphasizes that,
first, every quotation, whether by Acmeists or Futurists, is always a paradoxical
means of *self-expression* for the authorial ego.[7] In the case of Mandelstam, for
example, quotations are usual stripped of their initial context, only to be given
new meaning "according to the laws of Mandelstam's [own] text" (1988: 123).
Second, modernist intertextuality has always served the goal of the radical
revision of language and culture in particular and human behavior in general.
This kind of intertextuality has been accompanied by "expectations of an absolutely new text and an absolutely new culture" (ibid., 130).

Unlike modernism, postmodernism does not set itself the task of creating
a new metalanguage when it works with alien cultural languages. Its standpoint is deliberately nonserious: postmodernism *plays* with contexts, quotations, and discourses.

And indeed, there is hardly a scholar who would not find a connection
between the category of play and the most essential concepts of postmodernist
poetics. Here Roland Barthes's words are particularly instructive:

> "Playing" must be taken here in all the polysemy of the term: the text itself
> "plays." . . . and the reader plays twice over: he *plays at* the Text (lucid
> meaning), he seeks a practice which reproduces it; but, so that this practice is
> not reduced to a passive interior *mimesis* (the Text being precisely what

resists this reduction), he *plays* the Text; we must not forget that *play* is also a musical term." (1989: 62–63, emphasis in the original)

Here "play" refers to a kind of antisymmetrical strategy linking the author, the text, and the reader. As Barthes understands it, the literature of the postmodern era aims, on the whole, at overcoming *power,* which is embodied in the mechanisms of language, and thereby it asserts its complete and total freedom:

> Only writing, as a matter of fact, can assume the *fictional* character of the most serious, even the most violent dialects, can replace them in their theatrical distance.... Moreover, only writing can *mix* languages (psychoanalytic, Marxist, structuralist, for example), can constitute what is called a *heterology* of knowledge, can give language a festive dimension. Last, only writing can be deployed *without a site of origin;* only writing can baffle every rhetorical rule, every law of genre, every arrogance of system: writing is *atopic.* (1989: 110; emphasis in the original)

It is the category of play that reflects the most salient connection between the literature of postmodernism and relativist philosophy, or, on a larger scale, relativizing discourses in the twentieth century. Regardless of the level at which this postmodernist play is taking place, its logic is always the same: antihierarchical, antiteleological, antistructural. Such are the characteristics of the postmodernist interpretation of play.

The meaning of play, however, is the same for the avant-garde model of the world as well. As Jan Van Baak demonstrates, the concept of de-hierarchization is manifested at every level in the poetics of the avant-garde: "In extreme cases, de-hierarchization can lead to the sense that the combination of elements of the avant-garde world is deprived of any orderliness (anomy)" (1987: 2). But in this case, all the artistic elements, even those that seem unrelated to each other, are in a state of incessant and irreconcilable conflict. Van Baak sees this conflict as the most distinctive feature of avant-garde art.[8]

Postmodernism, while carrying on the avant-garde tradition, nevertheless eliminates its basic conflict: the combination of heterogeneous elements now takes on a thoroughly playful character; any conflict that may remain is *staged* or *simulated.* Postmodernist play replaces avant-garde fragmentation with an unstable, conditional, illusory, yet nonetheless *total and integrated playful involvement,* consolidating the text's heterogeneous elements and codes.

What is unique about postmodernist play? After all, strictly speaking, an element of playfulness has always been present throughout culture: it simply performs different functions and appears in different forms. In his classic monograph *Homo Ludens* (1980, orig. 1937), Johan Huisinga describes the following characteristics of play:

1. First and foremost, . . . all play is a *voluntary* activity. Play to order is no longer play: it could at best be but a forcible imitation of it. By this quality of freedom alone, play marks itself off from the course of the natural process. It is something added there to and spread out over it like a flowering, an ornament, a garment. (Ibid., 7)

2. As regards its formal characteristics, all students lay stress on the *disinterestedness* of play. Not being "ordinary" life it stands outside the immediate satisfaction of wants and appetites, indeed it interrupts the appetitive process.

3. Play is distinct from "ordinary" life both as to locality and duration. This is the third main characteristic of play: its secludedness, its limitedness. It is "played out" within certain limits of time and place. It contains its own course and meaning. Play begins, and then at a certain moment it is "over." It plays itself to an end. (Ibid., 9)

4. Inside the playground an absolutely and peculiar order reigns. Here we come across another, very positive feature of play: it creates order, *is* order. Into an imperfect world and into the confusion of life it brings a temporary, a limited perfection. Play demands order absolute and supreme.

5. The exceptional and special position of play is most tellingly illustrated by the fact that it loves to surround itself with an air of secrecy. Even in early childhood the charm of play is enhanced by making a "secret" out of it. This is for us, not for the "others." [What] the "others" do "outside" is no concern of ours at the moment. . . . A play-community generally tends to become permanent even after the game is over. (Ibid., 12)

Strange as it may seem, postmodernist play does not completely fit this model. The principle of intertextuality erodes the isolated and complete nature of the act of play. The antihierarchical tendencies of postmodernist play render Huisinga's thesis about the order of play questionable. Finally, the association of participants of literary play in a particular group is rather typical of modernist or avant-garde literary movements. Conversely, postmodernism, at least in Russian literature, has never given rise to groups comparable to such well-known associations of Russian modernists and avant-gardists as Hylea (the Cubo-Futurists), the Poets' Guild (the Acmeists), or OBERIU (the later Leningrad avant-garde). Moreover, Huisinga's definition quite accurately describes modernist aesthetics in general—the sacralization of art, aesthetic "life-construction" (*zhiznestroitel'stvo*),[9] and the juxtaposition of the laws of aesthetic play as reflecting a "higher reality," on the one hand, and the logic and laws of everyday life, on the other. If we use Huisinga as our guide, modernism is one of those cultures in which play is based on serious ideal contents, on a foundation of sacred mythologies and rituals. According to Huisinga, such cultures include ancient Rome, the Middle Ages, and Neo-Classicism. By contrast, postmodernism most closely resembles those cultures in which the nature of play is illusionist and predominantly aesthetic (the Renaissance, Baroque, Rococo, and Romanticism).

In other words, modernism continues the cultural tradition of myth-making play, whereas postmodernism is closer to the demythologizing tradition. Any myth presents us with a certain symbolic language as an *absolute equivalent of reality*. All of modernism is based on this global semiosis, which tries, first, to fill in all historical and cultural space, to uncover the symbolic meaning of each element of reality, and, second, to reveal the "real" meaning of each artistic statement by ascribing to it the significance of a life event. Even Socialist Realism, with its simulative mythology, aggressively tries to pass itself off as highbrow realism, ultimately displacing historical and factual reality.

Conversely, demythologizing cultural play results in a metamorphosis in the opposite direction. It shows that sacred symbols are nothing but a language that describes reality from one perspective or another, but no perspective is adequate. Postmodernism goes even further, demonstrating that reality itself is but a combination of various languages and language games, a colorful crazy quilt of intertexts. As a result, the search for equivalents of reality recedes, allowing play with the conventions of language to come to the fore. The most detailed analysis of such a playful strategy has been provided by Bakhtin (1968) in his work on the culture of carnival (an analogous type of play can be found in the folklore wondertale), which allows us to argue that in postmodernism we find a carnival of cultural languages, complete with all the features we expect from carnival. The differences between postmodernist play and play in its classical version reflect, first and foremost, the universal nature of carnival play, which was repeatedly emphasized by Bakhtin. In the context of postmodernist poetics, this universality makes it impossible to separate play from a more "serious" dimension, though in the "historical" carnival laughter is needed for the renewal of serious, sacred categories. In the postmodernist text, everything is subject to parody, everything is turned inside out, even the laws of the text's construction, the rules of the game themselves. As a result of this transformation, they lose their absolute meaning and become relative. Here is the source of "double coding" (Charles Jencks) in postmodernist poetics.

This is why, according to Umberto Eco, "with the modern [game], anyone who does not understand the game can only reject it, but with the postmodern, it is possible not to understand the game and yet to take it seriously" (Eco 1984: 68). While deconstructing its own rules, postmodernist play loses its esoteric nature, and it therefore does not require any special organizational groupings, such as clubs or unions, for those "initiated" into the rules of the game.

At this point, a particular structure of postmodernist intertext also arises, manifesting itself on all textual levels—from the verbal trope to the model of the world. This is a structure that entails a constant "code-switching" from one cultural language to another—from the low to the high, from the archaic to the new and fashionable, and vice versa. This process leads to a continuous state of entropy and disorder and yet to a radical philosophical freedom at the same time. Moreover, these states manifest themselves not only in the contents of the postmodernist work but also in its form, in the logic (or, to be more accurate, the antilogic, or "paralogy," according to Lyotard [1984: 60]) of its structure.

A typical feature of this intertextual play is the appearance of an author-creator (or, rather, his or her double) in the text itself. Such a double is often deliberately indistinguishable from the biographical author. Such is the case with the protagonist of Borges's "Borges and I," the author in Kurt Vonnegut's *Breakfast of Champions,* numerous representations of the author in Vladimir Nabokov's fiction, Venichka in Venedikt Erofeev's *Moscow to the End of the Line,* the novelists in Andrei Bitov's *Pushkin House* (these works are discussed in Part II) and Sasha's Sokolov's *Between Dog and Wolf* (see Part III, Chapter 7). This is more than simply laying bare the device. Rather, it is a manifestation of a philosophical principle: the author-demiurge, who, according to the traditional rules of the game, is supposed to be outside the text, now turns into an object of play, one of many involved in the process of intertextual recoding and de-hierarchization. Such devices theoretically undermine the possibility of finding some ultimate, conceivable, stable "frame" that might encompass and organize the continuous process of playful crowning and uncrowning. In this respect, postmodernist play is the opposite of the modernist mythology of the creative process, which views play as the form in which the author-creator realizes his or her divine freedom to the fullest.

## Subverted Dialogism

"After the decline of structuralism in the United States, a new, poststructuralist, postmodern, deconstructionist Bakhtin was born," writes Gary Saul

Morson (1992: 5). "Thus a thinker whose entire life was dedicated to understanding moral responsibility became an antinomialist and nihilist." Morson's exasperation is certainly not unwarranted. And yet . . . Why not look at the situation differently? What if Bakhtin had indeed outlined trends in twentieth-century culture that, by the end of the century, have developed in a direction quite different from what Bakhtin himself had in mind?

In this respect, Matei Calinescu's point of view is quite telling. He argues that the culture of modernity always reflects "the monistic orientation" of consciousness (1980: 169). According to Calinescu, even modernism, the final stage of modernity, is monistic, though this monism is of a particular kind—"negative monism," or "negative monologism," as Calinescu calls it. By this, he means the total rejection of all traditional concepts of truth, order, harmony, good and evil, and the ideal, all of which can be found in the avant-garde, Socialist Realism, and modernism to varying degrees. Unlike all of these movements, postmodernism engages in a dialogue with traditions, "looking at the past neither as an example (the normative and selective part of traditionalism) nor as an enemy (the adversary concept of the past upheld by modernism), but as a vast repertoire of alternatives, as an open-ended and ongoing creative debate, provides a great possibility for a fruitful cultural dialogue" (ibid.). Calinescu therefore views the postmodern period as "the age of dialogism," with the dialogue's nature being both intra- and intercultural at the same time.[10]

Drastic changes take place not only in relation to the past (tradition) but also to the present and the future. The philosopher Zygmunt Bauman traces the postmodernist of the conscience to the fact that contingency and the discrepancy between what is and what should be are no longer perceived as deviations from the "correct" logic of development but rather as the norm, as destiny ("contingency as destiny"):

> The residents of the house of modernity had been continuously trained to feel at home under conditions of necessity and to feel unhappy at the face of contingency; contingency, they had been told, was the state of discomfort and anxiety from which one needed to escape by making oneself into a binding norm and thus doing away with difference. Present [postmodern] unhappiness is the realization that this is not to be, that the hope will not come true and hence one needs to learn without the hope that supplied the meaning—the only meaning—to life . . . having been trained to live in necessity, we have ourselves living in contingency. And yet, bound to live in contingency, we can. . . make an attempt to transform it into our destiny." (Bauman 1993: 12)

Existence based on the logic of necessity requires the present to be sacrificed for the sake of the future, which is supposed to bring the reign of

Truth and Law. The delegitimation of such requirements, and of various utopias along with them, shifts the emphasis from the future tense to the present progressive—the *here and now* is, according to Bauman, the "axiologiocal center" of the postmodernist understanding of the world. There is an obvious connection between this concept and prosaics, which Gary Saul Morson and Caryl Emerson define as the core of Bakhtin's aesthetics and ethics:

> Prosaics is suspicious of systems in the strong sense, in the sense used by structuralists, semioticians, and general systems theorists: an organization in which every element has a place in a rigorous hierarchy. . . . According to Bakhtin's prosaic way of thinking order needs justification, disorder does not. The natural state of things is *mess*. . . . Bakhtin also presumed that, at least, in culture, mess was the normal, and at times even the healthy, state. (1990: 27–28, 30)

Moreover, the dialogue between contemporary theories of postmodernism and Bakhtin's more concrete concepts is clearly evident. Brian McHale considers the polyphony of worlds, not just of voices and ideas, to be an artistic innovation of postmodernism. "Postmodernist fiction," he writes, "by heightening the polyphonic structure and sharpening the dialogue in various ways, foregrounds the ontological dimension of the confrontation among discourses, thus achieving a polyphony of worlds" (1987: 166). In fact, this concept was already elaborated quite clearly by Bakhtin in his *Problems of Dostoevsky's Poetics:*

> In actual fact, the utterly incompatible elements comprising Dostoevsky's material are distributed among several worlds . . . these worlds, these consciousnesses with their individual fields of vision that combine in a higher unity, a unity, so to speak, of the second order, the unity of a polyphonic novel. The world of the ditty combines with the world of Schillerian dithyramb, Smerdyakov's field of vision combines with Dmitry's and Ivan's. Thanks to these *various worlds* the material can develop to the furthest extent what is most original and peculiar in it, without disturbing the unity of the whole and without mechanizing it. It is as if varying systems of calculations were united here in the complex unity of Einsteinian universe." (Bakhtin 1984: 16. Emphasis in the original.)

Bakhtin himself describes this method of organizing artistic material as *raznomirnost'*, "variety of worlds" (ibid.).

What differentiates postmodernism from polyphony (which was described by Bakhtin and can be traced primarily in the intellectual modernist fiction of the twentieth century, from Proust and Thomas Mann to Faulkner and Camus) is the fact that the ambivalent postmodernist mosaic consists of "second-order" worlds. These worlds are artistic amalgams of entire cultural systems and organic cultural languages. Further developing Bakhtin's argument, one could say that we are dealing with third-order polyphony and self-reflective versions of "variety of worlds" (*raznomirnost'*). They are unique in their lack of a consistent evaluative emphasis, whether unambiguously nihilistic or positivist and idealistic, all of which is typical of various types of modernism. The ambivalent nature of these formulae allows for contradictory readings and rereadings, which are frequently manifested in the plot dynamics of the postmodernist text (for instance, in Umberto Eco's *Name of the Rose,* or in Borges's stories).

According to Bakhtin, a crucial condition for the dialogic "variety of worlds" is "overcoming time in time" (ibid., 29). He writes: "Only such things as can conceivably be linked together at a single point of time are essential and are incorporated into Dostoevsky's world; such things can be carried over into eternity, for in eternity, according to Dostoevsky, all is simultaneous, everything coexists" (ibid.). According to Michael Holquist, simultaneity, understood, in this case, as the simultaneous existence of historically remote cultural languages in a polyphonic text, plays a fundamental role in Bakhtin's philosophical aesthetics. It is this very category that determines the profoundly relativist nature of Bakhtin's theories (see Holquist 1990: 20).

Clearly, this relativist principle is brought to the forefront of postmodernist poetics. Simultaneity is first expressed in the ease with which the languages and models of cultural systems separated by hundreds, if not thousands, of years are combined in the single artistic world of a postmodernist work. This trend is, of course, typical of twentieth-century culture in general. Postmodernism, however, does not simply continue this tendency in terms of content but implements cultural and philosophical simultaneity in a specific artistic structure, the *chronotope*. Here the chronotope is understood in a wider sense, the way Bakhtin uses this terms in his analysis of the Greek or chivalric novel as genres, without going into the details of the spatial and temporal imagery of individual work, more as a metachronotope of a particular cultural language. Bakhtin's "The Forms of Time and Chronotope in a Novel" includes a definition that looks almost as though it were deliberately included as a description of the postmodernist metachronotope *avant la letter*. This is the "creative chronotope" (*tvorcheskii khronotop*), in which, according to Bakhtin,

> an exchange between work and life occurs, and which constitutes the distinctive life of the work. . . . However forcefully the real and the represented

world resist fusion, however immutable the presence of that categorical boundary line between them, they are nevertheless indissolubly tied up with each other and find themselves in continual mutual interaction, uninterrupted exchange goes on between them, similar to the uninterrupted exchange of matter between living organisms and the environment that surrounds them. As long as an organism lives, it resists a fusion with the environment, but if it is torn out of its environment, it dies. . . . Of course, this process of exchange is itself chronotopic. (1981: 254)

This chronotope, in which a relationship develops between the author-narrator (creator) and the implied reader, is one of the ever-present, albeit peripheral, elements of any literary text. In postmodernism, however, the significance of this element is broadened to the point of becoming universal. In this chronotope, there is no more need for the category of time, since the act of reading is instantaneous. This, by the way, is the source of an entire spectrum of devices that are unique to postmodernism and related to imitating the spontaneity of the writing process, its instantaneous nature.

A very important feature of this chronotope, which penetrates all of postmodernist poetics, is the shift of artistic emphasis from the result of a creative act to the unfinished and unfinishable process of creation itself. Its open-endedness acquires an ontological significance in postmodernism; it is presented as a universal metaphor for human life—both for cultural life and for existence in general.[11] This characteristic of postmodernism sparks an association with the aesthetics of the baroque. "The receivers of the baroque work, being surprised at finding it incomplete or so irregularly constructed, remained a few instants in suspense; then, feeling compelled to thrust themselves forward and take part in it, they ended up finding themselves more strongly affected by the work, held by it" (Maravall 1986: 220). The Baroque belief in the primacy of spectacle is comparable to the postmodernist theory of the *video-text* (Frederic Jameson); one can also trace a certain similarity between the Baroque and postmodernist conceptions of time and death.[12] Yet while pointing out these typological similarities, one must not overlook the different semantic functions played by analogous devices in the Baroque and postmodernism. The openness of a Baroque work is determined by the desire to grasp and reflect the transitional and ephemeral, in other words, to describe the features of an *aesthetic object*. Such an object is mimetically reproduced in the poetics of artistic text. Postmodernism unequivocally replaces a wordless object with the polyphony of *aesthetic subjects,* which are engaged in dialogue with the voice of the author, which, in turn, breaks down into multiple voices (the intertextual "death of the author" [see Barthes 1989: 49–55]). Therefore, open-endedness in postmodernist texts results from radical changes in the structure of the subject–object relationship that forms the basis of any creative act. It is the prevalence of the "creative chronotope" that primarily reflects this change. Naturally, a unique relationship between the author of a literary work and his characters cannot help but arise within the "creative chronotope."

According to Bakhtin, the literary protagonist in the polyphonic novel is, first of all, a figure potentially equal to the author ("What the author used to do is now done by the hero, who illuminates himself from all possible points of view." [1984: 49]); second, s/he is the living embodiment of an incomplete, self-aware idea. This idea "is inter-individual and inter-subjective—the realm of its existence is not the individual consciousness, but the dialogic communion between several consciousnesses" (ibid., 88). Finally, due to these particular circumstances, the protagonist himself "does not merely dissolve in himself all possible concrete traits of his image by making them the subject of his own reflection—he has no such traits at all, he has no fixed definition, there is nothing to say about him; he figures not as a person taken from life, but rather as the subject of consciousness" (ibid., 48).

All these features of this type of character are given *maximum emphasis* by postmodernism. The postmodernist protagonist fulfills his authorial ambitions not only by constantly engaging in the act of writing (usually representing a considerable share of genres interpolated in the postmodernist text). He also tries to live his life according to aesthetic laws (for instance, Nabokov's Humbert in *Lolita* or Van in *Ada*). By so doing, such a character may become the embodiment of a cultural formula: The ups and downs of his life, inevitably accompanied by the character's own reflections upon them, reveal the relativism of cultural models. Or, more often, the character's personality forms the cultural field in which contradictory aesthetic systems intersect and begin their dialogue. The character's consciousness, posture, and actions frequently manifest their "intertextual" nature; this is why the postmodern protagonist is so often an academic, a literary scholar, a writer, a historian, or, on the contrary, why he sometimes assumes the role of a naive child. Paradoxically, both features may be combined in one and the same character, as is the case, for instance, in *A School for Fools, Pushkin House,* or *Moscow to the End of the Line.* All this conspires to endow the main character with the quality of "outsideness" (*vnenakhodimost'*), which Bakhtin considers a trait belonging solely to the work's author. This position of outsideness is what enables the main character to become the center of the intertextual dialogue, while at the same time avoiding being locked within some specific cultural formula.

Finally, the erosion of the main character's stable traits reaches its logical conclusion in postmodernism: the image of a specific human being, an individual with his or her own life, is replaced by a mask, which is always culturally polyvalent, or "dissolves" and turns into a bundle of conflicting cultural associations.[13] This disappearance of human individuality becomes particularly evident in Russian postmodernism, which employs the tradition of nineteenth-century Russian psychological realism. It is the main weakness of postmodernist poetics, one that is preprogrammed, as it were, and therefore impossible to rectify.

The postmodernist solution to the problem of the protagonist is to take the characteristics of the dialogic character to the point where the distinction between character and author disappears; according to Bakhtin's definition, the author himself is also characterized by *outsideness, uncertainty,* and *intersubjectivity.* In other words, the image of the postmodernist protagonist is constructed according to the same blueprint as that of the author/creator.

And vice versa. The postmodernist text deliberately puts author and character on an equal footing. The means may vary: giving the protagonist the same name as the biographical author; breaking down the authorial consciousness into "sub-voices" belonging to both the narrator and the characters; or even the establishment of an overt rivalry between author and hero. In the dialogic context, Roland Barthes's concept of the "death of the author" merely testifies to the fact that the postmodernist author not only retains his responsibilities for arranging contacts and conflicts among worlds, languages, and types of writing, but, to a far greater extent than Bakhtin could have foreseen, becomes involved in the dialogue as an equal participant. The cultural dimensions of this dialogue simply do not leave the author any "neutral space."

The constant tension between the author's role as "director" and "character" results in postmodernist fragmentation, irony, and self-referentiality, thereby contributing to the creation of a consistently playful situation. These characteristics of postmodernist style, as well as the emphasis on quotation, are often highlighted in discussions of postmodernism. However, they are nothing but the external manifestations of deeper constructive processes related to the transformations of dialogism.

Even these brief comparisons (which will be presented in more detail when we turn to particular literary texts) are sufficient to lead to an inevitable conclusion: dialogism cannot be treated as merely an individual element of postmodernist poetics, for it is the structural frame defining the unique nature of postmodernist intertextuality and playfulness. In other words, it functions as the key to the postmodernist artistic paradigm. Such a perspective allows us to posit that the process of literary evolution from modernism to postmodernism, which frequently occurs within the *oeuvre* of a single author (Joyce, Beckett, Nabokov, Brodsky), is connected to the more or less smooth transition from the monological principles of modernism to the dialogical principles of postmodernism.

We have seen, however, that dialogism itself undergoes considerable modifications in the context of other elements of postmodernist poetics. According to the logic of these modifications, the disproportional expansion of each element in the dialogical structure *to its limit* can result in the transformation of dialogue into the dissonance of a street festival: Polyphony can easily become cacophony, with all the voices overlapping and merging into an indistinguishable rumble. It should be noted, though, that these processes began not with postmodernism but with the modernist fiction of the twenties and thirties.[14]

This phenomenon is similar to the Second Law of Thermodynamics: when literature concentrates on the self-consciousness of the writing process and turns into a closed system, it results in a sharp surge of entropy that is manifested primarily in the artistic realization of the relative and transient nature of all ontological and epistemological boundaries, which had previously been thought to be unshakable. The dialogic system is supplanted by a postmodernist aggregate (hypertrophied dialogism) that reflects the chaotic entanglement of self and other, text and context, and various types of writing and cultural languages. The postmodernist version of dialogism demonstrates that at the end of the twentieth century it is impossible to take a cultural stand that would be both stable and distanced. Doing so is just as impossible for the author as for the narrator and the characters, since simultaneity eliminates temporal distance, and the dissolution of the boundaries between the author, the narrator, and the main character strips "outsideness" of its value: The author, protagonist, and reader are all locked within a universal "creative chronotope" from which there is no exit.

Bakhtin defines outsideness as "a founded axiological posture of consciousness that constitutes a precondition for aesthetic creativity" (1990: 205). But does this mean that aesthetic creativity is incompatible with the postmodernist artistic paradigm? Does postmodernism's "anti-totalizing" drive also undermine the structural foundation of the artistic consciousness itself? A positive answer to these questions implies that postmodernism should be interpreted as the death of art, as the triumph of a technological (computerized) collage made of the fragments of cultural values, as cultural self-destruction. Such masochistic concepts enjoy considerable popularity and respect (here one need only name Ihab Hassan or Gerald Graff).

However, a negative response is also possible: No, postmodernism is not the negation of art but is rather a logical stage in art's evolution, and the features it shares with the Baroque are no accident. Consequently, one might see a self-contained model of the world taking shape in postmodernism as well. By extension, this suggests that postmodernist aesthetics is discovering a new philosophical strategy, one that will provide a key to solving the mystery of the self-regulation of chaos and that looks for harmony *within* chaos rather than on its surface.

## Dialogue with Chaos as a New Artistic Strategy

In September 1981, Stanford University hosted an international symposium on the problems of chaos and order as applied to different cultural and scholarly areas. In his presentation "Order out of Chaos," Ilya Prigogine, a Russian-born Belgian chemist and winner of the 1977 Nobel Prize, shared his discovery of "dissipative structures." The concept of "dissipative structures" is the result of Prigogine's reinterpretation of the Second Law of Thermodynamics. They emerge in the process of self-organization of closed systems that are in extremely unbalanced conditions, that is, in a chaotic state. Prigogine concludes:

> The concept of laws, of "order," can no longer be considered as given, and the mechanism of the emergence of laws and order out of disorder and chaos has to be investigated. . . . On one side, as mentioned, we are moving to a pluralistic view. On the other, there is a trend to find a new unity in apparently contrasting aspects of our experience. . . . It is obvious that this new development brings the sciences and humanities closer together. Traditionally, the sciences dealt with universals and the humanities with events. It is a humanistic interpretation of nature in terms of events which diffuses now into science proper. It is not astonishing therefore that some concepts which have been recently emphasized find their application both in the sciences and humanities. As an example, I may mention the concept of "nonlinearity." It is essential for the occurrence of dissipative structures, but it is obviously also essential for the understanding of any form of society, be it an insect or human society. (Prigogine 1984: 43–44, 59–60)

The French theoretician Edgar Morin believes that "we should learn to think order and disorder together. . . . Science is applying itself more and more profoundly to a dialogue with randomness. But for that dialogue to be more and more fruitful, one should know that order is relative and relational and that disorder is uncertain. . . . Today the dialogic presence of order and disorder shows us that knowledge ought to try to negotiate with uncertainty. This also means that the purpose of knowledge is not to discover the secret of the world or the master equation, but to dialogue with the world" (Morin 1984: 105–6).

Michel Serres, a historian, views the myth of Babel as a general model of human knowledge; first, because human knowledge is always an open-ended project and, second, because knowledge also exists within "an un-integrable multiplicity" (1984: 226). "Order and disorder, the one and the multiple, systems and distributions, islands and seas, noises and harmony, are of the subject as they are of the object. . . . What fluctuates is order and disorder. What fluctuates is their vicinity and common border, their rela-tionship and mutual penetration" (ibid., 233). It is this logic, according to Serres, that establishes the direction for the development of knowledge and culture as a whole.

The opinions quoted above are not unusual but rather represent concep-tual common ground for scholars of different disciplines, representatives of the humanities and natural sciences, experts in poststructuralism and neo-Freudianism, theoreticians and experimenters. Thus in his introduction to Ilya Prigogine's and Isabelle Stengers's *Order out of Chaos* (1984), one of the major publications to bring chaos theory beyond its previous confines within individual natural sciences by giving it a general philosophical and methodological treatment, the well-known sociologist and historian Alvin Toffler calls the book a "lever for changing science itself, for compelling us to reexamine its goals, its methods, its epistemology—its world view" (ibid., xi). Without a doubt, the dialogical interpenetration of chaos and cosmos has created a new cultural and scholarly paradigm. There are nu-merous other examples of this paradigm's implementation: Thus, Mitchel Feigenbaum's "chaotic attractors" and Benoit Mandelbrot's theories of fractals examine the formation of temporal and locational structures of order *within* chaotic conditions, the regularity of coincidences between ran-dom-variable functions. These and other theories have outlined the vision of "self-organizing chaos" as the basis for a new paradigm of knowledge:

> Self-organization is the act whereby a self-propagating system, without out-side influence, takes itself from seeming irregularity into some sort of order. It seems to reflect a tendency for a dynamical system to organize itself into more complex structures. The structure can be spatial, temporal, or opera-tional (functional). The time which the structure lasts varies from one case to another. . . . To the extent that there is order within the chaotic regime, the word chaos (since its normal usage implies utter confusion or total disorder) is a misnomer. But it's too late now. (Williams 1997: 233–34)[15]

Postmodernism quite naturally takes its place alongside these theories.

When speaking of chaos in the literary context, we use this term as a metaphor for a universal artistic model of the world, one that can be traced back to the earliest forms of artistic consciousness. The opposition "chaos/cosmos" is the foundation of any aesthetic activity and is expressed at various points in time in more specific binary oppositions, such as *nature/culture, periphery/center, the diabolical/the divine, the impersonal/the personal, absurdity/meaning, standard/creativity,* and so forth.[16] However, in classical art, chaos appears to be external to the work; the artist overcomes chaos of material in the creative process and presents to the reader a ready snapshot of objective harmony, a completely "transfigured" chaos. The elements of the world model of chaos are certainly present in any artistic world, but they lack independent meaning and are subordinate to the internal logic of the work's harmonizing conception. The works of such nineteenth-century writers as Gogol, Dostoevsky, and Tolstoy certainly contain numerous images that could be said to represent the world model of chaos (for instance, the Kuragins in *War and Peace,* or Svidrigailov in *Crime and Punishment*). However, these images are subordinate to the author's fairly elegant artistic conception, which reflects a certain philosophy of harmony between the individual and the world. Therefore, this is not a case of struggle between destructive characters and those who personify creative and harmonizing trends but rather of the interaction between the semantics of chaos, as reflected in particular characters, and the will of the author who places them in his artistic structure. In the novels of the nineteenth century, including even those of Dostoevsky, where the transformation of the classical artistic system is particularly marked, all models of chaos, without exception, are determined by the author's idea of harmony.[17] This particular determinism is considerably weaker in modernism and disappears completely in postmodernism.

In modernism, the relationship with chaos is for the first time *realized* as the foundation of art and presented as art's central *content.* At this point, chaos is no longer treated as external to the aesthetic act but is rather incorporated within it. Still, in modernism chaos remains an impersonal formation, a mere *object* to be manipulated by the artist/subject. The various strategies that follow from such an understanding of the world result in different trends within modernist and postmodernist art. They all have one thing in common: a radical rejection of the search for harmony in life. Symbolism, for instance, seeks harmony in the unknowable. The "high modernism" of Marcel Proust or Thomas Mann presents the disjoined and illogical subjectivity of the human creator as a universal model of harmony. Surrealism also constructs harmony out of the chaos of the unconscious. The culture of modernism has, as a matter of fact, created a new understanding of harmony: harmony is identified with *freedom from the metaphysical power of reality/chaos.* The various movements within modernism disagree only on the methods of achieving this kind of harmony. This strategy reaches its extreme in the avant-garde (as well as in Socialist Realism, which is a paradoxical implementation of avant-garde discourse). The avant-garde myth is based on two related theses: first, the concept of the present reality's chaotic nature, which is demonstrated by the dismantling of all forms of culture, including the language of art itself in its traditional forms; second, the movement toward some abstract, rationally delineated utopian project for harmony. As a result, the process of dismantling traditional forms of world ordering and world perception becomes a purpose unto itself: The liberation of destructive forces is interpreted as the only path to greater harmony.

The difference between modernism and the artistic systems that preceded it lies in the fact that the modernist writer sees an opposition to chaos not in the "objective" law of harmony, which is merely articulated by the artist (as in classical art), but in the (fully self-conscious) subjective and free self-expression of the artist's personality, which embodies the only possible truth of being, one that is *a priori* relative. Here we see a peculiar self-reflection of art directed at universal models of the creative process. Modernism mythologizes the creative duel between artist and chaotic reality, endowing this duel with universal artistic and philosophical meaning. As Susan Strechle notes,

> modernism conceives its charge as replacing reality's chaos with the orderly truth of art. . . . No longer a mere observer of reality, the modernist becomes the maker of a clockwork universe. Empowered by the ordering activity of mind, the artist takes a position of absolute authority over the text: she or he becomes the mystified and absent presence, the *deus artifex,* or godly maker (1992: 17).

This is certainly the polar opposite of traditional monologism, but an opposite that is itself monological—"negative monism," as Matei Calinescu would have it.[18]

The paradoxical nature of the modernist world view results from mixing together ostensibly "chaotic" material, to be transformed into a harmonious image of the world *right before our very eyes*. This paradoxical character of modernist poetics is manifested in such essential features as a permanent inner conflict (Jan van Baak), or the predominance of "catachresis" (Igor Smirnov and Renata Dering), on all textual levels.

Though postmodernism would seem to continue the experiments of modernism and the avant-garde, it nevertheless differs from them significantly by incorporating dialogism. First of all, it is postmodernism that demolishes the completeness and objectivity of the artistic conception of chaos. In the context of total dialogism, chaos is not only constantly challenged to come up with a rebuttal but also *becomes subjective,* an equal participant in the dialogue with the artist.

In this context, the perception of the very idea of culture, as well as of cultural symbols, changes drastically. Each individual "cultural semioimage" (to use Yakov Golosovker's expression [1987: 119 and passim]) aspires to transcend chaos and maintains this intent regardless of any transformation it undergoes. However, in the simultaneous "creative chronotope" of the postmodernist text, the conflicting ideas expressed by such "semioimages" either overlap and cancel each other out, demonstrate their own ambivalent evaluative nature, or create the "Brownian" effect of disordered movement: They model chaos.

What is more important is that the dialogical emphasis changes the stance of the artist and creator of harmony. Postmodernism demonstrates a major artistic and philosophical attempt to overcome the binary opposition of chaos and cosmos, which is fundamental for classical and modernist types of culture, and to redirect the creative impulse toward a *compromise* between these universals. Taken to its limits, dialogue with chaos has precisely this objective. This understanding of culture was probably expressed for the first time in Joyce's *Finnegan's Wake.* Umberto Eco describes the novel's semantic structure:

> Were Joyce to describe this, he might say something: the form of the universe has changed in an incomprehensible way; I have felt that our millenary interpretive criteria no longer work, and thus I give to you a substitute of our world, an endless world and a meaningless whirl. At least this substitute is a human product, posited, not given, founded on the cultural order of language as opposed to the order of nature. . . . *Finnegans Wake* is that great epiphany of the cosmic structure resolved into language. (1992: 77)

However, creating the image of ontological chaos via the image of language, literally in language, has a major advantage: Chaos becomes comprehensible. As a result, in spite of the apparently chaotic cultural and linguistic form of Joyce's novel, Eco argues that "a medieval rhythm runs unobserved under the entire discourse of the book and emerges clearly when one hears the text recorded directly by Joyce. There is a sort of 'cantata,' a uniform rhythm, the diabolic reintroduction of a type of *proportio* in the very core of disorder" (ibid., 81).

Eco describes this paradoxical combination of order and disorder using the Joycean term "chaosmos"—the purest expression of the concept of compromise between chaos and cosmos. Not surprisingly, the chaosmos of *Finnegan's Wake* resembles Ilya Prigogine's theory of "dissipative structures." The new world model finds its realization through the concepts of the natural sciences and through art.

In *Chaosmos: Literature, Science, and Theory,* Philip Kuberski compares the ideas of quantum mechanics and relativity theory with works by Joyce, Eliot, and Lacan, demonstrating that the seed of this philosophy started to grow in the late forms of modernism. In this respect, postmodernism has to be viewed as the direct progeny of modernism, as an explicit manifestation of deep changes in modernist discourse that began in the twenties and thirties: "Texts such as *Finnegan's Wake* and *The Waste Land,* which abandon the linear and abstracting tendencies of modern literature, show how chaos and cosmos can be reconciled and yet appreciated distinctly within the dynamics of a multileveled, multitemporal, plurivocal language, whose surplus of meaning begins to resemble the 'noisy' but engendering status of chaos" (Kuberski 1994: 47). But it is only in the postmodern period that the philosophy of chaosmos becomes truly universal.

The search for a radical compromise between chaos and cosmos, and between binary oppositions in general, forms the particular logic of postmodernism, which Lyotard calls "paralogy." Lyotard uses this category in order to describe the new scientific consciousness (while relying on the work of such a "chaos theoretician" as Benoit Mandelbrot):

> Postmodern science—by concerning itself with such things as undecidables, the limits of precise control, conflicts characterized by incomplete information, *"fracta,"* catastrophes, and pragmatic paradoxes—is theorizing its own evolution as discontinuous, catastrophic, nonrectifiable, and paradoxical. It is changing the meaning of the word *knowledge,* while expressing how such a change can take place. It is producing not the known, but the unknown. And it suggests a model of legitimation that has nothing to do with maximized performance, but has as its basis difference understood as paralogy. (Lyotard 1984: 60)

Lyotard stresses that "paralogy" is the opposite of the idea of consensus. "Paralogy" arises as a result of skepticism about the possibility of achieving consensus on any issue. "Paralogy" embodies "a power that destabilizes the capacity for explanation, manifested in the promulgation of new norms for understanding" (ibid., 61). As Steven Connor notes, "paralogy" is interpreted here as "contradictory reasoning, designed to shift the structures of reason itself" (1989: 34).

All postmodernist compromises, including the compromise between chaos and cosmos in particular, are paralogical: Rather than resolving contradictions, they lead to a new intellectual space for the constant interaction of binary oppositions. Of course, such a space cannot help but be the source of new conflicts and new contradictions; yet such constant interaction is also the inexhaustible source of new artistic and philosophical meaning.

Without addressing this illogical combination of compromise with instability and perpetual conflict, it is impossible to understand the postmodernist artistic consciousness in general and Russian postmodernism in particular.

The most meaningful images in Russian postmodernism prove to be multilayered paralogical compromises between various binary oppositions. Thus the image of trash becomes particularly important for the Russian conceptual artist Ilya Kabakov. In a dialogue with Boris Groys (Groys and Kabakov 1996), Kabakov defines trash as a philosophical compromise between life and death: First he says that "trash is as close to death as possible: it is death made visual" (ibid., 320), but on the very next page he asserts that "life itself is a pile of trash" (ibid., 321). Moreover, trash for Kabakov is a "metaphor . . . for a mediocre, gray, and constant existence; first and foremost, for an existence without action" (ibid., 322). At the same time, it embodies something extremely individual and personal: Trash is "intimately mine, belonging only to me" (ibid., 328). Trash occupies the transitional zone between memory and oblivion: "It is a kind of intermediate and internally fragmentary object, one side of which points to memory, while the other side points to oblivion" (ibid., 329). Kabakov's discussion of trash is a particularly illuminating example of postmodernist "paralogy": For Kabakov, the question of trash is anything but abstract; over the course of the past decade, he has turned actual trash into the subject and material of his installations and albums.

Postmodernism in Russia attempts to overcome what Iurii Lotman and Boris Uspenskii call the "essential polarity" (1985: 31) of the Russian cultural tradition, which renders any compromise between binary oppositions virtually impossible:

The basic cultural values (ideological, political, and religious) of medieval Russia were distributed in a bipolar field, and divided by a sharp boundary without an axiologically neutral zone. . . . Intermediate neutral spheres were not envisaged. Behavior in earthly life could, correspondingly, be either sinful or holy. This situation spread into extra-ecclesiastical conceptions: thus secular power could be interpreted as divine or diabolical, but never as neutral.

The presence of a neutral sphere in the medieval West led to the appearance of a certain subjective continuity between the negated present and awaited future. . . . The neutral sphere of life became a norm, and the greatly semioticized high and low spheres of medieval culture were forced into the category of cultural anomalies.

Russian culture of the medieval period was dominated by a different value orientation. Duality and the absence of a neutral axiological sphere led to a conception of the new not as a continuation but as a total eschatological change. . . . These underlying structures of development are what allows us to speak about the unity of Russian culture at the various stages of its history. (1985: 31, 32, 33)

At the same time, one cannot help but agree with Mikhail Epstein that the uniqueness of Russian postmodernism in world culture can be defined in terms of the dualist maximalism of the Russian tradition. Russian postmodernism is capable of making a "paralogical" compromise between traditional Russian binarism and Western ternary models.

> In order for Russian culture to adopt the ternary model, it needed to add neutral and mediating zones without renouncing the productive aspects of binarism. It is this very dualism . . . which may prove to be Russian culture's invaluable contribution to the contemporary, homogenized "post-historical" state of Western culture. (1997: 55)

Earlier I speculated that, as a result of postmodernist transformations, dialogism could stop being a systematic principle, which can lead to the dialogically organized universe's loss of its internal organization, its mutation into a chaotic conglomerate. At this point, we can amend this thesis: The close interaction between postmodernist poetics and the world model of chaos, which is expressed in the breakdown of the artistic system's traditional structures, does *not inevitably* result in the fragmentation of artistic unity. The formation of a new, "nonclassical," "chaosmic" system within an artistic whole is also a *possibility* due to the artistic strategy described above, a strategy aimed at the formation of explosive "paralogical" compromises between binary oppositions and the destruction of stable cultural hierarchies while identifying "dissipative structures" in chaos, which in postmodernism is equal to the mixture of different voices and images of the cultural past and present. This artistic strategy might be called *dialogue with chaos,* a strategy that marks the boundaries between modernism and postmodernism. The formation of a new artistic strategy is likely to give new meaning to features that were obviously present in modernism but would become the principles of artistic world modeling only in postmodernism (intertextual play, dialogism).

Such a systematic organizational principle is described by Gilles Deleuze in "Rhizome Versus Trees." Deleuze isolates several different systems of cultural world modeling. Classical culture develops the concept of the world tree, a hierarchical, multitiered structure based on binary oppositions. It always includes a "trunk," that is, the system's base, and "roots," which are causal relations determining the dynamics and functioning of the system as a whole. The culture of modernism transformed this model into a "bush" with "multiple roots," none of which is primary. The unity of this system is defined not by the qualities of the object but by the intentions of the subject. Here binary oppositions are less pronounced, and the system is less cyclical, even though it is clearly connected to the world-tree model. In any case, it preserves the representational relationship between culture and reality: "The world has become chaos, but the book remains the image of the world: radicle-chaosmos rather than root-chaos" (Deleuze 1992: 29). This system, in turn, leads to a modern world model—a rhizomatic one.[19] On a somewhat simplified level, one can distinguish three groups of principles that, according to Gilles Deleuze, characterize a rhizomatic system:

1. heterogeneity, the playful combination of different semiotic codes without undermining their internal integrity; multiplicity, the impossibility of singling out the system's base. Rhizomatic multiplicity also denies any kind of transcendence, any additional dimension that would extend beyond its immediate multilinear space;
2. fragmentation—"A rhizome may be broken, shattered at a given spot, but it will start up again on one of its old lines, or on new lines" (ibid., 32). This principle is related to the transformation of the relationship between culture and reality, which are no longer connected by representation or mimises. The book and the world form a fragmented yet internally integral rhizome;
3. the rhizome is deprived of any transcendent deep structure, whether temporal or spatial—it is all *here* and *now;* hence the rhizome's incomplete nature: it has neither beginning nor end in any dimension but is always in the middle of its dynamics, always in the process of development based on the interaction of heterogeneous elements characterized by a single space–time status.

"In contrast to centered (even polycentric) systems with hierarchical modes of communication and preestablished paths, the rhizome is an acentered, nonhierarchical, nonsignifying system without a General, and without an organizing memory of central automation, defined solely by a circulation of states" (ibid., 36). At this point, the similarity between the rhizomatic system and postmodernist poetics becomes clear. The first group of rhizomatic principles resembles specific features of postmodernist play; the second resonates with the poetics of intertextuality; the third group corresponds to the postmodernist version of dialogism. Of particular importance here is the connection between simultaneity as a precondition for dialogue, with open-endedness as its major feature, and what Deleuze defines as "cartography and decalcomania: a rhizome is not amenable to any structural or generative model" (ibid., 36).

The artistic attempt to model chaos by mixing cultural languages, to search for "rhizomes" and "dissipative structures" hidden inside chaos and transforming it into chaosmos, is based on a contradictory interpretation of chaos. From the very beginning, chaos is perceived both as debunking all kinds of rules and providing a form of paradoxical survival for old cultural systems and for the creation of new ones. The postmodernist author constantly has to maintain an unstable balance between, on the one hand, the temptation of universal cultural teleology, a certain metalanguage that could rise above the chaos of multiple simultaneous cultural languages, and, on the other, the fascination with chaos as a supreme manifestation of freedom from any cultural and ontological limitations. Such a strategy is certainly unlikely to be stable and lasting—it is obviously a transitional artistic system. The question is, however, What is the direction of this transition?

This is clearly only a working hypothesis. It is essential to conduct a theoretical investigation of the specific mechanism of dialogue with chaos, drawing examples from Russian literature. Western theories of postmodernism pay special attention to such stylistic categories as postmodernist irony (Alan Wilde, Margaret Roze), parody (Linda Hutcheon), "double coding" (Charles Jencks), "pastiche" (Frederic Jameson), and carnivalization (Ihab Hassan, Matei Calinescu). Brian McHale's idea of postmodernist genres as successors to the Menippean tradition is also related to carnivalization. The list could be even longer. However, simply providing an inventory does not really address the question of the functional interconnection between this device and others, no matter how much postmodernist writers like to provide lists. It is this interconnection that lays the foundation for dialogue with chaos as a completely new artistic strategy.

We will try to solve this problem by other means: by analyzing the individual texts that, in our opinion, have played a major role in the emergence and development of Russian postmodernism. We will begin this analysis with works that appeared in Russian literature in the late sixties and early seventies, simultaneously with the rise of the postmodernist consciousness in the West, even if Soviet culture's isolation from its Western counterpart makes it completely independent. Today, literary scholars of radically different schools of thought unequivocally recognize these texts as classics of Russian postmodernism, which to a larger extent predetermined its further development in the history of Russian literature.

# II.
# Culture as Chaos

# 2

# Sacking the Museum

## Andrei Bitov's *Pushkin House*

*Where this axiologically "bodied" atmosphere is absent,
where the position of outsideness is fortuitous and unstable,
and where the living axiological understanding is totally immanent to a life experienced from within (practical-egoistic
life, social life, moral life, etc.)—any axiologically prolonged
and creative dwelling on the boundaries of man and his life
is impossible, and the only thing one can do is to mimic and
simulate a likeness to man and his life. . . .*

—Mikhail Bakhtin (1990: 204)

The post-Thaw crisis of socialist metanarratives, which became apparent in
the end of the sixties, has, to paraphrase Mandelstam, revived the Russian
modernists' "longing for world culture"; at the very least, the question of a
possible return to culture acquires vital relevance. Hence the emphasis on the
metafictional "modeling of modeling" (see Segal 1979) becomes crucial: it is
impossible to return to culture without thoroughly examining the mechanism
of transmission of cultural traditions, a mechanism that was apparently lost
or destroyed in the Soviet era.

Socialist Realism, however, is a grandiose metanarrative, legitimizing absolutely all spheres of spiritual and practical activity. Jean-Francois Lyotard
claims that Stalinism was founded on the absorption of both fundamental
forms of narrative legitimation: Party ideology subordinated the institutions
of both knowledge (science) and power (the state) (Lyotard 1984: 36–37). At
the same time, totalitarianism, which would appear to be the polar opposite
of classical culture, persistently reworked the classical tradition, creating its
own canon, its own Pushkin, Gogol, Lermontov, and Tolstoy (see Freidberg
1962). Moreover, totalitarian culture paradoxically continued the inherent
features of modernism and the avant-garde, reproducing them in a hyperbolic
form. Thus Boris Groys calls the socialist state "a total work of art," perhaps
even exaggerating the continuity between avant-garde and totalitarian culture in his *Total Art of Stalinism:*

[T]he Stalin era satisfied the fundamental avant-garde demand that art cease representing life and begin transforming it by means of a total aesthetico-political project. Thus if Stalin is viewed as the artist-tyrant who succeeded the philosopher-tyrant typical of the age of contemplative, mimetic thought, Stalinist poetics is the immediate heir to constructivist poetics. (1992: 36)

We have already mentioned Mikhail Epstein's model,[1] which sees postmodernism as resulting from the ideological simulacra of Socialist Realism that produce a fictional reality. But we should recall that there can be no talk of postmodernism and the postmodern condition until there is a *recognition* of the simulative nature of the cultural and historical context. Just how does the realization of total simulation, so central to totalitarian culture, occur in the literature of the sixties, and how is it reflected in postmodern fiction? Andrei Bitov's novel *Pushkin House* (1964–71) provides the perfect opportunity to address these questions. Bitov's most important achievement in *Pushkin House* is the exposure of the simulative character of the Soviet mentality and Soviet culture long before Baudrillard and his followers; that is, he draws the reader's attention to the primacy of imaginary constructs, of images without real referents, of copies without originals. It is in *Pushkin House* that this radical transformation is first established, the transformation that is perhaps the most important consequence of the Thaw. It is the beginning of postmodernist time.

Bitov's novel, which was banned in Russia for eighteen years (its first printing in the author's homeland was in 1988), tells (and retells) the life story of a young literary scholar, Lev Nikolaevich Odoevtsev (Lyova), the son of the famous scholar who, during the height of the Stalinist repression, renounced his own father, a truly outstanding thinker by the name of Modest Platonovich Odoevtsev. The novel consists of Lyova's childhood, his attempts to get to know his grandfather after the latter returns from the camps, his disillusionment when Modest Platonovich sees him as the image of his treacherous son rather than as an intellectual heir, his articles and research, his friendship and rivalry with another student, named Mitishatyev, and his convoluted relations with three women. The climax of the novel occurs when Lyova and Mitishatyev virtually destroy the Pushkin House's museum of the history of literature, and the two former friends fight a duel with pistols found in that very same museum. This sensational event takes place on the day of the fiftieth anniversary of the October Revolution (1967): When Lyova is on duty at the academic institute, his work gives way to drunken revelry, revelry to a fistfight, and the fight to the duel and the destruction of the museum. Over the course of the days remaining before the workweek begins, Lyova and his friends hastily clean up the museum and replace some of its most valuable pieces with copies, only to discover that no one takes any notice of the obvious frauds and forgeries. Such is the story of this complex metafictional narrative. Decades later, it is difficult to see why this book would be banned, and yet the authorities had their reasons. The censors often prove to be the most incisive readers.

That *Pushkin House* serves as a transition among various traditions has been quite clearly noted by the novel's many critics, who nonetheless diverge in their evaluation of its merits. Thus the traditionalist Iurii Karabchievskii departs from his overall positive appraisal of *Pushkin House* when he reproaches Bitov for his excessive devotion to "play" at the expense of life (Karabchievskii 1989: 67–103), while the postmodernist Viktor Erofeyev calls the novel "a monument to times past" for its traditionalism and overly authoritarian style (1988: 202–4).

For their part, Western critics have seen a striking resemblance in Bitov's novel to the aesthetic parameters of postmodernism: "In fact," writes Rolf Hellebust, "the first impression of a Western reader exposed to *Pushkin House* is that the author seems to have used the subversive literary devices of every postmodern writer he has read as well as some he has not. These include the essayism of Musil, the paratextual apparatus of Borges, Nabokov's exposure of fictional artifice, Eco's concern with intertextuality, and the repetition and narrative multiplicity of Robbe-Grillet" (1991: 267).

No less relevant to this novel are its ties to the modernist tradition in general and to Russian metafiction in particular. All of the features of metafiction are clearly present in Bitov's novel. His heroes are literary scholars, and the text of *Pushkin House* includes their entire articles (or their drafts and fragments), analyzing and reifying the very process of literary creation and cultural development. Even the author-narrator himself repeatedly lapses into reflections on the literary scholar's themes, as, for example in the appendix to the third part of the novel: "Achilles and the Tortoise (Relationship between Hero and Author)." The author-creator finds his double in the narrator-novelist, who constantly complains of defects in the novel's construction, changing his plans for future sections of the narrative on the fly; in the end he even meets up with his hero and asks him provocative questions (naturally, the author knows the answers the hero would give; he is, after all, a novelist). The freedom of time and space resulting from these metafictional games easily allows for the same events to be retold in different manners, for the resurrection of dead heroes, and for references in the beginning of the novel to its end; it also blurs any sort of plot connections through appendices and commentaries. Finally, a large role is played by semiparodic references to classical Russian literature in the titles of chapters, in epigraphs, and so forth.

Dubravka Oraić defines the metafictional character of *Pushkin House* as a special form of quotation that arose "in the Sixties and Seventies, when the megaculture of modernism had either already ended or was in the process of collapse" (1994: 106). Oraić's model also includes Anna Akhmatova's "Poem without a Hero," Valentin Kataev's *Grass of Oblivion,* and the lyric poetry of Joseph Brodsky. The paradigm of the "citational museum," as Oraić calls it, is comparable to the "citational dialogue" that is so typical of the Acmeist tradition:

> Montage in avant-garde citational dialogue is intellectual, insofar as the paradigmatic order of European culture at the pinnacle of the megaculture of modernism has been shaken, so that once again it behooves [modernists] to achieve mastery in the estranged processes of quotation. In the postmodern quotational museum, at the end of the megaculture of modernism, an ideal order of contemporary art has yet to arise; or if it does exist, it is threatened (especially in totalitarian societies such as those that existed in the Soviet era), and therefore it is necessary to create and fortify it in anthologized examples. . . . This younger nostalgic consciousness appeared outside of the avant-garde cultural system, but it rests upon the avant-garde and the modernist tradition in counterbalance to the Socialist Realist canon, which is still strong in its obsolescence, and to totalitarian society. . . . In all its essential characteristics, postmodern self-referentiality is a *reconstruction of the avant-garde citational dialogue*—but with a difference: now the dialogue is conducted with the avant-garde and modernist traditions themselves. (Ibid., 106–7; emphasis in the original)

In other words, Bitov's novel attempts to use metafiction to restore the tie to modernist tradition that totalitarian culture destroyed; the echoes of Vaginov, Mandelstam, and Nabokov in *Pushkin House* are not clearly intentional.[2] But between Bitov's novel and pre-postmodernist metafiction stand Socialist Realism and totalitarian culture with their own conception of classical culture. As Boris Groys argues, "[T]o the Bolshevik ideologists . . . point zero was the ultimate reality. The art of the past was not living history that could serve as a guide to the present, but a storehouse of inert things from among which anything that seems appealing or useful could be removed at will" (1992: 41). Thus it is particularly important that the plot of *Pushkin House* reaches its climax when this storehouse of classical heritage that pretends to be an academic museum is all but destroyed. Such violence is the only kind of dialogue with a frozen, simulated cultural heritage available to the metafiction of the post-Thaw, post–Socialist Realist culture of postmodernism.

Socialist Realism is never actually directly addressed in *Pushkin House.* It is only considerably later, in "The Near Retro" (1987), that Bitov reveals the Socialist Realist associations behind many of the novel's motifs. But this does not mean that images of totalitarian consciousness are absent from the novel, which is precisely the point, since Bitov does not work with the models of Socialist Realist literature themselves (that would be the task of Sots-Art); instead, he addresses the most universal models of the Soviet mentality.

It should come as no surprise that the simulation of reality is directly defined by the author of *Pushkin House* as the central theme of the novel. In the very beginning, when explaining the essence of the method he had chosen, Bitov writes:

> *We are inclined in this tale, under the roof of Pushkin House, to follow in the hallowed traditions of the museum, not shying away from echoes and repetitions—on the contrary, welcoming them in every way, as if we even rejoiced in our lack of inner independence. For that, too, is "in key," so to speak, and can be understood in relation to the phenomena that have served us here as theme and material; namely, phenomena utterly nonexistent in reality. So, if even the container we must use was created before our day and not by us, this fact also serves our purpose, as if closing the circle.*
> And so we are re-creating the hero's contemporary non-existence. (1987: 5; italics in the original)

It is significant that here, in the very beginning of the novel, the simulation of reality is presented as closely dependent on the "hallowed traditions of the museum" of the Pushkin House—in other words, on the Golden Age of Russian literature. This dependence is all the more paradoxical in that the novel's protagonists, who have preserved an organic link with the traditional culture buried beneath Soviet civilization, are the only ones who look *real,* and in this sense they are, according to Bitov, aristocratic. Here I have in mind the protagonist's grandfather, Modest Platonovich Odoevtsev, and Uncle Dickens, a family friend who has returned from the camps and who Lyova at times even imagines is his real father.

It is the grandfather whose drunken monologue constitutes a merciless diagnosis on Lyova and his whole generation:

> All of the positivism of contemporary spiritual life is negative. False concepts are wiped out and replaced by nothing. . . . You never seem to be utterly sincere—do you hear, Lyovushka, I don't doubt your sincerity, being sincere seems important to you—but you're never utterly sincere *yourself.* . . . Neither facts nor conditions nor reality exists for you—only the concepts of them. You simply have no suspicion that life exists! (Ibid., 64, 75, 76)

The entire novel essentially confirms this diagnosis, except that the novel as a whole lacks Modest Platonovich's tone of irascible scorn: the one true fact turns out to be that reality has been entirely replaced by current *conceptions* of reality.

As for Uncle Dickens, his originality in spite of the falseness of simulated reality is nonverbal, but no less convincing for that:

> Lyova had always had the childish idea that [Uncle Dickens] was reading a different *War and Peace* from everyone else, not in the sense that he was reading it his own way, but that he really had a different book by the name of *War and Peace,* with a different Natasha, a different Bolkonsky, also by Tolstoy, but a different Tolstoy.... Uncle Mitya—bluntly put, the rare outline of his soul—created the fact alongside him by his plain use of words. And Lyova would swallow his saliva, tasting in his mouth the metal of authenticity: it had happened, but it had, all of it had happened. (Ibid., 31)

Two traits clearly link Modest Platonovich with Uncle Dickens, all the while underscoring their exceptional and "rare" character in the concept of freedom. First, there is their extreme, truly modernist individualism: "Both men found their own solitary paths to that end, unique impossible paths characteristic of no one else.... They displayed the religiosity and ferocity of the *kulak,* but their property was their identity" (ibid., 90). Second, they are united by their capacity for an unrehearsed *understanding,* as opposed to a prefabricated knowledge that simulates reality. Modest Platonovich declares this principle in his monologue:

> The present-day system of education must be a more serious business than I thought. I thought it was just crass and ignorant. But no! Try to teach a person not actual understanding but the concept that he understands and grasps what's happening—now there's a staggering pedagogical phenomenon! ... that what distinguishes the wise man from the foolish, exactly and precisely, is not the level of his explanations of what is happening but the "unpreparedness" of those explanations in the face of reality ... intelligence is the capacity for the birth of a mirroring thought, synchronous with reality; it's not quotation, not recollection, not preparation according to any model, even the highest, not performance. Intelligence is the capacity for reality at the level of consciousness. (Ibid., 76, 77)

And as for Uncle Dickens, "[w]hen he put on a shirt he seemed to be *understanding* the shirt; when he tied his necktie, he was understanding the tie" (ibid., 32).

The combination of individualism and an aptitude "for reality on the level of consciousness" results in that internal freedom whose absence comprises the central problem of both the protagonist and the novel as a whole. Moreover, the view of freedom posited by Modest Platonovich and Uncle

Dickens bears a distinctly modernist character: the individual's self-sufficiency is expressed in the creation of one's own, unprepared intellectual reality. Such, apparently, is the author's ideal of freedom. At the very least, this is the case in the beginning of the novel, which sketches the portraits of Modest Platonovich and Uncle Dickens.

The simulation of reality in *Pushkin House* can be understood as the spiritual mechanism of the entire Soviet period, a mechanism that has removed Modest Platonovich and Uncle Dickens from life and put Lyovushka Odoevtsev in their place. The scene of Stalin's death, which was significant for many if not all of the "sixties generation,"[3] takes on a symbolic role. Bitov's perception is unique in that the death of Stalin is portrayed not as liberation from the tyrant's yoke, or even as the uneasy expectation of new and unpredictable turns of the wheel of history, but rather as the *apotheosis of simulation*. In this case, we have a simulation of universal grief: "All the others, heartbroken, had just forgotten outright about such a trivia as the quiz.... One and all—and Lyova the only one alone. Well, maybe one or two, Lyova thought, with a detective's logic. But they couldn't have all pretended the same thing . . . ? . . . It was lonely for Lyova to be so self-aware amid this elemental popular woe" (ibid., 135).

The motif of the sociohistorical simulation of life is developed most explicitly at the end of the novel, when the mass exultation over the impending anniversary of the Revolution is combined with the fantasmagorical *refusal to acknowledge* that Lyova and Mitishatyev have wreaked havoc on the institute's museum. Both cases are marked by theatrical imagery, dreams, a parade of phantoms, and, most important, the careless crudeness of the whole performance:

> We're not excited by all this, but Lyova was having fun. He realized, accurately, that he was dreaming it all: the soap-scrap faces (the blurred background of extras in the dream); the cracks in the scenery (wind blowing in); the cardboard horse, deliberately made to rear (from close up, right on stage, how obvious that he's a drawing!); the little wrinkles, the billowing shadow on the Admiralty backdrop; the general negligence, the hack melodrama, of a dream. (Ibid., 284)

And here is the scene following the removal of the traces of the demolition of the museum:

> No one noticed a thing! . . . As life returned to normal, Lyova was deeply wounded by the contempt it showed for his defects and oversights. This was the turn of events he had least expected. Life itself was so negligent that Lyova's little rough spots, in this unbroken sea of common negligence,

proved to be excess diligence . . . but 'negligence' was the motto of today's reality. . . . Lyova is thinking that when he does raise his eyes it's perfectly possible that someone will smartly haul up the rope and furl the landscape in a neat little roll. (Ibid., 333, 334, 337, 339)

The juxtaposition of situations so widely divergent in scale conceals the possibility of interpreting the phenomenon of total simulation as the consequences of *ignoring a catastrophe* as well as the possibility of an attempt to exist as if *nothing* had happened. But a simulation is not only the consequence of a catastrophe; it is itself a catastrophe predicated upon the disappearance of reality, which is in turn expressed in the elimination of cultural integrity and the disappearance of a living cultural order—an order unlike that of the museum.

The post-Stalin Thaw years, according to the convictions of the novel's author, not only did not remove simulation as a fundamental attribute of Soviet reality but even refined it: Simulation acquired a more organic, and therefore more latent, character: *"The curtain has been dropped, not only between the country and the world, but every place there's anything to hang it on. A fluttering multitude of gauze curtains, and one of them curtains man from himself"* (ibid., 111; italics in the original). The product of this newly organic degree of simulation in the novel is the "Myth of Mitishatyev." Mitishatyev is more than the protagonist's double; here we have a pure specimen of the new breed of man resulting from total simulation. In this sense he is truly mythological, because he visibly acts out the Soviet myth of the "new man," which in turn harks back to Nietzsche's equally mythological concept of the superman. Mitishatyev's status as a "superman" lies in the fact that he is a true *genius of simulation,* completely unequipped for any other mode of existence:

> In their schooldays, too, . . . Mitishatyev had looked older than everyone else—he could even look older than a teacher—as if he kept varying his age as a function of his companion, so as to be always slightly older than he. If anyone new came along, especially someone completely opposite to him, Mitishatyev pounced on that person with obvious pleasure, but he always managed to pass for one of his kind, even a bit more than one of his kind. Whether talking to a pace-setting worker, a front-line soldier, or an ex-convict, he became almost more of a pace-setter, front-liner, or convict than his companion, though he had never worked or fought or been in prison. But he never overplayed it. By and large he stayed on an equal footing, just barely implying his superiority: if he had been in his companion's trenches or prison camp, it was just for maybe a day or a month; but still, even though just for maybe a day, he'd been there. (Ibid., 189)

Essentially, Mitishatyev achieves a new level of simulation. If people like Odoevtsev's grandfather or Uncle Dickens may still be contrasted with the "classical" Soviet world by virtue of their own genuine existence, which demonstrates the possibility of reality in spite of the power of fictions, then Mitishatyev's simulation rules out any relationship to reality, thereby excluding even the potential for reality as such. According to Baudrillard, this is the level of the *hyperreality of the simulacrum:* "The territory no longer precedes the map, nor survives it. Henceforth, it is the map that precedes the territory—Precession of the Simulacra—it is the map that engenders the territory whose shreds are slowly rotting across the map" (1993: 343). It is worth noting that Mitishatyev is just as much a literary scholar as Lyova Odoevtsev, and, as Lyova's double, he is equally drawn into the field of interaction with the classical tradition of Russian culture: It is no accident that Lyova fights his duel with Mitishatyev. The influence of the simulacrum on paradigms of order (and the emphasis on the Pushkin House's status as museum is a clear marker of petrified orderliness) is also described by Baudrillard: "Transgression and violence are less serious, for they only contest the *distribution* of the real. Simulation is infinitely more dangerous, however, since it always suggests, over and above its object, that *law and order themselves might be really nothing more that a simulation*" (ibid., 358; emphasis in the original). But in *Pushkin House* Mitishatyev does not undermine tradition; instead, Mitishatyev's very presence is evidence of the transformation of all possible cultural orders into simulation. It is in this sense that Mitishatyev is Lyova's tempter, trying to hold on to faith in the stability of cultural memory and cultural tradition.

It is also telling that Mitishatyev himself is quite conscious of his "superhumanity": "The minute he walked in, Mitishatyev announced he was the messiah, he had reached the summit and was capable of moving heaven and earth. Prior to him there had been, to use Gorky's expression, Christ–Mohammed–Napoleon (he gave other names, however), and now him, Mitishatyev" (199). The ironic reference to Satin, from Gorky's *Lower Depths,* who in turn was without a doubt paraphrasing Nietzsche, connects Mitishatyev with both the Socialist Realist canon and the traditions of modernism. Strange as it may sound, Mitishatyev in his way embodies the same modernist philosophy of freedom as Modest Platonovich and Uncle Dickens. Both the "aristocrats" and the "plebeian" Mitishatyev are guided by the same strategy: they subordinate life to the "creative chronotope," turning it into a literary text. But if Grandfather Odoevtsev and Uncle Dickens, as true modernists, strive to achieve immunity from any external influences in order to perceive the world from an absolutely independent position, Mitishatyev creates a fictitious hyperreality in which he is strong and free, a hyperreality composed exclusively of "external influences" that belong to no one: they are copies without an original. In other words, simulacra.

Naturally, such freedom is defective, since it completely excludes individuality, which has been replaced by the "figure of the void," by a stream of reflected reflections. But at the same time, we are also faced with a kind of parody, a twisted likeness of the modernist project of spiritual freedom.

Moreover, Mitishatev is often bothered by his unsuitability for any non-simulated existence. This is a particular kind of inferiority complex, which is most sharply expressed in his anti-Semitism: "After all, why is it we dislike Jews? Because under all circumstances they are Jews. Someone doesn't seem to be Jewish at all anymore, you get friendly, and suddenly— he's still very much a Jew! What we dislike about them is their *belonging,* because we ourselves don't belong" (ibid., 293; emphasis in the original). Hence his envious desire to be Lyova's equal: " 'No-o! I do not have my own life!' Mitishatyev howled, and he kicked the cupboard. The door panel cracked and caved in. . . . 'And it's a lie that you have one! You don't either! If you did, you wouldn't hate me so—' " (ibid., 306–7).

Mitishatyev's mythological character is also revealed by the fact that, at various points in the novel, nearly all the characters discover some resemblance to him, starting with Lyova ("Lyova suddenly discovered that they simply swapped texts, he had begun to sound so much like Mitishatyev" [ibid., 194]). Through Lyova ("a likeness of a likeness"), Mitishatyev is compared to Albina and her husband, and even an episodic character such as the deputy director of Lyova's institute also turns out to be Mitishatyev: "His glance was peculiar: you wondered whether one of his eyes was false, but when you looked closely it was not" (ibid., 249). Moreover, the author projects Mitishatyev's complexes (which are reproduced and reflected by Lyova) onto the reader: "Villainous? Villainous. But let the reader pay his own accounts. . . . All lies, and all true" (ibid., 181). Thus the author deprives Mitishatyev of all his concreteness, turning him into a collection of qualities common to *everyone.*

A more complex drama of simulative existence is played out in the psychological world of the novel's protagonist, Lyova Odoevtsev. It is this aspect of the theme of simulation that has received the most treatment in the critical literature. "Lyova is constantly reflecting," writes Natal´ia Ivanova. "But his thoughts, to use one of Bakhtin's early terms, are not 'co-experiencing' (*uchastnye*). The distance between reflection and life is the basis of Lyova's constant search for an 'alibi in being': he does not feel responsible in any situation" (1988: 182–83). Ivanova's assessment seems more accurate than that of Vladimir Novikov: "[N]owhere can Mitishatyev find what Lyova, despite all his faults and all his intellectualism, has: inner freedom" (ibid., 230–31). Where could he find inner freedom if even Lyova is firmly in the grip of notions that exceed understanding, if Lyova is not capable of confirming his reputation as an intellectual through actions, if he does not have the strength to overcome Mitishatyev's power over him ("it was just that the myths about Mitishatyev had long since become more real in his consciousness than the truth itself" [Bitov 1987: 190]). Even the comparison at the end of the novel between Lyova and Pushkin's Yevgeny from *The Bronze Horseman* is not in Lyova's favor. Yevgeny rebelled against the Bronze Horseman—what about Lyova? Does running away from a policeman count? Lyova himself is aware that

> they needed him just as he was, a man who had made an outrageous mess of things and conscientiously eaten it up, licked the bed clean . . . a slave who has suppressed his own revolt by his own strength is both a profitable and a flattering category of slave for the slaveholder: this is precisely how power is recognized, and precisely how it is maintained. (Bitov 1987: 339)

Alice Stone Nakhimovsky posits that it is impossible to understand the protagonist of *Pushkin House* outside of his cultural and historical contexts, his intertextual surroundings:

> The men of the nineteenth century—the grandfather, the poets, the family friend that Leva once imagined as his real father [Uncle Dickens—M.L.] are all individuals; the men of the twentieth century are slaves . . . Leva therefore is zero; his talent and his heritage are possibilities which are contained in him but which are unrealizable. Here lies the difference between the version of *Fathers and Sons* and the original. In Turgenev's nineteenth century novel, the generation fight over the direction of the future. Here there is no fight for the future because there will be no future. "Lyova will have no future," says Bitov. There is only the generation of the sons, hopelessly chasing after its own past. (1988: 202–3)

It is important to understand the source of the "contemporary non-existence of the hero." After all, both his lack of "co-experiencing" (Bakhtin 1990: 61) and his inner nonfreedom have the same general cause: a kind of *metaphysical fear*. This is not the fear of reality, as it might seem; on the contrary, it is fear of further simulation that demands the most serious, genuine attitude toward itself. It is the fear of relationships ("Everything's relationships now" [310]), for they inevitably end in deceit and humiliation.

> The fundamental driving force of his subject was fear. . . . Fear in everything, fear *of* everything; of everything one's own, and now of movement, a gesture, an intonation, a taste, the weather. . . . Something is always reminding us of something. . . . Someone's voice speaks another's words, at that moment you are lifting the cup to your mouth in the gesture of a brother who drowned in infancy . . . the weather, like the taste of a cigarette, reminds you

of another time of life, another locale, another emotion . . . but you yourself discover you have already *had* this thought, some other time, about the cup and the cigarette. Horror! (290; emphasis in the original)

This fear conceals an additional, equally important nuance: Here we have more than just the fear of being deceived by someone else but the fear of being deceived *by oneself,* the revelation of one's own simulation, one's own imitation of something that is also not real. Unlike the other representatives of his generation in the novel, Lyova *sees* the simulative nature of reality and understands how dangerous the appearance of one's own originality is against the backdrop of universal simulation: "The most indecent thing, the most ruinous and hopeless, is to become visible, permit interpretation, reveal yourself. . . . Just don't reveal yourself or what's yours—that is the principle of survival, thought Lyova. Invisibility!" (332).

Yet is it even possible to express "what's yours" in an atmosphere of total simulation (setting aside for the moment the question of risk)? This question can be put differently. Essentially, the first part of *Pushkin House* is a realistic description of the postmodern condition, which is expressed first and foremost in the phenomenon of total simulation. The problem of self-expression is connected with the "axiological center" of modernist culture: Expressing oneself and one's own in this context means acquiring freedom. The uniqueness of Grandfather Odoevtsev and Uncle Dickens can be explained by the fact that they are the products of a modernist culture and modernist consciousness that have miraculously survived into another era—the era of the simulation of collective as well as individual values. It thus comes as no surprise that these characters die almost as soon as they appear in the novel. But Lyova is from another generation, and his attempts to find and express himself and "his own" are more of a cultural experiment: Is it possible to return to the values of modernist culture in this new, postmodern condition?

At first glance, Lyova does not justify the expectations of him: Simulation is second nature to him. The leitmotifs of immobility and the imitation of imitations are constantly present in the smallest narrative details about Lyova, from Lyova's behavior to the syntax of the author's remarks:

In movements taught by the movie camera, he sneaked up to the door like a guerrilla mining a train. (Bitov 1987: 287).

Lyova politely heard out the story of her daughter and her drinking son-in-law, and it struck him that he had already heard this story somewhere, or perhaps read it (253).

. . . Lyubasha. Beloved woman, unloved woman, any woman (185).

. . . reasoned philologist Lyova Odoevtsev in a mathematical way, gravitating toward the natural sciences (176).

Even this little bit was enough—winning a fight (304).

His thoughts were coherently tangled (331).

At the same time, the novel's network of characters is distinctly polarized between Modest Platonovich (the strength of an individual rooted in the past, the embodiment of originality, the fervor of modernist values) and Mitishatyev (the strength of the impersonal, dependence on the present moment, the apotheosis of simulation, parodic "superhumanity"). All the other characters are paired together in the same fashion: Uncle Dickens / Lyova's Father, Albina / Faina, the naively honest Blank / Gottich (probably a KGB agent). But Lyova is somewhere in the middle: From his grandfather's point of view, he represents simulated reality, but from Mitishatyev's perspective he is provocatively aristocratic in his involvement in the true reality of culture. This duality is the key to Lyova. Even as he strives to dissolve in the stream of simulation, he cannot bring himself to do so completely: Originality gets in the way. It is no coincidence that at the climactic moment Bitov's description of Lyova blurs the boundary between the protagonist and . . . Pushkin:

But how very visible Lyova had become! So visible it was impossible to miss him. Only yesterday he had been lying on sharp splinters on the floor, his gaze had pierced holes in the windows, the floor was strewn with *thousands of pages that he had spent a whole futile and banal lifetime writing, a snow-white sideburn had fallen off him—he had been the most visible man on earth! His wrath, his passion, his revolt and freedom."* (Ibid., 332; emphasis added)

It is particularly revealing that Bitov projects the modernist theme of freedom through self-expression onto the symbol of traditional culture: Pushkin. Bitov is not the only writer of the sixties and seventies to see modernist culture as part of a long line connected to the great tradition that has survived the abyss of Soviet pseudoculture (Brodsky, for example, does the same). In this sense, Bitov's novel inherits the Acmeist version of modernism, which understood the dialogue with cultural tradition as the most important condition for the freedom and self-expression of the creative consciousness.[4]

But *Pushkin House* contains a far more interesting and demonstrative level of simulation. Lyova's drama is doubled on the level of the relationship between the author and the novelistic form. Bitov builds his text as a system of attempts to imitate the classical Russian novel. Hence the epigraphs and chapter titles, the hero's genealogy, and the paraphrases of classical motifs. But, on the one hand, "[t]he literary allusions in *Pushkin House* are intentionally self-evident and almost comically abundant. . . . For most of the novel, citations to nineteenth century works result in a parody of the present. It is a parody which is fully appreciated by the characters, who recognize the futility of their attempts at recreating the past" (Nakhimovsky 1988: 198). On the other hand, the narrator himself constantly draws attention to the failure of these attempts. He is unable to rewrite "a famous trilogy, the *Childhood, Adolescence, Youth* of our hero" (Bitov 1987: 18); although early in the novel the narrator promises to retell the story of Lyova's family from a different perspective, later he admits that "Quite frankly, we like the first variant of Lyova's family better. It's more to our taste" (100). The plot does not move forward: "*We stand on the shore of the story we have longed for from the very beginning, it is swelling before us like a breaker—but there's no ford, it turns out, we can't cross here: we are swept backwards, towards the beginning of the narrative*" (ibid., 110; italics in the original). The second part continues the first from another perspective. Lyova the man is not the same as Lyova the literary protagonist.

The repeated references to the novel's failure certainly give Bitov's fixation on classical models a parodic spin. In the finale, parody gives way to outright travesty, as evidenced by the titles of the chapters: "Bronze Folk" and "Poor Horseman" (cf. Pushkin's *Bronze Horseman* and Dostoevsky's *Poor Folk*). The novel's climax, which is so deliberately clumsy, is in the spirit of metafiction:

> Lyova started. . . . For a third time, the author could not bear the shoddy melodrama of life and turned away to the window. A party-cracker shot rang out. . . . A groan, a crunch, an authorial gnashing of teeth. Space went askew behind the author's back. Lost its balance, lurched. The author rushed to catch it—too late—a tinkle of glass rained down. (Ibid., 310)

Just as Lyova, who cannot imagine himself outside the world of literature, participates in the sacking of the literary museum, so, too, does the author, who consciously looks back at the traditions of the nineteenth-century Russian novel, appear to turn his "novel-museum" into ruins just as consciously.[5] Yet in this case the novelistic form is the most important link between simulated reality and real cultural memory and tradition. The very goal of the "citational museum" (Oraić) is threatened: the re-creation of the "paradigmatic order of European culture" destroyed by totalitarian aggression.

Does it then follow that any contact with cultural tradition is fruitless for the contemporary consciousness that has been poisoned by simulation and is destructive for the tradition itself? This question can only be answered by examining the *model of culture* created in the novel, for it is on this model that both Lyova's inner freedom and the author's reconstructive project depend.

Twice Modest Platonovich Odoevstev, the most "programmatic" of all the characters, expresses the same thought, first in the beginning of the novel and then in the end. During his meeting with Lyova, Modest Platonovich tells his grandson:

> Now, you think that 1917 destroyed, devastated our previous culture. But it didn't; it canned and preserved it. What matters is the break, not the destruction. The authorities froze there untoppled, unmoving: they're all in their places, from Derzhavin to Blok—the sequel won't shake their order, because there won't be a sequel. Everything has been turned upside down, but Russia is still a land off-limits. You can't get there. (Ibid., 64)

The novel closes with a quote from a text called "Sphinx" written by Odoevtsev in the twenties and given to the author by Lyova:

> The ties have been broken, the secret forever lost ... a mystery is born! Culture remains only in the form of monuments contoured by destruction. A monument is doomed to eternal life, it is immortal merely because all that surrounded it has perished. In this sense, I'm not worried about our culture—it has already been. It's gone. It will exist in my absence, as a meaningless thing, for a good while longer. ... All has perished—and in this very hour the great Russian culture has been born, this time forever. ... To our descendants, Russian culture will be a sphinx, just as Pushkin was the sphinx of Russian culture. (Ibid., 352, 353)

And here he pronounces a formula that sounds like a universal diagnosis: "Unreality is a condition of life" (ibid., 354).

The meaning of these words is clear: They link the protagonist's simulated being, his "unreal time" (ibid., 341), with the cultural world of the Russian classics. Odoevtsev's ideas provide the vague contours for a model of Russian culture: Here death becomes preservation, broken ties give a sense of classical completion, and greatness is predetermined by nonexistence. However, on the whole, this conception of culture acquires a closed and incomprehensible character (specifically because of the impossibility of penetration); its context is the total destruction of reality, and its effect is either muteness or lack of understanding.

Naturally, both Lyova's and the author's connection to the classics is paradoxical. The destruction of the traditional novelist form embodies this internally contradictory tie. In order to gain a clearer understanding of this connection, it would be appropriate to borrow from the "deconstructive" lexicon of Jacques Derrida, since the actions of the author-narrator in effect constitute the deconstruction of the classical tradition. Here, first of all, one finds conscious *repetition,* realized not only through the chapter titles and epigraphs but also through the constant identification of the novel's characters with artistic models of behavior: "the superfluous man," "poor Yevgeny," "the hero of our time," "the petty demon" and "demons," romantic love and the "duel." However, this repetition leads to deformations and differences, erasing the previous meaning: This effect is connected with the fact that everything real within the classical context inevitably becomes simulation in the contemporary world. In essence, this is the difference between *mneme* (live memory) and *hypomnesis* (its simulation), discussed by Derrida in "Plato's *Pharmacy*":

> Nevertheless, between *mneme* and *hypomnesis,* between memory and its supplement, the line is more than subtle; it is hardly perceptible. On both sides of that line, it is a question of *repetition.* Live memory repeats the presence of *eidos* ["image," in the Platonic sense—M.L.], and truth is also the possibility of repetition through recall. . . . But in the amnesic movement of truth, what is repeated must present itself as such, as what it is, in repetition. The true is repeated; it is what is repeated in the repetition, what is represented and present in the representation. It is not the repeater in the repetition, nor the signifier in the signification. The true is the presence of the *eidos* signified. (1991: 136; emphasis in the original)

The Soviet classical museum is the direct realization of the "*amnesic moment of truth,*" the repetition of the phenomenon in numerous details (such as Grigorovich's inkwell, which Mitishatyev throws out the window), but without the "presence of the *eidos.*"[6] Lyova is an active and self-conscious part of this cultural process. But even the simulation of memory contains the trace of *eidos,* of what Derrida calls the truth, and what we, paraphrasing Bitov's novel, might call lost reality.

There is a crucial repetition at the very core of the novel's construction: the life led by Lyova is *just as simulative* as the forgotten "truth" of the Russian classics, which is perceived from without and is relevant precisely because of its nonexistence. Here difference gives way to *différance,* the paradoxical form of connection / repulsion / reproduction / erasure described by Derrida: "The play of a trace which no longer belongs to a horizon of Being, but whose play transports and encloses the meaning of Being: the play of the trace, or the *différance,* which has no meaning and is not. Which does not belong. There is no maintaining, and no depth to, this bottomless chessboard on which being is put into play" (1991: 75). This definition seems quite applicable to the way of thinking presented in *Pushkin House,* despite the fact that Bitov could not have been influenced by Derrida. In essence, this is the next logical stage in the development of the idea of "the world as text" that brings the free play of signifiers into history and contemporary reality. Such an understanding removes the contrast between simulation and reality, including the reality of culture. Simulation becomes a kind of life, an inevitable form of existence in culture. The paradox of ambivalent presence/absence, repetition/destruction, writing/erasure of the *life-as-text,* is expressed by Bitov in his own "terminology." In the beginning of the third section, the author-narrator plays with the double meaning of "Pushkin House": On the one hand, it is the title of the novel that is in an incomplete state of writing and reading; on the other hand, "Pushkin House" is a metaphor for the (completed) text of the Russian classics. And yet each meaning leads to an ironic conclusion:

> *Or perhaps as is, without a roof? So that it stands amid the chips, its windows letting in the four directions: the southern draft, the eastern forest, the western neighbor, the northern byroad?*
> *People will say, How can anybody live in a house like that?*
> *I will answer, "In Pushkin House? Nobody does. One man tried, just for three days, and what happened? It's impossible to live in Pushkin House."*
> *"You're muddled us with your allegories," the reader will say.*
> *I will answer, "Then don't read" . . .*
> *Nobody lives in Pushkin House. One man tried. . .* (Bitov 1987: 246, 247; italics in the original)

The incomplete construction of the house (as both novel and cultural whole, the "break" discussed by the elder Odoevtsev), the breakdown in aesthetic communication ("Then don't read"), the self-destruction of culture ("One man tried")—these are the paradoxical conditions for the existence of the protagonist, the activity of the author, and the reality of culture.

The very same deconstruction of cultural tradition takes place even more strikingly in the "creative chronotope" of the protagonist, Lyova Odoevtsev. Yes, Lyova cannot achieve a state of natural existence within a ruptured cultural reality, as his grandfather and Uncle Dickens do. They are the bearers of *mneme,* while he himself belongs entirely to the realm of *hypomnesis.* Clearly, culture takes on the traits of a simulacrum only when one looks from the outside: "[T]o be misunderstood is the sole condition for the existence of culture" (ibid., 353), writes the young Modest Platonovich Odoevtsev in the twenties. Almost everyone is doomed to the position of misunderstanding "outsiders." Except for those rare specimens who have miraculously remained within the preserve of cultural memory despite the change in eras. But the sterile, consumerist understanding discussed by Modest Platonovich is also alien to Lyova: "Now you're going through Tsvetaeva and Pushkin, next you'll go through Lermontov and somebody else, and then you'll stumble on Tyutchev and Fet: you'll make the one a genius, the other a great man. You'll drag up Bunin. . . . This inflating and devouring of reputations will pass for the growth of contemporary culture" (ibid., 65). Consumption is the same as forgetting, and this is the path of Mitishatyev, not of Lyova.

Lyova's own attitude toward cultural tradition is most clearly expressed in his article "Three Prophets." Here again, we have an emphasis on repetition, since Lyova not only discovers that at the age of twenty-seven, Pushkin, Lermontov, and Tyutchev had all written their own poems addressing the concept of the poet as prophet,[7] but he also openly projects himself onto his chosen subjects and onto his relationship with them: "Pushkin he deified. In Lermontov he perceived his own infantilism, and took a condescending attitude. In Tyutchev he frankly hated someone (we don't know whom)" (ibid., 239). Lyova accuses Tyutchev of a defect from which he himself suffers:

> He asserts his opinion about another, but he himself is not there. He is categorical in his appraisal—and puts nothing in the other pan of the scales (does not appraise himself). . . . The subject is a grudge. A complex one, moreover, with many facets and many turnabouts. Very secret, very deep, hidden almost from Tyutchev himself. . . . Here, without reference to Tyutchev, Lyova wrote a good many more pages sketching a psychological picture of such an emotion. He wrote with knowledge and passion. The experience of his sad love for Faina was evident here. As, in its turn, the experience of his attempt at a rapprochement with Grandfather was evident in his reckoning about Tyutchev's attraction to Pushkin, the lack of response to this attempt, and, in that case, a "devaluation" of the very object of attraction ("I didn't want you all that much," and "Fool yourself!"). (Ibid., 230, 233, 237)

This repetition does not imply a single correct interpretation. On the one hand, the thought suggests itself that Lyova reads his own meanings and plots into the reality of culture, that he attempts to achieve "the truth" of the classical tradition at the price of transforming the life of culture into the free play of simulacra. Neither Pushkin, nor Lermontov, nor Tyutchev replaces each other; their worlds exist and intersect without causing each other any harm. The fervor of Lyova's article comes from the "replacement" of Tyutchev by Pushkin, "in Pushkin's favor. In his name. . . ." (ibid., 227). However, the effect of this replacement turns out to be more long-range than the young Odoevtsev had thought: By rejecting Tyutchev, Lyova essentially rejects himself, for his attitude toward Tyutchev is the same as his interpretation of Tyutchev's attitude toward Pushkin: "[T]he positions and principles expressed in [Lyova's] article, when consistently followed, preclude the possibility of the article itself, even the very fact of its apparent enviousness, its need to assert itself by overthrowing someone. A kind of Salierism in those who fight Salieri" (ibid., 241). It would seem that everything is repeating itself again: the Pushkin–Tyutchev relationship is projected onto that of the grandfather and Lyova, and, finally, Lyova feels a similar attraction/repulsion toward Tyutchev. However, the repetition is intermittent, and it is Lyova's misfortune that he happens to live during a time of cultural rupture. Lyova's participation in the cultural dialogue deconstructs the very idea of dialogue itself; after the establishment of the hyperreality of simulacra, no continuity with the past is possible. Moreover, the "Three Prophets" article is not only unpublished but, as we find out in the end, even withdrawn from circulation by Lyova himself, while the sequels to the article, "The Middle of the Contrast," "The *I* of Pushkin," and "The Brilliant Latecomers" (ibid., 347), will never be written.

On the other hand, Lyova's calculations sound quite convincing (after all, Bitov himself published this article in the journal *Voprosy literatury* under his own name long before the novel was ever printed in Russia). And the theme of simulative relations linking Lermontov and Tyutchev to Pushkin is examined using major texts (Pushkin's and Lermontov's "The Prophet," Tyutchev's "Madness") that articulate the cultural self-consciousness of each of these poets. The reference to nihilism and "a kind of Salierism in those who fight Salieri" leads to numerous associations with the entire history of Russian literature after Pushkin (from Chernyshevsky and Pisarev to the Futurists and Socialist Realists). Lyova's article makes one stop and think about a shocking question: Perhaps the mechanism that inevitably leads to the replacement of life (Pushkin) with simulation (Lermontov, Tyutchev) is part of culture itself? If this is true, then the gap between Lyova's generation and that of his grandfather is perfectly normal within the framework of cultural dynamics; Lyova's ignorance of Tynianov's article "Pushkin and Tyutchev" is particularly telling, as the article lays the foundation for the rough and broken movement of cultural consciousness.[8] If that is the case, then Lyova really is an "heir" who is so sensitive to the sore points of the deformation of Russian culture. If this is so, then Lyova's conflict (or more broadly, the contemporary conflict) becomes universal. Behind the "repetitions" lies the shadow of a deep context that produces similar shifts and breaks in ties and meanings from century to century:

What had Tyutchev, for example, done to Lyova? And what, after all, had he done to Pushkin?. . . He is to blame only for the recognition, Lyova's recognition of himself, his impartial confrontation with his own experience. Tyutchev is to blame that Faina happened to Lyova, Grandfather happened; he is to blame for being born too late and emerging too late, like Lyova (each in his own epoch). (Ibid., 241)

Thus the target of this pointed deconstruction is not only Lyova but the entire mythology of classical culture. This deconstruction is even more transparent in the climax of the plot. On the night of November 7 (the anniversary of the October Revolution), a drunken Lyova, who worships Pushkin, ransacks the Pushkin House literary museum along with Mitishatyev. Then Lyova quickly replaces the damaged items with cheap copies (the attentive reader will note that we are retelling the same episode for a second time—why not succumb to the charms of our author's style?). It would seem that a kind of "allegory" is being played out, one that re-creates the revolutionary destruction and imaginary "reconstruction" of culture carried out with the direct participation of the Soviet intelligentsia—a ritual micromodel of Soviet cultural history repeating what happened "in the beginning." But Bitov focuses attention on something else: Lyova's very efforts to cover up the damage to the museum are also fictitious. In any case, the author deliberately weakens the plot motivations here—the exhaustion of the plot is not hidden but, on the contrary, emphasized: "Because we can't bear to continue, the author will concoct a hackwork *success* for Lyova. . . . We have glad news for the reader—Uncle Dickens is still alive! At least, he'll come back to life again and die again, for the sake of the novel" (ibid., 325). This parody of literary tricks (particularly those of Dickens) once again equates the fictionality of life with the fictionality of literary conflicts. Everything comes together: the author's simulation of the novel, Lyova's simulation of "participation" in culture, and, finally, the simulation of classical Russian culture itself. This last phenomenon is best illustrated by a particular detail: Pushkin's death mask has been broken (which is essentially the reason that Lyova challenges Mitishatyev to a duel), but all is not lost: "Albina, graceful, happy to have Lyova dependent on her, foolishly unloved Albina, will say, 'Lyovushka, that's nothing! We have lots of [masks].' And she'll go downstairs to the storeroom, where they lie in stacks, one inside the next" (ibid., 326–25). The motif of the mask becomes an unexpected link to the masquerade of festivity for the anniversary of the Revolution described in the previous chapter, as well as Mitishatyev's own masquerade. Where, then, is the original and the copy? Where are the remainders of a broken culture, and where are the contemporary simulations of culture and life in culture? The boundaries have been erased. Or they never existed at all.

As Grandfather Odoevtsev predicted, classical culture has become an epic legend for Lyova, completely closed to dialogue precisely because it is separated by "an absolute epic distance" (Bakhtin 1981: 13). The greater Lyova's piety toward Pushkin, the more this distance becomes insurmountable. And therefore contact with classical culture can only be imitated through simulacra of the classics created by Lyova in his own image. Is Lyova to blame? Has classical tradition truly ceased to exist? Apparently, the answer to both questions is "yes." But it would clearly be a mistake to reduce all the novel's paradoxes to the social and psychological defects of the sixties generation, which only appeared to stand against the totalitarian mentality but actually was complicit in inheriting a totalitarian simulation of reality and cultural succession. Bitov is building an artistic model that allows for several different readings. This playful ambiguity in the novel's artistic construction suggests that, for Bitov, the tragedy of culture and of the cultural tradition consists of the fact that culture can never be adequately perceived. Synchronically, without any temporal distance, cultural values are not recognized as values; but given the "absolute epic distance," culture becomes a dead monument to itself. This is a universal paradox of cultural development. Soviet history only intensified it, maximizing the rupture and rendering the lack of understanding total. The parallels between Bitov's artistic logic and the methodology of deconstruction indeed confirm the universality of this paradox and its importance for the postmodern conception of cultural movement in general.

The *sacking of the museum* of Russian culture and the simulation of its restoration—this is only the first step in Bitov's "deconstruction": the dismantling of the hierarchical opposition between the pre-Revolutionary culture and its contemporary "heirs" (an opposition that was taken for granted by both "Soviet" and "anti-Soviet" ideologies alike). Has Bitov taken the "second step": Does the novel allow for the formation of a nonhierarchical artistic model of culture? In other words, does this novel contain a new way out of the dead end of total simulation?

In order to answer these questions, we will focus our attention on the relationship between the author and the hero in *Pushkin House,* a theme that Bitov himself identifies in the final "Appendix" to the novel.

Using the terminology of Bakhtin's "Author and Hero in Aesthetic Activity" (1990: 4–256), we can identify three basic "axiological contexts" in Bitov's novel:

- the context of the hero, Lyova Odoevtsev;
- the context of the author-narrator (whom we shall call the "Novelist");
- the context of the author-creator (whom we shall call the "Author").

As Bakhtin argues, this last values context encompasses all others, resulting in artistic completion, and therefore this context has a feature that all other axiological contexts lack—temporal, spatial, and semantic *outsideness* (transgredience): "The outside standpoint of the aesthetic *subjectum* constitutes the necessary condition for integrating the contexts that form around several heroes into a single formal-aesthetic, axiological context (this is especially the case in epic genres)" (Bakhtin 1990: 212).

However, in Bitov's novel this extremely important condition for artistic integrity is noticeably weak: Outsideness is subject to reflection and is thus decreased in importance—the mystery of artistic form is replaced by communal voyeurism:

> *We have always wondered, since our earliest, most spontaneous childhood, where the author was hiding when he spied on the scene that he describes. Where did he so inconspicuously put himself?. . . As we read and check against life, we will be struck that the spirit of the dormitory and communal apartment, before its incarnation in the real world, arose in literature, in the author's similar relationship to the scene. He is a communal inhabitant in it, a neighbor, a new roommate.* (Bitov 1987: 56, 57; italics in the original)

Hence the conclusion:

> *If the conventionality, the subjectivity, the particularity of the solution are not declared to us, we may still read it, out of condescension, as we applaud a bad singer, but we find it difficult to share and believe by living through it. How does he know? What makes him think so? . . . God alone, if it is first agreed that He exists, can see from above. But only Lev Tolstoy has permitted himself to write from God's standpoint, and we won't even discuss here the extent of his competence in those efforts.* (Ibid., 57; italics in the original)

These thoughts are included not simply for effect. By undermining outsideness and arguing for the "*the subjectivity, the particularity of the solution*" and rejecting the "divine" viewpoint of the demiurge Tolstoy while looking back at Dostoevsky, who "*never conceals his status as the heroes' new roommate: he inhibits them, they don't forget that he can see them, that he is their audience*" (ibid., 57), Bitov is striving for a very specific artistic effect: *to bring the artistic context of the Novelist, who refuses to hide his own subjectivity, as close as possible to the context of the impersonal Author*. Moreover, he creates the illusion that the Novelist's context *engulfs* that of the Author, along with the Author's outsideness.

No less paradoxical is the relationship between the Novelist and the hero, Lyova Odoevtsev. It is not by chance that Bakhtin proposes differentiating between the "axiological contexts" of the heroes and the author. In essence, all the processes discussed above touch upon these values contexts: the context of the Novelist = "literature" (culture); the context of Lyova = "life" (contemporaneity). But, first of all, the antithesis of literature and life, of the cultural classics and contemporaneity, is consistently problematized in the novel, while the motif of life simulation blurs the boundaries between them once and for all. Second, the model of culture undergoes a kind of deconstruction, which not only develops the internal connection between cultural tradition and its contemporary destruction but also roots both this destruction and the simulation of life in the logic of culture. The combination of these axiological contexts forms the deep structure of the plot of *Pushkin House;* as a result, the *identification* of Lyova with the Novelist becomes more apparent. Bitov's 1987 commentary to *Pushkin House,* "The Near Retro," make it even clearer: The explanation of the *realia* surrounding the *heroes* becomes thoroughly confused with the personal reminiscences of the biographical author, who himself becomes the main character. But even with the commentary, the novel provides ample justification for identifying the Novelist with his hero. First, there is the basic psychological resemblance: the hesitation and musings of the Novelist contain the same flaws that had just been ascribed to Lyova Odoevtsev. For example, Lyova's inability to take action resembles the Novelist's admission that *"little by little I'm beginning to see that if I keep on like this, I'll never get to the game itself. It will wither away and become superfluous. Either there will no longer be any need of it, or, simply from overanticipation, I will no longer feel like playing"* (Bitov 1987: 212; italics in the original).

The Novelist's and the protagonist's already equal footing takes on a new dimension closer to the end, when a purely ethical conflict arises. The question of the author's responsibility toward his hero arises, a question that is exacerbated by the fact that the Novelist puts himself in his hero's position and understands that nothing is more bitter than knowing that the "implementation of this supreme will rests not with God but in the private hands of some actual author . . . unbelievable that someone, in respect to us, has appropriated to himself both fate and destiny and has seized the power of the Lord. This is the most terrible deprivation of rights we could ever imagine—the lack of a right to God" (Bitov 1989: 343).

The two axiological contexts come closest together in the realm of artistic time. By the end, the plot has returned to the point where the Novelist is located—the point at which the narration began ("Somewhere near the end of the novel we have already attempted to describe," warns Bitov on the novel's very first page [Bitov 1987: 3]). This is where the first part was leading, and it is also the point where the plots of the second and third parts come together. But the most important thing is that all these temporal circles are carefully noted by the Novelist himself: "What have we achieved, though, by merging the author's and the hero's time?" (ibid., 319), he asks in the Epilogue. And in the appendix to Part Three, "Achilles and the Tortoise (Relationship between Hero and Author)," he answers, "The writer's sole happiness (for the sake of which, we used to suppose, all is written) is to *coincide completely* with the hero's present, so that his *own* present, being tiresome and unsuccessful, will disappear. This, too, is unattainable" (ibid., 341). It is extremely important that this chapter contrasts the present time of the hero or the novel ("We wander in time present," ibid.) with the historical, *nonpresent* time of the author: "In our unreal time [*nenastoiashchee vremia*], tragic endings are inappropriate" (ibid.).

Bitov defines the novel's present as the "the line along which the past rips from the nonexisting future, tracing out the discontinuity of reality which has riddled us with holes. Any point of the present is the end of the past, but also the end of the present because there is no possibility of living, and yet we live" (ibid., 340). In essence, this is the same as Bakhtin's "creative chronotope." With one qualification: The novel's present is the *here and now* of the creative chronotope. For Bitov, the novel's present is the *only possible reality,* with its own original character, in spite of all the simulacra of history, of daily life, of social and individual psychology, and, finally, of cultural tradition. The way to this seemingly paradoxical conclusion has been paved by the merger of the axiological contexts of the Author, the Novelist, and the hero. This chain reaction gives unity to a novel that seems to be dissolving into various versions and commentaries.

As a result of this "merger," it is the values context of the literary hero (an open fiction, living only in the novel's present) that takes on the *outsideness* that originally belonged to the author-creator. Bitov's hero can therefore go through the same situation again and again, returning to the key points of his plot. Paradoxically, this weak, unfree character, whose being is restricted to the novel's present, proves to be freer than the all-powerful author-creator, who is dependent on extratextual reality. Only at his character's side does the Author (and not the Novelist) achieve the greatest possible measure of freedom. However, outsideness in Bitov is largely deprived of formal and aesthetic meaning; instead, it takes on the semantics of culture and philosophy: this is outsideness in relation to total simulation, which completely replaces natural life with itself, with simulation at the heart of the mechanisms of the creation of culture and the perception of cultural tradition.

At the same time, the novel's present, and the cultural and philosophical outsideness that is imprinted in it, is an unattainable horizon of originality ("This, too, is unattainable," [ibid., 341]). For many reasons. First of all, because it is impossible to get away with combining incompatible values contexts without incurring some form of punishment: The laws of art resist, and the total coincidence of the Author, the Novelist, and the hero would kill the novel as an artistic text; therefore, the novel's present would also die. As Bakhtin writes, "[T]he hero . . . may coincide *as a human being* with the author, and that, in fact, is what occurs most of the time. But the hero of a work can never coincide with the author—the *creator* of that work, for otherwise we would not get a work of art at all" (1990: 222; emphasis in the original).

Second, it is not for nothing that the Novelist's meeting with Lyova at the end of the story is so farcical. Both are "He/I" (Bitov 1987: 346). Naturally, the novelist "knows the answers to his questions" (ibid., 347) in advance; after all, the novel's present is the author's transfigured recent past, and the attempt to return to the lost present with the help of the hero is still a simulation: "[T]he author has been stealing each subsequent chapter from his own life, writing it by using exclusively the events that had time to happen while the preceding chapter was written. The distance grew shorter, and the close familiarity of his own movements became comical" (ibid., 351).

The all-powerful author therefore cannot completely belong to his/her creation. "Achilles will never catch up with the tortoise" (ibid., 341). But apparently, this is a case in which participating in the race is more important than any (inevitably Pyrrhic) victory.

As in modernist metafiction, Bitov's novel problematizes reality, the cultural context, and the text itself. As in metafiction, the models of historical reality and culture, which were initially in opposition, turn out to be profoundly similar. The metafiction of Rozanov, Vaginov, Mandelstam, Nabokov, and Kharms dealt with death: the death of culture, the death of civilization, the death of creativity, the death of the final repositories of culture, and, finally, the death of true reality. This death was depicted as a tragedy.

For Bitov, death is replaced by the simulation of life, which drastically changes the tone of metafiction: Instead of tragedy, we have (self-)irony, the bitter smile, sarcastic analysis. Bitov is making the same attempt made in the metafiction of the twenties and thirties, the attempt "to *resurrect* life by means of literature itself and its formal devices" (Segal 1979: 13–14; emphasis in the original), but the result is a tragicomic fiasco. And Bitov's novel is the story of this fiasco, the revelation that the viscious circle of simulacra allows for no exit. Even the death of the hero, an intellectual born and bred, who seemed to oppose Soviet totalitarian "monoculture," turns out to be a fiction. Even the classical tradition is powerless against simulation; on the contrary, simulation proves to be the normal form of cultural dynamics and succession, and the very motif of the cultural *museum* actually marks the triumph of simulation.

Simulation reveals itself to be the same death of culture and reality as in earlier Russian metafiction, but now tragic angst has become everyday, ordinary; indeed, it is decidedly comfortable. Which leads to a hypothesis: If the metafiction of the twenties and thirties described (and even embodied) the *threshold of the death of culture,* Bitov's *Pushkin House* establishes the *afterlife* of culture. After all, what are simulacra if not shadows that have already crossed the threshold and gone beyond death's reach? The novelist is immersed in the same afterlife as the hero; witness the ruins of the traditional novelistic form. But most important of all is the fact that after death culture itself reveals its simulated side, becoming its own shadow and thereby providing for its conservation and continuation.

This is how an entire world-model arises, a model where simulation welds together past and present, cultural tradition and reality, novelist and hero, "form" and "content." It makes perfect sense that the search for inner freedom with which the novel begins proves senseless: Within the simulative context, one can speak only of the freedom of simulation, the freedom of nonexistence. Such freedom is fully realized by Mitishatyev (with his parodic Nietzscheanism), but it is clearly insufficient for Lyova Odoevtsev, the Novelist, and the Author. Thus the modernist problematic becomes postmodernist: *The question of freedom is replaced by the question of context.* And from the looks of things, this replacement appears to have taken place as the novel was written, changing the author's conception. In any case, the first part ("Fathers and Sons") was written as a "well-wrought" modernist work, while the clear signs of postmodern poetics are brought to the fore in the third part ("The Poor Horseman"). The second part ("Hero of Our Time"), which describes Lyova's vacillation among Faina, Albina, and Lyuba, is deliberately amorphous:[9] It serves as a cushion for the sharp rupture taking place within the novel itself.

The similarity between Bitov's artistic strategy and certain elements of Derridean deconstruction can, in fact, be explained by the search for a way to overcome the simulative context; after all, overcoming the power of context can be understood as one of the most important problems of deconstruction. For Bitov, the most radical version of overcoming context, which is paradoxically combined with a near obsession with context, is the outsideness of the author-creator in relation to his own work. Hence the only possible present turns out to be the very process of playfully deconstructing the simulacra of life and culture, a process that can neither be completed nor lead to a positive result: It may only be cut off, as Bitov cuts off his own novel, ending the narration with literally nothing:

> We coincide with him in time—and what more do we know of him?
> NOTHING

(Bitov 1987: 351)

These words bring the "fictional" part of the novel to a close. Open-endedness differentiates this result from the one proposed by metafiction. The result of metafiction would be the text itself, whose reading is an ontological act. For Bitov, the result is the impossibility of creating such a text, since, in the afterlife of culture, the text can be nothing more than a simulacrum, which imitates something that turns out to be still another simulacrum, and so on *ad infinitum*. The only solution is to recognize this impossibility by deliberately revealing the text's own contexts, its own simulated character, and, therefore, its own unreality.

Bitov's artistic structure has a *deliberately postmodernist character*. The impossibility of implementing the modernists' means for overcoming spiritual nonfreedom pushes the author of *Pushkin House* toward combining thoroughly modernist approaches with postmodernist results. The basis for these transformations is the decidedly realistic depiction of what might be called the Russian postmodern condition of the sixties and seventies.

# 3

# From an Otherwordly Point of View

## Venedikt Erofeev's *Moscow to the End of the Line*

*His quirky, or simply bizarre position—as he called it, "in*
*my otherworldly point of view"—is truly consistent.*

—Olga Sedakova, from her memoir about
Venedikt Erofeev (Frolova et al. 1991: 98)

More than enough has been written about the carnivalesque character of
Venedikt Erofeev's *Moscow to the End of the Line.* Indeed, the book's
connection to the "festive tradition," to blasphemous travesties that wove
together sacred images and the motifs of the "lower bodily stratum," to
questions of the "serious laughter" of the "ultimate questions of being," are
all more than apparent. However, it is telling that all the critics who have
written about Erofeev's carnivalization are forced to make allowances for
the unique, nontraditional *semantics* of these traditional forms in *Moscow
to the End of the Line.* Thus when Svetlana Gaiser-Shnitman points out the
book's connection with the "generic memory" of Menippean satire, she
notes that an equally large role in the "poem's" poetics is played by the
semantic structures of such decidedly uncarnivalesque genres as the spiritual quest, prose poems, ballads, and mystery plays (Gaiser-Shnitman
1984: 257–65). The author calls his text a *"poema"* (narrative or epic
poem), which evidently refers to Gogol's *Dead Souls,* in turn referring to
Dante's *Divine Comedy* and the epic poems of Homer. Elena Smirnova
notes that *Moscow to the End of the Line* truly corresponds to the Gogolian
understanding of this genre; Erofeev's protagonist

goes beyond the narrow confines of existence to the limitless dimension of
being. . . . And in this new dimension, Venichka's trip to Petushki proves to
be merely a pretext for the broadest possible formulation of the question of
the meaning and essence of human life throughout human history. This is the
solution to the troubling riddle of the word "poema." I should add that the
same holds true for *Dead Souls.* (1990: 59)

Mark Altshuller adds that the "journey from Moscow to Petushki is the soul's symbolic journey from darkness to light, the journey Gogol had in mind for Chichikov, and which Dante carried out" (1982: 83). The asymmetrical relationship between Erofeev's poem and the carnival tradition is also analyzed by Andrei Zorin, who notes Bakhtin's dislike of the "entropy" of the poem's ending. He argues that in *Moscow to the End of the Line* "the element of folk laughter in the final analysis deceives the hero as well. . . . The carnivalesque unity of the hero and the folk . . . is not meant to be" (Zorin 1991: 121). For his part, Mikhail Epstein argues that "Venya's values, which had been turned topsy-turvy by carnival, once again begin to turn themselves upside down. . . . Yet this is no longer carnival, but rather its after-life: all previous traits that had been overturned by carnival are now restored in a kind of new, 'noumenal' dimension . . . the carnival itself becomes car-nivalized, which leads to a new realm of the serious" (1995b: 17).

Surprisingly, these critics are echoed by the authors of memoirs about Venedikt Erofeev, who constantly emphasize the deep, programmatic seri-ousness of the life of this "professional tippler": "Venichka has the sense that a successful, everyday life is a substitute for real life, which it destroys; and this destruction has a partly religious nuance" (Vladimir Murav'ev, in Frolova 1991: 90); "One probably shouldn't say so, but I think that he was imitating Christ" (Galina Erofeeva in Frolova 1991: 89); "Venichka lives on the edge of life. And what's important is not his final illness, not the dangers so common to the drinking man, but his lifestyle, even his inner lifestyle—'in view of the end'. . . One can sense that this lifestyle is more than trivial drunkenness; it's a kind of service. Service to the pub?" (Olga Sedakova in Frolova 1991: 98).

These quotes allow us to make a hypothesis about the paradoxically serious and even *tragic* carnivalesque character of Erofeev's poem (and apparently, his philosophy of life), which is implemented within the frame-work of dialogic poetics in general. One can also suppose that such a transformation is connected with the general logic of the postmodern dia-logue with chaos that obliges the artist to identify the very creative process with the creation of fictitious simulacra and even with death. However, the power of the influence of *Moscow to the End of the Line* on the entire subsequent development of Russian postmodernism and contemporary Rus-sian literature leads to the thought that this writer did more than simply use the implicit postmodernist artistic paradigm; rather, he gave it a truly origi-nal feel, bringing it into the context of the Russian cultural tradition. How did he do it? What is the aesthetic mechanism behind these transforma-tions? What is the artistic and philosophical point of this synthesis (if a synthesis was really achieved)?

We shall try to answer these questions by concentrating first and foremost on the meaning of dialogism in *Moscow to the End of the Line*, which was written in 1970 (Erofeev 1994).

The first and most obvious feature of Erofeev's dialogism is its stylistic ambivalence. This is not only the "familiarization of high style and unexpected and comic *mésalliances*" (Gaiser-Shnitman 1984: 257). Instead, one should concentrate on the conflation of high and low styles that results in a true *intersection* of absolutely incompatible meanings. Here is a typical example:

> And later (listen carefully), later, after they had found out why Pushkin died, I gave them Alexander Blok's poem "The Nightingale Garden" to read. There, at the center of the poem—if you throw out all of the perfumed shoulders, the unilluminated mists, the rosy towers in smoky vestments—there at the center of the poem you find the lyric hero dismissed from work for drunkenness, whoring, and absenteeism. I told them, "It's a very contemporary book." I told them, "You'll find it useful." And so? They read it. But, in spite of everything, it had a depressing effect on them—Freshen-up disappeared immediately from all the stores. It's impossible to say why, but black-jack was forgotten, vermouth was forgotten, Sheremetievo International Field was forgotten, and Freshen-up triumphed. Everyone drank only Freshen-up. Oh, to be carefree! Oh heavenly birds, who neither sow nor reap. Oh, the lilies of the field are dressed more beautifully than Solomon! They drank up all the Freshen-up from Dolgoprudny Station to Sheremetievo International (Erofeev 1994: 37; Erofeev 1995: 52).[1]

This passage's stylistic trajectory can best be described as a downward parabola. In the beginning a highly poetic style is ironically reproduced ("the perfumed shoulders, the unilluminated mists, the rosy towers in smoky vestments"), only to be lowered sharply, first by vulgarity ("for drunkenness, whoring, and absenteeism"), then by the quote from Lenin ("It's a very contemporary book"). But the final part of this passage is a provocative return to the poetic key; moreover, the name of "Freshen-up" cologne is a semantic echo of Blok's "The Nightingale Garden" and is placed within a biblical stylistic context ("Oh, the lilies of the field are dressed more beautifully than Solomon"). Here the high style is lowered not simply to discredit it but to attain a different form of existence in the "lower" meanings. In other words, in Erofeev's style the high and the low do not destroy each other or cancel each other out but instead form an ambivalent unity of meaning. In fact, all the most stylistically vivid passages are built on the dialogical intersection of high and low meanings: from the famous words about the spit on each step of the social ladder to the chapter about cocktails, from the description of "the most beloved of trollops" (Erofeev 1994: 43) to the meditation on the hiccup.

This same principle determines the logic of the construction of the model of culture in Erofeev's poem. The numerous cultural quotations in *Moscow to the End of the Line* have been described in detail by several scholars (see Paperno and Gasparov 1981; Levin 1992; Gaiser-Shnitman 1984; Altshuller 1982). On the basis of their observations, it can be said that this is not simply a lowering of traditional cultural themes. Even the parodic story about unrequited love for the famous Soviet harpist Olga Erdely (where the harpist is depicted as a one-ruble "hag of a woman, not so very old but drunk as they come" [ibid., 75]) realizes the high theme of resurrection through love, which was invoked a few pages earlier in Venichka's story about his own resurrection. And the comic list of writers and composers who drank in the name of art and for love of the people (only "Privy Counselor Goethe did not drink a gram" [ibid., 84], according to Venichka) becomes a kind of authorial confession that paves the way for the poem's end: "He (Goethe) remained alive but it was as if he committed suicide. And now was completely satisfied. This is even worse than real suicide"; it is no accident that "the man with the black mustache" says about Venichka himself that "with you, it's not like with other people, it's like Goethe" (ibid., 87). This sort of relationship to culture is most apparent in the book's treatment of biblical motifs. Paperno and Gasparov note:

> Each event exists simultaneously in two dimensions. A hangover is interpreted as an execution, death, crucifixion. Getting a hair of the dog that bit you—that's resurrection. After resurrection life begins: the gradual intoxication that ultimately leads to a new execution. The hero speaks openly about this at the end of the story: "For isn't the life of man a momentary booziness of the soul as well?" However, such an interpretation of these everyday events in turn has the opposite effect on the story's biblical motifs. They often take on the tone of parody, jokes, puns: the high and the tragic are irrevocably tied together with the comic and the obscene. Moreover, this gives the biblical text a cyclical character: the very same chain of events is repeated again and again.... The reversed order of events points to the vicious circle within which they move." (1981: 389–90)

It is important to note that some of the New Testament parallels are deliberately distorted. Thus, for example, it is not Venichka/Jesus who resurrects Lazarus but Venichka who is himself resurrected by a "bad woman": "twelve weeks ago I was in a coffin, I had been in a coffin for four years already, so that I had already stopped stinking. And they said to her, 'Look, he's in a coffin. Resurrect him, if you can' " (Erofeev 1994: 90); the reference to the star of Bethlehem occurs only immediately before the final crucifixion. Meanwhile, other New Testament quotes are presented in surprising detail. Thus the four killers with "a touch of something classical about them" (ibid., 158) correspond to the four executioners from the Gospels: "Then the soldiers, when they had crucified Jesus, took his garments, and made four parts, to every soldier a part" (King James version, John 19:23), "because it was the preparation, that the bodies should not remain upon the cross on the sabbath day, (for that sabbath day was an high day,)" (John 19:31).

In this case we may speak of a conscious combination of the principles of citational accuracy and citational confusion. The very model of culture this creates is in the zone of "unprepared contact" with current, "lower" reality: it turns out to be simultaneously canonical and yet *open-ended.* The image of culture loses its aura of epic legend and becomes the object of radical *novelization.* In fact, Bitov obtains this same effect by means of ironic reflection in *Pushkin House.* As with Bitov, this leads to the relativization of the model of culture, which loses its absolute meaning. But the originality of *Moscow to the End of the Line* lies in the other side of the same process: This very "low" and thoroughly "extracultural" context turns out to be the place where eternal cultural plots come to an *unpredictable* conclusion. Skipping forward a bit, we should note that the unpredictability of the realization of the New Testament line is expressed first and foremost by the fact that the final crucifixion of this new Jesus is not accompanied by resurrection: "And since then I have not regained consciousness, and I never will" (Erofeev 1994: 164). This is why both high *and* low are so drastically reduced by Erofeev: The travesty inevitably leads to tragic seriousness. But the pivotal embodiment of dialogical ambivalence is the central figure of the poem: Venichka Erofeev himself, who is the central character, the narrator, and the author's double all at once. This is emphasized by the fact that the author and the main character have the same name, as well as by a number of autobiographical signals, such as references to the places where the poem was written ("While working as a cable fitter in Sheremetievo, Autumn, 1969" [ibid.]) right next to the description of this same cable work in the story about Venichka's short career as a foreman (the chapters "Kuskovo-Novogireevo," "Novogireevo-Reutova").

The cultural archetype of *holy foolishness* serves as the basis for the poem's protagonist—Venichka Erofeev, the author's double. Venichka's connection to the tradition of Russian holy foolishness has been noted by Svetlana Gaiser-Shnitman, Irina Sluzhevskaia, Mikhail Epstein, Olga Sedakova:

> Among the many contrasts in *Moscow to the End of the Line* one finds the most profound one: an entirely different ethic is surrounded by the aesthetics of abomination [*bezobrazie*]. To call it the ethic of the harmonious [*blagoobrazie*] would be going too far, but one can, in any case, speak of a

kind of strange, perhaps otherworldly harmony. When Venichka (the hero, not the author) informs us of his chastity and the expansion of the intimate sphere, and when the *Song of Songs* is quoted in the drunken "love" scene, this is not just a collection of pretty words. The star of Bethlehem over the hiccups and vomit (and the proof of God's existence using the example of the hiccup), the temptation on the roof of the temple (transferred to the commuter train), as well as many other oddly used biblical themes, are more than mere blasphemy. This is not so strange to anyone who has read the lives of holy fools, for example." (Sedakova 1991: 264)

From this point of view, a number of the riddles of Erofeev's poem are resolved. The enigmatic and paradoxical nature of the poem itself corresponds to the aesthetics of holy foolishness, in which "paradox fulfills the function of the aesthetic dominant" (Likhachev, Panchenko, and Ponyrko 1984: 10–11). Thus the artistic meaning of the main character's drunkenness becomes clear. Venichka's drinking, which is described in such detail and with such care, is a typical symbolic gesture of "wise holy foolishness," which is supposed to renew the eternal truths with the help of wild behavioral paradoxes. The holy fool's typical "willful martyrdom" may not be necessary, but it is desired, like the stigmata of St. Theresa referred to in the poem: "And, all in blue flashes of lightning, the Lord answered me: 'So what did St. Teresa need her stigmata for? It, too, was unnecessary, yet she desired it.' 'That's the point,' I answered in ecstasy. 'Me, too, I desire this, but it's not at all necessary.' 'Well, since it's desired, Venichka, go on and drink' " (Erofeev 1994: 26–27). At the same time, Venichka's drunkenness also reveals the features of the fool's "holy madness," a madness that allows for direct and familiar conversation with angels, and even for inviting the Lord to have a drink ("*Share with me my repast, Lord*" [ibid., 27; italics in the original]). This is why Erofeev so persistently uses religious terminology to describe drunkenness. "What am I to drink in Thy name?" (66), asks Venichka; the fabulous cocktail recipes seem quite at home here (note that so many of them bear biblical names, such as "Balsam of Canaan," "Jordan's Waters," and "Star of Bethlehem"), as does the ritual of their preparation; for example, the "Tear of a Komsomol Girl" absolutely has to be mixed with a sprig of honeysuckle and by no means with a dodder. The result is thoroughly spiritual: "After only two goblets of this cocktail, a person will become so inspired that it is possible to go up to him for half an hour and, standing one and a half meters away, spit in his fat face without his saying a thing" (ibid.,71). Note that this "inspiration" is like an exaggerated version of the meekness of the holy fool. And the angels who try to convince Venichka not to drink the whole bottle, as well as the man on the train who says "tran-scen-den-tal!" (ibid., 30) after every swig, are also perfectly at home here. It is also typical that, as Panchenko has observed, the suffering of the old Russian holy fool contains an indirect reference to the pains of the Savior (Likhachev, Panchenko, and Ponyrko 1984: 114), which explains why the parallels between Venichka's travels and the Gospels are so persistent. And the journey plot itself corresponds to the tradition of the holy fool's "wanderings from house to house." Therefore the "sinfulness" of many of Venichka's actions and declarations should be no cause for concern, since even love for a whore has its counterpart in the lives of holy fools: "God told Osia to go unto his whore of a wife and love a wife who loves evil and is an adulteress" (ibid., 85).

The process of drinking is also constantly surrounded with artistic associations; the same metaphor repeats itself with a folkloric insistency: He drank, "throwing back my head like a pianist, conscious both of the grandeur of the fact that it was just beginning and of what lay ahead" (Erofeev 1994: 44, also pp. 53, 78). Scholars of this cultural tradition have noted the peculiar theatricality of the holy fool's behavior (see Likhachev, Panchenko, and Ponyrko 1984: 81–116); various theatrical metaphors work for this version as well, for example: "Perhaps I was rehearsing something out there? . . . Perhaps it was the immortal drama of *Othello, the Venetian Moor*? I was playing it alone—all the roles at once." (Erofeev 1994: 29). But even most important is that this is the way that the "holy fool's" position is extrapolated onto the creative process. It is no accident that the process of wandering is also described using the terminology of literary criticism: "The devil knows in which genre I'll arrive in Petushki. All the way from Moscow it was memoirs and philosophical essays, it was all poems in prose, as with Ivan Turgenev. Now the detective story begins" (ibid., 73). The fact that the protagonist and the biographical author share the same name renders this extrapolation all the more apparent.

"Old Russian holy foolishness contains echoes of the idea that the tsar and the outcast are one and the same," writes Panchenko (Likhachev, Panchenko, and Ponyrko 1984: 139). This is also one of the central motifs of the poem, which is once again reflected in the features shared by the drunken hero and his all-powerful, extratextual author-creator. But this is not all. Venichka, as he recalls his work on the brigade, calls himself the "little prince" (Erofeev 1994: 37), while his drinking companions, who are appalled by how he "infinitely expanded the sphere of intimacy" (ibid., 30), that is, by his refusal to urinate in public, tell him to "[c]ut out thinking that you're better than anyone else. That we're small potatoes and you're tops" (ibid., 31). Venichka is famous for the fact that "in his whole life, he has never passed gas" (ibid., 33). This would seem to be typical carnivalesque exhaltation, and yet it is always accompanied by the tones of truly regal dignity: "Oh, the ephemeral! oh, that most helpless and shameful of times in the life of my people" (ibid., 15); "how all of you scattered about *my world*" (ibid., 24); "I like it that my country's people have such empty, bulging eyes. . . . I like *my people*" (ibid., 28; emphasis in the original).

Venichka's responsibility for *his people* (we will return to the other connotations of this constantly repeated phrase) can be seen even more clearly in his many sermons and prophecies, which, once again, are those of the holy fool: "Everything should take place slowly and incorrectly so that man doesn't get a chance to start feeling proud, so that man is sad and perplexed" (ibid., 14); "universal chicken-heartedness" is a "predicate to sublime perfection" (ibid., 21); "we must honor . . . the dark reaches of another's soul. We must look into them even if there's nothing there, even if there's only trash there. It's all one; look and honor it, look and don't spit on it" (ibid., 94), "pity and love for the world are one" (ibid., 96); "that day of days" will come (ibid., 113). The meaning of these sermons is profoundly dialogic. Thus Erofeev's typical hatred for the idea of heroism and heroic deeds[2] is quite understandable in a dialogic context: The righteous man is complete unto himself and therefore is absolutely closed to dialogic relations. At the same time, sinfulness and weakness of heart are, strangely enough, requirements for openness to understanding and pity, the first sign of open-endedness and readiness to change.

This philosophy clearly coincides with Zygmunt Bauman's conception of "contingency-as-destiny" (1993: 14). Bauman, we recall, argues that the crisis of the idea of the One Law and Absolute Truth that is at the heart of the postmodern condition gives rise to a decidedly new life strategy. The acceptance of the illogical accident of existence as the only possible fate not only leads to a particular kind of discomfort but also acts as a new condition for the inner freedom of the individual:

> Living in contingency, means living without a guarantee, with just a provisional, pragmatic, Pyrrhonic, until-further-notice certainty. . . . Awareness of contingency does not "empower": its acquisition does not give the owner advantage over the protagonists in the struggle of wills and purposes, or in the game of cunning and luck. It does not lead to, or sustain, domination. As if to make the score even, it does not aid the struggle against domination either. It is, to put it bluntly, indifferent to the current or prospective structures of domination" (ibid., 15, 16).

In other words, this kind of consciousness is really free. This philosophy of freedom in the lawless accident of the world, of freedom without guarantees, of freedom that inevitably leads to suffering, is all quite close to the hero of *Moscow to the End of the Line;* it determines the meaning of his holy foolishness.[3] Dialogism turns out to be the direct expression and consequence of this freedom.

From the point of view of the holy fool, it is clear why Erofeev's poem does not fit within the confines of the carnivalesque culture of laughter. The holy fool straddles the boundary between the funny and the serious, embodying what Panchenko calls the "tragic version of the world's laughter" (Likhachev, Panchenko, and Ponyrko 1984: 72). Typically, Venichka, who calls himself a fool and "blissful" ("*blazhennyi*," the traditional synonyms of the holy fool), himself justifies these terms first and foremost by invoking "world sorrow" and "inconsolable grief" (an explicit reference to Kramskoi's painting of the same name):[4]

> I am sick in my soul, though I don't look it. Because, since that time, as I remember my condition, I do nothing but simulate mental health, expending everything, without a scrap left over, all powers, mental, physical, whatever. This is what makes me boring. . . .
>   I am not saying that now the truth is known to me, or that I've approached it close up. Not at all. But I've gotten close enough to it so that it's convenient to look it over.
>   And I look, and I see, and for that reason, I'm sorrowful. And I don't believe that any one of you has dragged around within himself this bitter, bitter mishmash. I am in a quandary over saying what this mishmash is composed of, and, all the same, you would never understand, but mostly there's "sorrow" and "fear" in it. "Sorrow" and "fear" most of all and, then, muteness. (Erefeev 1994: 46)

Medieval holy foolishness, like ancient cynicism, might be considered the "postmodernism" of its own era. "The life of the holy fool, like the life of the cynic, was the conscious negation of beauty, the refutation of the universally accepted idea of the beautiful, or, to be more precise, it turned this idea upside down" (Likhachev, Panchenko, and Ponyrko 1984: 80). The holy fool, like the postmodern writer, enters into a dialogue with chaos, striving to find the truth in filth and obscenity. " 'Grace will descend upon the worst of them'—this is what the holy fool has in mind" (ibid., 79). This is why the model of the holy fool become so significant for Daniil Kharms, one of Russian postmodernism's most radical precursors.[5] Such a similarity in strategy most likely explains why Venedikt Erofeev and the most recent postmodernists (Sasha Sokolov and Yevgeny Popov in particular) are drawn to the cultural archetype of the holy fool.

However, in the case of *Moscow to the End of the Line,* one must also consider the historical and literary factors. In her study of Bulgakov's *The Master and Margarita,* Marietta Chudakova writes:

The resistance to social humiliation by the individual, the "piecemeal" that pretends to homogeneity, led to the equation of hero (who, as has already been noted, is clearly identified with the author) with Christ himself, and his departure allowed for the possibility of interpreting the "appearance of the hero" as an unrecognized Second Coming. This would be repeated in *Doctor Zhivago* . . . It's plain that no further progress could be made in this direction. It was time for a change of heroes and a change of literary cycles. (1991: 16)

With his holy-foolish version of Christ, Venedikt Erofeev both completes this great tradition and shifts it by 180 degrees. The complex ambivalence of *Moscow to the End of the Line* moves the imitation of Christ into an entirely new dimension: A new paradigm arises, in which the serious repetition of Christ's path is inseparable from the travesty of the Gospels as the surrealistic daily life of a Russian alcoholic. It's impossible to imagine such a combination in Bulgakov or Pasternak; for them, the New Testament contexts are the repositories of eternal, absolute values. But Erofeev adds a new twist to this tradition: The New Testament plot is subject to a Menippean "testing of a philosophical idea, a discourse, a *truth*" (Bakhtin 1984: 114). It, too, is relative, lacking any stable value. Thus Erofeev's poem serves as a bridge from the spiritual tutelage of the Russian realist classics of the nineteenth and twentieth centuries (Bulgakov's orientation toward Gogol and Pasternak's toward Tolstoy) to the unrestrained playfulness of postmodernism. The position of the holy fool is perfect for combining moral sermons with playful freedom while also picking up the threads of the literary tradition of Russian holy foolishness, which goes back to Rozanov, Remizov, Leskov, Dostoevsky, and the old Russian classics before it was broken off with Kharms.

The vision of chaos in *Moscow to the End of the Line* is formed as a system of several semantic fields. First, there is everything connected with "the life of the people," such as drinking, the life of the gutter, and the descriptions of Venichka's traveling companions. These motifs are symbolically concentrated in the description of the people's eyes in the chapter "Karacharovo-Chukhlika" (which is paraphrased again in the chapter "43rd Kilometer—Khrapunovo"):

On the other hand, my people have such eyes! They're constantly bulging but with no tension of any kind in them. There's complete lack of any sense but, then, what power! (What spiritual power!) These eyes will not sell out. They'll not sell or buy anything, whatever happens to my country. In days of doubt, in days of burdensome reflection, at the time of any trial or calamity, these eyes will not blink. They don't give a good Goddamn about anything. (Erofeev 1994: 28)

Here one phrase virtually annihilates the other, both semantically and stylistically. The portrait of the people's fragmentary face proves to be the mirror image of the *face of chaos*. It expresses nothing, but at the same time, despite its lack of connection, logic, and meaning, it expresses everything. The phrase "my people" works not only to create the distance between the holy-foolish tsar and his subjects; it is also an expression of belonging: "I like my people. I'm happy that I was born and grew up under the gaze of those eyes" (ibid., 28); "Now, after 500 grams of Kubanskaya, I was in love with those eyes, in love like a madman" (ibid., 72). It is because he is both inseparable from his people and unable to lose himself among them that Venichka is able to conduct his dialogue with the popular face of chaos. Venichka's attempts to systematize and rationalize the process of drinking are particularly revealing.[6] The direct result of this tactic, Venichka's "notorious individualized charts" (ibid., 38) showing the amount of alcohol consumed by each coworker, as well as the famous cocktail recipes, combine mathematical precision with fantastic ingredients: "I then examined with care, intently and close up, the soul of every shitass" (ibid., 40), recalls Venichka. But he also looks into his own soul and draws up an "individualized chart" (ibid., 38) for himself ("the beating of a proud heart, the song of the stormy petrel—in other words, pure Gorky—or like Aivazovsky's trashy painting of the ninth wave" [ibid., 39–40]), philosophically and experimentally analyzing the reasons why "from the first shot through the fifth I would ripen, but beginning with the sixth, and through the ninth, I would go soft. I'd go so soft that on the tenth I would have to shut my eyes" (ibid., 61). Here Venichka takes a different path toward the inner harmonization of the abominable: the path of analogy. Hence his comparison of the sixth through ninth shots with the symphonies of Antonín Dvořák: "You must drink the sixth, seventh, eighth, and ninth immediately, at one go, but drink them in an ideal sense—that is, drink them only in your imagination" (ibid., 61). When each participant in the train-car symposium tells a love story ("like in Turgenev" [ibid., 91]), each story casts an ironic light on a cultural subtext (the story of the man with black mustaches of his friend's resurrection, Mitrich's Wagnerian Loengrin, and a kind of metatext of the Russian classics, including Pushkin, Anna Karenina, and Liza Kalitina narrated by "the woman with the complicated story and a scar and no teeth" [ibid., 101]). As a rule, Venichka reinforces these subtexts: "And I sat there and understood old Mitrich, understood his tears—he was simply sorry for everything and everyone. . . . First love or ultimate pity, what's the difference?" (ibid., 95–96).

Another level of chaos (the sociopolitical) is formed from the stereotypes of Sovietspeak and the Soviet mentality as a whole. Once again, these stereotypes are more than simply parodied by Venichka. He uses this abominable language for his own improvisations about traveling around the world ("The playthings of monopoly's ideologues, the marionettes of the arms kings, where do they get such appetite?" [102]).[7] Moreover, Venichka's dream-like reminiscences about the Cherkassovo Revolution (in the chapters "Orekhovo-Zuevo—Krutoe" and "Voinovo—Usad") testify to his perception of the logic of the historical absurd. At the very least, the chronicle of the Cherkassovo Revolution, with its storms of buildings and its decrees, looks like a travesty of 1917.

But *Moscow to the End of the Line* embodies another level of the presentation of chaos: the *metaphysical* level. It is manifested first and foremost in the chronotopic structure of the text. The poem's metaphysics is most visible in the trajectory of Venichka's drunken wanderings: When he heads in the direction of the Kremlin, he always ends up at Kursk Station, where the train leaves for Petushki; however, the actual road to Petushki brings Venichka to the Kremlin, where he meets his terrible demise. And if Petushki is truly heaven ("Petushki is the place where the birds never cease singing, not by day or by night, where winter and summer the jasmine never cease blooming. Perhaps there is such a thing as original sin, but no one ever feels burdened in Petushki" [ibid., 43]), then the Kremlin is directly associated with hell (Kuritsyn 1992: 296–304). Therefore, Venichka's strange trajectory has a distinct metaphysical sense to it: He who is curious about hell comes to heaven, while he who seeks heaven ends up in hell.

This is looking-glass logic, enchanted space, a vicious circle. Only in this metaphysically distorted reality can the poem's space–time continuum make sense: "Five minutes, seven minutes, a whole eternity I flung myself about like that, surrounded by four walls, grabbing myself by the throat, entreating God not to offend me" (Erofeev 1994: 27); "Our tomorrow is brighter than our yesterday and our today. But who'll see to it that our day after tomorrow won't be worse than our day before yesterday?" (ibid., 45); "they gave a glassful to the young one, who clasped it happily to his left nipple with his right thigh, tears gushing from both nostrils" (ibid., 85). And on the sad journey back from Petushki to Moscow, space disappears entirely, to be replaced by the absolute darkness outside the train's window. Time disappears as well: "What do you need the time for, Venichka? . . . Once you had a heavenly paradise, you could have found out the time last Friday, but now your heavenly paradise is no more, what do you need with the time?" (ibid., 155).

It is perfectly clear that this metaphysical face of chaos does not move Venichka to rapture; on the contrary, he feels something closer to ontological horror. And yet Venichka does not recoil from the world's absurdity; instead, he tries to overcome chaos with words and faith.

His program for dialogue with chaos is expressed most clearly in the discussion of hiccups in the chapter "Kilometer 33—Electrougli." The drunken hiccup acts as a pure case of disorder and, therefore, as a model of human life and humanity itself: "It is not so with every individual's triumphs and failures, ecstasies and afflictions—isn't there the slightest hint of regularity? Is it not thus that the catastrophes in the life of humanity follow one another in confusion? Law is higher than us all. The hiccup is higher than any law" (ibid., 65). Then the hiccup is compared to the Right Hand of God, while the transition from hiccups to God is deliberately smoothed over by the narrator's style:

> [The hiccup] is indiscernible and we are helpless. We are deprived of freedom of will and are in the power of the arbitrary which has no name and from which is no escape.
> We are mere trembling creatures while it is omnipotent. It—that is, the Right Hand of God which is raised above us all and before which only cretins and rogues do not bow their heads. He is incomprehensible and, therefore, He is. (Ibid., 65)

In other words, the symbol of chaos comes to signify the higher divine logic, which humanity cannot understand. And it reconciles us to chaos. Moreover, the *faith* that a Higher meaning is hidden within chaos gives Venichka strength, becoming the source of his own Joycean *epiphany:*

> . . . a believer in overcoming who is without any thought of rebellion, I believe in the fact that He is good and that therefore I myself am good.
> He is good. He leads me from suffering toward the light. From Moscow toward Petushki. Through the torments of the Kursk Station. Through the purgation at Kuchino, through the fancies of Kupavna to the light of Petushki. (Ibid., 66)

Is this program carried out? What are the consequences of dialogue with chaos, particularly with metaphysical chaos? The answer to this question is found in the last part of *Moscow to the End of the Line,* where Venichka once again speaks with mythological and legendary "emissaries from eternity," like the angels in the poem's beginning.

In the final section of the poem, the action's internal tension rests on the contrast between the increasingly illusory linearity of the movement (the chapters are still named after the stations from Moscow to Petushki) and the insistency with which the actual space of the text becomes circular (he has yet to realize that he overslept Petushki and is heading back to Moscow).

The finale of this process in the chapters combining both ends of Venichka's journey in a single point: "Petushki. Sadovy Circle" and "Petushki. The Kremlin" (ibid., 156, 160). This metamorphosis is expressed not only by the fact that the train takes the road back, closer to Moscow, but also by the fact that all the most important motifs of the first part are symmetrically rewound:

- the memory of the woman and the child, Venichka's son, "the little one who knows the letter Ю like his own five fingers" (ibid., 49);
- the motif of "Inconsolable Grief," Kramskoi's painting;
- Christian quotes and paraphrases (from Peter's denial to "lama savahtan");
- Goethe and Schiller;
- important verbal formulae either repeat themselves or are paraphrased, such as: "Oh, the ephemeral. Oh, vanity. Oh, that most infamous and shameful of times in the life of my people" (ibid., 153); "Talife cumi, as your Tsaritsa said when you were lying in your coffin" (ibid., 153–54); " 'Why are you silent?' the Lord, all in blue lightning, asks me" (ibid., 155). (Compare with "And, all in blue flashes of lightning, the Lord answered me . . . The Lord was silent" [ibid., 26–27].)

The emissaries of chaos (the Furies, Satan, the Sphinx, Mithridates, king of Pontus, the "Worker and Collective Farmer" statue, and the four killers) all give this circular structure a definite meaning. Venichka's attempts to organize chaos from within fail miserably. The emissaries of chaos kill Venichka, with no hope for a subsequent resurrection. The "bad infinity" of the circle triumphs over the line of human life.

Against the backdrop of these repetitions, the confusion of the images of God and the angels stands out sharply. The good angels are not only compared to bad children who laugh devilishly at a man's terrible death: "And the angels burst out laughing. . . . They are shameful creatures . . . should I tell you how they burst out laughing just now?. . . They laughed, and God was silent" (ibid., 162–63). It is particularly telling that this happens after Venichka's prayer about the Cup ("Trembling all over, I said to myself, *Talife cumi*! . . . This isn't *Talife cumi*, it's *lama savahtan*, as the Savior said. . . . That is 'Why hast thou forsaken me?'" [ibid., 162]), while the analogous scene in the Gospels is followed by an angelic visitation: "There appeared an angel unto him from heaven, strengthening him" (Luke 22:34). Thus even God's cold silence contains a note of wordless agreement with the killers. Venichka's attitude toward chaos changes as well. If in the chapter "Usad—105th Kilometer" he says, "So there remains only one way out: accept the dark" (Erofeev 1994: 132), in the chapter "Petushki. Station Square" he sees his death differently: "And if I die sometime—I'm going to die very soon—I know I'll die as I am, without accepting this world, perceiving it close up and far away, inside and out, perceiving but not accepting it" (ibid., 154).

Why does Venichka's dialogue with chaos end in defeat? Why is his death final and irrevocable?

The first and most important reason is connected with Venichka's holy-foolish position in relation to the chaos that surrounds him. Venichka *errs* when he calculates the hidden internal logic of chaos. He cannot help but err, since that is the cost of "holy madness" and drunken absurdity. Such is the inevitable result of dialogic *interaction* with chaos rather than monologic influence on it: Dialogue requires involvement. And the position of the holy fool corresponds perfectly to this kind of tragic involvement in chaos.

Even reliable figures turn out to be ambiguous upon a second examination. The dream that causes Venichka to miss the heavenly Petushki comes upon him after the dangerous sixth shot of alcohol. The action of *Moscow to the End of the Line* takes place on Friday, during Venichka's thirteenth trip to Petushki. Viacheslav Kuritsyn interprets this "thirteenth Friday" as a symbol of the unruliness of diabolical forces (Kuritsyn 1992: 303). Elena A. Smirnova sees a reference to the thirteenth of Nisan in the Greek calendar, when Jesus was betrayed (1990: 62). But no less important is the fact that thirteen is the number of Christ himself, since he has twelve apostles. In other words, one and the same number (and numbers for Venichka are an essential instrument in the search for stability within chaos) has both diabolical and divine connotations.

Is Venichka to blame if Chaos proves stronger than he? If so, then this is a case of tragic guilt. The reason for Venichka's defeat is not his error—on the contrary, his error is the result of the correctness of his chosen path. The entire artistic construction of the poem and first and foremost the correspondences or confusion between the first part (before Petushki) and the second part (after) clearly testify to the fact that *literally everything that is imbued with divine meaning turns out to belong just as much to chaos.* The New Testament plot does, indeed, repeat itself. But it repeats itself *incorrectly.* The New Christ is betrayed not by Judas (who is not even mentioned in the poem, nor is he doubled by any of the poem's characters) but by God and the angels. In other words, the spiritual values contained in this timeless plot cannot withstand Menippean testing in an atmosphere of total ambivalence. Carnival, according to Bakhtin, embodies the "joyful relativity"

(1984: 107) of being. In Erofeev's work, this "joyful relativity" is experienced as an *objective* source of tragedy. Even the symbol of the purest and brightest character in the poem, Venichka's little son, who "knows the letter Ю " and "loves his father like himself" (Erofeev 1994: 49), becomes, by the end of the poem, a fiery sign of death, a bloody symbol of the absurd: "[A] clotted red letter 'Ю' spread across my eyes and started to quiver. And since then I have not regained consciousness, and I never will" (ibid., 164).

Developing David Bethea's hypothesis that the four men who kill Venichka may constitute an allusion to the Four Horsemen of the Apocalypse (Bethea 1989: 275), Vladimir Tumanov suggests that Venichka undergoes "something like an aesthetic Apocalypse" (1996: 109): "Venya's death lacks a key element of the biblical narrative and especially of John's Revelation, for his apocalypse is without hope, i.e., without *resurrection*. By stressing the disappearance of his consciousness at the moment of his grotesque crucifixion, Venya not only makes his narrative 'impossible,' but also indicates that there is *nothing* after his death. . . . This is all the more paradoxical because throughout the text the hero sees himself as an alcoholic Christ" (ibid., 109).

At the same time, this paradox is the ultimate expression of postmodernist aesthetics: The repeatedly reinforced identity of author and character renders the "death of the author" literal. Moreover, one cannot help but see this ending as an unintentional reinterpretation of the theme of the "death of the author." In retrospect, this finale produces an unexpected effect: it turns out that we have before us the confession of a man who has already moved into the next world, a confession written from an "otherworldly point of view." But in Erofeev's work, the "death of the author" takes on extremely important significance. In essence, this position becomes the tragic value that contrasts Venichka and his double, the author-creator, with the relativistic world around him. For in this reality, death proves to be the only possible *stable, unambiguous category*. And the view from death is the only possible—tragic—genuine one. In the end, the reader gets the chance to take a new look at the entire poem after understanding its paradoxes and the very emphasis on the dialogue with chaos, as the result of this otherworldly point of view, which was acquired by the author-creator and paid for at the cost of the hero's demise.

To sum up, it is important to understand the logic of the semantic mechanism of dialogue with chaos, which Erofeev developed with ingenious artistic intuition.

First of all, we are in the presence of the renewal of the carnivalesque or, more precisely, the Menippean tradition, but from a particular point of view: From this tradition, Erofeev primarily draws on dialogical ambivalence, which is given a universal meaning that also determines the poem's style, its artistic structure, and the meaning of its cultural context.

Second, the principle of total ambivalence becomes the basis on which the world model of chaos is formed within the poem, a model that reaches all the levels of the text (the system of images, the narrative structure, the chronotope, the associative backdrop) and manifests itself throughout three intersecting semantic subsystems (the image of the people, the motifs of "Soviet-ness," and the metaphysical dimension of chaos).

Third, such a poetics radically relativizes the spiritual absolutes that have been fossilized in cultural symbols and that in turn prove to be incomplete: They need only be completed in "inconclusive present-day reality" (Bakhtin 1981: 39); they must undergo the Menippean test of drunken freedom, of "slum naturalism" (Bakhtin 1984: 115); and in the final analysis, they cannot withstand the test.

Fourth, the cultural archetype of holy foolishness takes on a particular significance, undergoing an essential renewal, since in Erofeev's work it is interpreted as

- the expression of the tragic side of the carnivalesque "joyful relativity" of being;
- preaching, as practical examples of a dialogic relationship to the world, or, more precisely, to the absurd, to the filth of existence—and this dialogic perception of the world gives rise to the unique freedom of the holy fool: freedom from finalization, from the ready-made laws of life;
- the holy fool acts as an individual combining existence on a high metaphysical level (the daily coexperiencing of the Gospels) with involvement in the "lower" world; he therefore tries to understand from within the Idea, the harmony, the logic hidden within the various versions of world chaos and for this purpose enters into an intimate and inevitably deadly involvement with chaos.

Fifth, close correspondences are established between the hero/holy fool and the author-creator, as a result of which the hero's tragic defeat turns into the "death of the author." But this very "death of the author" is equivalent to the acquisition of that point of view which allows one to find solid ground within shifting chaos and, as a consequence, provides for a productive dialogue with chaos, the result of which is the poem itself.

# 4

# The Myth of Metamorphosis

## Sasha Sokolov's *A School for Fools*

> *The psychology of the moron, which is devoid of determin-*
> *ism, was adopted by my generation as the literary norm of a*
> *character's self-consciousness. It was honest because it was*
> *not prejudiced. This psychology was real and parodic; it was*
> *a kind of revenge on the official [propaganda].*

> —Alexei Parshchikov (1995: 11)

According to D. Barton Johnson (1987: 207), Sasha Sokolov's novel *A School for Fools* was completed in 1973, when the author "obtained a sinecure as a game warden in a primitive hunting preserve set aside for the Soviet elite" (ibid., 207). This experimental fiction, narrated from the point of a mentally ill boy, presented a very negative vision of contemporary Russia and therefore had no chance of being published in the Soviet Union. This novel appeared for the first time in Russian only in 1976, when it was brought out by Ardis Publishers in Michigan after Sokolov's emigration in 1974. In Russia, *A School for Fools* was published only after perestroika, in 1989 (in the journal *Oktiabr'*).

Given the obvious stylistic and structural differences between Sasha Sokolov's novel and Erofeev's *Moscow to the End of the Line,* there is nonetheless an important similarity: The heroes of these works are both holy fools. In both works, moreover, the holy foolishness of the hero forms the structure of the artistic world, insofar as the holy fool acts as the central narrator in both cases (Karriker 1979: 610; Johnson 1987: 207). But there is indeed a substantive difference: As we have seen, the hero of Erofeev's poem, by entering into a dialogue with chaos, tries until the very end to preserve internal autonomy in relation to the elements of ontological chaos and social absurdity; the tragic failure of these efforts causes Venichka's death. As for *A School for Fools,* D. Barton Johnson writes that "through the kaleidoscopically chaotic prism of the young man's schizoid mind we see a number of incidents reflecting both his disordered perceptions and his attempts to come to terms with his psychic abnormality vis-à-vis the surrounding world" (1980: 207). In other words, chaos does not surround the narrator from without, as in *Moscow to the End of the Line,* but is found *inside* his ailing consciousness from the very beginning.

Schizophrenia, however, is a no less convincing justification of polyphony than the dialogic intensity of Erofeev's narrator. Aside from the divided consciousness of the central narrator, the pupil at the school for fools, the two voices of his consciousness are able to fight with each other harshly enough; aside from the voice and outlook of the "author of the book" ("Dear student so-and-so, I, the author of this book, have a pretty clear picture of that train" [Sokolov 1977: 43]), it is only in the first chapter, "Nymphea," that we imperceptibly enter into the zone of the teacher Pavel Norvegov's monologue ("what do I fear, geographer Pavel Norvegov, an honest suntanned man from suburban zone five, a modest pedagogue, but one who knows his business" [ibid., 27]), into the stream of consciousness of the boy's mother ("I wasn't in a special hurry looked first at carpeting and signed up for a meter and a half for a meter seventy-five for three years from now" [ibid., 48]), which, in addition, is interrupted by the voice of the woman next to them in line ("I'll be standing here the whole time if anyone says anything I'll say you were behind me and as for pajamas you're wrong to argue with your wife I know those pajamas a very worthwhile buy they'll be" [ibid., 49]), and also by the railway men's discussion of Japanese poetry, which is gradually imbued dialogically with the motifs and intonation of the poetry itself (ibid., 52–56).

The second chapter, "Now. Stories Written on the Veranda," is extremely significant in this context. One cannot agree with John Freedman, who considers these stories the fruit of the narrator's (the "student so-and-so's") literary ambitions: "Literary creation offers the schizophrenic young boy the perfect escape from the confines of the world he inhabits" (1987: 276). In fact, these stories are distinctly different in tone and manner from the rest of the narrative, even though they contain a great number of thematic echoes from it; it would be logical to suggest that these stories were written by the "author of the book," a psychologically healthy person with his own point of view, who depicts the very reality that has already appeared in the first chapter, refracted through the perception of "student so-and-so." Second, these very stories are frequently constructed as first-person monologues—and the voices of these narrators are correlated with the characters who have already appeared in the first chapter—the father-prosecutor, the teacher Norvegov, Veta, her father, Professor Acatov, Rosa Windova, and the narrator's classmate. The polyphonic structure of the narrative becomes a kind of "garden of forking paths," encompassing the simultaneous existence of most of the possibilities and variants of *modus vivendi* in a single, very local chronotope. As John Freedman himself observes, in "*A School for Fools* meaning emerges rather than exists, and every eventuality is possible at any given moment. The literary fact exists and we have had the opportunity, if only briefly, to experience simultaneously several different possibilities" (1987: 268). As many scholars have noted (Karriker 1979; Johnson 1980; Toker 1987), Sokolov usually presents several different versions of the same character in any given work; in *A School for Fools,* this is true not only of the primary narrator but of all the other characters as well: the schoolteacher Veta Acatova/the branch (*vetka*) of acacia/the station prostitute/the "simple girl"; the assistant principal Trachtenberg/the witch Tinbergen; the professor Acatov/Leonardo da Vinci; the geography teacher Pavel/Savl Norvegov/the immortal prophet; the postman Mikheev/Medvedev/The Sender of Wind. However, if the division of one person and voice into several hypostases can be attributed to the delusions of the mentally ill narrator and explained in the spirit of the "epistemological dominant" (see McHale 1987) of classical modernism, then the question of the *ontology of polyphony* in *A School for Fools* remains open.

It is significant, for example, that the second chapter, "Now. Stories Written on the Veranda," which is clearly distanced from the point of view of "student so-and-so," intersects with his worldview, not only thematically, but also structurally. Thus, even in the second chapter, all the stories are written in the present tense: Both for the storytellers and for the primary narrator, *"in time nothingness is in the past and future and it contains nothing from the present"* (Sokolov 1977: 22; emphasis in the original); the various narrators also constantly play with cyclical structures. Moreover, the stories from the second chapter form certain pairs, once against suggesting different takes on what are essentially the same human conflicts and characters ("The Last Day" and "Now," "Three Summers in a Row," and "A Sick Girl," "The Tutor" and "Dissertation," "The Locale" and "Amid the Wastelands," "As Always on Sunday" and "The Guard"). Thus objective significance is clearly attached to the abnormal perceptions of "student so-and-so"—in other words, it is *ontologized.*

The simultaneous existence of two absolutely different models of chaos is the most significant expression of *polyphonic ontology* (or *ontologized polyphony*) as a central narrative device in *A School for Fools,* Fred Moody observes in his study of *A School for Fools.* "One's awareness of chaos as the fundamental condition of being can become either a gift or a burden, despair or inspiration, as Sokolov's use of transformation throughout the novel reveals" (1979: 26).

What is absolutely certain is the connection between chaos, the school for fools, and the life that unfolds behind the school's walls (first and foremost in Chapter 3, "Savl," and Chapter 4, "Skeerly"). There is also the "slipper system" of the school principal Nikolai Gorimirovich Perillo, symbolizing the absurdity of violence (the Russian word *gore*—trouble, woe, misfortune—can be heard in his fanciful patronymic). Moreover, the teachers who possess strength and power and the idiots who have to obey them merge together into one indivisible whole:

> O people, teachers and pupils, how fatuous and filthy you are in your ideas and your deeds! But are we the ones to blame for our idiocy and animal lust, are our hands the ones that scribbled on the doors of the stalls? No, no!—he will exclaim—we are nothing but weak and helpless servants and non-servants of our Principal, Kolya Perillo, and it is he who has inspired us with debauchery and weakmindedness . . . and his hands are the ones which guide ours when we are drawing on the walls here, and he is to blame for our idiocy and our lust" (Sokolov 1977: 113).

It is significant also that the detailed description of the administrative activities of the angry Perillo, who, as they said in school, "served in the same battalion with Kutuzov himself" (ibid., 116–17), is completed in the next passage, which shifts the motif of violence into an openly idiotic dimension:

> The idiots, they are the ones who hang cats on the fire escape, they are the ones who spit in each other's faces during the long recesses and take jam pirozhki away from each other, they are the ones who secretly urinate in each other's pockets and trip each other, they are the ones who twist each other's arms and gang up on weaklings, and they are the idiots who scribbled all over the doors to the stalls. (Ibid., 117)

The description of the song sung by the choir of idiots is also revealing: The song "reached us bloodied, snowswept, in the torn and filthy dress of a girl whom someone forced to do everything they wanted" (ibid., 173).

In the second place, many of the motifs of "normal," "adult," and "historical" life turn out to be linked to this image. Thus, for example, the fictional—or is it real?—story of the life of the "ordinary girl with the ordinary dog" (ibid., 68), who will "catch taxis, go south, raise children, stand in line for hours, grow irremediably old, dress in fashion, curse the government, live through inertia, drink medicine, curse her husband, be on a diet, go away and come back, put lipstick on, desire nothing more, visit parents, consider it all over and velveteen (worstedcambricsilkchintzmorocco) very practical" (ibid., 69)—is imperceptibly shifted into the realm of chaos. Even "adult" love comes to resemble a nightmarish phantasmagoria, as in the narrator's version of the "horrific children's fairy tale about a bear," "Skeerly" (ibid., 144):

> When I recall *Skeerly*—although I try not to remember it, it's better not to remember—it occurs to me that the girl might not be a girl, but a certain woman acquaintance of mine, with whom I have close relations, you understand, of course, you and I are no longer children, and it occurs to me that the bear is not a bear either, but some man I don't know, a man, and I can almost see him doing something there in a hotel room with my acquaintance, and the accursed *skeerly* resounds repeatedly, and I get sick with hate for the sound." (Ibid., 145)

It is worth mentioning that Trachtenberg, the associate principal of the school for fools, participates in this tale along with the folkloric bear, which clearly connects the tale to the insane world of the school for fools. Trachtenberg is pictured here as a "graybearded witch with the sleepy face of an old woman who has died but then been forced to awaken and live" (ibid., 145).

Even the historical episode, the arrest of the biologist Acatov, is presented as the continuation of some kind of bizarre fairy tale: The people who arrest him may well be the insect parasite larvae he had been studying. Moreover, this chaotic aggression is connected with the process of the disappearance of time: They "took the Academician away somewhere for a long time, and somewhere there, where precisely is not known, they beat him in the face and in the stomach so that Acatov would never again dare to assert all this nonsense. And when they released him it turned out that many years had passed, and he had aged" (ibid., 74). All the motifs relating to the father-prosecutor, his newspapers, his work, his misanthropy, as well as to the narrator's memories of the trips to see his music teacher (who was also his mother's secret lover), also develop the vision of aggressively chaotic social relations and everyday "adult" life.

The involvement of all of these themes and motifs with the image of chaos is expressed by the repetition of *signs of death* marking each of these elements of the narrative. Such marking may be indirect: The "paradigmatic" character (Johnson 1980) of Sokolov's novel attaches particular significance to the repetition not only of the images of death but also of their contextual equivalents. Thus, for example, in the first chapter, "Nymphea," the motif of chalk and a chalky color already becomes one of the symbols of death:

> the miners suffered their illnesses and died, sick with a special disease which in conversations among themselves they called 'the chalky.' Chalk dust set-

tled in the workers' lungs, penetrated their blood, their blood became weak and anemic. The people paled, their pellucid white faces glowed in the murk of the night-shift hours, they glowed against a background of astonishingly clean curtains in the windows of the hospital, they glowed in farewell against the background of pillows on which they would die and after that the faces glowed only in the photographs of family albums." (Sokolov 1977: 45)

In this context, the fact that in front of the façade of the school for fools stand "two small old chalk men, one wearing a plain cap, the other a military forage cap" (ibid., 110) acquires particular significance, as does the presence of the chalk girl with a small deer (or with an "ordinary dog"?) and the chalk bugle boy, from whose lips protrudes a piece of rusty wire instead of a bugle. And if the "two old chalk men"—and these, of course, are Lenin and Stalin—extend the motif of the chaos of power and violence, and if the "chalk girl" is transformed into the heroine of the fairy tale about *Skeerly,* then the chalk boy corresponds directly to the central narrator, insofar as the piece of wire protruding from his lips is associated with the very same needle with which "student so-and-so" threatens to sew his mouth shut, "so as not to eat his mother's sandwiches wrapped in his father's newspapers" (ibid., 111). The notion that "[t]he station itself was called *Chalk,* and the river—the misty white river with chalky banks—could have no other name than the *Chalk*" (ibid., 44) completes the picture of death and the total simulation of life.

Thus the image of the chaos of social simulacra, already familiar to us from Bitov's *Pushkin House,* is translated into a language of constantly flowing, suggestive metaphors, but the meaning of the simulation of normal existence is invariant, and what is more, it sounds like a final verdict: "The scientist writes: if you want to know the truth, then here it is: you have nothing *here*—no family, no work, no time, no space, nor you yourself, you have made this all up" (ibid., 201; emphasis in the original).

This world is foreign and hostile to the hero-narrator. The world created by the hero's imagination opposes it—quite a modernist contrast. However, insofar as the consciousness of the narrator is affected by insanity, it turns out that internal chaos is opposed by external chaos—and this is already the mark of postmodernism. Distinctive verbal avalanches play an extremely important role in sketching the contours of this interior world; virtually devoid of punctuation, they represent streams of metaphors, idioms, quotations. These verbal outpourings, on the one hand, create an image of anomaly, of chaotic consciousness, since the laws of logic and sense connections do not hold; on the other hand, rhythmic and phonetic relationships come to the fore. The resulting metaphoric combinations now begin to exist absolutely independently: The woman Veta Acatova arises from a branch of acacia (*vetka akatsii*) and a railroad branch (*zheleznodorozhnaia vetka*); the river Lethe ("*Leta*") emerges from the word "*bi-lety*" (tickets). The Land of the Lonely Nightjar, "the solicitous bird by the name of Nachtigall" (ibid., 17), the winter butterflies and the dragonflies simpetrum, the Sender of Wind, and many others similarly take shape through an associative "chain reaction," giving the impression of the total absence of control over the self-contained energy of words and sounds.

Is such a stream of consciousness chaotic? Formally, yes. But the difference between the creative chaos of "student so-and-so's" sick consciousness and the chaos produced by the school for fools as a metaphor for a sick social order can be explained in terms of chaos theory. " 'Chaos,' as used in the term 'chaos theory,' refers to *deterministic* chaos, which is a form of chaos within which patterns periodically appear and disappear. Most of us are familiar with *entropic* chaos, which never resolves into patterns. It simply deteriorates into total disorder, never to return" (Van Eenwyk 1997: 45). But what kinds of patterns "periodically appear and disappear" within the consciousness of the narrator? Perhaps mythological ones?

Thus lexical items that appeared earlier come together in a single, frankly mythological picture by the end of the first chapter:

> When our dachas are veiled in dusk and *the heavenly dipper*, tipped over the earth, spills out its dew on *enchanting Lethe*'s banks, I emerge from my father's house and walk quietly through the garden—quietly so as not to awake you, *the strange person who lives beside me*. . . . I smear the oarlocks *with thick dark water* dipped from the river—and my path is quieter than the flash of stars vanishing into the past, my path lies around the second bend, to the *Land of the Lonely Nightjar*, bird of the good summer. My path is neither too short nor too long, I will compare it to the path of a *tarnished sewing needle* stitching a wind-severed cloud." (Sokolov 1977: 72–73; emphasis added)

About the specific nature of the images in *A School for Fools*, John Freedman notes that

> each one is "not real" in the traditional sense, yet neither is it a merely fantastic image. If it is a metaphor, the reference remains obscure. But the beauty it evokes is immediate, and the image it provides is concrete. It acquires the lilting simplicity of a folkloric description which the reader accepts unquestioningly, without pretense or prejudice. . . . But such suppositions trivialize the image contained in the phrase itself, which demands to be accepted as self-contained and non-referential. Sokolov's choice of a schizophrenic as narrator fundamentally alters our reception of the images he supplies." (1987: 271)

Freedman's assessment of the imagery of *A School for Fools* is very close to Olga Freidenberg's conception of primordial metaphorical archetypes, which are the basis of mythological consciousness. According to her theory, these archetypes do not refer to any objects; the table does not symbolize the sky but rather *is* the sky—and this paradox is the basis of mythological consciousness (see Freidenberg 1936). In this context, the boy's stream of consciousness takes on the significance of ritual incantations, bringing mythological archetypes into the humdrum existence of the suburban zone.

The narrator's defining feature is that he is an *eternal adolescent*: His desire for love, his conflicts with his parents, his search for a wise teacher, his dreams of acceptance by society—none of them will ever be fulfilled. And this is that surplus of knowledge available to the author and reader but not to the schizophrenic narrator. But this strange situation connects the entire plot of *A School for Fools* to the ancient ritual of initiation, the rite of passage, which the narrator is undergoing and which he will never complete.

According to Mircea Eliade, every rite of passage refers to the beginning of time and constitutes a ritual death:

> Every repetition of the cosmogony is preceded by a symbolic retrogression to Chaos. In order to be created anew, the old world must first be annihilated. . . . In the scenario of initiation rites, "death" corresponds to the temporary return to the Chaos; hence it is the paradigmatic expression of the *end of a mode of being*—the mode of ignorance and of the child's irresponsibility. Initiatory death provides the clean state on which will be written the successive revelation whose end is the formation of a new man. (1975: xiii)

"In other words," as John R. Van Eenwyk writes, commenting on Eliade, "entropic chaos becomes deterministic" (1997:161). He emphasizes that the concept of death for "entropic" (before initiation) and "deterministic" (during and after the rite of passage) kinds of chaos has a very different meaning: "The idea of entropy is often elaborated into a model wherein death becomes the ultimate unraveling. The opposite of this idea is contained in models that refer to rebirth, renewal, and rejuvenation. In these models, death gives way to a new state of order, to new configurations and patterns that replace—and sometimes improve upon—the old ones" (ibid., 159).

This explains why the motif of death penetrates both the realm of the school for fools as a metaphor for social life and the realm of the narrator's dreams and fantasies. Death is a sign of chaos; in the context of the school for fools, death signifies ultimate destruction, while in the consciousness of "student so-and-so" the already dead world, which is able only to simulate its life, is given hope for rebirth and rejuvenation.

It is, of course, quite significant that the world created by the irrational perceptions of the narrator, like the universe of mythology, follows a cyclical model.[1] Therefore death in this universe is not final; the River Lethe can flow in both directions, and the dying teacher Norvegov can unceremoniously discuss the details of his own demise with "student so-and-so." Time in *A School for Fools* has a cyclical structure, just as in Eliade's interpretation of mythological time:[2]

> The philosopher wrote that in his opinion time has a reverse side, that is, that it moved not in the direction we suppose it should move, but in reverse, backwards, because everything which was—all this is just going to be, he said, the real future is the past, and that which we call the future has already passed and will never be repeated.... And I also thought: but if time is rushing back, that means everything is normal, therefore Savl [another name for Pavel Norvegov—M.L.] who died precisely at the time when I read the article, therefore Savl still *will be,* that is, will come, will return. (Sokolov 1977: 130)

In both Sokolov's novel and Eliade's concept of myth, the cyclical movement of time turns out to be inseparable from the regeneration of life and the triumph over death. The absence of linear order is turned into endless metamorphoses, which become the fundamental element of the mythology created by the narrator of *A School for Fools.* By incorporating everything that catches his eye (himself included) in the process of continuous metamorphoses, the narrator pursues one principal aim: to regenerate reality, which has been annihilated by the chaos of social simulacra. These metamorphoses happen on various levels of the narrative. First, there is the purely linguistic level, such as the aforementioned reciprocal transformations of words united by a single context or by a rhythmic, phonetic resemblance. A typical example of this type of metamorphosis occurs when "Supervisor so-and-so, a man who hopes to be promoted," "Semyon Nikolaev, a man with an intelligent face," and "Fedor Muromtsev, a man with an ordinary face" (ibid., 52–53) read verses by Japanese poets;[3] in name and language they themselves gradually become Japanese: "Ts. Nakamura: last year at this time the weather was exactly the same, the roof started to leak at my house, it soaked all the *tatami,* and there was no way I could hang them up outside to dry. F. Muromatsu: too bad, Tsuneo-san, this kind of rain is no use to anyone, it's just a bother" (ibid., 55).

Second, metamorphoses occur on the level of objects. The most significant example is the transformation of the freight train covered with writing in chalk into the pure manifestation of language, consisting "of clean words and curse words, fragments of someone's heartaches, memorial inscriptions, business notes, idle graphical exercises, of laughter and curses, howls and tears, blood and chalk, of white on black and brown, of fear of death, of pity for friends and strangers, of whacked nerves, of good impulses and rose-colored glasses, of boorishness, tenderness, dullness and servility" (ibid., 46–47). What is more, this freight train becomes the "passing book . . . of life" (ibid., 47) for all of Russia.

Third, we have the metamorphoses of voices and characters, as discussed above. The most interesting metamorphoses happen to the narrator himself, who is transformed into the white river lily Nymphea Alba, a waltz, an adult, an engineer, Veta Acatova's ecstatic lover, an entomologist, and so on. The most convincing of these metamorphoses (especially for the narrator) are the transformations into Nymphea Alba and into a waltz. These metamorphoses are engendered by an aesthetic shock and accompanied by his *disappearance:*

> And I tried to take the oars, I stretched out my hands toward them, but nothing happened: I saw the grips, but my palms did not feel them, the wood of the oars flowed through my fingers, past the phalanges, like sand, like air. No, on the contrary, I, my former and now no longer existing palms, let the wood flow through like water. . . . After taking several steps along the beach, I looked back: there was nothing resembling my tracks on the sand behind. (Ibid., 38–39)

Of course, the model of the world created by "student so-and-so" cannot be completely reduced to the cyclical structures of myth. First of all, Sokolov's hero's perception of the world, unlike that of the historical bearer of mythological consciousness, excludes faith in any kind of "absolute reality." Sometimes he is aware that "[b]oth the dacha and the city, between which you race all summer, . . . are only fruits of your somewhat disordered imagination" (ibid., 201). Even a complete departure from the ordinary perception of the world, which makes it possible for the narrator to enter the realm of myth, would return neither him nor us to the solid ground of real absolutes. Mythological time is colored in the shades of postmodern simulation. This occurs because a mentally ill boy is presented in the novel as the creator of a new myth of eternal life.

Scholars have long noted the connection between the narrator's insanity, creativity, and surrealistic freedom. Moreover the hero himself recognizes this feature of the chronotope of *A School for Fools* as a form of freedom from the "false" time of "normal" reality: "Dear mama, I don't know if one can be an engineer and a schoolboy together, perhaps some people can't, some are unable, some haven't been given the gift, but I, having chosen freedom, one of its forms, I am free to act as I wish and to be whoever I want either simultaneously or separately, can it be you don't understand this?" (ibid., 107).

Fred Moody holds that the "narrator's fiction is an attempt to create for himself a world in which can be found equivalents to his own schizophrenia. His mental deficiency is a metaphorical representation of the artistic impulse, an indication of the creative basis for the novel, as the rhymes and reflections in the described world are imposed upon it by the consciousness that creates and orders it" (1979: 15).

The emphatic fictionality of "student so-and-so's" mythology brings him closer to the novel's author, who is both a character participating in the narrative (as "we") and the "outside" narrator. Hence the conversations between the "author of the novel" and "student so-and-so," in which the "author" acts as a kind of student of the "student," who tries to follow "student so-and-so's" method as far as possible: "Student so-and-so, allow me, the author, to interrupt you and tell how I imagine to myself the moment when you receive the long-awaited letter from the Academy, like you, I have a pretty good imagination, I think I can. Of course, go ahead, he says" (Sokolov 1977: 212); "Student so-and-so, your high evaluation of my humble work pleases me very much, you know, of late I have been trying hard, I write several hours a day, and the rest of the hours—when I'm not writing, that is—I meditate about how to write better the next day, how to write so that all future readers will like it, and, above all, naturally, you, the heroes of the book . . ." (ibid., 218–19). Certainly, the comparison of creativity to insanity, and insanity to creativity, is nothing new, especially against the backdrop of modernist culture. Still, an artist who resembles a madman while in the ecstasy of creation is one thing, but a snotty youth (" 'The one thing I would advise you as a scientist is to use your handkerchief more often,' Acatov says to him" [ibid., 132]), a "backward dolt of the special school" suffering from schizophrenia and sexual complexes, is another matter entirely.

The fourth chapter, "Savl," is crucial to understanding the relationships between the narrator's insanity and creativity. This chapter consists entirely of essays written by "student so-and-so" in various genres: fairy tales ("Skeerly"), oaths, utopias, pastorals, and, finally, the essay "My Morning." But the greatest expression of his creative impulse in this chapter and in the entire book remains his *shout*. The teacher Norvegov calls this shout the highest spiritual accomplishment:

O, with what rapturous effort and pain I would shout, if it were my lot to shout even half of your shout! But it isn't my lot, how weak I am, your mentor, before your talent, given from on high. So shout then—most capable of the capable, shout for yourself and for me, and for all of us, deceived, defamed, dishonored and stupefied, for us, the idiots and holy fools, the defectives and schizoids, for the educators and the educatees, for all those to whom it has not been given and whose salivating mouths have already been shut, or will soon be shut, for all those who have been innocently muted, or are being muted, tongues torn out—shout, intoxicated and intoxicating: bacilli, bacilli, bacilli! (Ibid., 136–37)

The primary purpose of this shout is to fill "the emptiness of empty chambers" (ibid., 137) and spaces. In any case, in the boy's meditations on the cyclical nature of time, it is this emptiness that corresponds to the moment of nonexistence that must be present in what others call time: "Sometimes a day doesn't come for a long time. Then you live in emptiness, not understanding anything, quite sick. And other people are sick too, but they keep quiet" (ibid., 33–34). Thus the shout in the emptiness of empty chambers, like the construction of a personal mythology, is meant to overcome death, to fill in nonexistence, and to regenerate life ("What's it called? It's called *life*" [ibid., 188; emphasis in the original]). This association is further underscored when the student, while thinking up a "cry of a new type" (ibid., 163), exclaims, "I am Nymphea!" (ibid., 164). Yet the cry itself is monstrous; it is inseparable from the "entropic chaos" of the school for fools:

> to the kind of ultramundane terror which your mad cry caused the pedagogues and the students, and even the deaf-mute stoker. . . . And did I not see the faces of your fellow pupils, which are infinitely obtuse anyway, become even more obtuse from your shout . . . in an answering, albeit mute, cry, and all the dolts of the specschool howled in a monstrous, deafening chorus and sick yellow saliva flowed from all these frightened psychopathic mouths. (Ibid., 135–36)

As this passage vividly demonstrates, despite the poetry of the metamorphoses that replace the linear movement of time with cyclical infinity, the world created by the feelings and fantasies of "student so-and-so" nevertheless remains a part of chaos. It is also significant that, in spite of his obvious opposition to death, the narrator himself, like his favorite characters in the myth he has created, also bears the mark of death. "Student so-and-so," who has vanished like a ghost as a result of metamorphoses, leaves no traces in the sand; elsewhere, he says of himself that "I was quite certain (am certain, will be certain) that I will soon die, if I have not died already" (ibid., 35). The teacher Norvegov has already died, and now he converses with the narrator on the shores of the "enchanting Lethe" (ibid., 73) (the river's actual name is "Chalk," which is equated with death in the novel). Every mention of Pavel/Savl's beloved girlfriend Rosa Windova is accompanied by the morbid paraphrase of the *Song of Songs:* "O Rosa Windova . . . dear girl, sepulchral flower, how I want your untouched body!" (ibid., 30, 153–54).

This is why one can compare the narrator's strategy of mythologism with the scientific theory of "strange attractors," which examines the deep and unstable structures of order that spring up *within* chaotic systems (we refer to them in Chapter 1). This is why we must once again raise the question of the interplay between the chaotic world of simulacra and the chaotic imagination of the narrator, who creates his mythology of metamorphosis before our very eyes. It is clear that this is more than a simple and categorical contrast.

It is this very correlation that becomes the focus of the fifth and final chapter of *A School for Fools,* "Testament." All of the most important themes and motifs from the preceding chapters are repeated here. The motifs linked with the school for fools ("we, the prisoners of the special school, slaves of the Perillo slipper system" [ibid., 178]) are repeated, but here the motifs of the mythology of metamorphosis attain a lofty significance. Thus, the motif of adolescent love for Veta Acatov is united with the motifs of resurrection and cyclical time:

> Most of all I would like to say—and to say it before a very long separation—to say what you have long known yourself, of course, or what you are just surmising. We all make surmises about it. I want to say that there was already a time when we were acquainted on this earth, you no doubt remember. The river is called. And now we've come again, we've returned in order to meet again. We are Those Who Came. Now you know. Her name is Veta. Veta. (Ibid., 189)

The trip along the River Lethe and the student's transformation into Nymphea are repeated, but now this episode is directly linked to the motif of surrealistic freedom:

> I walked a certain number of steps along the beach and looked back: there was nothing resembling my tracks left in the sand, and in the boat lay a white water lily, called by the Romans Nymphea Alba, that is, white lily. And then I realized that I had turned into it and no longer belonged to myself, or the school, or you personally, Nikolai Gorimirovich,—to no one on earth. From this time forth I belong to the dacha river Lethe, which streams against its own current at its own desire. And long live The Sender of Wind! (Ibid., 192)

However, this monologue immediately changes: "Mama, mama, help me, I'm sitting here in Perillo's office, and he's calling *there,* for Doctor Zauze. I don't want to, believe me" (ibid., 193; emphasis in the original). Here we have evidence of the hero/narrator's simultaneous existence in his own mythical world and in the terrifying phantasmagoria of the school for fools.

Of particular importance in this regard is the episode when Savl/Pavel Norvegov and the narrator(s) discuss the idea that "you have *nothing* here—

no family, no work, no time, no space, nor you yourself" (ibid., 201; emphasis in the original). The first attempt at clarification is made by the student(s): "And here we said: Savl Petrovich, but nevertheless something *is,* this is just as obvious as the fact that the river has a name" (ibid., 201–2; emphasis in the original). At first glance the argument of the student(s) seems strange. Indeed, this is a direct reference to the first chapter ("The river was called" [ibid., 12]) and its construction of an eternal myth from the petty and insignificant details of "suburban zone five." In other words, the creative—or schizoid—imagination of the narrator itself is a product and producer of simulacra. Next comes Savl/Pavel Petrovich Norvegov's explanation: "Now I shout with all my blood, the way one shouts of vengeance to come: there is nothing in the world—except The Wind! And The Sender?—we asked. And The Sender too—replied the teacher" (ibid., 202). The Wind and The Sender of Wind are component parts of the hero/narrator's myth, that is, this point in no way contradicts the first objection. But the meaning of these images is much wider in this particular context.

Savl's spiritual freedom is association with The Wind—hence his nickname, *vetrogon* (which literally means "chaser of wind" and is roughly equivalent to "airhead").[4] The Wind is also associated with revenge on the world of simulacra; this is the idea behind Savl's prophesies in the first chapter, while Savl's connection with The Wind is transformed into a symbol of his mythical power:

> Give me time—I'll show you which of us is right, some day I'll give your lazy, squeaky ellipsoid such a whirl that your river will back up, you'll forget your false books and newspapers, your own voices, names, and ranks will make you vomit, you will forget how to read and write, you will want to babble and whisper like aspen leaves in August. An angry crosswind will blast away the names of your streets and back alleys and the asinine signs, and you will want the truth. . . . And then I will come. I will come and bring with me the ones you have murdered and humiliated and I will say: there is your truth for you, and retribution against you. From horror and sorrow the obsequious pus which pollutes the blood in your veins will turn into ice. Fear The Sender of Wind, you sovereigns of cities and dachas, cower before the breezes and crosswinds, they engender hurricanes and tornadoes. (Ibid., 28)

In this context, D. Barton Johnson's theory about the role of wind in Sokolov's *A School for Fools* makes sense: This is a metaphor for the Holy Spirit (1980: 226–27).[5] But The Wind is inextricably linked to the motif of emptiness, that is, of death; The Wind in *A School for Fools* is a moving void. In the very first chapter, Leonardo da Vinci/Professor Acatov declares that nothing is opposed to the present and then adds: "*[I]inasmuch as there would have to be emptiness present where nothing is supposed to be,* but nevertheless—continues the artist,—with the help of windmills I can produce wind at any time" (Sokolov 1977: 31; emphasis in the original) (as always in Sokolov, the logic here is purely associative). Returning to the episode at hand, we observe that it is the *ambivalence* of the motif of the wind that brings this fragment to a logical end, uniting the poetry of the myth of free creative metamorphoses with the ugliness of the world of idiots: "Water rumbled in the bowels of the unpainted radiators, outside strode the inexorable, indestructible polyped street, our stoker and guard rushed from one open boiler to another in the basement, with a shovel in his hand, muttering, and on the fourth floor the quadrille of fools boomed like cannon, shaking the foundations of the entire establishment" (ibid., 202).

The clash of world models in the last chapter proves not only that neither one is capable of overpowering the other but also that the mythical world of the hero and the absurd world of the school for fools *cannot help but interact* with each other—they have a common denominator: their chaotic nature, expressed in their common attraction to death ("chaotic attractor" of a kind). But for this very reason, the virtual immortality of the dead Pavel Norvegov in the chapter's finale is followed by bitter words that refute the myth of resurrection, renewal, and rejuvenation; the narrator tells us that even the

> rhododendrons growing every minute somewhere in Alpine meadows are far happier than we, for they know neither love, nor hate, nor the Perillo slipper system, and they don't even die, since all nature, excepting man, is one undying, indestructible whole. . . . Only man minds and feels bitter, burdened as he is with egotistical pity for himself. Remember, even Savl, who devoted himself entirely to science and its students, said, after dying, it's dammed maddening. (Ibid., 227–28)

And at the same time, the central episode of this chapter—the parable Savl tells about the carpenter—is important, first of all, in that its metamorphoses connect the formerly diametrically opposed poles of *A School for Fools*: creator and executioner, free bird and enslaved victim, executioner and victim. Together they form an ever-changing whole. In addition, death here means overcoming schizophrenic dissociation, reducing all variants of existence to one single point, thereby putting an end to all metamorphoses:

> Oh foolish man, do you really not yet realize that there is no difference between you and me, that you and I—are one and the same carpenter, don't you realize that on the cross which you have created in the name of your sublime carpenter's craft, you have crucified yourself, and when they were pinning you down, you pounded in the nails yourself. Having said this to himself, the carpenter died. (Ibid., 185)

In *A School for Fools,* the strategies of dialogue with chaos are more complex than in the works of Bitov and Venedikt Erofeev. Strictly speaking, all the
internal dynamics in Sokolov's work are determined as much by dialogue with
chaos as by a *dialogue of chaoses*—the dialogic interaction of the chaos of
freedom (deterministic) and the chaos of violence (entropic). And here the
metamorphoses take on a meaning that exceeds the mythical world created by
the narrator: *The metamorphoses themselves become the language of dialogue
between opposing destructive and creative models of chaos.*

But this is also the reason that the unavoidable coexistence and ambivalent interpenetration of these world models does not lead the author to
despair. The conclusion of *A School for Fools* is astonishingly joyous:
"Merrily gabbing and recounting pocket change, slapping each other on the
shoulders and whistling foolish songs, we walk out into the polyped street
and in some miraculous manner are transformed into passersby" (ibid.,
228). The image of the "polyped street," which Sokolov usually described
as part of the terrible chronotope of the school for fools,[6] and the miraculous transformation of "student so-and-so" and the "author of the novel"
into a small part of the "polyped street," cannot help but be interpreted as a
symbol of the endlessness of metamorphoses and, consequently, of life;
moreover, one of the principal preconditions of this endlessness is the in-
separability of the chaos of freedom and the chaos of violence (as is also the
case with Venichka). It is worth noting that this very conflict between the
ambivalent transformation of values and their opposites in Erofeev's *Moscow to the End of the Line* was a source of sublime tragic tension. The
transformation of the dialogue with chaos into a dialogue of chaoses *cancels out tragedy* in *A School for Fools.* This novel may well mark the first
time that chaos is accepted as the norm rather than a frightening abyss, as a
source both of creativity and of torment and suffering. It is also very important that Sokolov and his narrator are creating a new mythological
world, rewriting the myths of initiation, transforming the rite of passage
into endless stasis. While Bitov was dismantling the contemporary cultural
consciousness, Erofeev tried to combine the "noise" of multiple cultural
voices with a new reading of the Gospels, which are brought into contact
with "inconclusive present-day reality" (Bakhtin 1981: 39). Sokolov goes
even further than Erofeev—to the basic structural and existential model of
any mythology, both Judeo-Christian and pagan, "primitive," prehistoric.
These universal patterns of myth are presented as newly born in the consciousness of "student so-and-so"—that is, they are newly born for and
within the realm of chaos. Eliade asserts that fundamental change can occur
in the mythological consciousness only by reentering the beginning of time
(*illo temporo*) (see Eliade 1975: x–xiii). *A School for Fools* in a sense is

establishing the *illo temporo* for the fundamental cultural shift: It is now chaos, rather than order, that is considered the existential norm. Of course, the postmodernist "remodeling" of the cultural experience is not complete, but its prospects are outlined in the novels of Bitov, Venedikt Erofeev, and Sokolov. The lack of a sense of tragedy in *A School for Fools* can also be explained by the fact that chaos is now seen as a source of opportunity rather than of danger. This vision can be compared to the opinion of those "connoisseurs of chaos" who find that chaos has advantages over order: "First, flexibility depends on chaos. Second, chaos offers more choices than order. Finally, to the degree that adaptation requires flexibility chaos is essential for growth" (Van Eenwyk 1997: 168).

The consequences of these transformations can be found in the entire subsequent history of Russian postmodernism from the end of the seventies through the beginning of the nineties, when the Soviet "order" finally collapsed.

# 5

# Active Nonbeing

The artistic discoveries of Bitov, Venedikt Erofeev, and Sokolov compel a return to the most hotly debated theoretical questions of postmodernism, particularly the problem of artistic unity. The entire aesthetic of postmodernism espouses a movement "from the work to the text" (to use the title of Roland Barthes's famous essay [see 1989: 56–64]), from the illusion of a unified image (totalitarian in its nature, as the most radical postmodernist theoreticians allege), to a fragmented, self-sufficient and self-referential text. Postmodernism's theoretical and practical revolt against any ideologies founded on the ideals of Unity and Hierarchy cannot help but impinge upon the category of artistic unity. Even the most cursory glance at *Pushkin House, Moscow to the End of the Line,* and *A School for Fools* leads to profound doubts as to the efficacy of such traditional bearers of artistic unity as thematic unity, the distant, God-like author, and, most important, the author's model of the *harmony* of the world and humankind. It would be tempting to argue that the theoretical underpinnings of postmodernism are incompatible with the generic qualities of literature: Where the doctrine of postmodernism triumphs, literature as art is dying, and vice versa; where artistic laws triumph, there is no room for the speculative aesthetic of postmodernism. In that case, however, one first would have to come to agree upon the absolute and fixed criteria of artistic value, and second . . . Second, in the case of Russian postmodernism, to say that writers illustrate any sort of aesthetic doctrine is highly problematic. We have already mentioned that, when they were writing their texts, Bitov, Venedikt Erofeev, and Sokolov were completely isolated from postmodernist theory, which in any case was only just taking shape in the West.

At the same time, when we analyze texts by Bitov, Erofeev, and Sokolov, we are repeatedly convinced that we are dealing with not only a linguistic object but also a *work,* that is, semantic worlds that do not hide their pretension to universality: Venedikt Erofeev's and Sokolov's use of mythological themes and structures makes this pretension perfectly clear.

But what is mythologized by the authors of *Pushkin House, Moscow to the End of the Line,* and *A School for Fools?*

In *Pushkin House,* it is the simulacrum, fictitious existence ("The Myth of Mitishatyev"), ruptures, incoherence, and incomprehension as the only form of cultural and historical succession.

In *Moscow to the End of the Line,* it is a tragic inability to distinguish between the sacred and the profane, heaven and hell, sin and heroism, and death and resurrection.

In *A School for Fools,* it is the abolition of time, the disappearance of the self, emptiness as the equivalent of the Holy Spirit, and death as the space in which all the sense and nonsense of existence come together.

In essence, all three examples mythologize various aspects of *chaos*—whether chaos be existential (Bitov), ontological (Erofeev), or phenomenological (Sokolov). The authors of these texts come to know the *impossibility* of building a harmonious world and experiencing self-actualization in relationship to chaos; that is, in the fragmented picture of the world they recognize their "fragmentariness," a simulated spirituality that engenders catharsis, albeit one that is altogether different from that of traditional culture.

But when analyzing *Pushkin House, Moscow to the End of the Line,* and *A School for Fools,* we have noticed that in all these works the concept of *death* plays a very significant role in the process of reuniting different fragments and fractures of the former cultural orders into a new unity based on "deterministic chaos." Generally, the concept of death forms a special relationship between *continuity and discreteness, fragmentation and wholeness* characteristic of a work of literature. Iurii Lotman notes the motif of death as completion, which is inextricably linked "with the possibility of understanding reality as something comprehensible"; at the same time, he emphasizes that the "literary work, by introducing the theme of death into the plot, in so doing must expose it to negatio" (1994: 418, 422). Yet in the works examined in the previous chapters, death—contrary to expectations—invariably plays a *positive and constructive* role in the structure of the artistic world. Death is a kind of common denominator, revealing the afterlife of culture and "contemporary life" (Bitov), which moves the hero into the author's customary position as outsider (Erofeev) and serves as the basis for the dialogic metamorphoses of the chaos of "student so-and-so's" poetic consciousness and the cruel insanity of the "school for fools." In *Moscow to the End of the Line,* death acts as the "final" and perhaps only stable value in a catastrophically ambivalent world.

Undoubtedly, such a motif of death is analogous to the ritual/mythological conception that considers death part of a regularly repeating cycle and even as the indispensable condition for the cycle's renewal. John R. Van Eewyk argues that this mythological cyclicity is very close to the scientific model of "deterministic chaos" (see Van Eenwyk 1997: 157–71). It is also apparent that the authors of these texts avoid rationalizing the role of death in their work—in a sense, they follow the logic common to both myth and "deterministic chaos": "Myth is an example of what Bateson and Prigogine would regard as a participative universe—a universe which is unified and completed only through observation and representation" (Kuberski 1994: 81).

The narration in all three texts discussed above endlessly circles around the concept of death and its "paradigmatic" synonyms: simulacra, emptiness, darkness, insanity, drunken oblivion, destruction. None of these categories can be described in positive terms but only negatively, "apophatically," as Mikhail Epstein would say.

This philosophical strategy was articulated most explicitly by the artist Ilya Kabakov—another acknowledged classic of Russian postmodernism—in his essay "On Emptiness" (included in his installation "Fly with Wings"). Kabakov describes the feeling of aggressive emptiness (quasi existence, permanent destruction) as a major ontological problem for contemporary Russian culture:

> A gigantic reservoir, the volume of emptiness in question that represents "our place" is not emptiness per se—a "vacant place" in the European meaning of the word. This approach will characterize emptiness as a space not yet filled, not yet mastered, undeveloped or developed poorly, a little, and so on. . . . This European, rationalist notion of emptiness as a field where it is potentially necessary to apply human forces, so that the place "awaiting human labor" can be mattered, is entirely unsuitable for our phenomenon of emptiness. . . . [T]his emptiness presents itself as an extraordinary active volume . . . transforming being into its antithesis, destroying construction, mystifying reality, turning all into dust and emptiness. This emptiness, I repeat, is the transferring of active being into active nonbeing, and most importantly, this emptiness lives and exists not by its own power, but by that life which surrounds it . . . this very emptiness inhabits the place in which we live from "sea to shining sea." (Berry and Miller-Pogacar 1995: 91, 92, 93)

This may well be a definition of the subject of Russian postmodernism. If so, how can one represent the absence of all imaginable qualities, emptiness, death, "active nonbeing"? Tracing this "hole in the fabric of being" (ibid., 93) in terms of its outlines would seem to be a perfectly natural approach. This explains the frequency of repeated motifs, themes, and circular structures in the works of Bitov, Sokolov, and Erofeev. Of course, these repetitions are not literal—the same motifs and themes are always reiterated with some variation. The ability of the author to improvise on a recurring theme becomes proof of creativity and stylistic virtuosity (one need only recall Erofeev's repeated depictions of the ritual of drinking or Sokolov's constant references to chalk, the wind, and the river). The narrative's circular trajectories inevitably make the area of death visible, but they are never the same: The play of repetitions and differences serves as a source of nonlinear, self-reflective, dialogically constructed plots. Only the constant presence of absence, emptiness, death, and destruction provides "axiological center(s)" for the texts; they may be negative, apophatic, and more repulsive than attractive, but they are still powerful and intriguing.

Such a structure is actually quite similar to "chaotic attractors" or, more specifically, to fractals (the most graphic models of self-organized chaotic dynamics). Based on the principle of self-similarity on all possible scales, they always reflect but never duplicate themselves: "Never repeating—yet always resembling—themselves, they are the epitome of contradiction: infinitely recognizable, ultimately unpredictable" (Van Eenwyk 1987: 54). "Chaotic attractors" and fractals look like capricious loops and curves, "infinitely deep, never quite joining, never intersecting" (Gleick 1987: 140); this geometry is explained by the obligatory presence of the "empty void" that "corresponds to the physical impossibility" (ibid., 135). In other words, the empty void is outlined by the infinitive fractal curves and loops circling around it, and their very circulation is explained by the gravitation of this "zone of impossibility." The rhizome as described by Deleuze is another variation on the same type of structure—"chaosmos, rather than root-chaos" (1992: 29).

The rhizomatic or fractal model of artistic unity, as it is presented by Bitov, Erofeev, or Sokolov, is fundamentally different from models rooted in classical culture. It embodies the artistic and philosophical idea of *self-organizing chaos*. Such artistic unity gives the impression of total independence from the author's effort to organize the artistic world. It goes without saying that this is a carefully constructed illusion of spontaneity rather than the "real thing." But if this illusion is actually achieved, then the results could exceed the limits of a rational and determinist view of the world. In this sense, Venichka's mystical epiphany and the surreal freedom of the narrator of *A School for Fools* are far from accidental.

At the same time, we cannot help but recognize that the rhizomatic model of artistic unity cannot possibly be stable; by its very nature, it verges on entropy and is drawn to self-destruction. It is a clear example of *paralogic compromise*—here, between unity and fragmentation, between authorial control and spontaneity. As we have seen, such a compromise cannot help but be explosive and unstable.

The conflict between the author (who abdicates his prerogatives in favor of the narrator and hero) and the world of simulacra (which are equated with chaos and death) is at the heart of all three works. This conflict is intensified when the author/hero discovers the power of simulacra and total simulation within both himself and the models inherited from cultural history, including the most authoritative and sacred ones. This conflict unfolds against the backdrop of the very process of this open-ended text's creation, in the playful deconstruction of the simulacra of life and culture. Bitov, Erofeev, and Sokolov represent, respectively, the epic, dramatic, and lyrical paths for the development—but not the resolution!—of this conflict.

The epic path of Bitov is the attempt to find a way in which the author and hero, literature and life, the contemporary world and cultural tradition can all coexist on the shaky ground of total simulation.

The dramatic path (which in Erofeev's case is primarily tragic) is expressed in the author/hero's attempts to "cast a spell" on chaos, to organize it creatively from within, at the price of sacrificial self-destruction. Such are the conditions of dialogic *inter*-action.

The lyrical path of Sokolov requires the acceptance of the chaos of simulacra/death, which is *experienced* by the narrator-hero as both a source of ontological horror and the necessary precondition for freedom and creativity; moreover, the lyrical discourse itself, with its arbitrary associations and impulsive metamorphoses, suits the incomprehensible logic of chaos perfectly.

All three paths inevitably lead to questions. How does the postmodernist mythology of chaosmos, which is the basis of the rhizomatic model of unity, interact with other, preexisting cultural mythologies and corresponding models of unity? How does this interaction affect relatively traditional generic and stylistic forms? These questions will be addressed in Part III.

# III.
## The Poetics of Chaosmos

# 6

# Context: Soviet Utopia

The works discussed in Part II rise far above the "current" literary process. Clearly, they hark back to "far-off" historical and literary contexts. As often happens, contexts much closer at hand served as springboards for the emergence of the works of Andrei Bitov, Venedikt Erofeev, or Sasha Sokolov, in which postmodernism reached its maturity. In turn, these works were a powerful catalyst for postmodernism's development as an artistic system.

Postmodernism is characterized by its relativizing, antihierarchical, and playful approach to any and all authoritative discourses. By transforming itself into a pseudoclassical myth, Socialist Realism aesthetically formed the particular metadiscourse that, in turn, served as the ideological foundation of Soviet civilization. In the works of Bitov, Erofeev, and Sokolov, the existential aspect of this discourse was recognized as one of the forms of ontological chaos. But on the level of style, ironic games with this metadiscourse had already begun in the sixties, in a literary movement that would come to be called "Youth Prose." "Youth Prose" undermined authoritative style through the use of unofficial language, slang, confessional narratives, and a tone that, although still relatively cautious, was increasingly skeptical of the highest authorities.[1] Demythologizing irony was even more radical in fiction that was not initially intended for publication; the *samizdat* and *tamizdat*[2] texts of Abram Tertz, Yuz Aleshkovsky, Vladimir Maramzin, and Alexander Zinoviev were unacceptable to the Soviet regime not only ideologically (like the works of Alexander Solzhenitsyn, Vasily Grossman, or Lidia Chukovskaya), but *stylistically.* These works attempted to undermine authority through irony, rather than simply shifting the ideological polarities within the framework of an inflexible discourse. Such authors as Vasily Aksyonov, Vladimir Voinovich, Fazil Iskander, Vladimir Vysotsky, and Mikhail Zhvanetsky, who were close to "Youth Prose" but whose inclination toward irony and lack of stylistic inhibitions set them apart, invariably overstepped the bounds of ideological loyalty, and in the seventies and eighties, the best of their works could only be published either abroad or in *samizdat.*

In her study *Russian Experimental Fiction: Resisting Ideology After Utopia* (1993), Edith Clowes identifies a single meta-utopian tendency that ironically deconstructs utopian discourse. This tendency encompasses such works as Abram Tertz's *The Makepeace Experiment,* Vasily Aksyonov's *The Burn* and *The Island of Crimea,* Vladimir Voinovich's *Moscow 2042,* Alexander Zinoviev's *Yawning Heights,* Yuz Aleshkovsky's *The Plain Little Blue Scarf,* and Fazil Iskander's *Rabbits and Boa Constrictors.* As Clowes demonstrates, these works are marked by a whole complex of such postmodern qualities as the fictionalization of history, the blurring of boundaries between elite and mass art, the use of parody to subvert the Russian author's traditional authority over the reader, and the creation of narrative structures founded on semiotic play and directed not only against utopian consciousness but also against any kind of monologism. These structures are skeptical of any given ideological totalities:

> Russian meta-utopian writing and discrete trends in recent Western fiction and social thought share a number of features. All play with realized utopian orthodoxies fixed in conventional, popular literary forms. They call for a consideration of the ways in which we limit our collective memory and imagination. And, finally, there is a strong suspicion of binary models of thinking that deny an imaginative middle ground. Taken together, these shared concerns are the hallmark of the "meta-utopian" mentality. (Clowes 1993: 219)

This chapter will examine several strategies within meta-utopian literature, paying special attention to the correlation between its poetics and the postmodern artistic paradigm.

## Vasily Aksyonov: Utopia as a Fantasy

> *One of the properties of the wondertale is that it is based on poetic fiction and is a distortion of reality. In most languages the word tale is a synonym for lie or falsehood. "The tale is over; I can't lie any more"—thus do Russian narrators conclude their stories.*

> —Vladimir Propp (1984: 79)

Initially, Russian postmodernism was a phenomenon largely of *samizdat* and *tamizdat;* we recall that the works of Erofeev, Sokolov, and Bitov discussed in the previous section would not be printed in the Soviet Union until the end of the eighties. It would fall on Vasily Aksyonov, the writer whose sardonic literary portraits of the life of Soviet youth in the early sixties firmly identified him with "Youth Prose," to be the first to publish a stylistically postmodern work in a Soviet journal: *Surplussed Barrelware* (Zatovarennaia bochkatara). It was printed in 1968, almost simultaneously with the aforementioned classics of Russian postmodernism. What makes this particular tale remarkable is not only the lack of stylistic inhibition, so unusual for the time, although that was certainly a part of it. Far more important, however, is the tale's new interpretation of Soviet utopian discourse.

The plot of this story is extremely simple. The driver Volodya Teleskopov is bringing empty barrels (the "surplussed barrelware" of the story's title) to Koryazhsk, the regional center. Along the way he is joined by Gleb Shustikov, a marine; Irina Valentinova, a schoolteacher; Vadim Afanasievich Drozhinin, a scholar; the retired activist Mochenkin; and others. During their travels, strange things happen to them: All of them have lyrical dreams about a "Good Person," and all of them grow strangely attached to one another and to the barrelware, without which they cannot even imagine their lives. So when the bureaucrats in Koryazhsk refuse to accept the empty barrels, the group decides to continue their journey with their beloved barrelware, only now they have no apparent destination whatsoever.[3] The tale's style may appear parodic, and, indeed, each of the heroes hyperbolically reproduces a certain typological model of Socialist Realism: the village schoolteacher, the gallant sailor, the old Stalinist who writes denunciations of everyone out of sheer force of habit, the Soviet "refined intellectual" (Aksyonov 1985: 27) who is the best friend of the people of the nonexistent country Khali-Galia, the reckless young man who models himself after the dead poet Sergei Esenin, the old woman who zealously advocates scientific research —each is rendered in an appropriate style. Moreover, their dreams exploit these models in order to distill entire branches of Socialist Realism parodically. "The author of 'Barrelware' is a parodist of plenitude, of multiple texts, including his own," Laura Beraha (1997: 218–19) quite convincingly argues. Thus the dreams of Vadim Afanasievich are rendered in the style of the Soviet political potboiler, whose goal was always to reveal the "ulcerating sores of capitalism": "Junta appeared, twisting her pale lips in a diplomatic smile. She wore stiletto high heels and a threadbare fox-fur stole around her neck. Everything else on her dripped and oozed dark-blue. Her little clay feet trembled under the weight of her huge body" (Aksyonov 1985: 37). Heroic production novels about the "wind of distant wanderings" find themselves parodied by the dreams of the driver Gleb Shustikov: "Our favorite midshipman Reinvolf—Kozma Yelistratovich, comes in: 'At ease! At ease! Today, you cream of wheat, is the final tug-of-war competition with submariners. Everybody gets a double portion of butter and meat, a triple of compote.' 'Will we get some doughnuts, comrade shipman?' 'Atten-tion!' " (ibid., 69). The distinct tones of

"Youth Prose" resonate in the speech patterns of the teacher Irina Valentinovna Selezneva: " 'Do you remember the passage in Hemingway? Don't you recall the place in Druon? As Zhukhovitsky said . . . you remember, don't you?' Goodness me! What impudent rogues—I'm supposed to recall everything just because they bought me a 'Kamikaze–Mind Blower' cocktail. But the Polish magazines from countries all over the world came flying down from up above, from up above" (ibid., 39). Moreover, each character is surrounded with his or her own stylistic aura of quotations, not only in the dreams but in the main narrative itself; in this story there is no discourse but the discourse of others. Even apparently neutral descriptions are still stylistically marked, in one way or another corresponding to the discourse of the characters.

Characteristically, even the loud, garish epithets used to describe the barrelware are apparently lifted from newspapers, as the story's epigraph makes clear: "Having surplussed and surfaced herself in yellow-flower bloom, the barrelware surged and surgeoned at her hoopseams and went sauntering off" (ibid., 26). By contrast, the Good Person who walks through the dew (the image uniting the dreams of all the characters) is the specific, although probably unrecognized, dream of utopian discourse, a dream that acquires the characteristics of each of the protagonists as each one dreams of the Good Person in turn: from the Errant "Knight" in the dream of lab assistant Stepanida Efimovna to the "tasty young and juicy Resume" (ibid., 75) from old Mochenkin's dream. By the end of the story, even the impersonal narrator blends with the other characters into a single "we":

> Volodya Teleskopov was sitting on the embankment, with his head hung between his knees, and we were looking at him. . . . "Let's go," we said, and jumped down one by one from the platform. . . . We followed Volodya along a narrow path on the bottom of a ravine, through a carpet of buttercups, ferns, and burdock; at eye-level, tall lilac candles of willow herb were swaying in the glass twilight. Then we caught sight of our truck, which had found shelter under a sandy precipice, and in it was our misfortunate, desecrated, surplussed barrelware. Our hearts sank on account of her alluring tenderness which was dissipating itself with the sunset, at dusk. (Ibid., 89–90)

This transformation can be interpreted within the context of the Socialist Realist utopia, for which the formation of the collective "WE" was always a crucial accomplishment. Similarly significant are the final "rehabilitation" of the good-for-nothing Volodya Teleskopov ("we didn't recognize the former rowdy in him" [89]); the rehabilitation of the old man Mochenkin, who sends a letter to all the appropriate authorities ("I ask all my reports and denunciations to return *in back*" [ibid., 89, italics in the original]); and the appearance of the departing Enemy with the cigar and crimson waistcoat, in whom each of the characters once again recognizes his personal enemy, from the Tempter to Señor Siracuzers. And the story's crowning "Last Common Dream" about the Good Person who "always waits" might also be understood as a sign of utopian moral apotheosis. On the other hand, here one can easily find a typical example of postmodern intertextuality, blurring the boundaries between "self" and "other," depriving the author of any advantages over his characters.

For the purposes of the present study, it is the intertextual aspect that proves essential, since it lends new meaning to the story's parodic style. Theoretically, the conflation of the author with his parodic characters emphasizes the characters' literary nature. They do not represent reality; rather, they are purely linguistic models, simulacra created by Socialist Realist discourse. Thus Gleb Shustikov and old Mochenkin are joined by such characters as "Romance" and "False-Science."

The absence of a mimetic dimension completely transforms the utopian discourse itself. Utopia always considers its own possible application to *reality*. In Aksyonov's novel, the presence of "reality" itself seems problematic. In Aksyonov's hands, the Soviet utopia turns into a kind of *children's fairy tale*.[4] The barrelware becomes a magical being, leading the unlikely traveling companions to the magic kingdom;[5] in his letter to his girlfriend, Volodya Teleskopov writes: "Simka, you want the truth? I don't know when we'll see each other again, because we go not where we want to go but where our dear barrelware wants us to go. Understand?" (ibid., 76) The ups and downs of their journey are identical to the fairy-tale motif of "testing," and each ordeal concludes with the former enemies making peace with the wandering heroes on the basis of their common love for the barrelware. As in fairy tales, hostile territories are conquered by using only one kind of weapon: moral qualities. The endpoint of the journey, the city of Koryazhsk, where the bureaucrats damage the precious barrelware, is directly associated with the fairy-tale kingdom of evil; for example, the express train in which the main villain departs is depicted as a dragon with a "yellow head, blue mustache, and huge blinkers" (ibid., 89). The repeated dreams of the characters create a special type of fairy-tale chronotope in which *all is possible,* in which miracles are a matter of course. This, together with the playful style, gives the stories a fairy-tale atmosphere.[6]

Fairy tales originate from the ruins of myth, the reinterpretation of sacred motifs in a purely playful, fantastic manner—like the tall tale (*nebylitsa*), the pure fiction. In essence, this same process takes place in the stories of Aksyonov. He basically *removes the spell* of the Soviet utopian myth by transforming it into *belles lettres* rather than a "reflection of life." In this case, the text obeys only the laws of literary play. The completely unrestrained interactions of the text's simulacra create a playful effect that determines the artistic tonality of the entire tale. This is why *Surplussed Barrelware* firmly resists any allegorical readings—in the foreground of the tale is the poetics of play, the joy of literary self-sufficiency.[7] Aksyonov was one of the first to reveal that Soviet discourse was *unreal* and that, as a consequence, there is no need to polemicize with it, to oppose it with other discourses; far better simply to play with it, as with any literary model.[8]

The true distinction between utopian and fairy-tale traditions lies not in the combination of motifs (utopian motifs also occur in fairy tales) but in the motif's relationship to the proffered model of "reality." Utopia always proposes a program of transformation in order to achieve universal social happiness. A fairy tale's ultimate achievements are the result of miraculous, unbelievable adventures, that is, they stem from a reality that is *fictional* by definition. Vladimir Propp defines the fairy tale as "deliberate and poetic fiction [that] never passes itself off as reality. . . . In the Russian folktale there is *not a single* credible plot. . . . Neither the teller nor the listener treats it as reality. . . . Nothing is quite improbable here" (Propp 1984: 18–19). The fairy-tale miracle does not demand faith; it requires only imagination. Much of the "confessional fiction" of the sixties, in which Aksyonov got his start, was permeated with a faith in the utopian transformation of life. The unabashed deconstruction of utopian discourse into that of the fairy tale was certainly proof of a crisis in this faith, a "delegitimation" of the final versions of Soviet discourse such as "socialism with a human face" or "Leninist socialism" (*Surplussed Barrelware* was published in March 1968, five months before the invasion of Czechoslovakia, which dealt a death blow to the Thaw). As Aksyonov remarked in a later interview, "one can only hope for a miracle; there are no logical bases for hope" (Mozeiko, Briker, and Dalgard 1986: 25).

Aksyonov's *In Search of a Genre* (first published in 1978) can be seen as a kind of sequel to "Barrelware." The comparison is suggested not only by the shared theme of the journey but especially by the profession of the primary hero: Pavel Durov is a magician. Yet if fantasy united the author-storyteller with his characters in 1968, ten years later the key to the plot becomes the magician's public loneliness, the obsolescence of his profession. It is worth noting that *In Search of a Genre* begins and ends with the hero's journey to the underworld: In the beginning, Durov, who has spent the night at the highway patrol station, intrudes upon the quiet discussion of the ghostly victims of car crashes, and in the end, Durov, who has been killed by an avalanche, awakens in the Valley of Miracles. Essentially, the fossilized, fairy-tale motif of the journey to the underworld comes alive.[9] In

*Surplussed Barrelware*, this motif is completely supplanted by the utopian archetype of the search for happiness, the dreams of the Good Person. In *In Search of a Genre*, utopian motifs appear *only and without exception* in relation to death. Thus, after the discussion with the "goners" at the highway patrol station, Durov dreams of a "miraculous time of life, which either was, or is, or will be. . . . All three sorrows, the past, the present, and the future, combined in this miraculous time of life" (Aksenov 1991: 220). By the end of the novel, this literally realized "afterlife" is presented as the incarnation of a dream of happiness: "The air of love now surrounded us, filled our lungs, straightened out our collapsed bronchia, saturated our blood, and gradually became our world. The air of love" (ibid., 324).

The wanderings of Durov, who is seeking his genre, are doubled by inserted episodes, "scenes" featuring someone who is either Durov or his author-double; they present the "genre" from within. In these "scenes," the magic "genre" becomes identical to the technique of literary creation (the rhyme in prose, the meditations of the artist, the work on the novel in Venice, etc.); the discussion of "genre" becomes self-referential. Typically, the author rhymes in the scenes about rhyme, and in Venice, he works on a novel about "how he worked on a novel in Venice" (ibid., 291). As Boris Briker puts it, "*In Search of a Genre* manifestly contains two quests for a genre: the quest, or rather artistic experiment of the author, and Durov's quest for his genre. Hence, the title of the work [*In Search of a Genre*] and its generic subtitle ["in search of a genre"], set in a different sized type, coincide. Durov's 'genre' and that of other artists is a multidimensional phenomenon, and, in one of its dimensions, it also subsumes the genre of Aksyonov the writer" (Briker 1986: 149).

The story's numerous characters are also engaged in the search for a "genre," the search for a miracle. Moreover, these characters do not act as objects of Durov's manipulations but as completely independent creators. All of them are guided in their conduct not by a practical but by a fantastic, at times exclusively artistic, logic. Take, for example, the "gold prospector" Lyosha Kharitonov, who fulfills his dream of a trip from Tyumen to the sea in the "miracle on wheels"—an automobile put together at the junkyard. Or Mamanya, who traverses all of Russia, sometimes hitchhiking, other times on foot, in order to reconcile her daughter and husband. Moreover, Mamanya's literary artistry is emphasized by one of her particular qualities: "So she usually mumbled, and each word in her gibberish danced for her, as if it were made of mother-of-pearl; in each one, repeated a hundred times, she saw a special kind of color. Mamanya loved words. She did not admit this secret even to herself" (Aksyonov 1991: 256). In this context, even the euphemisms of the locksmith Efim Mikhin come across as complex alliterative avant-garde "trans-sense" (*zaum*΄). Inside the shell of official rhetoric, the poetic impulse moves the bartender Alka from the beer bar as she hunts for her good-for-nothing boyfriend, who, though he loves and wants her, irrationally leaves her; as he sails off into the cold sea, his final monologue is rendered in a stylized stream of consciousness. The musician he happens to meet turns out to be from a Thaw-era jazz session (which for Aksyonov is absolutely equivalent to poetry). And Ekaterina, Durov's female acquaintance, does a rather professional job bringing a dead duckling back to life—that is, she accomplishes yet another miracle. And these are only a few of many such examples. Moreover, the random characters not only recapitulate the stock images of socialist mass culture, but they also, as a rule, seek an individual poetic genre despite these very same stereotypes. Second, even creativity within the framework of clichés (such as those of Lieutenant Zhukov or Alka the bartender) does not provoke Durov's haughty disregard; and this, too, is a kind of search for a "genre." Durov can even borrow from other people's creative impulses, as is the case when he completes the dream that collapses before Lyosha Kharitonov's very eyes with the appearance of the "pink iceberg" in the middle of the warm sea, or when he buys the amateur poem from Arkadius that nudges him toward his trip to the Valley. However, he still fails to find his own genre, his own miracle that could have justified his search.

The reasons for this divergence are left unarticulated and are probably more metaphysical than social or psychological. Thus, the image of space in the first chapter proves essential: "I was no longer worried by my wrecked car, by my masculine pride, or by continuing my trip, but by the *tatters of space. All around me I suddenly started to discover holes, threadbare patches, and crudely ripped seams*" (ibid., 205; emphasis added). This description may serve to justify the fragmentary narrative of *In Search of a Genre*. But it is also more than that. "Genre," in Durov's interpretation, is aimed at the "miracle of mass trust and revelation" (310); it is directly associated with the dreams at the highway patrol station and the revelations of the Valley "after death." However, the most important symbol in the story represents something entirely different: Mona Lisa hides her famous smile from Arkadius with the palm of her hand. This is the kind of miracle that is possible in a space that is being torn apart at the seams. The characters of *Surplussed Barrelware* were united, even if this unity was illusory. In *In Search of a Genre*, even this kind of unity is impossible. This story is about a magical game in a reality that is disintegrating into discrete plots.

Aksyonov's novel gives new life to the identification of creation with death. The wondertale archetype of the journey to the next world is superimposed upon a metafictional structure that embodies that same artistic logic: After utopia has transformed the world into fairy-tale fiction, the creator may realize his aspiration for harmony only beyond the boundaries of life, that is, in death. This is why, in the final analysis, *In Search of a Genre* turns out to be *a search for death*: Even in the doomed camp on the dangerous mountain slope, the last practitioners of the "genre" gather together, each one following his own internal impulse rather than any external summons. Genuine miracles occur only in the "true Valley": the Valley of the Afterlife.

Hence the peculiar otherworldly utopianism of *In Search of a Genre*. It is, of course, somewhat reminiscent of the dual worlds of Romanticism and even more of the "departures" of Vladimir Nabokov's heroes (Luzhin from *The Defense,* Martyn Edelweis from *Glory,* Cincinnatus C. from *Invitation to a Beheading*). This is an example of the general principle of "secondary styles" discussed by Renata Dering-Smirnova and Igor Smirnov:

> "Secondary styles" make real that which can only exist in the realm of thought; that is, the second terms of [a number of] oppositions are marked: life is not death, waking = not dreams, the present = the non-past (or non-future), fact = non-fiction, sanity = not-insanity, a message = a non-secret. . . . In order to understand immediate reality, the hero of secondary styles must find himself on the edge of doom, drift off to sleep. . . , return to the past or catch a glimpse of the future. (Dering-Smirnova and Smirnov 1980: 7–8)

Against the backdrop of this general principle, Aksyonov's particular resolution of the conflict becomes clear. His Pavel Durov actually longs for utopia, that is, for a complete fulfillment of dreams in reality. The impossibility of this utopian wholeness leads to the fairy-tale image of the "true Valley." This particular image of reality is presented as a pseudo–fairy tale or, more precisely, an *anti-wondertale,* as the ruins of a collapsed utopian project.

Typically for Aksyonov, the five protagonists of his 1980 novel *The Burn,* all of whom share the same patronymic (Appolinarievich) and all of whom represent possible diverging paths of the autobiographical hero, the adolescent Tolya von Steinbok, once again merge into a single hero, the Last Victim, who finds God only on the threshold and beyond the threshold of nonexistence. The yearning for utopian wholeness, for a "common fate," also motivates Pavel Luchnikov, the hero *The Island of Crimea* (1981), ultimately resulting in the destruction of the beautiful world of the Island and the death of the central characters. These novels are built on distinctly fairy-tale principles; one need only recall that the parallel fates of the five characters of *The Burn* recapitulate the fairy-tale model of the identical tests faced by the brothers who have each gone off in different directions at the fork in the road, while the portrayal of *The Island of Crimea* clearly comes from the archetype of the land of milk and honey. On the one hand, these fairy-tale qualities make a mockery of the hypocrisy of the Soviet utopia in its everyday manifestations; on the other hand, these very qualities are fraught with utopianism, pure and romantic though it may be. Luchnikov's defeat, for instance, demonstrates that Aksyonov himself has a quite sober view of the limits of such an approach, although it is impossible to name a work where he stepped beyond them.[10]

Aksyonov provides one of the clearest examples of fairy-tale play as a means of polemicizing with utopian discourse. The fairy tale's "genre memory" enables the creation of a closed, playful world in which all mythologemes turn into the impossible rules of a game that does not require any faith. Thus the freedom of creative play triumphs over the iron laws of Soviet discourse. Faith and truth stand in contrast to a kind of aestheticism: the joy of imagination and good-natured horseplay. Fairy-tale play more clearly expresses the tendency of the literature of the sixties to demythologize than did various forms of "Socialist Realism with a human face," primarily because it did not argue with the ideological discourse on any particular questions (however important those questions may have been); rather, it pushed the socialist mythology aside, turning the Single True Teaching into merely one of many magic tales of human devising. Similar processes may be noted in the fairy-tales of Fazil Iskander, in the fairy-tale cycles of Vladimir Vysotsky and Yuli Kim, and in such synthetic texts as Ludmilla Petrushevskaya's and Yuri Norstein's animated film *Fairy Tale of Fairy Tales* or Grigory Gorin's and Mark Zakharov's film *That Notorious Munchausen*.

On the other hand, the fairy-tale tradition has its own far from insignificant utopian dimension, which is why folklorists call the wonder tale one of the first utopias in the history of culture (see, for example, Anikin 1991: 136–37). Moreover, unlike myths, the "axiological center" of fairy-tale play is connected first and foremost with moral categories, with the cosmos of *private* life (injustice in the family in the beginning of the fairy tale is interpreted as analogous to the intrusion of the forces of chaos into an ordered world, while marriage in the end constitutes the restoration of world order). This is why fairy-tale play in the fiction of the sixties and seventies not only parodies and deconstructs the Soviet utopian myth but at the same time itself provides the basis for the formation of a new utopian discourse that might be called the *moral utopia of individual freedom*.

Despite the fact that many authors of the sixties generation perceived the Soviet world as anti-order or pseudo-order, as the senseless spinning of wheels, fairy-tale characteristics are actually a form of dialogue with this discourse and even have as their aim the *liberation and renewal of utopian-*

*ism.* Here we seem to encounter a particular kind of postmodern dialogue with chaos. Yet incipient utopianism is also the direct result of a progressive tendency that is so typical of the avant-garde in particular (Surrealism, Expressionism) and the culture of modernity in general. Therefore, it is impossible to call the meta-utopian literature of the sixties either postmodern or incompatible with postmodernism. Rather, it is an idiosyncratic hybrid, one without which the portrait of Russian postmodernism would be essentially incomplete.

However, the meta-utopian literature of the sixties and seventies cannot be reduced to the poetics of fairy-tale play. The tradition of carnivalization plays no less a role.

## Yuz Aleshkovsky: Bodies versus Ideas

> *This sense of the world, liberating one from fear, bringing the world maximally close to a person and bringing one person maximally close to another (everything is drawn into the zone of free familiar contact), with its joy at change and its joyful relativity, is opposed to that one-sided and gloomy official seriousness which is dogmatic and hostile to evolution and change, which seeks to absolutize a given condition of existence or a given social order. From precisely that sort of seriousness did the carnival sense of world liberate man.*
>
> —Mikhail Bakhtin (1984: 160)

In the first part (Chapter 1, "Intertextual Play"), I noted that the philosophy of postmodern demythologizing and antihierarchical play was in large part modeled on Bakhtin's theory of the carnival. If this is so, then in Russian literature from the sixties to the eighties one cannot find a more carnivalesque writer than Yuz Aleshkovsky. The poetics of the lower bodily stratum, the "slum naturalism," the eccentricity of plot and style, the reliance on coarse language, the blasphemous defamation of official dogmas and symbols of truth, the comic grotesque and in general "unrestrained carnival word—familiar, cynically frank, eccentric, eulogistic-abusive" (Bakhtin 1984: 130)—all of the most important components of the carnivalesque tradition, including the drama of confrontation with "that one-sided and gloomy official seriousness which is dogmatic and hostile to evolution and change" (ibid., 160), appear in Aleshkovsky's fiction with exceptional precision and in an utterly natural, unmannered style. In the context of car-

nivalization, those aspects of Aleshkovsky's poetics which initially provoked shock and disdain but then brought a flood of applause seem quite
ordinary: the literary legitimation of "the noble gems of foul language,
the only natural and characteristic part of the Russian language that
remained in Soviet language" (Bitov 1991: 202), or the primordial, genuine, national character of Aleshkovsky's perception of the world. That
Aleshkovsky's foul language takes on the significance of a special type of
antidiscourse is another thing entirely: While colliding with official versions of Soviet discourse (literary, bureaucratic, political, or utopian), he
parodies, deflates, undermines, and ultimately countermands the power of
the myth over the consciousness of the hero. As Aleksandr Arkhangel'skii
writes, "Aleshkovsky's principled noncanonical stance and flashy 'un-liter-
ariness' are links in a single chain, since we have before us an author who is
clearly hostile toward *any* myth, whether it be historical, philosophical, or
linguistic, regardless of its 'ideological bent.' He knocks loose the literary
covers of the mythologized consciousness" (1991: 6).

Theoretically, the hero of Aleshkovsky's fiction is very typical of the literature of the sixties. On one hand, we have the "simple man," the folksy nonconformist, the bearer of life's harsh truths. On the other hand, this hero, as a rule,
is a victim of the Soviet system, who harbors no illusions about its nature. And
yet the narrator-protagonists of Aleshkovsky's *Nikolai Nikolaevich* or *Kangaroo* have nothing in them of the victim, of the martyr, nothing that would
remind us of, say, Solzhenitsyn's Ivan Denisovich or Shalamov's *zeks*. On the
contrary, Aleshkovsky's heroes are far more self-confident and decisively energetic than those of the "Youth Prose" of the sixties. But the paradoxical laws of
the carnival tradition refract this typically "sixties" conflict, so that in
Aleshkovsky's work man feels completely human only in a situation of extreme abasement and dehumanization: when he is a guinea pig in scientific
experiments (*Nikolai Nikolaevich*), or convinced that he is a "moral freak of all
times and nations" (*Kangaroo*), or drunk to the point where he no longer seems
human and is raped by his own wife (*The Mask*), or ends up in an insane
asylum (*The Plain Little Blue Scarf*).

Finally, all of Aleshkovsky's work is permeated by a frenzied, anti-Soviet
critique, but once again the forms taken by this subtext common to all of the
literature of the sixties are suggested by the logic of carnivalization. First,
there are the spectacular paraphrases of communist ideological discourse:

> Churchill's being tried in Moscow City Council for his Iron Curtain speech.
> Ukrainian secret-agent partisans—guys with a clear conscience—have seized
> power in Switzerland, and we're in possession of almost all world capital.
> What else? The Leningrad party organization thinks its leader was taken

away just in time, and for good reasons. We've sent air balloons over Africa to drop tracts inciting the overthrow of the white colonizers, Latin America's in turmoil. Everything's going to collapse, basically because of the foundation of the People's Republic of China. (Aleshkovsky 1986; 139)

Second, and far more important, Aleshkovsky's ideologized reality takes on an absurd, phantasmagorical character: We need only recall the show trial in the case of the "vicious rape and murder of an aged kangaroo in the Moscow Zoo on a night between July 14, 1789, and January 9, 1905" (ibid., 23). Such grotesques are not without their epic scope: All of Aleshkovsky's characters are highly *historical.* Thus the title character of *Nikolai Nikolaevich* gets drawn into the frantic struggle against "Weisman-Morganism"; Fan Fanych from *Kangaroo* plays a significant, if hidden, role in the abolition of NEP, meets Hitler, changes the course of the Yalta conference, plays the role of a defendant in an anniversary show trial, and is acquainted with the nineteenth-century radical author Nikolai Chernyshevsky; the drunks in *The Mask* make up the history of the Brezhnev era; Leonid Ilich Baikin from *The Plain Little Blue Scarf* is quite directly connected with the tomb of the unknown soldier in Moscow; Frol Vlasych Gusev reconstructs the tragicomical picture of the October Revolution, having private conversations with live abstractions from the Communist hymn "The International": Outraged Reason, which, so the story goes, was ready to march off into Fatal Combat, and which also robbed a poor veterinarian (*The Hand*); and finally, the drunken policeman from "Ru-Ru" proclaims a prophecy of the coming era of "perestroika and glasnost."

Aleshkovsky invariably depicts all the decades of Soviet history as a kind of pseudolife, as a disguise for the real and normal characteristics of existence—hence the phantasms, the grotesque, and the absurd. In the seriocomic world of Aleshkovsky, there is only one force that is beyond the control of the senility of history and thus essentially free; it is a time-honored power: the simple and majestic laws of *natural* existence, of the life of the Flesh, literally "the collective ancestral body of all the people [whose main themes] are fertility, growth, and a brimming-over abundance" (Bakhtin 1968: 19). Here we find the main artistic meaning of the lavish "poetics of the lower bodily stratum" in the fiction of Aleshkovsky. Here we find the main reason for the triumphant tenacity of such protagonists as the former pickpocket turned sperm donor and sexual giant Nikolai Nikolaevich: His truth is the truth of the natural norms of being, and therefore his cynicism is more moral than any official morality, his coarseness more chaste than governmental boorishness. In Aleshkovsky's fiction we often find a conflict between flesh and reason, as when Stalin's left leg revolts against its owner (*Kangaroo*). But always and invariably, it is the flesh that wins the argument, it is physiology that proves to be the last refuge of true wisdom.

The philosophy of carnivalization, however, presupposes the impossibility of saying "the ultimate word of the world and about the world" (Bakhtin 1984: 166), the principled unfinished and unfinishable truth that must endure an unending series of metamorphoses. It is these particular qualities that determine the deep-rooted proximity of this poetics to the aesthetics of postmodernism, which accentuates the impossibility of concluding a dialogue with chaos. In Aleshkovsky's work, carnivalization undergoes a radical transformation. Aleshkovsky is, by nature, a moralist who firmly knows the truth and who passes this certain knowledge to his favorite heroes, who in moments of pathos, at times even abandoning their characteristic manner of speech, speak in the unmediated voice of the author. In Aleshkovsky, dialogue is always distinctly formal: It is either an appeal to a conventional interlocutor, who listens in silent agreement (*Nikolai Nikolaevich, Kangaroo, The Mask*), or the obvious clash of two truths and two positions, in which one of them has to be surrounded by the author's sincere sympathy and the other is just as clearly discredited and ridiculed. Such is the case in *The Plain Little Blue Scarf,* where the "sad tale" of the life of Leonid Ilich Baikin alternates with the messages and appeals of Vliul (whose name is an abbreviation formed from the first letters of the name Vladimir Ilich Ulianov [Lenin]), Baikin's roommate in the insane asylum, who thinks he is Lenin and fairly accurately reproduces Lenin's mythologized style. The monologic nature of Aleshkovsky's artistic constructions also makes itself known in the way in which any image, any given plot construction can usually be reduced to a simple allegory, one that inevitably illustrates the antithesis of wise Nature and the pathological System.

Practically all of the unhappiness and suffering of Aleshkovsky's heroes is explained as the result of exclusively *social causes* and specifically as the result of the satanic power of the "shitty and soulless System." Even when the wife in *The Mask,* sick of the constant drunkenness of her husband, "screws" her husband with an artificial penis as he sleeps, Aleshkovsky sets the scene so that there can be no doubt that the hero is actually the people who have been violated by the Communist system. Thus while the suffering Fedya sleeps, not noticing the insidious intrigues of his spouse, he dreams of a troika of birds, in which the shaft horse is Marx, the trace horses are Engels and Lenin, and the coachman is Stalin. Nor is it coincidental, first of all, that, upon awakening, Fedya hears the words "The distance from Lenin to the anus of the victim is eight [meters]. From the road, it's ten. From Marx-Engels—forty" (Aleshkovsky 1993: 408). Nor should we forget that the artificial penis is made of a material that happens to be called "Politbu-ron." Such sociopolitical rebuses in the fiction of Aleshkovsky are legion. All of this appreciably shrinks the boundaries of the carnivalistic game and the carnivalesque perception of the world. Carnivalization does not result in a de-hierarchization of the model of the world: One hierarchy, an official one, gives way to another, nonofficial one; one utopia supplants another. In essence, it is Aleshkovsky's "lower bodily stratum" that serves as the foundation for his own utopia—a utopia that cannot be overthrown by any political regime. Aleshkovsky's utopia, as a rule, triumphs in the end of each of his works. And this utopia, too, is of a mythological cast, assuming a universal and timeless dimension.

Especially pronounced is the reduction of carnival to an image that is central to all of Aleshkovsky's fiction: the image of the people. This presumably genuinely ambivalent folk hero, this sinner and cheat who laughs at the world and at himself, endures humiliation, and manages to survive even in the most hopeless situations—by the end of each work, he always finds the Main Truth (which is known to the author from the very beginning) and becomes a straightforwardly righteous man.

The picture is a bit more complicated in *The Plain Little Blue Scarf,* one of Aleshkovsky's better works. The hero of this story, who, due to harsh circumstances, changes his name from Pyotr Vdovushkin to Lyonya Baikin, remains unchanged from start to finish, his new name notwithstanding. From the trenches of the front to the Brezhnev-era loony bin, he firmly despises the "ratty Soviet regime" with its chiefs and commissars and instead believes in ruined, bitter, and majestic LIFE (a philosophical theme that the story expresses as a musical one: the popular Soviet war-time song about the "plain little blue scarf"). The life of Vdovushkin-Baikin turns into the unusual—earthly—hagiography of a perfectly normal man. He tirelessly battles with the devil, whose ugly face constantly peers out from behind the shoulder of every Party bureaucrat (which is why Baikin calls them all by the same name, Vtupyakin). And he himself endures tortures in the name of the sinful values of human existence, as everything that lends meaning to his life is taken away: his home, his wife, and even his own biography.

But *The Plain Little Blue Scarf* happens to be the exception that confirms the rule. In *The Mask, The Hand,* and "Ru-Ru," which, like "Scarf," were written at the end of the seventies and the beginning of the eighties, the schematic aesthetics of the peasant chapbook triumph once again: Here, too, peasants with Party membership cards in their pockets, who had adequately served the authorities they hated, suddenly turn into rebels and dissidents behind the curtain. Yes, utopianism is present in the carnival from the very beginning,[11] but that does not mean that carnival can be reduced to utopia.

Of all the carnivalesque genres, the greatest influence on Aleshkovsky's work is the folkloric anecdote (which also holds true for Voinovich, Iskander, and Zhvanetsky). Strictly speaking, both the main plots and the subplots of many of Aleshkovsky's books are essentially anecdotal. It is well known that one of the branches of the novel grows out of the anecdotal tradition. Phylogeny repeats ontogeny, and Aleshkovsky builds the novel from the anecdote once again. Except that the anecdote becomes overgrown with details and offshoots and sometimes lengthens to the point of becoming difficult to read (as in the case of *Kangaroo*), all without managing to become a novel. Why? Probably because the artistic philosophy that guides Aleshkovsky cannot grasp the complexity of the world. As a result, the world ends up looking one-dimensional and flat and, therefore, not novelistic.

If we use Bakhtin's dichotomy of "epic" and "novel" as a point of departure (Bakhtin 1981: 3–40), then it is more accurate to say that in all Aleshkovsky's works, starting with the legendary, folklore-inspired songs ("Comrade Stalin, you're a great scientist," "The Cigarette Butt"), Aleshkovsky turns Soviet history into an unusual, comic *epic*. In terms of scale, one could even compare this epic with Solzhenitsyn's multivolume *Red Wheel*. Thus the extremes of the development of genre and style in the seventies and eighties come together. If all of Solzhenitsyn's work (especially his later books) is marked by the distinct stamp of what Bakhtin would call "single-leveled, absolute, heavy monolithically seriousness" (Bakhtin 1984: 125), then Aleshkovsky constructs an artistic world that may be understood as the thoroughly carnivalesque, "low" double of Solzhenitsyn's fiction. Yet in the case of both Solzhenitsyn and Aleshkovsky we find a single *monologic* artistic paradigm. Hence the reduction of carnivalesque utopianism and the transformation of the playful style into the conventionally allegorical, as well as the domination of the epic model over that of the novel.

Aleshkovsky and Aksyonov are not exceptional. On the contrary, they are more than typical of meta-utopian literature. The wealth of playful forms is invariably and paradoxically combined here with predetermined meanings, with the absolutism of social categories and with monologic tendencies. At the risk of oversimplification, one might say that this trend is marked by duality. On the one hand, the playful element of travesty is directed toward the total deconstruction of Communist discourse and the Soviet myth to which it gave birth: This is a realm of poetics that is undoubtedly saturated with dialogic and potentially postmodern tendencies. On the other hand, while destroying the Soviet myth, the authors of this fiction create their myth in its image: the mirror image of the Soviet myth, recapitulating its structure entirely and illustrating extra-artistic discourse ("anti-Soviet," liberal-democratic, dissident) in the exact same way. Once again, monologism takes center stage, usually appealing either to modernism (Aksyonov, Tertz, Maramzin) or to prerealist artistic systems (hence the significance of the Swiftian tradition for Zinoviev, fairy tales and anecdotes for Voinovich, and the folkloric-epic tradition for Iskander). At the same time, the playfulness that is so characteristic of all of these authors is noticeably transformed: It loses its ambivalence, becomes formalized and subordinated to the straightforward logic of the satiric grotesque.

And it is here that the duality of the play with utopian discourse becomes evident. "Play's autonomy promises, if faintly, the possibility of creating a necessary order in the midst of absurd falseness," writes Allen Thiher. "The play metaphor is in some respect a two-edged sword: with regard to the writer's revolt against acceptance of what is, it cuts both ways. In some writers I think that it works both ways at once, for they attempt to revolt against fallen discourse at the same time they feel compelled to accept the play rules that prescribe what kind of games can be played in the chaos" (Thiher 1984: 156, 158). Or, continuing Thiher's thought, one can find a peculiar sort of "elective affinity" between the logic of the overthrown discourse and the rules of the overthrowing play (thus, for example, Aleshkovsky's polemic with the ideology of utopia awakens the utopian potential of carnival, just as it roused the utopianism inherent in the magical–fairy tale tradition in Aksyonov's fiction). And therefore, the *dictatorship of the rules of play* proves to be structurally symmetrical to the dictatorship of the discourse—in this case, of utopian discourse. So how can one free oneself from the dictatorship of the rules of play?

Purely theoretically, one can argue that the uniqueness of postmodern play stems from the fact that the very rules of play become the subject of play and these rules are being subverted *ad infinitum.* To a limited extent, the very convention of playfulness that lies at the heart of the text as such and that establishes the relationship between the author-creator and the implied reader is subverted. It follows, then, that the central problem of postmodern play proves to be the creation of a *playful context* that re-encodes the author-creator's play and expands the playing field into infinity.

Here two basic paths can be found. The first is connected with the playful framing, the theatricalization of the text, the performance, the creation of multilayered structures that also encompass the level of reception; the regular violation of boundaries between fact and fancy. Not all of these devices work well in fiction. Some, such as performance, are much more closely related to poetry. And yet Brian McHale, whose work has isolated a large number of postmodernist devices, assures us that such an effect is also achieved in fiction (McHale 1987: 99–215). It may be assumed that in this case an artistic structure is formed in which a concrete textual world is actually a *metonymy* for the boundless *creative chronotope,* which swallows up the world outside the text as well. This path is oriented on the creation and actualization of an *external* playful context.

Jacques Derrida's theory of deconstruction suggests another path: Work with the *internal* context of discourse, or the "archi-writing." According to him, each sign functions as a moving game of differences and references to other signs, a game that is present only in the here and now. Accordingly, each sign bears the traces of those signs from which it distinguishes itself and to which it refers: these are symbols of *différance,* and they form the internal and always playful context of any text, no matter how serious. As Derrida emphasizes, *différance* is always "the displaced and equivocal passage of one different thing to another, from one term of opposition to the other.... Figures without truth, or at least a system of figures not dominated by the value of truth, which then becomes only an included, inscribed, circumscribed function" (Derrida 1991: 70). According to Derrida, such are the characteristics of the "internal" context of any contemporary text. Derrida's tactics of deconstruction are, in fact, directed toward exposing this game of differences, or the "archi-writing," which, as a rule, opposes the direct meaning of the discourse.

The writer of postmodern fiction can take a similar route by developing his own deconstructive devices, all the more so since Derrida's own methods have often been characterized as purely artistic rather than scientific, which then explains their supposedly universal applicability.[12] Of course, this is not a question of imitating Derrida or even of Derrida's influence on Russian literature; rather, it is a matter of the *typological* similarity of aesthetic strategies. In particular, we already saw how the metatext of the Russian classics deconstructs itself in Bitov's *Pushkin House.* Apparently, the immanent logic of postmodernist evolution assumes certain invariant routes: What took shape in the poststructuralist philosophies of the European tradition would in Russia be embodied in literary forms and in literary poetics, in keeping with the culture's long-standing traditions. Work with the internal context directs the author to make a serious attempt to master the rules of another's discourse and reveal within it the presence of cultural voices that are alien to it, voices that both re-encode this discourse and its rules of play and are re-encoded by them at the same time. One might say that this endless re-encoding is achieved with the help of the mutual reflections of at least two mirrors placed in front of each other.

From this point of view, it is apparent that the limits of the postmodern literature of the sixties generation were precisely that its complicated and inventive play was restricted to the text, barely touching upon the external discursive context. In the final analysis, the serious and straightforward utopian discourse that formed this external context defined and encompassed the values spectrum of textual play. The power of that discourse was still so serious and humorless that the text itself was created as a form of *isolation* from that power—an isolation that ruled out any *interaction* with this authoritative discourse. Isolation from the external discursive context was seen as the condition for creative freedom—as it actually was. And yet freedom achieved at such a cost was to a large extent infantile, half-formed, not yet mature.

Without these attempts, however, more mature steps toward Russian postmodernism would never have been made. The postmodernists of the younger generation, despite their recent hostility toward their sixties predecessors, are actually greatly indebted to them. The writers of the sixties were the first to play with the Soviet myth, after decades of Socialist Realism's monopoly on culture, and hence they outlined the logic of subsequent postmodern play with myth and mythological discourses.[13]

# 7

# Context: Mythologies of Creation

Already in the first responses to the fiction of the "New Wave" (which appeared in the early years of Gorbachev's perestroika), critics noted that the *author himself* becomes the central character. Peter Vail and Alexander Genis observed that this fiction is characterized by "the insistence on the authenticity of the author-hero. From the author's point of view, no one is more authentic than the author himself. That is, the writer. Thus here we have an artistic, rather than social designation: The main character is the writer" (1989: 248). They explained this dislocation of the "axiological center" as "skepticism toward the importance of the social ideal," a special kind of escapism into the realm of art. Vladimir Potapov agrees, emphasizing that this "other fiction" (the term suggested by Sergei Chuprinin and immediately picked up by many, if not by all) is a type of "literature that is conscious of itself only as a phenomenon of language," where "the 'I' or 'ego' [of the author] is placed at the center of the perception of the world in order not to lose oneself completely, not to lose one's 'living soul,' not to become a toy for the will of another, for words, evaluations, judgments" (Potapov 1989: 252, 254).

Only when set against the literature of the late Brezhnev era could such an approach give the impression of radical novelty. The focus on the image of the author and the creative process in order to reveal the playful nature of artistic reality only testifies to the fact that, in actuality, the fiction of the "New Wave" was clearly a revival of certain aspects of the modernist metafiction of the twenties and thirties, especially that of Vladimir Nabokov.[1] However, it is patently obvious that the metafiction of the eighties could not help but be different from the metafiction of the thirties or even the end of the sixties (such as that of Bitov). All the cultural factors that stimulated the birth of Russian postmodernism in the sixties had, by the eighties, become the "commonplaces" of the mindset of an entire literary generation, the "generation of janitors and watchmen" as the popular singer/songwriter Boris Grebenshchikov called the young nonconformists at the time. This designation had serious social roots. Its most talented representatives cherished no illusions about publishing their works in the seventies. Born in the fifties, they were not old enough to get the chance to make their mark during the Thaw (1956–68). Refusing all ideological and aesthetic compromises with Socialist Realism from the very beginning, many of them consciously accepted their marginal social status, combining their literary activities with jobs as janitors, watchmen, firemen—professions that Russians traditionally considered to be inappropriate for members of the intelligentsia.

In fiction, this generation was represented by Tatyana Tolstaya and Vyacheslav Pietsukh, Yevgeny Popov and Viktor Erofeyev, Valeria Narbikova and Alexander Ivanchenko; eventually, works appeared by other authors whose cultural and aesthetic outlook was close to theirs: Vladimir Sorokin, Anatoly Gavrilov, Mikhail Berg, Zyfar Gareev, Dmitri Galkovsky, Vladimir Sharov, Irina Polyanskaya, Tatyana Shcherbina, Viktor Pelevin, Aleksei Slapovsky, and Anatoly Korolyov (these are only the most prominent of many). It would be logical to suggest that "New Wave" fiction is defined by the *reconceptualization* of metafiction and its modernist mythology of the artist as the demiurge of a subjective universe of absolute yet fragile freedom.

It should come as no surprise that the modernist theme of the transformation of one's own life into the object of literary creation would be appropriated by several very different "New Wave" authors. A particularly significant role was played by Tatyana Tolstaya, whose works captured the attention of not only Soviet and émigré critics but also Western scholars almost immediately after their publication.[2]

# Tatyana Tolstaya: In the Broken Mirror

*Writers surely create something, but their fiction is no longer seen best in terms of subject or even content, but rather as a structuring act that becomes its own reality. Thus even though all material claims yield only a void, it is a structured void, with the fictional writer's acts creating a systematic web of relationships that is sustained not by what it captures or spans but rather by its own network of constructions.*

—Jerome Klinkowitz (1992: 2)

Of all the "New Wave" writers, Tatyana Tolstaya has the greatest debt to the tradition of the fairy tale. This is particularly evident in her stories of childhood, such as "Loves Me, Loves Me Not," "On the Golden Porch," and "Date with a Bird." For the children in her stories, fairy tales and life are one and the same; there is no gap between fantasy and reality. They all participate in the fairy tale: the neighbor, Uncle Pasha, the "Caliph for an hour, enchanted prince, starry youth" (Tolstaya 1990: 48), whom the children see as the guardian of a treasure trove to rival Aladdin's; the cream of wheat "in the light blue plate, on the bottom the geese and swans are going to catch the running children, and the girl's hands are chipped off and she can't cover her head or hold her brother" (ibid., 14), and even human death ("The Sirin bird had suffocated Grandfather" [ibid., 130]). The fairy tale does not obscure the story's drama but rather gives it a language, and the child's internal cry that "the world is so frightening and hostile" (ibid., 13) is resolved with the fairy tale about Alyonushka and the geese and swans, while the fairy tale about Sirin the bird provides the key to understanding one's own mortality: "No one can escape his fate. It's all true, child. That's how it is" (ibid., 130). If in Sokolov's *A School for Fools* the child looks at the world through the prism of myth, then Tolstaya's use of the fairy tale first and foremost *aestheticizes* children's impressions, subordinating everything, no matter how frightening or incomprehensible it is. This is what gives Tolstaya's style a particular *festiveness* that reveals itself primarily in unexpected similes and metaphors: "self-important kasha, so pleased with itself" (ibid., 13); "The wind had walked from the south smelling of sea and roses, promising a path up easy stairs to heavenly blue countries" (ibid., 31); "dusty corn cobs" (ibid., 37); "a blue corpse rolled swiftly down endless corridors followed by a hurrying sorrowing little angel clutching to its pigeon chest a long-suffering, released soul, diapered like a doll" (ibid., 53).[3]

In the stories of childhood it becomes clear that Tolstaya's magic constitutes something much greater than simply borrowing fairy-tale imagery. Thus in the story "Loves Me, Loves Me Not," the fairy-tale context also includes elements of "the classics" ("Marvelous oilcloth paintings flickered: Lermontov on a gray wolf snatching up a swooning beauty; or him again wearing a caftan and aiming from bushes at swans with gold crowns; or doing something on a horse . . . but Papa dragged me on, farther, farther, past invalids with lollipops, to the lamp shade row" [ibid., 8]) and even of Soviet discourse ("And when she was five—like me—the tsar sent her a secret package to Lenin at Smolny Institute. There was a note in the package: "Surrender!" And Lenin replied: "Never!" And shot off a cannon" [ibid., 10]). Moreover, it turns out that even the child's antagonist, the hated nanny Maryvanna, also lives in the world of the fairy tale. In any case, the three poems by Maryvanna's uncle, which are reproduced in the story in their entirety, not only bear the distinct stamp of the romantic tradition, with its orientation toward some "other" reality that is unfailingly beautiful (the last poem, moreover, is marked by fairy-tale motifs in the spirit of Neo-

Romanticism); but as we (the readers, not the little heroine) understand, these poems give life and order to the terrifying and hostile world that surrounds Maryvanna, fulfilling the same function as the fairy-tale fantasies of the child. The paradox of the story stems from the fact that the primary antagonists are not the child and the adult but, in essence, two children and two versions of magic. As Tolstaya argues, the fairy tales of childhood are in many ways equal to the *fairy tales of culture*—like those by which Maryvanna lives, or Simeonov from "Okkervill River," or Sonya, or Sweet Shura, or Peters from the stories of the same names. The fairy tale becomes the *universal model* for the aesthetic creation of an individual artistic world, the only one in which it is possible to live, the only refuge from loneliness, domestic disorder, and the nightmare of communal apartments.

What resists such a fairy-tale interpretation of life in Tolstaya's work? Death? The consciousness of the end of existence? No, for the child's date with the bird of death does not replace the fairy tale. The fairy tale only becomes wiser and more bitter: Life loses its value when one does not know that the gloom of nonexistence is just a step away. Moreover, knowledge of death and the journey to death are an essential part of the fairy tale's "objective memory of the . . . genre" (Bakhtin 1984: 121).

It is not the end that resists the fairy tale but endlessness. *The circle*. "The world is ended, the world is distorted, the world is closed, and it is closed around Vasily Mikhailovich" (Tolstaya 1990: 63); "The day was dark, empty, brief; its evening had been born with the dawn" (ibid., 64–65); "he had simply felt around in the dark and grabbed the usual wheel of fate and if he went around it hand over hand, along the curve, along the circle, he would eventually end up with himself, from the other side" (ibid., 67)— these quotations are from a story that even calls itself "The Circle." But is it not this very same circle that crushes the life out of Ignatiev in "A Clean Sheet," is this not what he dreams of escaping at any cost, even if it tears his heart out? And is this not the very same circle, only on a larger scale, that Seryozha feels surrounding him in the story "Sweet Dream, Son," when he understands that the blame for the stolen "trophy" fur coat, for the poor, slandered cleaning woman Panya, for the hypocrisy of a life that's passed, falls on him? And is this not the very same circle that manifests itself in the images of everyday fate and reproduces itself in the spatial images of "The Fakir" ("Beyond the house the boundary road lay like a hoop of darkness" [ibid., 157]) and in the temporal images of the story "Fire and Dust" ("she looked back and saw that time was still flowing but the future wasn't coming any closer" [ibid., 108–9])? "To get off the tracks, drill a hole in the sky, leave through a drawing of a door" (ibid., 66), to break open the shell, to cut the enchanted ring with magic scissors (an image from "A Clean

Sheet"), or just to run away as far as the eye can see, into the darkness, into the night, like a "sleepwalker in a fog"—this is the constant desire of Tolstaya's heroes.

It is as if the ancient cultural archetype of the Wheel of Fortune were turned upside down to be recast in a new, thoroughly prosaic context. But the effect is actually the opposite: The dramas and tragicomedies of today's people are shown to be eternal and universal. At times, Tolstaya openly plays with the duality of this motif: "The spirals of earthly existence end around the corner on a patch of asphalt, in rubbish bins. Where did you think? Beyond the clouds, maybe? There they are, the spirals—springs sticking out from the rotting couch" (ibid., 40). A similar bipolarity was found in the fiction of the twenties. In 1929, the critic Naum Berkovsky wrote about Mandelstam's prose works that "[t]he 'coin' of the image is minted to have a fixed value. The generalized image is given not just for this particular stage but forever." (Berkovskii 1989: 391). The similarity is hardly coincidental. After all, Tolstaya's everyday circle, like the historical reality in the Russian metafiction of the twenties and thirties, is presented as a kind of *set design,* a system of essentially eternal signs that bear a superficial resemblance to "real" life. This is why the wildest fantasies and delusions end up being the most real, *"As real as a mirage"* (Tolstaya 1990: 40)—this is Tolstaya's formula, which she confirms in the plots of such stories as "Fire and Dust," "Sweet Shura," and "Sonya."

Helena Goscilo argues that Tolstaya's artistic world is thoroughly permeated by mythological motifs. Equally mythological is the motif of the circle, which dates back to cyclical models of ancient cultures (Goscilo 1996: 127–50). In the final analysis, it is mythological archetypes that can be glimpsed under the coat of many colors of everyday fate and cultural certainty. Mythological archetypes can also be seen behind the fairy tales of Tolstaya's heroes. For example, in the stories of childhood, enormous significance is accorded to images that go back to the archetypes of Heaven and the Fall.[4]

And yet the difference between myth and fairy tale is one of values rather than structure. Myth is founded on a belief in the authenticity of complexes of signs, while the fairy tale uses these very same signs as material for decidedly lighthearted play. As a rule, Tolstaya's stories encompass both approaches; they are based on the conflict between fairy tale and mythological worldviews.

Such a dual modality is embodied above all through the narrative many-voicedness of Tolstaya's fiction. In the stories of childhood, the mythological relationship is connected with the worldview of the child (or child-narrator) who lives in a world that s/he her/himself created, who firmly believes in its truth and is therefore utterly intolerant of other worldviews, no matter how similar they might be. Meanwhile, the adult point of view of the very same hero (as in "On the Golden Porch") or of an impersonal narrator evaluates this world as that of a fairy tale, as a lighthearted and wonderful game.

In other stories, the conflict between the fairy tale and the eternal/circular myth is played out far more subtly. Consider "The Fakir" (1986), one of Tolstaya's "programmatic" texts. "The Fakir" tells the story of Galina, an unhappy woman whose drab life is enlivened by her conversations with the fabulous Filin, a man whose every anecdote points to another, more cultured world. But by the end of the story, Filin is revealed as a fraud: Galina discovers that his life is no more colorful or cultured than her own; if anything, Filin's living conditions are far worse. The story's structure is a system of antitheses (Goscilo 1996: 101–7). But what is important is that these antitheses depict a paradoxically whole world model. Thus the contrast between the images of refined culture and civilization that make up the world of Filin and the images of wildness and entropy that surround Galya and Yura is particularly noticeable. On the one hand, we have "Mephistophelian eyes" (Tolstaya 1990; 157); a "dry silvery beard that rustled" (ibid., 156); the teacup collection, snuff boxes, old coins in the case of "God help me, Antioch, or something even grander, than that" (ibid.); little tartlets, which Pushkin himself fatefully declined to try just before his duel; a "curlicued palace," decorated with every sort of symbol of science and art imaginable, under "a real Moscow, theatrical sky" (ibid. 166). On the other hand, there is the world beyond the boundary road—"the viscous Precambrian of the outskirts" (ibid., 174), "thick oily cold darkness" (ibid., 166), "red squares struggling to push aside the polar murk" (ibid.), "the degree of noncivilization from which she and Yura were a stone's throw—over the city line, beyond the ravine, to the other side" (ibid., 168), the neighborhood of the "pathetic wolf," which "in its rough wool coat smelling of juniper and blood, wildness, disaster . . . and everyone is the enemy and everyone is the killer" (ibid., 167). Bestial images comprise one of the most complex leitmotifs of "The Fakir": "Galya, slithering into her panty hose like a snake, left instructions with her daughter" (ibid., 156); "there's no trouble finding cows in our suburb" (ibid., 159); "the yellow beetles of someone's headlights" (ibid., 166); "if you want, you can lie low and gradually turn wild, collecting portions of cold poison in your teeth" (ibid., 171); "Galya and Yura remained where they were. And the wolves giggled in the forest. For it was written: if you are meant to chirp, don't purr. If you are meant to purr, don't chirp" (ibid., 172). Typically, when Filin tells a story about a dog who sets the table and warms the food in anticipation of the arrival of his master, it is the dog who represents civilization and culture. But Galya remembers how their dog Julie did not permit the bard Vlasov to sing when he was their guest. Moreover, even a trip to the Bolshoi Theater, the citadel of culture itself, turns out to be a scandal for Galya with "this toad" (ibid., 163); afterward, while gazing at the dance of the little swans, Galya imagines how these swans must go back to live "in icy Zyuzino, and puddly Korovino, and even to that horrible city limits road where Galya howled silently at night, into that impenetrable misery where you can only run and croak inhumanely" (ibid., 174).

This, in essence, is how the mythological world is modeled, a world where the periphery borders on natural chaos but the center embodies the cultural logos. The motif of the "boundary road" appeals to the archetype of the world's edge: "[T]the invisible sky slipped down, resting its heavy edge on a beet field" (ibid., 166). On the other hand, "Filin's tower . . . a pink mountain, ornamented here and there in the most varied way" (ibid., 165) is nestled "*in the middle of the capital*" (itself a kind of double center). Filin himself is constantly compared to a king, a sultan, an all-powerful sovereign, a magician, a "giant, with a frightening black gaze" (ibid., 174), and even a god—that is, in other words, he is identified with the absolute magical center of the world of myth. With one very important proviso: This entire myth-world is not objective but is rather completely dependent on Galya's perspective—it is *her myth of Filin*. This is how the link between Filin's "wonderland" and the chronotope of the "boundary road" expresses itself, although the development of the plot changes the nature of this link fundamentally.

Typically, in contrast with Galya's mythological perception, the tall tales told by Filin are of a distinctly fairy-tale cast. First, all of these stories are clearly parodic, which is the first sign of their playful character; they tend to mock elements of Soviet mass culture (obtaining baking secrets with the help of political blackmail; the hunt for treasures swallowed by a parrot, in order to turn them over to the people by the very end; the partisan heroics in the spirit of Vasily Terkin; an episode from *The Lives of the Noteworthy*). Moreover, in nearly every story, we see a kind of postmodern collage in which stories about Goethe are told in the language of Daniil Kharms's anecdotes about writers: "So, the children were there, and the grandchildren. . . . Goethe picked on a wing and tossed it aside. He couldn't eat it. Nor the peas. The grandchildren said, Gramps, what's the matter? He got up, threw his chair down, and said bitterly: Once a week, she says, eat fish. He burst into tears and left" (ibid., 177–78). The same passage contains a line from a popular Soviet song: "As they say, farewell, Antonina Petrovna, my unsung song. . . ." (ibid., 177). In addition, these stories are almost always built on completely fantastic assumptions: A ballerina uses her well-trained leg to stop a steamship; a set of fine china is extracted unharmed from a German airplane shot down *with a single bullet;* and Goethe's uneaten game bird is kept in a museum in Weimar until 1932. Moreover, the narrator seems to be simultaneously aware and unaware that these assumptions are fantastic. Hence Yura's reaction to the story about the partisan: "Your partisan is a liar. . . . What a great liar. Fantastic!" (ibid., 164). To which Filin objects: "Of course, I can't rule out that he's no partisan at all but just a vulgar little thief, but you know . . . somehow I prefer to believe" (ibid.).

To a certain extent, Filin's story resonates with Galya's memories, and with the plot of the story as a whole. If all Galya's memories are variations on the impossibility of overcoming the boundaries between the mythologi-cal periphery of borders and the sacred center of culture, then all of Filin's stories, on the contrary, demonstrate the comic conventionality of any *hier-archical* cultural boundaries as such: Pushkin dies during his duel because of the confectioner Kuzma's drunken binge; a village peasant put milk in a real Wedgwood cup; the ballerina Doltseva-Elanskaya actually turns out to be "Dogin-Katkin-Mousekin" (which, in the context of "Fakir's" animal imagery, is particularly important); the Olympian Goethe is rudely barked at from a window, as in a Soviet store ("You're old, and so on. A real Faust. You should eat more fish—it has phosphorous to make your brain work" [ibid., 177]).

Filin proves to be an exemplary postmodernist, who perceives culture as an endless series of simulacra, and who constantly pokes fun at their con-ventionality. Moreover, it is his playful consciousness that defines Filin's special freedom. This freedom becomes quite clear when the exposure of Filin as a fraud defeats Galya but not Filin himself. In the end, Filin's exposure is portrayed primarily from Galya's point of view, as the collapse of *her myth.* In the context of Galya's myth of Filin, every detail proves significant: that the divine sorcerer turns into "that pathetic midget, that clown in a shah's robe" (ibid., 175) (the sacred is replaced by the playful), that it turns out that Filin is registered not in Moscow but in Domodedovo (that is, he, like Galya, belongs to the cultural periphery: "he was no better than they, he was just like them [ibid., 175]), and that near his door "[e]ven on the landing she could smell the boiled fish" (ibid.), and that Filin himself "looked terrible, worse than Julie [the dog]" (ibid.) (an animal connection). The hierarchical construction of the myth falls apart; the periphery pene-trates the center, destroying it from within.

But Filin is absolutely invulnerable to these catastrophes, because he resides within the myth. His *modus vivendi* is to transform the mythological beliefs and sacred symbols into a series of tall tales. This is why in the end

Galya finds Filin sitting at a table eating ordinary cod, which he solemnly calls "perch Orly," listening to the music of Brahms without putting on airs; and this is why, in response to Galya's reproaches, he responds, without the slightest bit of embarrassment, by telling incredible tall tales about an Antarctic explorer's ears falling off and about Goethe's humiliation. He is faithful to himself and to his strategy. Moreover, the difference between these stories and all his other compositions is that they are created on the spot, as an improvised reaction to a specific situation (the polar explorer who is the owner of the apartment, the fish dinner, the failed marriage). This episode reveals yet another essential but heretofore unnoticed aspect of Filin's "theater for himself": he creates his fantastic fairy tales from the ruins of his own life, turning what is apparently not the most successful life into a *context* for fairy tales.

And it is precisely at this moment that the undisguised voice of the author breaks in (naturally, as a kind of internal textual image). At first it follows Galya's voice in unison, entailing a change in the narrative's form: The impersonal narration, with its strongly diffuse heteroglossia, is transformed into something generalized, yet personal ("We stood with our arms extended—to whom?" [ibid., 178]). Finally, in the last paragraphs, the reader is presented with the author's own monologue. At first the author speaks in the mannered language of Galina's troubled feelings:

> Your tree with golden fruits has dried up and your words are just fireworks in the night, a moment's run of colored zephyrs, the hysteria of fiery roses in the dark over our hair. . . . Well, let's wipe our tears with a finger, smear them on our cheeks, let's spit at the votive lights: our god is dead and his temple is empty. Farewell. (Ibid., 178)[5]

By the story's finale, Tolstaya's prose-poetry is drawn from that same nightmarish, anticultural chaos that was embodied in the chronotope of the "boundary road":

> And now, home. The path is far. Ahead is a new winter, new hopes, new songs. Well, let's sing the praises of the outskirts, the rains, the grayed houses, the long evenings on the threshold of darkness. Let's sing the praises of the deserted lots, the grayish grasses, the cold of the mud under cautious feet, let's sing the slow autumn dawn, the barking dogs amid aspens, the fragile golden gossamer webs, and the first ice, the first bluish ice with a deep imprint of someone else's foot. (Ibid., 178–79).

If the images of the outskirts, slush, terror ("under cautious feet"), darkness, and the dog's barking stem from previous accounts of the "boundary road," then the "golden gossamer webs," the coda for the whole passage, clearly resonate with Filin's "golden fruits."

Here the narrator has inherited Filin's artistic strategy, revealing its internal mechanism at the same time. In short, the last three paragraphs of "The Fakir" show the *demythologization of Culture and the remythologization of its ruins.* The new myth, which is born as a result, knows that it is conditional and ephemeral, that it has been created ("Let's sing . . .") —hence its fragility. Indeed, this is no longer a myth but a fairy tale: The harmony of the mythological world is relativized and replaced by a thoroughly aesthetic relationship to that which in the context of myth appeared to be the negation of order, a negative harmony. The author's "creative chronotope" comes to the foreground, encompassing the antithesis of the chronotopes of the Moscow palace and the "boundary road," blurring their boundaries, turning them into the convertible elements of a single process of magical metamorphosis.

The principle of metamorphosis as a means of dialogue with chaos is already familiar to us from Sokolov's *A School for Fools.* The peculiarity of this principle in Tolstaya's work can be seen in the repeated instances of *metamorphoses* in the characters' and author's perspectives. The various perceptions that preserve the "memory" of distant cultural and artistic contexts are transformed, merging with each other. The mutual metamorphoses of mythology and the fairy tales of culture are the theme of Tolstaya's short stories. Here it is important to note that both mythology and the fairy tales of culture are shown to be *equally* inadequate attempts by the individual to defend her/himself, to shield her/himself from the bad infinity of the "circle," from the cruel absurdity of "everyday fate." Yet at the same time, fairy tales, including the fairy tales of culture (unlike myths), do not refute each other, for they do not pretend to a single possible truth. And here we find a significant divergence between the optics of the author and that of most of Tolstaya's heroes (with the exception of such "author-like" heroes as Filin, Svetka-Pipka, Sonya, and Korobeinikov). For characters like Galya, the collapse of the myth of culture is equivalent to a catastrophe, while for the author, this is only the beginning of a never-ending flow of fairy tales.

As a rule, it is in the end of a Tolstaya story that this divergence between the author and her beloved hero is revealed. Besides "The Fakir," similar endings can be found in "Peters," "The Okkervil River," "The Circle," "Sweet Shura," "Heavenly Flame," and "Sleepwalker in a Fog." The ending is always indicative of the artistic strategy selected by the author. Tolstaya's adherence to these particular methods may be explained as the author's attempt to overcome the hopelessness of the characters' lives through purely literary means.[6] But such an explanation can hardly be accepted, since a different kind of logic is revealed in her stories. As long as each of Tolstaya's characters lives in a world he or she created (whether it is one of myth or fairy tale is not important), the author's "creative chronotope" turns out to be quite similar to the chronotope of her heroes. The endings in which the author's "creative chronotope" comes to the fore do not contrast with the chronotope of the heroes; instead, the "creative chronotope" seems to absorb them, just as a general philosophy of art includes individual examples, thereby becoming richer and more complicated. The endings of Tolstaya's short stories, in which the author is the only one really to reach the light, turn these very stories into a kind of *confessional dialogue* between the author and herself, a dialogue about how not to be broken, how to overcome the existential hopelessness of life.

Moreover, it is crucial that the author's "creative chronotope" does not appear in Tolstaya's work out of thin air; it passes through the entire text unnoticed, expressing itself first and foremost in the system of metaphors, which in its turn dialogically corresponds to the voices of the heroes. Tolstaya's metaphors *animate* everything around them—the external world, which is so dead and hostile to the heroes, turns out to be alive, to make noise, to breathe:

> The warm, already dusty leaves of the luxurious linden splashed, whispered, conspired about something, huddling in a tangled green mass, giggling, prompting one another, plotting: let's do it this way; or how about this? Good idea: well, then, we're agreed, but it's our secret, right? Don't give it away! (Ibid., 91–92)

Just "Peters" alone contains a whole catalogue of such transformations: "Life got on tiptoe and peered into the window in surprise: why was Peters asleep, why wasn't he coming out to play its cruel games?" (ibid., 197); galoshes lie on the floor, "their insides laid with the flesh of flowering fuchsia" (ibid., 188); useless announcements "hung all through the summer, fading, moving their pseudopods" (ibid., 189); the spire of the Peter and Paul Fortress "murkily raised its index finger" (ibid., 190); the summer "rustled, wandered free in gardens, sitting on benches, swinging bare feet in the dust" (ibid., 196). Not to mention the "dead yellow macaroni, old people's brown soap" (ibid., 197), and, of course, the "the cold young chicken, who had known neither love nor freedom, nor green grass nor the merry round eye of a girlfriend" (ibid.).

In all of Tolstaya's fiction, abstract concepts, familiar things, the details of the desolate city landscape so willfully animated by the author, are inevitably in harmony with the character's inner state. These pictures, so reminiscent of Baroque allegories, tell more about the hero than does the omniscient author; they become a mirror for the human soul and seem to cry out, "We are also you!"

Does this means that the individual human being, with all his or her fairy tales, delusions, weaknesses, and defeats, *is identical to the cosmos*? Yes, and that the ancient image of "man as universe" is also part of her fiction's "creative chronotope." True, the archetype of the human macrocosm inevitably becomes prosaic: "his years around his face and his cheap socks far below, on the edge of existence" (ibid., 180). And a bit later, this portrait of sweet Shura is filled out by a reference to her clothing: "But her hat! . . . The four seasons—snow balls, lilies of the valley, cherries, and barberries —were entwined on the pale straw platter fastened to the remainder of her hair with a pin *this* big" (ibid., 30). In "A Blank Sheet," the metaphors are replaced by direct, extensive, openly stylized description: "Hand in hand with depression Ignatiev said nothing: locked in his heart, gardens, seas, and cities tumbled; Ignatiev was their master" (ibid., 78). Yes, there is irony, and, yes, the macrocosm is in ruins, but the old image has made the "mocking, meaningless, and alien [life]" become the "marvelous, marvelous, marvelous" (ibid., 198).

Such a philosophy discards the modernist opposition between the lonesome creator of living, individual realities and faceless, dead clichés. Certainly, the sources of this transformation can be found in the later versions of modernism and, in particular, of modernist metafiction. But even in Nabokov's *Lolita,* with its clash between the world of high poetry (for the sake of argument, the world of Humbert) and the world of mass culture (the world of Lolita), it turns out that each of them aspires to the role of the only possible mythology, and this is why they are impervious to one another, despite their internal similarity, and this is why they are inevitably destructive in relation to other worlds, and particularly in relation to themselves. Tolstaya's metamorphosis of cultural myths into fairy tales of culture not only destroys the hierarchies of modernist discourse; it also does away with modernism's tragic sense. The tragedy of the lack of understanding, which cuts the creator of harmonious orders off from a world of chaos, is replaced by a self-ironizing consciousness of the fairy-tale conventionality of any attempts to create harmony and of the fact that chaos itself is also formed by the Brownian motion of ghostly orders that are built one on top of the other and that do not understand each other.

In essence, Tolstaya's fairy tales offer a typical example of postmodernist irony. Alan Wilde writes that

[p]ostmodernism (postmodernist irony especially) has both less and more hope. Chary of comprehensive solutions, doubtful of the self's integrity, it confronts a world more chaotic (if chaos admits gradations) than any imagined by its predecessors and, refusing the modernist dialectic, interrogating both distance and depth, opens itself to the randomness and contingency of unmediated experience. Or at any rate intends to . . . [T]he defining feature of modernism is its ironic vision of disconnection and disjunction, postmodernism, more radical in its perceptions, derives instead from a vision of randomness, multiplicity, and contingency: in short, a world in need of mending is superseded by one beyond repair." (Wilde 1981: 129, 131)

As Wilde suggests, postmodernism communicates this philosophy through a special form of "suspensive irony" that supposes that "the perception and acceptance of a world disarray exceeds and defies resolution" (ibid., 133). Particularly appropriate is Aleksandr Genis's observation that postmodernism reifies the formalist understanding of irony "not as 'mockery,' but as a device for the simultaneous reception of two contradictory phenomena, or as the simultaneous attribution of one and the same phenomenon to two semantic orders" (Genis 1994a: 245). Moreover, postmodernist irony is expanded due to the fact that the semantic orders to which one and the same phenomenon belong are, as a rule, entire models of the world (chaos and cosmos) or discourses that are as old as world culture itself (fairy tale and myth).

All of these aspects are present in Tolstaya's work. The conceptual divergence between Author and Hero is, in fact, determined by the ability or inability to accept chaos that does not allow itself to be tamed by order. Characters such as Filin occupy an intermediate position: Enthusiastically creating "local," closed, and therefore fantastic and illusory orders, they model the author's sense of the world, moving from defeat to defeat. And so the stylistic artistry of Tatyana Tolstaya is founded on *a paradoxical combination of demonstrative make-believe, the conventionality of any "creative chronotope" (including that of the author), and the discovery of the ontological significance of this very conventionality.* It is possible to assume that such is the stylistic principle of all postmodern fiction that plays with modernist mythologies of creation. This playfulness may or may not be radical, but it will always be subordinate to the logic of postmodern irony. This very same fiction continues the important themes of Russian modernist metafiction; at the very least, the characteristics of the creative consciousness in its relations with "uncreative" chaotic reality remain the subject of play.

What is the range of this playful strategy? Might it be too narrow? To answer this question, we must turn to other writers' attempts to reevaluate the modernist philosophy of creation.

# Sasha Sokolov (1980): Chaos Speaks

*But Uncle Pyotr the drunk, he warned me, that semi-literate
game warden from a Volga village where I also worked as a
game warden and wrote my first book. "Sanka," Uncle Petya
told me, "don't go to America." Actually, when he gave me
his old man's advice, I wasn't even thinking about emigrat-
ing. And I was truly surprised: "Come on, Pyotr Nikolaevich,
where did you get that idea from? What do you mean, America?" "I can see it," he said, reading my fate, "you'll go...."
Strange, enigmatic, and tragic are the events that take place
in that God-forsaken place, where, besides me, Tchaikovsky
and Prishvin went for inspiration, but where the human soul
wasn't worth much more than a pair of boots. The Volga
flows there, and it's also the Lethe, which flows into the
Turkic sea of oblivion. Drinking its water..., you become forever a part of something inexplicable—in it, and in the destinies of those who were doomed by it.*

—Sasha Sokolov (Matich and Heim 1984: 206)

After *A School for Fools,* Sasha Sokolov began to write his next novel while
still in Russia. However, the bulk of the work on *Between Dog and Wolf*
(*Mezhdu sobakoi i volkom*) would be done after his emigration from the
USSR in 1975. According to D. Barton Johnson, "the first version was
completed in the spring of 1978" (1987: 216). Published in Russian by Ardis
in 1980, *Between Dog and Wolf* is an even more complex linguistic and
stylistic experiment than *A School for Fools.* This is probably the reason why
*Between Dog and Wolf* has yet to be translated into English, despite the fact
that many critics consider it to be Sokolov's best work. D. Barton Johnson
characterizes it as a "book of language and style. The narrative line is negli-
gible, but the language is of such richness and density that it largely supplants the more traditional concerns of the novel form" (Johnson 1987: 212).
This novel paradoxically continues the tradition of Russian literary *skaz*
(narration from the point of view of a character whose language is at once
substandard and ingeniously inventive) and creates an entire worldview out
of puns. In Johnson's opinion, the most important features of the novel's
poetics are indicated by the title, a phrase used to describe the moment
between sunset and dusk, when indistinct shapes suggest both something
friendly and something savage: Here everything happens in the twilight

zone, and for that reason it is impossible to distinguish one character from another, the real from the fanciful, the dog from the wolf.

Johnson finds the novel's single relatively stable foundation in the archetype of Oedipus, suggesting that Sasha Sokolov "allies himself with other modernist writers who have drawn upon myth as a way of structuring their highly fragmented texts. The Oedipus myth provides a frame of reference in the world between the dog and the wolf, that multidimensional twilight zone in which all is possible and nothing is certain" (ibid., 212). In *Between Dog and Wolf,* a traveling grinder, Ilya Petrikeich Dzyndzyrella, is the father to the "drunken huntsman" Yakov Ilich Palamakherov, who perhaps takes part in the events that would cause the grinder's death; moreover, the grinder and the hunter also love the same woman. Certainly, these elements of the plot point to the Oedipus myth, and yet this is only one possible interpretation that the text suggests without decisively confirming or refuting it. Leona Toker defines the central device of Sokolov's novel as "forking characters" (by analogy with Borges's garden of forking paths): "[T]he characters of the novel form groups whose members merge into another, so that each character seems to branch, or to fork into that of his neighbor" (Toker 1987; 354). Toker emphasizes that

> the novel's main structural idea is largely an effect of paronomasia. The world and the quasi-characters of *Between Dog and Wolf* are, in Nabokov's terms, "slippery sophism, a play upon words." Remarkably, one of the greatest pleasures of the characters of this novel is skating upon the frozen river: the more treacherous its thin ice, the more exciting the experience. The real (very real) risk of going under is precisely that element of disaster-as-prize which, as in Borges's "Lottery in Babylon," makes the participation in the game a matter of honor." (Ibid., 354).

Making adjustments for the forking characters and twilight zone, one can provisionally isolate three narrators. First of all, we have the grinder Ilya Dzyndzyrella, who appears in the chapters with the repeating titles "Zaitil'shchina" ("Itil" is an ancient name for the Volga, so this name means basically the same as "Zavolzh'e," or "Beyond the Volga") and "From Ilya Petrikeich"; and, second, the "drunken huntsman," the author of the chapters in verse ("Notes of a Drunken Huntsman" or "A Drunk's Journal"); and, finally, the faceless author himself, the improviser in the chapters called "Pictures from an Exhibition" and "The Hunter's Tale." If the first voice appears to be a kind of fantastic semi-*skaz* and the second is made up of parodic imitations of various classical canons and traditions, including Pushkin's and the modernists', then the third consists entirely of artistic transitions from one culture to another, from one stylization to another. Moreover, the tenth chapter ("Dzyndzyrella"), which contains Orina's confession, is quite close to the voice of Ilya Petrikeich. And in the last of the "The Hunter's Tale" chapters, Yakov Ilich's stream of consciousness (which, by the way, is neither strictly direct speech nor first-person narration) concludes with the transition to the Author's voice, which, as in other chapters, is filled with infinitive constructions:

> To cross, to cross, he fantasized, to turn into the freezing rain of Brumer and hang over the junk of the props of the suburb, over some impossibly far-off sign-post . . . to cover the yawning gaps of perspectives with glass—and to stretch out, to deepen the confusion of the crossroads, wire, and, destroying the appearance of the old-fashioned tailcoats . . . and the hats of garden scarecrows and other characters. (Sokolov 1980: 188–89)

One constantly finds such typically metafictional motifs, not only in this almost randomly chosen quotation, with consciousness of the theatricality and artifice of nature itself, but in the author's voice as a whole. The feeling of total simulation—"that everything that surrounds us in the unsolvable here exists only *as if*" (ibid., 64)—becomes an internal part of these chapters. But if in *A School for Fools* the ability to create a myth of the world from the fragments of a destroyed reality overcomes death through infinite metamorphoses, then in this novel creation is doomed to bring on death. "It would be wonderful, honestly, to off yourself on that barbed wire. . . . Where are you, hour of death, why have you lingered so far away, give me a sign" (ibid., 112), exclaims Ilya in a moment of genuine creative inspiration. This is followed by the story about how after her meeting with Orina (or more likely, her ghost), a hunter, Kaluga-Kostroma, eats spurge-flax and dies—further evidence of the suicidal fascination with beauty. Ilya himself yearns for Orina, and his entire confession is created because of this loss, although he insists that the very thought of "that woman" leads inevitably to misfortune and death. And only in the chapter "The Last One" (Poslednee) does Ilya attain peace, apparently after crossing the threshold of death.

Certainly, each of the novel's narrators acts as the creator of his own reality, and this is the main justification for the twilight ambiguity of the plot of *Between Dog and Wolf.* As in *A School for Fools,* the creative will expresses itself through metamorphoses. However, if in *A School for Fools* the metamorphoses serve as a form of dialogical interaction among multifarious models of the world, then in this novel metamorphoses, as a rule, are surprisingly one-dimensional. Here their logic is *metonymic* rather than metaphorical: the wolf turns into the dog; the fox tied to the railroad tracks turns into Ilya, who is also tied to those very same rails; the one-legged grinder turns into the lame tanner; the railroad inspector turns into the lieutenant and sailor, who happen to share a train car with Ilya; Palamakherov turns into his great-grandfather; Orina turns into a feeble-minded girl; Pyotr turns into Pavel; Kaluga turns into Kostroma; the hunter turns into the murderer . . . This is why the motif of universal interrelatedness is so important to the novel's thematic composition; "The river Volga, streaming, is your homeland" (ibid., 21), Ilya says to himself in the novel's first chapter. Then it turns out that the railroad inspector is his brother and Yakov Ilich Alfeev, his one-legged companion in misery, is possibly his son. The presumed family ties between Ilya with Palamakherov and Ilya and Orina have already been discussed. In the final chapters, this motif comes through loud and clear:

> Hey, our chain of generations doesn't break off here, it rings, it clanks, and the tea service on the very precipice won't hide from us. We're all humanity's children, my dear, and we have nothing against tossing back a shot. . . . Everything's already happened on the Itil, everyone has been there. Say someone comes by, and they call out to him: hey, stranger man, will you join us? But the new arrival cuts them off: you've forgotten, I'm one of you, you just don't have any memory of me, pour some. (Ibid., 166)

Typically, two completely contradictory conclusions bracket this passage: on the one hand, "we can't wait for a taste of nonbeing" (ibid., 166) and, on the other, "our life is eternal" (ibid., 167). This is hardly an accident. As in *A School for Fools,* time holds no power over the creative consciousness of Sokolov's characters and narrators. For Ilya, today is as it always was, "the moon [month] is clear, you can't keep track of the dates, the year is the current one" (ibid., 9), he simply takes "the future canoe into the pluperfect past" (ibid., 157). Lugging stylistic forms behind them, Yakov Ilich and the impersonal Author easily travel across centuries and cultures. But the continuous metonymic metamorphoses (based on proximity rather than similarity) form a special kind of eternity. It is the impersonal Author who defines it best, in his symbolic picture of the *procession of the beggars:*

> You'll see the shaggy and ugly beggars; their features are drawn. All this procession had to do was come down from the embankment and come close to the gardens where the scarecrows stood, hunched over, and step onto the firmament of the yard that has been killed by children's games and the prints of chicken feet, and everything accomplished . . . in overcoming distances turned out to be the simplest of fictions. With no intention of returning, not taking a single step backward, the procession has already been returned, shifted, displaced to the original borders, to the horizon, and, clearly not noticing what has happened, continues what it started—parading, marching,

striding, dragging, and shoving, instructing the one whose head leans backward and is crowned with an unfresh ribbon that, from far away, across the purifying crystal of emptiness, is astonishingly fresh. (Ibid., 148–49)

This eternity is homogeneous, one-dimensional, and therefore painfully inert. This is the eternity of Sisyphus. Nonexistence is the only possible means of surmounting it. Only on the threshold of death (or after it) do Sokolov's characters undergo a qualitative metamorphosis: After death, the whore (*zlobludichaia fria,* ibid., 161) Orina becomes the Romantic "incomprehensible stranger" (ibid., 115) recognized as "Life Everlasting" (ibid., 115, 164), while simultaneously bringing certain death to her admirers. The holy fool Ilya, whose "prophetic" name (the Russian equivalent of "Elijah") is nothing but fodder for irony when he is alive ("I thought I'd turn the stormclouds around, but I got lazy" [ibid., 95]), realizes the truly prophetic weight of his words in the afterword-afterlife, when he asks, "Or are my words enigmatic [*sokrovenny*] to you?" (ibid., 192). For his part, after his vision of death, Yakov Ilich Palamakherov, the apparently unsuccessful poet (judging by his semiparodic verse), reaches the level of genuine poetry, his voice merging with that of the impersonal Author.

This is why the creative consciousness that gives rise to metamorphoses is drawn inexorably toward death: Death is seen here as the only *real,* and therefore only authentic, metamorphosis. Sokolov himself calls his novel a book "about the continuity of human existence, about its isolation. About several incarnations of one identity, if you will" (Sokolov and Erofeev 1989: 198).

But in what form can the impersonal Author himself, and his double, the author-creator, be reincarnated? Critics have already observed that the novel's first epigraph (from Pushkin: "I like a friendly chat in season, / I like to share a friendly glass, / About an hour the people class / A 'wolf-and-dog time.' " [Pushkin 1963: 108]) and its second (from Pasternak: "The young man was a hunter") each refers to the two narrators, Ilya Petrikeivich and Yakov Ilich, respectively. But in addition to the epigraphs, the novel also has a dedication: "To my friends in dispersal," one which apparently belongs to the Author's discourse in the novel. This supposition relies not only on the fact that *Between Dog and Wolf* is Sokolov's first work completed "in dispersal," that is, in emigration. In this context, the motif of the motherland is particularly important, especially in the chapters narrated by the Author. Here Russia is a figurative synonym for Orina, both as the mother who abandons her child (in relation to Yakov) and as an unfaithful lover (in relation to Ilya). Moreover, the author, like Ilya, longs for his beloved, tries to meet her and runs away from her, hates her and pities her.

In Chapter 13 ("Pictures from the Exhibition"), the description of the procession's monotonous eternity is transformed into an authorial confession of love:

> You hide, you conceal, and if you were asked, from what, you wouldn't answer; perhaps you don't know the answer? No, you know, but you won't answer—that's all. You'll only answer someday, when you're done growing up and mourning, but, *as before, jealous of that far-off place for harboring aliens, you'll answer for everything. Silly girl, orphan, and child of this world's orphans, I'm calling you—look back,* do you know how clear and clean your unwashed face is and how much of the earthly sorrows of your sisters has come together in its unearthly features? Lonely and alone, one of all the lonely and alone, who are countless, twinkle-twinkle clearly. . . (Ibid., 152; emphasis added)

Despite the novel's customary confusion as to the utterance's intended addressee, here there can be no doubt: These words are about Russia. At the same time, Russia is metonymically presented as the Zaitil'shchina, that is, as the monotonous and frightened face of eternity. Alfeev (Yakov Ilich's metonymic double) explicitly compares Russia to a she-wolf: "Mother Russia is huge, playful, and howls like a she-wolf in the darkness" (ibid., 65). The she-wolf in the darkness is not simply a sinister image; in the context of the novel's title, it is an image of a double darkness, a double danger. Here the exodus from Russia represents the exodus from the bad infinity of Zaitil'shchina, a leap out of the darkness. But it is also death, for what are Zaitil'shchina, Orina, Russia if not "Life Everlasting": "Long-suffering, beaten, but with a generous, worn-out body—in a word, painfully beautiful" (ibid., 114)?

The correlation of these motifs with emigration, a subject never broached in the story proper, leaves no room for doubt. The private existential context of the biographical author is thus included within the narration. And in the phantasmagorical field of *Between Dog and Wolf,* emigration is one of the metamorphoses typical for this world. Moreover, through the images of Russia/the She-Wolf/Orina/Life Everlasting, the price of genuine metamorphosis, accomplished by the author *beyond the boundaries of the text of the novel* but interpreted aesthetically and metaphysically by the novel, becomes clear.

And yet this is not the only possible manifestation of the passage from creativity to death in the author's "conceptual context." In Sokolov's work, the novel's "twilight poetics" acquires a self-sufficient significance: *Death, the kingdom of shades,* is modeled in the very blurring of the outlines, the stratifications of the different versions of one and the same event, the ease of metamorphosis, the indifference to categories of time (which beget, in their turn, what D. Barton Johnson calls "chronological chaos" [1987: 209]). It is noteworthy that the specific devices of Sokolov's work with the word resonate with the devices of Derridean deconstruction. Consider the Volga: In the Russian cultural tradition, the Volga has long been identified with the River of Life; in its name, Sokolov exploits a false etymology to connect the Volga with the wolf (*volchii*), all the while maintaining the river's "higher" mythological significance. This is an extremely vivid example of Sokolov's realization of the "archi-writing," a game in *différance*.

In Tatyana's Tolstaya's fiction and in Sokolov's novel, as well as in many other texts of the "New Wave," something occurs that is indeed similar to Barthes's "death of the author." This is the death of the modernist author, or, more precisely, of the author-creator who embodies a singular authenticity amidst a world of illusions and destructive dissonance.

On the one hand, in all of these works somehow or other there appears a figure who is synonymous with the author-creator (who can by no means be reduced to the function of the narrator). Yet the demonstrative fictionality and artifice of the artistic world that this figure emphasizes does not reverse the profound *dependence* of the author on the reality he himself has created. Particularly telling are the instances in which the characters act as the author's doubles, as well as the aforementioned transformation of the text as such into an *ontological gesture by the author.*

On the other hand, the "creative chronotopes" of almost every character do not oppose the "creative chronotopes" of the author but rather complement them. Unlike in the modernist metafiction of the twenties and thirties, the chronotopes of the author and characters in the fiction of Tolstaya or Sokolov, in essence, prove to be alike: Permeated by a single system of motifs, they correspond with one another and respond to one another. All of them together create a model of culture and of existence as a game of supremely unstable, slippery, illusory states that, moreover, constantly turn into one another. Thus, through the never-ending "multiplication" of unique creative worlds, which are consequently uncorrelated to anything or anyone, the modernist tradition is transformed into the external context of artistic play.

By the same token, artistic play is invested with universal significance: There is nothing there that does not belong. The rapprochement of the "creative chronotope" with death definitively accords a mythological dimension to play, one that encompasses all possible forms not only of existence but of nonexistence. *But what is mythologized in the given situation is not a new variant of order but the fundamental impossibility of its establishment.* Thus such an interpretation of the world-model of chaos paradoxically resolves the modernist antithesis between the creator of illusory harmony and the chaos of an objective organization of the world. If chaos is sufficient to the kaleidoscopic game of creative chronotopes that fall apart only to arise from their own ruins, then the author-creator is not alienated from that chaos but rather *is drawn into* unending play. Certainly, this is not harmony, but neither is it a cry of despair.

The next move in this game extends the kaleidoscopic structure of the author's own identity. Undoubtedly, this is the most radical transformation of the modernist conception of art; it is a direct continuation of experiments such as the ones analyzed above. The texts of Lev Rubinshtein, one of the best known Russian conceptualists, offer the most vivid illustration of this trend.

# Lev Rubinshtein: Creation of the Kaleidoscopic Self

> *Reconstructing language in my texts means giving it new, positive codes. In general, I absolutely seriously think that the main vector of my work is positive, although many think otherwise.*

—Lev Rubinshtein (Rubinshtein and Abdullaeva 1997: 181)

Now let us turn to texts that straddle the boundary between prose and poetry but that still address the same set of philosophical and aesthetic problems as the fiction of Tolstaya and Sokolov. Lev Rubinshtein's verse fiction is remarkable particularly for the fact that it lays bare the devices of the postmodernist remytholologization of the concept of the creative consciousness.

Rubinshtein's work has already prompted a rather wide range of interpretive approaches, each of which focuses on some particular aspect of his poetics and is therefore incomplete. Thus Mikhail Epstein, in the first articles about the new poetry, compares Rubinshtein's cards with the works of Ilya Kabakov, a move he justifies on the basis that both of them satirize linguistic trash, clearing out the deadwood of language. In his polemic with Epstein, Viktor Lettsev showed that Rubinshtein's vulgar speech formations serve as a trampoline for leaping beyond the boundaries of rationalistic discourse: "The function of such texts may perhaps be compared to that of Zen koans: paradoxical questions, riddles, and problems that have no logical solution on the level of discursive thought" (1989: 112). Andrei Zorin, whose short but densely packed article accompanied one of Rubinshtein's first publications, wrote that, first of all, the "card" structure of Rubinshtein's texts has a world-modeling function, giving rise to a "model that disregards connections between cause and effect. . . . His cosmos turns out to be populated by voices calling out to each other in a bodiless void."

Second, it is Zorin who first noted the unique rhythmicality of Rubinshtein's texts, where the very act of leafing through cards lends rhythm to the work, while the card itself becomes the quantum unit of rhythm and meaning. The combination of the apparently arbitrary order of the statements with an internal, hidden rhythmicality that cannot be recognized by such standard formal characteristics as meter and rhyme creates a field of free associative play that is nonetheless subtly organized by the author:

> The internal dynamics [of Rubinshtein's texts] are born from the torturous attempt of consciousness to free itself from the spell of an excess of variations, to express itself in the mechanical movement of time. Hence the particular weight given to the pauses, the zones of silence between the fragments. . . . The sensation of the necessity and impossibility of a final statement brings Rubinshtein's poetic thought closer to the concept of romantic irony (cf. the role of the fragment in the aesthetics of German romanticism)." (Zorin 1989: 100)

The poet himself defines his aesthetics as the "optimal realization of dialogical thought," with special attention to the "problem of *languages,* that is, of the relations among various linguistic spaces, various linguistic genres, and, in certain cases, among literary genres." However, in keeping with the tenets of dialogue, he immediately qualifies himself: "Now, in contradiction to everything I have just said, I'll say that in general I don't think it's productive to describe a particular artistic system, especially one in which self-description is an intrinsic part. Any system is interesting precisely at that point where it reveals its capacity to get outside itself, to break the ranks" (Rubinshtein 1991: 344–45).

Let us take the author's advice, and, accepting these words as a more or less adequate description of his artistic system, let us look for the points where that system "reveals its capacity to get outside itself." And in order to avoid repeating what others have already said, let us change the analytical perspective: Instead of interpreting Rubinshtein's work as a whole, we will examine the principles by which a specific text is constructed: the piece with the expressive title *That's Me* ("Eto—ia") (from the publication "It Is Impossible to Encompass Everything That Exists" in the literary journal *Novyi mir* [1996]).

At first glance, this is a typical postmodernist enumeration, a "register" in which the important and unimportant are separated only by commas: photographs from a family album, people's names, unconnected phrases, titles of books, inscriptions, short dialogues, stage directions—in essence, the way things always are in Rubinshtein's work. And yet *That's Me* does not contain a straightforward denial of verbal or mental clichés, since these very clichés are almost entirely absent from the text: The words here are either completely neutral ("These are my parents. Probably in Kislovodsk. Inscription: '1952' " [ibid., 1996: 69]) or are rather individual. Here there are none of the mysterious and paradoxical formulas that Lettsev discusses, although the text itself as a whole may be taken as a special kind of puzzle: Why this whole register or collection, in its mere appearance a heap of words and subjects—why "That's Me"? In other words, it is the visible unconnectedness of form that makes the question of the link among seemingly arbitrary elements of meaning the most important semantic problem of Rubinshtein's poetics.

It refutes the idea that Rubinshtein's world is populated by bodiless voices calling out in the void, although this idea is typical for the author. Strange as it may seem, the device of the photographs' names gives a very concrete and, in fact, bodily significance to words that are extremely general (indeed, to pronouns). In his earlier works, Rubinshtein achieved a similar effect by including "improper" language in the context of "cards" that were otherwise thoroughly bookish in style.[7] In contemporary poetics, the body apparently serves as the antithesis to hierarchical structures, as a sign of an organic, yet nonrational, link between things, as a shocking step beyond the bounds of the dictatorship of "spirituality."

But the most important thing is that the rhythm of a particular text is created *not only* by an equal alternation of the cards. The whole text is divided into several local rhythmic and semantic structures, which take each other's place in sequence. The first part (from the first to the thirteenth card) is given order by the mentions of snapshots where "I" was photographed: "6. Me with a sled. . . . 8. Third from the left me. . . . 13. And that's me in shorts and a T-shirt" (Rubinshtein 1996: 69–70). The intervals between these cards are filled by naming photographs of "others." "I" becomes a special kind of rhythm, emphasized in the first three cards: "1. That's me. 2. That's me too. 3. And that's me" (ibid., 69). Such a structure acquires the meaning not only of a formal but also of a semantic introduction: Mentions of myself, the constant presence of "my" portrait, allows for the arrangement in a single row of his parents, Misha with a ball, the market in Ufa, dear Elochka, and the deaf seamstress Tatyana in a swimsuit. It is significant that the final card of the fragment strengthens the rhythmic role of mentions of "I" with a metrical element: "And this is me in shorts and a T-shirt" (*A eto ia v trusakh i v maike*)—a fully accented iambic tetrameter.

The beginning of the following rhythmic fragment (cards 14–32) is designated as the beginning of a syntactic period: "14. Sitting." The rhythm of this fragment creates an alternation of various names and meditative phrases: "15. Lazutin Felix. 16. And someone's hand, writing something on a sheet of paper. 17. Golubovsky Arkady Lvovich. 18. And a droplet of rain running down the train window" (ibid., 70). The degree of rhythmicality here is quite high since the names are all given uneven cards and the meditations are given even ones. In addition, the meditative phrases correspond to each other not only by means of anaphora (which is often the case in Rubinshtein) but also through distinct syntactical parallelism. The meaning of this rhythmic structure is also illuminated by the play of "one's own" and "another's." At first glance, we have the alternation of a person (a personal name) and an impersonal detail. But anaphora, syntactical parallelisms, and the general expressiveness of the descriptions of these details affirm the opposite: In an item that is an object—whether a droplet of rain, a piece torn from a photograph, or "an open umbrella, slowly floating out from under a bridge" (ibid., 28)—the reflection of the "I," the author-as-subject, stands out, while at the same time a person's name turns into a dry sign, an impersonal index, and, in essence, becomes disembodied.

The third rhythmical fragment (Cards 29–55) starts by rhyming with the beginning of the preceding fragment: "14. Sitting: . . . 29. Standing" *(sidiat . . . stoiat)* (ibid., 71). And even the structure of this part takes the form of a complicated version of that of the preceding part. The list of names continues (cards 30, 33, 36, 39, 42, 45, 48, 51). The list of expressive details also goes on, although now such phrases are tied together by the anaphoric repetition "We see . . ." (34, 37, 40, 43, 46, 49, 52, 54). A third element is added to the rhythmic structure: the cards starting with the words "And the inscription . . ." (35, 38, 41, 44, 47, 50, 53). Special semantic relations arise among phrases with identical beginnings. For example, "And we see . . ." cards are all variations on the themes of pain, vileness, weakness: "And we see the teary face of the Italian TV journalist . . . And we see six or even seven bright orange pills in a child's trembling palm . . . And we see a pile of dog shit with fresh bicycle-tire tracks . . . And we see a child's finger hesitantly hunting-and-pecking Schubert's 'Trout' on the piano . . . And we discern in the semidarkness a silhouette of a huge rat sniffing the face of a sleeping child." We have a *video* list, one that is truly reminiscent of tele- and photo-montage. It quite naturally stands in contrast to, or perhaps enters into dialogue with, the *verbal* list, the list of inscriptions. Moreover, Rubinshtein deliberately intensifies the literary character of these cards, to the point where they resemble rhymed stanzas. They can easily be arranged in columns:

> Many years have passed since then,
> And you're the same as you had been,
> as once a poet said,
> whose name I did forget

The first two inscriptions do not fit into this minitext: "32. And the inscription: "What do I have to do with it?" . . . 35. Everyone's guilty, but you'll have to answer for it." But these "inscriptions," which precede the poetic "text within the text," are directly related to the self-description of the authorial "I." In these verses, the speaker philosophizes about what forces within him might stand against suffering, vileness, and weakness. However, the paradox here is the same as in the second part: That which pretends to the role of personal expression turns out to be the alien, tired word of the epigone's truisms.

In this fragment, the alternation of rhythmic structural elements is extremely regular: In fact one and the same "stanza" is repeated seven times, consisting of name + phrase "And we see" + phrase "And the inscription." A change takes place only in the finale of the fragment where the "three-line stanza" is substituted for the "two-line," "And we see . . ." is replaced with "And we discern" (ibid., 72), and in place of the name of the "other," the "I" appears again: "54. And we discern in the semidarkness a silhouette of a huge rat sniffing the face of a sleeping child. 55. That's me" (ibid., 72). Changes in such a steady rhythm are always a method of accentuating a semantically important point in the text. This holds true for Rubinshtein. The final card, "That's me," summarizes the whole fragment: All of this is me. Looking ahead, we see that the finale of the following fragment will be precisely the same: "63. All of this is me" (ibid., 73). In other words, the self-consciousness and self-awareness of the "I" arises through intersections with other people's names, the words of others supposedly said about this "I," and the names of unknown others.

This conclusion is fully applicable to the fourth fragment (cards 56–63), whose rhythm is formed by a repetition of intentionally bookish phrases that almost resemble quotations, beginning with: "And trembles . . . (a dueling pistol; a French novel opened to the middle; a silver snuffbox; a small tin cross; a silver samovar)." In addition, this fragment begins with a phrase that clearly calls up an association with the beginning of *Eugene Onegin* ("a large silver button on the traveling cloak of a young man who is going to visit his dying relative") and concludes with a reference to Poe's "The Raven": "a brilliant beak of a large black bird, sitting motionless on the head of a plaster bust of an ancient goddess" (ibid., 72). These are quotes, literary images of fate, primarily that of the suffering and unfortunate, but all this is also "me."

The rhythm of the largest, penultimate, fifth fragment (cards 64–102) is composed of such repeated elements as:

- remarks of concrete characters, which gradually turn into small scenes or dialogues of from one to three cards;

- the dividing stage direction "Exits," without fail heard after a person's remark or at the end of a scene;
- bibliographical information on scholarly articles and books with complete data—the name of the author of the imprint, pages, and so forth.

The main focus of this fragment consists of the fact that the names of all the "speaking" characters and of all the authors of books and articles have already been mentioned and heard in the first and second parts of the text. Here purely rhythmic links arise, distant repetitions semantically related among themselves according to the law of the subtext. There is a dual effect: First, what seemed to be an impersonal index acquires a voice and speech; second, the titles of books and articles sound like the text's own self-descriptions—like the author's attempts to define the essence of his composition: "The Current Labyrinth," "Season of Revelation," "We're Having Fun! And You?—A Repertoire Collection . . . for the Hard of Hearing," "Formula of a Wheel," "Several Questions of Unconventional Poetics" (ibid., 73–74).

Yet another pivotal point is that all these names first appeared after "Sitting" and "Standing." A certain group photograph from a family archive comes to life before our eyes, and all its characters "exit." In fact, "exit" becomes the main condition of their lives.

Here it would seem that any autobiographically colored elements that could be the bearers of the self-consciousness of "I" are completely absent. But in fact the "I" here is manifested indirectly—through "others." Only the consciousness and portrayal of "I" continually appearing next to those of "Govendo T. Kh." and "the aforementioned A.V. Sutyagin" unites these characters in the general space of the text, in fact in a single scene of the text, from which they all gradually exit. Thus the remarks they pronounce may seem puzzling only outside the general semantic field of the text. Thus, A.P. Gavrilin says: "We, for example, say: the wind is making noise. Right? . . . But it is not the wind at all but rather that which falls in its path: tree branches, roofing tin, stove chimneys. The wind, Lyubochka, is not making noise. What can it make noise with?" (ibid., 74). But this is a direct explanation of the ability of the "I" to manifest itself in the poem, a problem with which the structure of the text constantly plays. "I" is the wind, incarnating itself only in something else or through others but not reduced to roofs, chimneys, and trees remaining in some way separate from them.

It is no accident that when everyone *exits* in the finale the "I" nevertheless does not disappear. The rhythm of the final part (cards 103–19) returns to the rhythm of the initial fragment. But the rhythmicality of the final fragment is much greater. Here the same phrase, "And that's me," is distinctly repeated, whereas in the beginning "I" was invoked through varia-tions. The repeated maxim in its turn is anaphorically linked with phrases about others. Here, too, these phrases shape a text with verse rhymes, but now it is no longer torn apart by the refrain "And that's me"; on the contrary, the refrain becomes an integral part of the particular and tangible rhythmic design. We truly have an occurrence of "I," dissolved in signs of the existence of others. And in the finale of the text, for the first time, the phrase about "I" is unfolded—*only* about "I"—independently, although it exists in the words and images "of others":

113. And that's me.
114. And that's me in shorts and a T-shirt.
115. And that's me in shorts and a T-shirt with my head under the blanket.
116. And that's me in shorts and a T-shirt with my head under the blanket running along a sunny lawn, and my marmot is with me.
117. And my marmot is with me.
118. Exits. (Ibid., 76)

On the one hand, Rubinshtein's autobiographical "I" is free of any individual biographical or even external characteristics. At the same time, this "I" turns out to be a unique combination of alien and repeated elements of existence, from people and words to things and signs. The search for this combination, the elaboration of its design, is actually the meaning of life; the definitive discovery of "I" is the result of one's life. After this, one can only exit.

From this point of view, the very structure of the text becomes a plastic model of the "I," a model of moving (self-)consciousness. Its rhythmic structure acquires a special, philosophical meaning. The semantic parts of the text formed by a single rhythm realize certain not so much biographical as metaphysical phases of the formation of the "I," acting as essential aspects of the dynamic of self-knowledge, which in the face of constant instability seeks its definition in the world of fixed data about Others (hence the metaphor of the photo album). The rhythmic organization turns this text into a condensed synopsis of a *Bildungsroman*. Therefore the construction of the text as alternations of local rhythms flexibly incarnates the authorial model of self-identity and the process of its formation. The unstable, tempo-rary orders that take each other's place, which are built together into an arbitrary and, it seems, chaotic listing of everything, and all the rhythmic systems in Rubinshtein are interrelated. The creative consciousness arises precisely at the point of their mutual intersection. The concept of the cre-ative "I" is born as a result of the attendant short-lived systems characteriz-ing the unstable correlation of the "I" and the Other. These unstable systems in turn arise from the stream of alien forms of consciousness and soon go back into it. But the "I" is also a dynamic unity of these unstable rhythms, which join "I" and the Other in such diverse and contradictory ways. The construction of the text as alternations of local rhythms giving order to what appears to be utterly incompatible elements is reminiscent of "dissipative orders," one of the most important categories in scientific chaos theory. Rubinshtein's rhythm flexibly embodies his model of chaosmos: This is a series of orders that take each other's place, arranged in an arbitrary and apparently chaotic list of all and sundry. Moreover, as we have seen, these rhythmic orders in Rubinshtein's work are in dialogue with each other. It is precisely at the point where they intersect that the motif of "I" arises. *I as chaosmos,* as the combination of fleeting orders arising from the chaos of alien forms, to which it returns—this is what Rubinshtein's text leads toward. Truly, such a text deserves the name "That's Me."

This kind of postmodernist text would best be called "prosaic." Gary Saul Morson and Caryl Emerson (1990) define "prosaics" as an artistic philosophy of everyday and chance-filled existence. "Prosaics is the sort of worldview, to which disorder, lack of coordination and isolation are more inherent, than a system or a law" (Morson and Emerson 1990: 130). "In the center of attention in prosaics are everyday occurrence which in principle cannot be reduced to 'basic laws or systems' " (ibid., 34). Creative work in this conception is aimed at a search for and creation of the smallest links between "I" and the Other. These links are almost impossible to evaluate, but they remove the opposition of "one's own" and "another's," which is fundamentally important for Aleshkovsky's "carnivalesque" variant (the reduction of "one's own" to "another's") and Tolstaya's and Sokolov's "Baroque-like" variants (the creation of "one's own" out of "another's"). It is the very process of building these links (of rhythmic and semantic consonance, analogies, repetitions) that structures emptiness, turning human personality into a self-sufficient "dissipative order"—which is incomplete and not reducible to abstract totalities.

The mythologization of the very process of shifting through the fragments of bygone values (cultural values in particular) is a *postutopian* rather than anti-utopian model of artistic consciousness, one that rules out not only the very idea of linear development (whether progressive or regressive is of little import) but also the assumption of a stable natural order.

# 8

# Context: Mythologies of History

It should come as no surprise that postmodernism, with its emphasis on the playful subversion of all authoritative discourses, has a unique approach to the question of history. In her book *A Poetics of Postmodernism* (1988), Linda Hutcheon goes so far as to define this entire trend in fiction as "historiographic metafiction," positing that the combination of metafictional self-reflexiveness with a new artistic philosophy of history is what gives rise to postmodernist poetics. This approach could seem a bit narrow, since it cannot possibly encompass the entire radically diverse range of post-modernist literature, but it seems tailor-made for such significant postmodernist novels as Umberto Eco's *Name of the Rose,* E.A. Doctorow's *Book of Daniel* and *Ragtime,* Milorad Pavić's *Dictionary of the Khazars,* John Fowles's *French Lieutenant's Woman* and *A Maggot,* D.M. Thomas's *White Hotel,* Gabriel Garcia Marquez's *One Hundred Years of Solitude* and *The Autumn of the Patriarch,* the novels of John Barth, and, of course, numerous short stories by Jorge Luis Borges. What is different about the postmodernist interpretation of history? Using the work of Hutcheon and other scholars as a point of departure, I suggest concentrating on the follow-ing major principles:

1.  A rejection not only of the search for any kind of historical truth but of the very teleology of the historical process itself. This feature is cer-tainly connected to postmodernism's fundamental orientation toward relativism and multiple truths. As Linda Hutcheon writes: "Postmodern-ist discourse—both theoretical and practical—needs the very myths and conventions they contest and reduce . . .; they do not necessarily come to terms with either order or disorder . . . but question both in terms of each other. . . . The postmodern impulse is not to seek any total vision. It merely questions. If it *finds* such a vision, it questions how, in fact, it *made* it" (1988: 48; emphasis in the original). That is, postmodernism not only establishes multiple variations of the ordering of history but also uncovers the artificial status of such orders; they are not objective, not given, but rather are constructed by the mechanisms of culture and human consciousness. On the level of poetics, this quality reveals itself

in the way in which "postmodernism establishes, differentiates, and then disperses stable narrative voices (and bodies) that use memory to try to make sense of the past" (ibid., 118). In other words, in postmodernist poetics the concept of *culture as chaos* is projected on the image of history.

2. Hutcheon argues that postmodernism leads to a "metafictional rethinking of the epistemological and ontological relations between history and fiction" (ibid., 121). The point here is that in both postmodern literature and contemporary historical scholarship (Michel Foucault, the "New Historicism," Hayden White) the historical process is treated as a complex interaction of myths, discourses, cultural languages, and symbols, that is, as an open-ended *metatext* that is constantly being rewritten. The traditional Aristotelian opposition of history and literature as the real and the possible, as fact and fancy, is destroyed: "Historiographic metafiction shows fiction to be historically conditioned and history to be discursively structured" (ibid., 120).

3. The understanding of history as an open-ended text naturally gives rise to a particular aesthetic strategy: "Postmodern fiction suggests that to rewrite or to re-present the past in fiction and in history is, in both cases, to open it to the present, to prevent it from being conclusive and teleological" (ibid., 110). On the one hand, this describes the formation of a particular historical view of the present that in no way differs from the past; both past and present are constantly written and rewritten. On the other hand, here we also see the connection between postmodern philosophy and dialogical poetics, which attempts to expand the "zone of direct contact with inconclusive present day reality" (Bakhtin 1981: 39).

4. Finally, postmodern intertextuality and irony take on particular importance when this conception of history is given form: "Postmodern intertextuality is a formal manifestation of both a desire to close the gap between past and present of the reader and a desire to rewrite the past in a new context. . . . Among the many things that postmodern intertextuality challenges are both closure and single, centralized meaning. . . . The typically contradictory intertextuality of postmodern art both provides and undermines context" (ibid., 118, 127). As a rule, postmodern intertextuality is of a parodic or ironic cast, making problematic the subject's pretense to historical knowledge of both the past and the present. Hutcheon suggests that this is the fulfillment of Foucault's predictions that the "writing subject endlessly disappears" (Foucault 1977: 116), emphasizing the dependence of the creative subject on impersonal forms of language or discursive play.

To what extent can these principles be applied to Russian literary post-modernism? To what extent do Russian authors transform typically post-modernist artistic and philosophical concepts? This question is crucial, for Russian postmodernist fiction contains numerous examples of such play with various historical myths and mythologies of the ordering of history; Here we need only recall the works of Vladimir Sharov, in particular, his novels *The Rehearsals* (1992), *Before and During* (1993), *How Could I Not Be Sorry* (1995), as well as Valery Zalotukha's *Great Crusade for the Liberation of India* (1995), Dmitry Lipskerov's *Forty Years of Chanzhoe* (1996), and Yuri Buida's *Yermo* (1996) and *Boris and Gleb* (1997), among other recent works.

Even a cursory glance at these texts reveals their striking difference from the meta-utopian fiction of the "sixties" authors who also addressed the problem of historical discourses (Vladimir Voinovich's *Life and Extraordinary Adventures of the Private Ivan Chonkin,* Vasily Aksyonov's *Island of Crimea,* several chapters of Fazil Iskander's *Sandro of Chegem,* and practically all the fiction of Yuz Aleshkovsky). The authors of the sixties satirized the myths of Soviet history and historiography, but in revealing their absurdity, they tended to operate under the premise that Soviet myths distorted "normal," "rightful" history, which had nonetheless been imprinted in the memories of individuals (that is, sources that are unreliable by definition). As for the authors of the "New Wave," they either seek a kinship between Soviet historical myths and any possible attempt to give order to history forever and always, or go beyond the bounds of the "Soviet world" entirely in order to examine the problem of the absurdity of history and historical consciousness *in general,* as well as the question of the possibility (or rather, the impossibility) of "historical truth" as such.

Such a "new historicism" is central to the fiction of Vyacheslav Pietsukh, who himself was initially a history teacher by profession.

# Vyacheslav Pietsukh: "The Enigma of the Russian Soul" Revisited

> *Vyacheslav Pietsukh: Forgive me once again for repeating myself, but there is good literature and nonliterature.*
> *Elisabeth Rich: Only those categories?*
> *Vyacheslav Pietsukh: Only those. All these others are philologists' fancies. They also need to earn their bread. It's they who think up all kinds of postmodernisms. We simply*

*never had any postmodernists. What kind of postmodernists can you talk about? . . . [T]he avant-garde in general—this is pure experimentalism; I repeat, a laboratory. . . . And results in Russia, as a rule, consist of solid Russian Christian realism.*

—Vyacheslav Pietsukh (Rich 1995: 136–37)

Pietsukh's very style breaks the boundaries of "Soviet-ness," lending the narrative a strong intertextual dimension. Yet the point is not that Pietsukh paraphrases classical plots in his stories. Far more important is the narration's somewhat stylized tone, which breathes new life into the image of the unhurried, respectable, reliable *narrator,* an image that had been consigned to the realm of generic archeology. Pietsukh actually *narrates* his stories (and his novels, which are written in the exact same manner), using a narrator who is somewhat distanced from the author (unlike the narrators of Aksyonov, Aleshkovsky, Tolstaya, and Sokolov).

Pietsukh's narrator presents the author's thoroughly everyday plots in the light of the historical and cultural past. The parallels between the flood in a modest Moscow office and the *Decameron* ("The Flood"), an old woman's disappearance from a crowded communal apartment and *Crime and Punishment (The New Moscow Philosophy),* the story of the hostility between two neighborhoods and old Russian chronicles of war ("The Central–Ermolaevo War"), the fate of an unknown graphomaniac and Pushkin's tragic death ("Allusion")—all seem to arise spontaneously from absurd situations rather than from the author's master plan.

"[T]here is absolutely nothing surprising in the fact that, in our country, where life goes, there goes literature," says the narrator of "The Central–Ermolaevo War," explaining one of Pietsukh's key themes, "and, on the other hand, where literature goes, there goes life; not only do we write the way we live, but we live the way we write" (Pietsukh 1990: 219–20). According to this logic, Russian life throughout history, and especially recently, has been naturally literary, with the single stipulation that "literature is a finished version, while life is a rough draft, and not even a very good one" (ibid., 246). All these declarations draw attention to a purely postmodern blurring of boundaries between the sign and its referent, calling the dependence of "history" on "literature" into question.

The device that lies at the heart of Pietsukh's fiction is paradoxical: it might best be called *intertextual irony.* On the one hand, the natural literariness of Russian life compels the author to *recognize* literary-historical prototypes in the anecdotal conflicts he describes. Moreover, as a rule, this recognition is the prerogative of that very same narrator, a professional man of letters who invariably finds his way into Pietsukh's works. He is the one who locates the author's wild stories in the context of Russian cultural traditions. On the other hand, the direct intertextual connections to the Russian classics only emphasize the discrepancy between "real" events and the familiar stories from nineteenth-century Russian literature and history. Thus "Our Man in a Case," whose title refers to Chekhov's famous short story about the narrow-minded provincial teacher Belikov, presents a contemporary Belikov who is a rather nice, unusually refined, and vulnerable man, whose "fears were not abstractions of the 'what if that happens' variety but were well founded." (ibid., 35). His death prompts the narrator to comment: "[O]ne hundred years ago, Belikov the schoolteacher was sent off on his final journey with great pleasure, since he was considered a harmful anomaly, but at the end of this century, everyone felt sorry for Serpeev the schoolteacher. No, say what you will, life does not stand still" (ibid., 38). And vice versa: when two of our contemporaries try to resolve conflicts at work through a classic duel (with bows and arrows, no less—no other weapons could be found), when they fire eleven times (since neither of the duelists had ever held a bow in his hands), when an arrow finally hits one of them in the eye, then not only do the ideas of "life's rules" lifted from literature prove absolutely inappropriate, but the fundamental *impossibility* of these ideas become clear. What in the past had been tragedy now becomes tragi-farce. Such transformations are constant motifs in Pietsukh's fiction.

The "class" conflict between the *nouveau riche* and the intellectual ends with the two becoming pals, a friendship that somehow leads to the trashing of the *nouveau riche*'s car and furniture ("The Tragedy of Ownership"). The story of the local poet, which resembles Pushkin's family drama but ends with a concussion and sedatives rather than with the poet's death, in today's terms looks like the script for an absurdist performance piece ("Allusion"). The absurdity is only reinforced by the regular, heart-rending cry of "Comrades, what are you doing! Have you flipped [*ochumeli*] or something? Do you have any idea what you're doing?" (ibid., 48). In Pietsukh's contemporary *Decameron* ("The Flood"), the plague (*chuma*) is replaced by a burst water pipe, while Boccaccio's orderly system of stories is replaced by completely fantastic tall tales that nonetheless turn out to be gospel truth while remaining unbelievably absurd, like the story about the millions of rubles lost at a card game, which, of course, can never be paid back to the creditor.

Such is the "laughter of life" that results from natural literariness and eventually replaces traditional cultural patterns. The play with literary and historical archetypes compels us to see randomness in place of profound connections, gaps in place of centuries-old traditions, absurd impulses in place of unshakable "rules of life." In *The New Moscow Philosophy,* the lovers of wisdom who investigate the death of an old woman come to the conclusion that "something's happened to time. . . The Bible, Christ, the Roman Empire, Spinoza, the encyclopedists, 'liberty, equality, fraternity'— it's all still to come. . . . For a while now, our evil hasn't been what it should be, our good hasn't been what it should be, they've somehow been transformed by seventy-one years of building socialism" (ibid., 310). Soviet history, it would seem, has stranded Pietsukh's heroes in pretime, prehistory, and preculture.

Yet Pietsukh goes much further; quite often he projects Soviet discourse onto historically distant situations. "That's just the point, Stepan. It's never gone your way and it never will," says one of the "remnants of the Russian empire" who have miraculously survived the revolution and political oppression in "Three Men under an Apple Tree." "In our country, even in the time of Nicholas the Bloody [Nicholas I], the social was higher than the personal. Don't even get me started on Ivan the Terrible's struggle with the enemies of the people. And I'll say nothing about the large-scale collectivization under Mikhail Romanov" (ibid., 113). Such pronouncements reflect numerous theories on the "origins and meaning" of Soviet history (from those of the turn-of-the-century Russian philosopher Nikolai Berdyaev to Vasily Grossman, author of the 1961 novel *Life and Fate*). But far more important than this resemblance is the revelation that Russian history was always as inextricably entangled in the absurd as Soviet history, and therefore, the Russian literary classics never "reflected" anything; instead, they continually composed and modeled an *ideal* plan for life. At the same time, according to the author, Russian life itself has invariably been built with literature in mind. "People are required to live with literature in mind, like Christians do with 'Our Father' " (ibid., 333), according to the protagonists of *The New Moscow Philosophy,* Pietsukh's reinterpretation of Dostoevsky's *Crime and Punishment.* Thus the "natural literariness" of life, as we have seen, merely reinforces the permanent absurdity of existence rather than reversing it.

For Pietsukh, the category of "national character" becomes a form of ironic, provisional compromise with literary tradition, the historical past, and the present. This is what Pietsukh's literature models, uniting the present and the past. And yet when the author talks of Russia and the absurdity of Russian life and Russian history, he creates such a universal context that "Russian national absurdity" looks like an existential and timeless trait. This paradox is central to his story "The Central–Ermolaevo War," which would seem to be an artistic examination of the problem of "national character" and the peculiarities of Russian life.

The story's simple plot, which describes the protracted hostility between young men from two neighboring central Russian villages, is deceptive: From the very first lines of the story, its universal scale is clear; "The

Central–Ermolaevo War" is only an arbitrarily selected point in history, one that is no more or less significant than any other. As the narrator contends, the *"compositional"* nature of the Russian soul consists equally of Napoleonic Wars, senseless domestic tasks, arguments with one's wife, and a new religion. Naturally, a place can be found for the Central–Ermolaevo War as well:

> The enigma of the Russian soul is actually very easily explained: the Russian soul encompasses everything. By way of comparison the German soul or, say perhaps, the Serbo-Croat soul . . . Not that we have any grounds for supposing their souls to be in any way shallower than ours; indeed, they may well in some respects be more thorough-going, more compositionally sound if you like, as a bowlful of stewed fruit containing fruit is more compositionally sound than a bowlful of fruit consisting of fruit, vegetables, spices and minerals. That said, however, there is no getting round the fact that certain things they do lack. They may, for instance, be brimming with constructiveness but quite hopeless at negating the universe. They may be bursting with entrepreneurial flair, but lack any trace of that eighth note of the octave, that sense of 'let's watch the whole lot go up in flames.' Again, they may be long on national pride, but quite hopeless at building castles in the air. The Russian soul has the lot: constructiveness, negation, flair, pyromania, national pride and castles in the air. Building castles in the air is, in fact, a particular strength. Imagine for a moment that a Russian, from having nothing better to do, has dismantled a shed he actually very much needs, explained to his neighbor why Russia was victorious in the war against Napoleon, and given his wife a good thrashing with the kitchen towel; he then sits back on his veranda smiling peacefully at the loveliness of the day, and is suddenly struck by the thought that it's perhaps time he invented a new religion. (Pietsukh 1995: 237)

Characteristically, the universalism of national character in this description is defined by a combination of mutually exclusive elements, resulting in either destruction (dismantling "a shed he actually very much needs") or something frankly irrational ("it's perhaps time he invented a new religion"). This theme is elaborated in at least two aspects of the story. First of all, the history of the Central–Ermolaevo War is framed by reflections on the influence of place names, landscape, and climate on the Russian national character (in the spirit of Russian historians such as Vasily Kliuchevskii or Dmitrii Likhachev). But the narrator, as opposed to the authorities, deliberately interprets it either as something destructive or something totally irrational and illogical. The toponymy preserves the memory of "Fyodor Ermolaev who dynamited the local church in 1922" (ibid., 238), or is simply absurd, since "Golden Beaches boasts a wire factory and the entire town is ankle deep in sunflower seed husks expectorated by the local inhabitants . . . the launch visits Third Left Riverbanks rather less than daily, . . . the English teacher is the only person in Afrikanida who knows what 'subjective idealism' means" (ibid.). The climate "does indeed tend toward divisiveness" (ibid.), while the landscape is called "nothing special" and a "near-desert" (ibid., 240), although its very lack of anything specific or memorable "leaves you with a sense of obligation. What that obligation might be is anyone's guess" (ibid.). These are the parameters (or perhaps, the absence of parameters) that define the national character from within.

Second, the history of "The Central–Ermolaevo War" is permeated with a network of intertexts that lend it a universal significance. Several cultural languages are combined in this story without doing any damage to consistency. As noted above, one of the most important intertexts of this story is the tradition of the old Russian war chronicle: It is no accident that this little squabble is repeatedly called "internal strife." The story includes the "Battle of Ermolaevo" and a solar eclipse ("the last total eclipse of the sun in the twentieth century" [ibid., 252], emphasizes the narrator), which exerts a decisive influence on the conflict's outcome (this motif clearly recalls the medieval Russian chronicles, such as *The Igor Tale* and *Zadonshchina*). The story's characters themselves recognize the "genre memory" of the medieval Russian heroic military tale to some extent, although for them it is mediated through Soviet discourse and Sergei Eisenstein's film *Alexander Nevsky:*

> . . . there was only the eerie sound of bicycle chains whistling in the air, heavy breathing on all sides, wide shouting and cursing. Pyotr Ermolaev furiously dispatched the mechanics, his blows accompanied by the cry of Alexander Nevsky: "He who comes to us with the sword . . . !" For some reason he did not go on.
> Papa Carlo battled in silence. (Ibid., 251)

Certainly, Soviet war movies inspired the men to throw Molotov cocktails into the enemy's clubhouse, as well as to interrogate the "prisoner," Ablyazov the vet. During the interrogation, the good-natured Papa Carlo plays the role of the cruel inquisitor, while the hungover Ablyazov is forced to take on the role of heroic partisan, especially since "not only did he not know why Svistunov [the militiaman whose presence seems suspicious to the men from Central—M.L.] was snooping around in Ermolaevo, he hadn't even known Svistunov was there at all. His ignorance was, in a sense, a blessing, since he was delivered of the temptation to behave dishonorably. He grimaced in terror, and even smiled, but they seared his arm in two places all the same" (ibid., 248). A particularly remarkable signal of the characters' involvement in the world of Soviet rhetoric is the poem that Ablyazov, while hungover, writes just before the interrogation:

> The more you sing and make a racket
> The less you worry how much you get in your wage packet. (Ibid., 247)

His enemy, Papa Carlo, immediately responds: "That's a real poem, sinuous, and politically correct" (ibid.). Another example of "folk art" is the play written by Medical Orderly Serebryakov: *Home Remedies Spell Trouble.* The man whose Chekhovian name (Professor Serebryakov from "Uncle Vanya") is apparently meant to accentuate his intelligentsia roots stages his very own play by casting village youth in the parts, thus recapitulating a typical cliché of Thaw-era "Socialist Realism with a human face." But the play itself, which is described in such detail, ironically revives another cultural tradition, that of Neo-Classicism. Serebryakov himself explains his play, constantly skipping from one cultural language to another: "You have to appreciate, comrades, that what we have here is drama, almost tragedy. Because this, this *free-thinking* results in someone's becoming even more ill instead of recovering. One could weep, comrades, but you are hamming it up mercilessly. Now do let's start this scene again from the beginning" (ibid., 249; italics in the original). The heroes of this didactic drama are naturally called Vetrogonov ("empty-headed") and Pravdin ("truth"), and the story culminates when they hear the Voice of Reason. . . .

All these cultural languages hark back to highly hierarchical artistic systems, ones that are based on notions of universal Order and the concomitant Rules of Life; this, perhaps, explains why these codes are so intertwined. But the languages of these literary forms are imposed upon absolutely *absurd* and destructive events. Or, to put it more precisely, the absurd plot of "The Central–Ermolaevo War," which starts for no reason and ends because of a solar eclipse, arises from the *intersection* of these literary traditions.

Moreover, all participants in these events are strict followers of the literary Rules of Life: Pyotr Ermolaev plays Pravdin (from the Russian for "truth") and in the heat of battle pronounces the "legendary" words of Alexander Nevsky (actually from Eisenstein's film); during the solar eclipse he looks "so much like a priest preparing to commune with the heavens that it fair made your flesh creep" (ibid., 253). The nickname "Papa Carlo," which comes from Alexei Tolstoy's version of *Pinocchio,* is also associated with the role of *raisonneur.*

Particularly noteworthy is the description of Field Husbandry Day as a kind of deeply ritualized ceremony: This episode can be interpreted as a form of folkloric cultural Order. Here we have a calendar holiday, one that necessarily combines dances and fistfights. However, the holiday culminates in a "catchy song":

> *All the boys from Vologda*
> *Are hooligans and thieving gits.*
> *They jumped a peasant carting dung*
> *And robbed and left him in the shits.* (Ibid., 243)

Note, too, the use of the word "sentimental," so reminiscent of the literary movement that represented the world of the folk as the peak of natural harmony: " 'I heard a hunter came across a herd of wild cows twenty kilometers from your Ermolaevo,' says Papa Carlo. 'Perfectly ordinary cows they were, Sentimenthalers, only wild' " (ibid., 241). Pyotr Ermolaev dismisses these words as "unrealistic."

The combination of "correct" ideas with absurd actions paradoxically gives rise to a sense of the *fullness of life*—and this is typical of Pietsukh's other stories as well: "On the way home the men of Ermolaevo sang songs, and from time to time their leader shouted into the wind, 'This is living, eh lads? This, I reckon, lads, is life!' " (ibid., 245).

The sense of the fullness of life that grips the characters of the story compels one to understand the *historical value of the absurd*. And the universalistic context of the story does not suggest any other scale. The absurd, on the one hand, appears as a form of freedom and hence as the fullest realization of vital forces—the freedom from various, always limited, orders dictated by culture and history. But against the backdrop of the absurd and destructive "fullness of life," these cultural orders themselves, from medieval heroics to the Socialist Realist canon, are similarly unrealized utopias, various linguistic *shells* for *normal* human absurdity. The universality of the description of a 1981 model of internal strife convinces one that all other Russian internal strife, from the time of Prince Igor or Alexander Nevsky, followed the same course as the Central–Ermolaevo War: "[A] fundamental law of our life creates multi-talented characters, men with top-heavy destinies, and all sorts of peculiar goings on in which the spirit of the Mongol Horde is palpable" (ibid., 254).[1]

Here national character resembles a kind of "black box": At its entrance are the culturally regulated "rules of life," while at its exit are the absurd consequences and total ruins of any attempt to impose order. "The Central–Ermolaevo War" reveals a peculiar symmetry in the way in which purely external factors such as toponymy, landscape, climate, and celestial mechanics, as well as such factors as cultural languages and codes, influence "national character." In each case all influences are accepted and . . . lead to logically, absolutely unpredictable and usually absurd results. Why? Pietsukh argues that it is precisely because the "Russian soul" encompasses *absolutely all* possible and impossible influences of both culture and nature —and, we might add, it is therefore *chaotic,* according to Prigogine's definition of chaos as the realization of all of a system's possibilities simultaneously. "National character" is utterly lacking in any selectivity or the slightest immunity to these influences. The initial notion of "national character" as a historical constant becomes the complete "chaotization" and dehierarchization of any mythology of history, since all of them, regardless of the cause-and-effect relations that the particular mythology emphasizes, are deconstructed by the chaotic field of "national character," which transforms history into a consistently absurd notion, the only one capable of encompassing the fullness of being. It is "national character" that Pietsukh presents as the paradoxical chaotic mechanism for giving rise to an inevitably absurd metatext of history, one that is equally absurd in both the past and the present.

Moreover, the absurd effect arises at the expense of the *simultaneous* existence of the high cultural canon dictated by literature and the fantastic, grotesque repetitions of literary plots and conflicts. But where does this great literature come from? From the "rough draft" of normal absurdity—as its *mythology*. Thus history constantly plays itself out as the open-ended, paradoxical transition from order to the absurd, which is mythologized by literature as order and which gives rise to new absurdity. Moreover, it is specifically literature that becomes the teleological justification of historical absurdity. Polemicizing with the teleology of historical progress, Pietsukh proposes his own inverse teleology, which presents literature, or rather, literariness, as the "meaning of history." In Pietsukh's consistently absurd work, historical development takes place in changes not in the present or future but in the *past*; mythologized by history, the past is transformed from a "rough draft" into a "fair copy." If the absurdity of history abolishes the category of time (everything always take place in a disorderly "here and now"), then "natural literariness" directs time from the present to the past: The Central–Ermolaevo War exerts an influence on the epic tradition, but not the other way around. "National character" provides reliable isolation from any kind of "lessons of the past." It is no accident that for Pietsukh the voice of the narrator becomes an idiosyncratic pillar of stability; this voice is always registered in the present and always preserves a "common-sense" tone and cozy, old-fashioned style, no matter what he is writing about, whether it be the legendary past or the anecdotal present. This very "literariness" becomes the narrator's defense against chaos; an ironic defense, but a defense nonetheless. Pietsukh's narrator is not a character but rather a traditional literary function belonging to the space of literature; and he belongs to the "fair copy" rather than the "rough draft." It is the narrator's voice that delineates the boundary between the absurdity of life's "natural literariness" and the conventional order of mythologizing play with life.

Absurdity establishes a rupture with the unified logic of history: Causality loses its force. But the permanence of chaotic "national character" suggests a paradoxical logic (or *paralogy?*) based on absurdity. According to Pietsukh, history irrevocably unites order and entropy, which consequently are expressed in repetitions and unpredictability, in dynamism and inertia, in time and timelessness. Thus history takes on the characteristics of the rhizome, whose multiplicity is homogenous and whose fragmentary nature does not exclude wholeness or the capacity for regeneration from any point.

## The "Historical" Stories of Viktor Erofeyev: An Apotheosis of Particles

> *Having written my first essays on de Sade and Lev Shestov*
> *as long ago as the beginning of the seventies and having*
> *paid my dues to the literature of evil, I am nevertheless prob-*
> *ably closer to what may be called a "lickering aesthetics,"*
> *type of "negative capability" which I view as an attempt to*
> *escape the postmodern canon, and which combines sugges-*
> *tive, seditious invention with an alluring laying bare of the*
> *devices of any discourse.*
> —Viktor Erofeyev (1991: xxviii)

Viktor Erofeyev's short stories, like the fiction of Pietsukh, follow a "rhizomatic" model of history. His favorite narrative device is his idiosyncratic *skaz,* which binds together the locutions of different eras, weaving together paraphrases of classical texts with parodies of current *belles lettres,* superimposing naturalistic details on refined intertextual discourse. Moreover, in Erofeyev's work the clash of various languages of culture and history invariably leads not to synthesis, not to a universal metalanguage, but to a dissonance that saturates the entire text and displays a deliberate clumsiness and contempt for logic.

Extremely vivid examples of such multitemporal *skaz* can be found in "The Parakeet" and "Letter to Mother": They not only share a formal similarity (both are letters), but they can be seen as two parts of a single artistic project. Moreover, multitemporality here is not only a characteristic of the consciousness of the narrator but also a property of the chronotope. The speaker in the first story is a Russian torturer who belongs simultaneously to the era of the rack and to the era of pinching the scrotum "as a preventive measure" (Erofeyev 1990: 372) and who is fluent in the language of some kind of "medieval age" and highly contemporary "special" terminology. At the center of the other story, once again the main character and narrator is a Russian liberal living through some sort of generalized perestroika, which mixes civil-war detachments and Gorbachev's anti-alcohol campaign, the progressive thought of Alexander Herzen and "the idea of erecting a general monument to all the victims of our country's history" (Erofeyev 1993: 54), Orwell's *1984* and a loose paraphrase of a "very contemporary book" about dead souls (ibid., 52). These playful fusions, which can at times be found within the boundaries of a single phrase, work toward an image of history *without movement,* in which one time creeps into another but all times are subject to the same incontrovertible laws: the laws of the absurd.

But the essential difference between Viktor Erofeyev's stories and those of Pietsukh lies in the fact that, in Erofeyev, absurdity is expressed first and foremost *through the narrator's voice* (hence Erofeyev's devotion to *skaz*), while in Pietsukh's work the narrator is removed from the absurdity of history.

The protagonists of both "The Parakeet" and "Letter to Mother" are narrational Frankenstein's monsters, assembled from the bodies of their cultural ancestors. Each story's voice masks a certain archetypal discourse of the torturer and the liberal, refracted through the prism of Russian history and culture in a new way each time. In "Letter to Mother," the liberal consciousness is depicted as fundamentally open, one that is for this very reason eclectically oxymoronic and reliant on parodic quotations. It contains everything at once: a feeling for the people (" 'The proletariat,' said Zotov affectionately. 'You know, Viktor, it's a majestic thing!' " [Erofeyev 1993: 54]), an appeal to the people ("Mama, the people will need my book" [ibid., 50]), and the condescending disdain for the people ("the repentant savages" [ibid., 53]). Loyal ecstasy ("To the health of the liberator! May God help him! Amen!" [ibid.]) mixes with rebelliousness, as well as with rosy-cheeked, enthusiastic optimism and proud skepticism ("I don't believe it! I don't believe it! I don't believe it!" [ibid., 52]). There is no contradiction whatsoever between self-sacrifice and the "fashionably painted" automobile; the customary cautiousness and extreme romanticism ("not one step backward" [ibid., 51]). He finds himself in bed with the elderly "amazon," who turns out to be the spouse of a "loathsome man" who "had suddenly been thrown into the garbage dump of history" (ibid., 56), and he comforts himself by saying yet again, "We are building a new, new world. Nobodies will become somebodies!" (ibid.).

It is not abstract "national character" but rather a concrete voice (whose specificity is further strengthened by the fact that the narrator and the author share the same name) that absorbs various languages of culture that subsequently cancel each other out. But at the same time this voice accommodates the discourse of Russian liberalism, of Russian freethinkers. It accommodates but also deconstructs. Moreover, this deconstruction proves double-edged: Its target is both the intelligentsia's ideal of freedom and the concept of history perceived through the prism of this ideal (hence the story's references to Herzen, Dostoevsky, and other classics of Russian culture). In each case, the result is self-negation, the sign of "zero":

"Old man," said the artist, sad once again. "I've come to the conclusion that there was no Susanin."

"Then who lured the Poles?"

"Maybe there were no Poles, either," Zotov squinted. "There was no one. No one!" he suddenly shouted and, opening up his fist, showed me an absolutely empty palm." (Ibid., 55)

". . . the next night her husband arrived, he had been suddenly thrown onto the trash heap of history, he was a repulsive type, and she herself was a disgusting broad, to hell with both of them! To hell with them! And us? We'll build the new, new world, he who was nothing will become everything." (Ibid., 56)

The mentality represented by the narrator of "The Parakeet" (the torturer, who embodies the discourse of absolute power) is diametrically opposed to liberalism, and yet it is even more thoroughly saturated with oxymorons. But if the liberal's oxymorons are the consequence of his full openness to the outside, then the oxymorons of the torturer in "The Parakeet" are the consequence of his total isolation. Erofeyev's torturer is entirely certain of his dignity and high professionalism: "We tormented and tortured your son, Yermolai Spiridonovich, we couldn't have done otherwise, we've not been taught any other way" (Erofeyev 1990: 372). He is convinced of his own profound knowledge of people and the unconditional social usefulness of his trade; hence the patronizing and condescending tone of his letter to the father of the tortured boy. The most important thing for him is his firm knowledge of the *norm*. With wise, fatherly experience, the torturer submits his moral judgments:

I, thank God, know my business, I earn my bread, and therefore I have an idea of how our kind of people scream on the rack and how those who aren't our kind do. One of ours would never call me a barbarian, because he doesn't think that way, but your scoundrel admitted that he did. He behaved, I regret to inform you, rather cowardly. (Ibid., 373)

But at the same time, I like the humble sufferers, the ones who only fart and quack when they're on the rack, I respect them, and I wouldn't even swap a sufferer like that for a hundred Englishmen, because torture and suffering are a thing pleasing unto God, and what's an Englishman?—shit and nothing more! (Ibid., 375)

At this point (or was it, perhaps, earlier) we tore off his knackers to teach him not to shoot his mouth off like that about his father for no good reason, tore them off and tossed them right to the dogs: let them have a little treat . . . (Ibid.)

And all of the torturer's work, whose terrifying details lend a special persuasiveness to these edifying speeches, is dictated by the imperative to protect the norm from "alien" influences. He sees his main social and personal duty as nipping potential violations of the Norm in the bud, finding the symbol hidden behind any nontrivial action, such as forcing a dead parakeet to take "unnatural flight":

> Well, what if all of a sudden, contrary to our expectations, it up and actually was resurrected? In what terms would we explain this particular circumstance to our countrymen, so trusting in our best intentions? I become lost in fatal conjecture . . .
> WOULDN'T WE BE FINE FOOLS! (Ibid., 368–69)

Or course, such logic presupposes the potential guilt of everyone, without exception; even a "three-year-old sniveler" is under suspicion, the "villain still does not talk, or pretends not to" (ibid., 370). Only the torturer himself is above suspicion; he bears the heavy burden of responsibility to the Norms of the people's life. It is precisely the torturer's conviction of the existence of an unshakable order of things that also serves as the justification for his atrocities. As Serafima Roll argues, the main crime turns out to be "an attempt to inquire into the natural order of things" (Roll n.d.: 12)—for the attempt to resurrect a dead parakeet the hapless boy Yermolai Spiridonovich endures terrible tortures culminating in his gruesome death, all of which is described in the torturer's letter to the boy's father.

The combination of sadism and the unwavering attaching to maintaining the "norm" is not the only oxymoron. The very transformation of the *category* of the norm itself is paradoxical. What matters here is not even the executioner's musings on "mankind's great passion for torture" (Erofeyev 1990: 374) or how "a man will sell out anyone and anything, you just have to approach him slowly, don't scare him—just give him time!" (ibid., 375). Far more important is the stylistics of *skaz*. Thus the narrator's "terminology" of torture and Soviet bureaucratic clichés are easily transformed into the lexicon and style of folk poetics:

> And I struck him, your brown-eyed boy, right in the teeth with all my soul, because I'd grown weary, I took preventive measures, but my fist . . . well, you, Yermolaich, know. And so his teeth spattering in various directions, *just like pearls from a broken string—they spattered and tumbled.*" (Ibid., 372; emphasis added)

> When Yermolai Spiridonovich and I came to share that common opinion, we embraced in our joy: *a job well done, I say, is its own reward, bring us, my stalwarts, wine and viands, we shall make merry! And my stalwarts bring*

*us white salmon, suckling pigs and lambs, sundry soufflés and a wine that has the playful name, Madonna's Milk. We ate and then shot the breeze."* (Ibid., 375–76; emphasis added)

There is nothing forced about the conflation of the rack and the poetics of folklore; the transitions are entirely organic—and this is the most terrifying thing of all. If for Pietsukh the language of cultural symbols is a refined version of the absurdity of history, then Erofeyev reveals that what appears to be the norm, inculcated both in culture and in history, is open to any pathology, any atrocity. Not only that, but the dogged assertion of the norm (cultural or otherwise; the torturer constantly invokes the authority of "world culture") becomes the triumph of pathology and torture.

The constant paradoxes and dissonance of both "The Parakeet" and "Letter to Mother" determine not only the narrative structure but something broader: the representation of the (meta)historical discourses of the Russian mentality, which remain constant in time. *Skaz,* which is common to so many of Erofeyev's stories (such as "Life with an Idiot," "Berdyaev," "Death and the Maiden," "How We Cut the Frenchman's Throat"), forms the core of his poetics. Here one might use Foucault's term, the "decentralization of the subject": The voice of the narrator, when expressed through multicultural and multihistorical *skaz,* does not actually belong to the narrator as a character anymore; it is only the projection of multiple and multidimensional historical and cultural discourses. But the clash of these discourses and the fragments of cultural codes gives way to a *figure of emptiness* that swallows up the subject, the discourses, cultural codes, and history itself as the aggregate of all those factors. Moreover, it does not matter which of the discourses is accepted as a system of reading: the discourse of power or powerlessness, freedom or violation, liberalism or the ideology of the torturer. The result remains the same. For Erofeyev, the synonym of this figure of emptiness is the theme of death and/or insanity. It is death that turns out to be the moment of *unity* of torturer and victim in "The Parakeet":

"Well, Godspeed!" I said, and I led him by the arm to the ledge of the belfry. "Fly, Yermolushka! Fly, my pigeon!" Spreading his arms out to form a cross, he stepped into the emptiness. For just a minute I was almost seized by the torment of doubt: what if he were to ascend like a turquoise parakeet, to the demons' delight? With a certain disquiet I leaned over the railing and glanced below. Thank God! Smashed!" (Erofeyev 1990: 376)

In "Death and the Maiden," we have the monologue of a man who has recognized death as the magnificent mystery of *unity* and who therefore commits a senseless murder for the sake of existential self-actualization.

Murder is presented by the narrator-protagonist as "proof of the boundless possibilities of our reason, which has become the master of the most implacable and destructive force" (Erofeyev 1993: 131), "transforming blind chance into the triumph of will and handicrafts" (ibid.). It is worth noting that the hero's passion for death is inseparable from his strong desire for a woman—the murdered girlfriend. Comprehension of death once again turns out to be essential for living life to the fullest.[2]

Yet there, as in his other stories, Erofeyev contextualizes the discourse of his narrator. The narrator's reflections on death as a unique performance ("a strong feeling of genre" [ibid.]) is offset by apparently "alien," "healthy" opinions: "the most fashionable murder of the season" (ibid., 129), "the Komsomol burial service . . . after the service a young priest bursting with health spoke of the ties between science and religion" (ibid., 133). The narrator's speech is based on oxymoronic combinations of refinement and naturalistic vulgarity, but his victim speaks exactly the same language. This victim belongs to the same circle, in which "both foul language and 'Nabokov' are described as 'okay' " (ibid.). But the "unattainable example of Stalin's sense of humor" (ibid., 131)—the phrase "love conquers death," which runs through the entire story as a leitmotif—ultimately imparts a *discursive significance* to the protagonist's monologue.

Thus his imagined speech at the graveside of the girl he killed is begun with the famous words "Brothers and sisters!" (ibid., 136)—these are the very same words with which Stalin began his speech to the Soviet people after the Nazis invaded the USSR. Behind the protagonist's pathology we see the norm of Russian history, which invariably proves that love (for the tyrant, for power, for the idea) really does conquer death. The loss of a sense of *existential limits* as the norm of historical being, the identification of death with effective spectacle, and, in the final analysis, the transformation of death into a game: Here we find those conditions thanks to which the narrator attains unity with his beloved, with society, with history. This is an epic situation, but one that has been turned inside out: Here the blurring of ontological boundaries and concomitant values becomes the precondition for epic unity: "We're racing along the outlying road. The noise of the forest. And everything is good. Stalin is right. Gorky is right. We are all right. 'Man' has a proud ring about it. Love conquers death" (ibid., 137).

By analogy, the murder of the wife in "Life with an Idiot" ultimately identifies the intellectual narrator with the idiot (who is also a rapist, a murderer, a lover, and Lenin). The story begins with the narrator's punishment: He must choose a madman from a mental institution and live with him for a fixed period of time. One of the mental patients looks remarkably like the narrator himself, but he is rejected in favor of Volodya, the "idiot" of the story's title. By the end of "Life with an Idiot," the narrator has himself been committed to that very asylum and realizes that the man he rejected in the beginning was actually he. Erofeyev consciously provokes the reader's disgust and confusion. But the paradox of his fiction is that he completes the collapse of the "grand narratives" of Soviet culture, at times in literally nauseating detail, demonstrating the process in which words that once held power are literally transformed into excrement and carrion.[3]

In such a model of the world, the position of the martyr turns out to be the only reliable one. But typically for Erofeyev, this role, as a rule, is given to the child, who traditionally embodies the infinite renewal of life. Like Yermolai Spiridonych from "The Parakeet," and the boy from the story "Galoshes," these characters are at great pains to adapt to the conditions of the lethal game, and they seek understanding ("He kept trying to help me to understand, he aided himself, you see, with his little hand" ["The Parakeet," Erofeyev 1990: 369]). They gullibly accept historical norms and imitate them: "Each holiday, the boy imitated the street and weighed out the decorations: stars, slogans, portraits of the leaders; and he led a parade of tin soldiers and carved chess figures on the bed" ("Galoshes," Erofeyev 1993: 173). But even the everyday road from home to school demonstrates alienation from life; it becomes a procession around the circles of hell. "Galoshes" begins with the scene of the boy's death ("The boy feverishly grabbed hold of the fire escape. He was afraid of climbing higher, and as for going down, he was afraid of the stones. The third-grader stood below and threw rocks at him. One rock hit his back, the other hit his shoulder, the third, finally, ended up in the back of his head. He shouted weakly and flew down, back first" [ibid., 172]). Then come exile ("Grandma shoved the boy out the door" [ibid., 173]), spitting ("the third-grader magnanimously spat in his face" [ibid., 174]), and ridicule. Moreover, as he depicts the class as it laughs at the boy, squealing and barking, the author suddenly changes angles, which radically expands the temporal and spatial boundaries of this particular scene:

> They laughed: Gorianova, who went away on a two-year business trip with her husband; the fidgety Artsybashev would subsequently become a rather famous man of letters and join the writers' union. . . . Sokina, with her skinny legs, laughed, but the red-headed fool Trunina was lucky; her husband was a member of the Central Committee (true, of the Komsomol). . . . Yudina would outlive them all: on her ninetieth birthday, she would walk into the communal kitchen in a colorful bathing suit. The shocked neighbors would burst into applause. . . . Shchapov the warrant officer, who received a concussion in the colonial campaign, Chemodanov the karate expert, and Wagner, breastless Wagner, crowed with all their might. Baklazhanova, Mukhanov, and Klyshko laughed their way into the passageway, like some sort of fruit. (Ibid., 1993: 176)[4]

This infinitely expanding image of the cruelly laughing class is life itself, in its motley diversity. And the child in this scene—because of his suffering—looks like a saint (the teacher notices a halo around his head). The target of universal malice, he gains a unique perspective from which he can see the future lives of his laughing classmates.

Here life's continuity is based on the mythological paradigm of sacrifice, which lies beneath the oxymorons of plot and style in Erofeyev's stories. But, as in *Moscow to the End of the Line,* sacrifice does not serve as a renewal of being and does not presuppose resurrection. The cyclical order of myth is replaced by a structure that once again resembles the "dissipative orders," which, as specialists in self-organizing chaos assert, "can survive only by remaining open to a flowing matter and energy exchange with the environment. In fact, matter and energy literally flow through it and form it, like the river water through the vortex. . . . The structure is *stabilized* by its flowing. It is stable but only relatively—relative to the constant flow required to maintain its shape" (Briggs and Peat 1984: 169). One can apply this idea to Erofeyev's representation of history, with the sole stipulation that *here fluidity is paradoxically expressed in the endless self-destruction and self-negation of all the constituent elements of the system, but only by performing this function does the system continue to exist.*

In the fiction of Pietsukh and Erofeyev, history certainly lacks the aura of "objectivity." It is relative and pathological, born of cultural myths and the anecdotes that make a mockery of them. It is senseless and infinite, self-destructive and eternal. Nevertheless, in the works of these authors, the world of history is "already made"; the hero only participates in it while submitting to the logic of the game of history, the logic of a demythologizing reproduction of the mythology of history and culture.

On the other hand, the very nature of postmodernist playfulness thoroughly undermines such a fundamental category of history as *time.* In both Pietsukh and Erofeyev, history becomes timelessness, which is explained by the fact that the interactions of heterogeneous cultural languages and symbols in their works are expressed through the motifs of destruction, loss of meaning, and death. The perception of history *as emptiness filled with heterogeneous ideas of history* quite logically becomes the next step in the development of the historical consciousness of Russian postmodernism.[5] These ideas are also of a mythological cast, but they are myths that are aware of their status as creations, of their literary (rather than divine) origins. We have the opportunity to see how these myths are composed before our very eyes, *in order that they become real as soon as possible.* Moreover, if humor predominates in the works of Pietsukh and Erofeyev, in the form of parodic periphrases of various quotations, they are surprisingly earnest in their approach to history as a literary artifact. The difference, apparently, is a consequence of an altered relationship between the author and the historical character. Each occupies an opposing position in relation to history: The character looks at history from within; the author looks from without, thereby creating the distance necessary for the ironic deconstruction of "historical consciousness." In this sense, Pietsukh's author-narrator, who directly comments on his characters' actions, and Erofeyev's extra-textual author, who hides behind the *skaz* narrator, have much in common: The deliberately literary style of Pietsukh's narrator creates the essential ironic distance no less effectively than the conspicuous absence of an authorial voice in Erofeyev's stories. When the authorial voice is not only not hidden but also pointedly identical to that of historical characters, then we have a new situation in which the author locates himself within the historical context and takes part in its creation, just like the characters. In this case the play with mythologies of history cannot be separated from metafictional devices: Metafiction becomes metahistory. The literature of the past decade gives us a number of striking examples of this phenomenon, such as Mikhail Kuraev's *Captain Dikstein*, Mark Kharitonov's *Lines of Fate* (winner of the first Russian Booker Prize in 1992), Vladimir Sharov's *Rehearsals* and *Before and During*, Anatoly Korolyov's *Gogol's Head*, Alexei Slapovsky's *The First Second Coming*, Alexander Kabakov's *The Composer* [Sochinitel'], Mikhail Shishkin's *The Same Night Awaits Everyone*, and Viktor Pelevin's *Chapaev and Void*. Yet the postmodern paradigm by no means applies to all of these works. Perhaps this very interpretive strategy is located on the periphery of postmodernism. But what new perspective does it bring to the postmodern conception of history?

# Sasha Sokolov (1985): Self-Portrait on a Timeless Background

*In the end, everything is a gag.*

—Charlie Chaplin

To answer this question, let us turn to Sasha Sokolov's novel *Astrophobia* (*Palisandriia* 1985), which is perhaps the most original and thorough Russian example of what Linda Hutcheon calls "historiographic metafiction." Although this novel appeared a few years before the works discussed above, it can be read as an idiosyncratic summation of the end of the "New

Wave." D. Barton Johnson argues that, in *Astrophobia,* Sokolov wanted to create "his own inverted *Lolita:* Nabokovian nympholepsy superseded by Sokolovian gerontophilia. He dreamed of creating a new erotic lexicon. The other [intention—M.L.] was 'to write a novel that would end the novel as a genre.' Parody was the key: parody of the numerous subliterary genres that flood the mass market—the political thriller, the adventure tale, the pornographic novel" (Johnson 1987: 217). Perhaps it would be appropriate to say that Sokolov is looking back at Nabokov's *Lolita* rather than reacting against it; after all, in Russian literature it was Nabokov who first parodied mass culture in all its genres; moreover, the author of *Lolita* made his parody the most important element of a new, postmodern conception of culture. How does this type of parody change in Sokolov's novel? And why not follow Barton Johnson's example and look at *Astrophobia* against the backdrop of *Lolita*? Such an approach would enhance our understanding of the evolution of Russian postmodern fiction.

As in Nabokov's novel, Sokolov surrenders all the prerogatives of authorial power to an "unreliable narrator"—here, the Kremlin Orphan and subsequent ruler of Russia, Palisander Dalberg, who is writing his memoirs for a grateful posterity. Neither the parodic epigraph ("To Whom It May Concern"—in English in the original text) nor the foreword of the Biographer, written in 2757, is incompatible with the unmistakable style of Palisander himself. As a matter of principle, Sokolov erases the boundaries of the autobiographical character-narrator's worldview: It is, by definition, universal from the very start. Thus the very first pages of this quasi autobiography establish the contradiction between the author as powerful emissary from the magic space of language and the author as a character living in concrete space and time.

If Nabokov's Humbert tries to subordinate reality to aesthetics, Sokolov's Palisander is himself something of an artifact. First, there is his fantastic genealogy: He traces his ancestry to "a German of Georgian descent" (Sokolov 1989: 38) who beheaded his beloved mother-in-law, Marie Stewart, "thereby assuming a place of pride and envy among the Progressive Sons-in-Law of the Renaissance" (ibid.); he is the grand-nephew of Lavrenty Beria, and he grew up in the arms of Stalin, Andropov, and Brezhnev. Palisander is mentioned in the prophecies of Nostradamus (the Kremlin will collapse if the last of the Dalbergs perishes). His appearance is no less exotic than his lineage: He has seven fingers on each hand, and his fingers are so thick that they don't fit into a telephone dial. He is bald from birth ("my inherited alopecia had kept and would keep me from growing so much as a hair, gray or otherwise, on my body" [ibid., 268]) and is of a dwarfish stature. Later it is revealed that he is a hermaphrodite who has spent his entire life in "splash-baths" (ibid., 56 and passim) filled with dirt, who literally hides his face under numerous masks and whose sexual potency exceeds even the highest expectations. Palisander suffers from astrophobia, a fear of the stars; he is gifted with every possible talent and knows an unbelievable number of languages (including Etruscan and Chuvash); his confidantes include not only Kremlin leaders and their decrepit wives but also Samuel Beckett, Solzhenitsyn (a.k.a. Soloukhin), Voldemar (Vladimir) Vysotsky, King Juan Carlos of Spain, Muamar Qadafi, Igor Stravinsky, Carl Gustav Jung, and even the Ayatollah Khomeini's runaway wife, with the Esenin-like name Shaganeǒ (legless). Unlike Humbert, who is in constant conflict with his mass cultural surroundings, this modernist monster/superhero is perfectly at home in this quasi-historical setting, which is itself the main subject of Palisander's memoirs.

Sokolov uses Palisander to model an *idyllic simulacrum* of Soviet history. The idyllic principle runs through the entire tradition of Russian autobiography, from Aksakov to Nabokov; the portrayal of childhood in idyllic tones is completely canonical. But the combination of this tradition with the topos of bloody Soviet history yields an unexpected aesthetic effect. Sokolov endows the Kremlin with a mythological continuity: Except for Beria, who hangs himself on the hands of the Spassky Tower clock, no one really dies in this novel. It turns out that even the last tsar lives in the Kremlin under the name of Nikolai Aleksandrovich Bulganin (and is a member of Stalin's Politburo, no less). And all the details of Kremlin life— from childhood games to the Novodevichy Monastery, which has been transformed into a government House of Massage, from the description of the verse improvisation competition in the Kremlin's solemn Georgievsky Hall to the touching image of Andropov in a cap—bear witness to the idyllic eternity of Soviet history. Bakhtin notes:

> Idyllic life and its events are inseparable from this concrete spatial corner where the fathers and grandfathers lived and where one's children and their children will live. . . . The unity of life of generations (in general, the life of men) in an idyll is in most instances primarily defined by the *unity of place*, by the age-rooting of the life of generations to a single place, from which this life, in all its events, is inseparable. The unity of place in the life of generations weakens and renders less distinct all the temporal boundaries between individual lives and between various phases of one and the same life. The unity of place brings together and fuses the cradle and the grave. . . childhood and old age. (Bakhtin 1981: 225)

This characteristic of the idyllic chronotope explains not only the deliberate anachronisms of Palisander's autobiography but also the fact that until his departure from the Kremlin he is completely unaware that he is "unsuitably—inappropriately—unacceptably—and—above all—irreparably on in years" (Sokolov 1989: 301), portraying himself as a youth of eighteen years (blurring the boundaries between "various phases of one and the same life"). Even Palisander's gerontophilia is the ultimate expression of the conquest of generational boundaries, the maximum (and perhaps excessive) closeness between youth and age. Yet as soon as Palisander leaves the Kremlin, his sexuality leads to persecution and debasement.

This is not just an idyll but the simulacrum of an idyll. Sokolov emphasizes the simulated character of this idyllic world primarily through style. And here, too, we see the essential difference between *Astrophobia* and *Lolita*. If *Lolita* represents the complicated, dramatic clash between modernist and mass-cultural codes, then *Astrophobia,* as Alexander Zholkovsky has argued, does something entirely different:

> [*Astrophobia*'s] dominant can be defined as a post-modernist repudiation of the ideological partisanship of the Soviet era in favor of an all-inclusive aestheticism. Hence Sokolov's mock remythologization of the Kremlin *and* of Silver Age decadence *and* of dissident and émigré literary sensibility, in particular its interest in supermen and graphomaniacs. Since Palisander's polymorphism is an emblematic embodiment of this eclectic posture, one may seek a key to the stylistic secrets of the novel in the way the panoply of discourses are successfully fused into a linguistic vehicle for the new aggregate self. (Zholkovsky 1987: 380)

Yet in Sokolov's novel, there is nothing even remotely resembling a conflict between these codes: They idyllically blend together into a semi-fantastic, semi-parodic style, one that is strikingly refined. One need look at only a few examples of this stylistic playfulness in order to feel how the novel was written:

> Meanwhile, yours truly, draped in a billowy chlamyd, made his way along the fire-wall path to the Kremlin's Torture Clinic with a pinch of his feces (borne in a matchbox by his nanny Agrippa) for analysis, or on an errand for the good of the arts, among which he always favored sculpture (see my personal entries in the ledgers of Madame Tussaud's and other such establishments). (Sokolov 1989: 83)

> I have a heightened sense of harmony and rhythm and an excellent ear. "I say, old man," Stravinsky once said to me, "you're a perfect pitcher!" (The occasion was a benefit in his honor, and I had just taken childish delight in firing back the a-sharp of a Prokofyevian tuning spoon that had fallen to the floor, a victim of Rostropovian obscurantism. (Ibid., 40)

> I requested some modeling clay and plaster of Paris and indulged in a little sculpting not far from the barracks. If I soon captured the imagination of the

sailor lads, it was not so much for my polyfigural forms as for their red-blooded contents. I gave them all away as soon as I finished them. There is nothing more rewarding to an artist than to see the calloused hands of a simple soldier quivering with desire to touch his work. (Ibid., 209)

> The Locum Tenens [Leonid Brezhnev] and his wife made believe they did not recognize me [after the assassination], but I am not one to bear a grudge and waved something at them whenever we met. (Ibid., 273)

The most profound difference between this stylistic scale and the inner dialogism of Humbert's confession, or the ambivalent juxtapositions in Venichka Erofeev's narrative, consists of the basic *lack of conflict* between the stylistically incompatible layers of Sokolov's novel. In *Astrophobia* everything is united—and this *in-different* unity is also aesthetically flaw-less. [holkovsky rightly compares the novel's stylistics with prose poetry. But it must be emphasized that the variety of styles here does not result in a multiplicity of voices; indifference equalizes all codes within one essen-tially monological stream. The artistic philosophy of the self in *Astrophobia* is the direct result of the novel's style.

One of the recurring motifs of *Astrophobia,* and of postmodernist fiction in general, is the motif of time, or rather its disappearance. Timelessness sets in immediately after Uncle Beria hangs himself on the clock hands. In addition, all the important Kremlin personages belong to a secret society of watchmakers, while Palisander himself, after becoming tsar, acquires the title "Your Eternity." Certainly, this timelessness comes as a bit of a shock: "Well, listen, then. The day before yesterday at sixteen minutes to nine an anachrony [*bezvremen'e*] began, a time to dare and a time to create" (ibid., 68), announces Andropov at the very beginning of the novel. Palisander accepts this formulation implicitly, and, "daring and creating," he puts his own personal spin on the notion of timelessness.

Throughout the book, Palisander's slogan (which he allegedly borrowed from Berdy Kerbabaev, his coworker at the government House of Massage) is "There is no death!" (ibid., 157 and passim). But there is no death precisely because there is no time. We find indirect evidence of the connec-tion between the two motifs in the denouement of the novel: As soon as Palisander comes to Russia to announce the end of timelessness, the novel itself quickly ends, but the epilogue begins with the words "Life broke off. It broke off tastelessly and slowly, like a trashy novel that closes with the magniloquent death of its hero" (ibid., 383). The epilogue is dedicated to describing the process of death. On the other hand, Palisander constantly recalls his many incarnations, and there is no death for him because he lives eternally, changing only his appearance. But the theme of incarnation is realized in the plot through the condition of "already was" *(uzhe bylo—déjà vu),* a state that Palisander experiences repeatedly:

> [T]he time will come when all the recreated *déjà-vus* and all their variations will merge beyond perspective in a single *déjà-vu.* And I shall be unable to determine in which of my beings I am as I run now, at this moment, and what this moment is, what this someone is doing here, and who this someone is, that is, the being behind the—if you will excuse the expression—letter I. To be honest, I am unable to come to grips with it even now, yet I go on running." (Ibid., 345)

But how do all these instances of "already was" differ from the hero's timeless recollections about the future? The narrator makes no secret about equating these concepts; indeed, he also equates them to the narrative style itself: "Anachrony is harmful, disastrous. It eats away at the structure of a narrative, robbing it of its clarity, its very identity. Like Palisander we began to wonder in which of his incarnations all this occurs" (ibid., 347). In fact, in *Astrophobia* timelessness (anachrony) and eternity act as synonyms, and the very style that smoothes over the contradictions between starkly contrasting elements itself embodies the image of anachronic eternity (*bezvremennaia vechnost'*) that consists of undifferentiated instances of "already was."

The plot of the novel also provides the very same model of eternity. In the course of his life, Palisander manages to reconcile polar opposites even as his transformations take on an increasingly universal character: The privileged Kremlin orphan becomes a dissident and makes an attempt on the life of the "Locum Tenens" Brezhnev; the sexual outlaw becomes a prostitute; the youth is also an old man; finally, this "man's man" turns into an androgyne and starts to refer to himself as "it" *(ono).* Yet here we have the same mechanism as that of the style of the novel and the image of eternity/timelessness: The erasure of differences between polar opposites devalues and depletes both poles. In the final analysis, existence becomes indistinguishable from nonexistence: Both of them are equally simulated. As Palisander himself confesses in the final chapters: "Do not weep for me, O Russia, do not weep. For thou art no more. I am no more. We are gone. We have crossed over. We have fallen off . . . Where's your country? . . . 'Forget her,' an inner voice responded, 'forget her Name. Your country is Chaos'" (ibid., 373, 380). We already know that the transition from simulation to chaos is completely natural for postmodernism. But Sokolov goes one step further, identifying chaos with the monotonous eternity of timelessness, an image that, in turn, is an inextricable component of the novel's style. Moreover, the stylistic perfection of *Astrophobia* presents a new take on chaos:

chaos becomes *pleasant.* One might say that Palisander, the novel's narrator and quasi author, approaches chaos as he would a warm mud bath, taking it with undisguised pleasure.

It is important to note that the artistic model of the world in *Astrophobia* is *inert,* since all the transformations that occur change nothing: All conditions are equally simulative. The absence of time is a metaphor for the impossibility of movement. In his commentary to *Astrophobia,* "Palissander —c'est moi?" (Sokolov 1992: 264–68), Sokolov rather insistently speaks of his lost taste for plot, although in this novel (if we compare it, for example, with *Between Dog and Wolf*) not only is the overarching plot much more distinct, but it even has a completely identifiable story line. However, Sokolov appears to be correct: Both the overall plot and the narrative line in *Astrophobia* are a fake, since in the gelatinous eternity of *déjà vu* nothing can happen.

The stylistic play in *Astrophobia* finally turns into a *mythological perspective:* a system of stylistic devices directly modeling absolute eternity. Here those characteristics which Palisander gives himself as fictitious author and consequently as the source of this stylistic play are also important: "[T]he whole world from my point of view—my vantage point, if you will—is a motley medley, the universe frowzy and diffuse" (ibid., 114); "You were the ideal lover for the elderly—death" (ibid., 124). Such phrases merely emphasize that which is embodied in the whole architectonics of the novel. Palisander is an inextricable part of the world that he is describing, and therefore he becomes the personification of mythological chaos, its voice. Zholkovsky sees clear links between *Astrophobia* and the myth of Narcissus (1994: 226–29), yet here we find a more complex form of mythology, one that turns the archetypes of classical myths inside out. The mythological consciousness knows no boundaries between subject and object. As Olga Freidenberg put it, in the world of myth, "[e]ven an enemy is a friend, is me myself; even death is immortality" (Freidenberg 1936: 115). And as if to prove Freidenberg right, Palisander argues that Majorette, the woman who sadistically tortures him, is Palisander himself. Yet a completely different logic is at work here nonetheless. In myth, man is a part of the universal cycle of life–death–birth; he is an integral part of the world, a participant in its highest natural laws. But the eternity of *Astrophobia* rejects the category of natural laws; this is an eternity of uniform repetitions, an eternity of timelessness, an eternity of *déjà vu,* an eternity of the inert idyll of simulacra, in which there is no difference between executioner and victim, male and female, young and old, life and death. It is precisely because of this uniformity and lack of boundaries that Palisander's memoirs create a model of eternity with such ease, and in the final analysis his "I" really is the whole universe. Nothing in this novel goes beyond this limit, nor can it. This worldview might best be called *narcissistic mythologism.* Such a worldview is more closely tied to modernism and the avant-garde than to postmodernism proper. The protagonist, who has all the preroga- tives of the author's position, achieves the maximum degree of modernist freedom: His monologic consciousness swallows up the universe with- out a trace. But this freedom completely cancels itself out. In the uniform eternity of *déjà vu,* there can be no independent acts: Everything has al- ready happened—and, as we have already seen, each phenomenon easily becomes its opposite. No wonder Palisander, who has built his own individ- ual eternity, admits defeat in the novel's epilogue:

> You were so carried away that at times you imagined the text you were reading exempt from the time warps and whirlpools of relativity. You were mistaken. Although literature has till now been merely a timid exercise, a clumsy form of hieroglyphics, a tribute to human boorishness and savagery, nothing is exempt: every word of mine shall be lost. . . . And—listen closely, now!—everything that happened, happened in vain. The abyss yawned, life cracked, and slowly it broke off. (Sokolov 1989: 261)

Moreover, the epilogue, which is formally ascribed to the hero, stands out against the general background by virtue of its style, while the words "The author threw up" (ibid., 384) refer not only to Palisander but also to the impersonal author-creator. For behind every change in Palisander's stylistic tone hides a distinct authorial position. Palisander exhaustively subjects each of these positions to *reductio ad absurdum*: the position of eyewitness- memoirist and historical chronicler, of pornographer and epic author, of dispassionate anthropologist and muckraker. It should come as no surprise that Sokolov intended "to write a novel that could end the novel as a genre" (Johnson 1987: 27). To some degree, he succeeded: All the possible autho- rial positions are imprinted in *Astrophobia* through style, and the difference among them, as well as the value of each of them, is reduced to zero. They all represent the same narcissistic myth, and they all embody the *"déjà vu"* model of eternity: the endless repetition of events, devalorizing time itself. By the end of the novel, the author-creator is left with nothing; even deconstructive play with various languages of culture is no longer an option. Play presupposes freedom, but freedom does not exist without the possibility of *changes*—a possibility excluded in the narcissistic myth of *Astrophobia.*

Thus *Astrophobia* occupies a special point in the development of Russian postmodernism: the point where postmodernist play with mythologies of history crosses over into Sots-Art.

# 9

# Context: Mythologies of the Absurd

Sots-Art is such a typical example of Russian postmodernism that it is often *mistaken* for Russian postmodernism; that is, the part is substituted for the whole, and confusion results. It is telling that the Sots-Artists themselves prefer to be called conceptualists, accenting the fact that they work not only with Soviet-Socialist language but with the language of every conceivable ideology. Sots-Art originated in painting (Vitaly Komar and Alexander Melamid, Ilya Kabakov, Erik Bulatov, Grisha Bruskin) and in poetry (Dmitri Prigov, Timur Kibirov, and others); by contrast, its role in prose has been rather limited. In essence, the only true Sots-Art fiction writer is Vladimir Sorokin, although elements of Sots-Art poetics play an important role in the works of Yevgeny Popov, Zufar Gareev (*Park*), Anatoly Gavrilov, Arkady Bartov, and Viktor Pelevin (*The Life of Insects*) and in Sasha Sokolov's *Astrophobia*.

The creators of Sots-Art are consciously oriented toward working with a particular cultural context. However, this context in and of itself is distinct from the contexts of the mythology of creation or history with which other Russian postmodernists work, such as Tatyana Tolstaya, Viktor Erofeyev, or the author of *Astrophobia*. The main context for this aesthetic is clearly Socialist Realism: The conceptualists first immerse themselves in official Soviet culture, only much later expanding their scope to any politicized mythology, any authoritarian idea (although, as a rule, even the most abstract idea is marked by these authors with the stamp of "Soviet-ness" [*sovkovost'*]—see, for example, Prigov's cycle *Moscow and the Muscovites*).

There are several approaches to understanding the Sots-Art play with Socialist Realist myths and languages, structures and motifs. Mikhail Epstein, who was the first critic to analyze Sots-Art (conceptualism), proposes a fundamentally avant-garde interpretation. In his opinion conceptualism uses a device that is the opposite of "defamiliarization" (*ostranenie*), the formalist notion that forces the reader to look at a familiar object as though seeing it for the first time; according to Epstein, the conceptualists strive for the automization of perception, the conscious stereotyping of entire ideologies, an effort that is directed toward an effect similar to "apophatic theodicy":

> A humbling of speech, a deflation of meaning—these are ways of pointing to another, silent reality for which there are no and can be no words. . . . Nihil-

ism affirms the strength, pride, truth of negation. Conceptualism drapes negation in the tattered rags of mediocrity and senselessness. Nihilism *affirms
negation*. Conceptualism negates affirmation. (Epstein 1995a: 65)

In this interpretation, Sots-Art is simply one of many variants of conceptualism as the latest avant-garde trend, distinguished only by the fact that out
of all ideologies it chooses to play with Socialist Realism.

Boris Groys views Socialist Realism as an extreme expression of avant-
garde utopianism and sees in Sots-Art not the continuation of the avant-garde
impulse but rather its "removal." Thus, for example, in analyzing the poetics
of Komar and Melamid he demonstrates that they not only do not "unmask"
the Stalinist myth but rather "remythologize" it, penetrating through the
Socialist Realist structure into the "Soviet unconscious," where Soviet myths
fall into an associative network that unites them with other mythologies:

> Komar and Melamid therefore regard their "Sots-Art" not as a simple
> parody of Socialist Realism, but as the discovery within themselves of a
> universal element, a collective component that unites them with others, an
> amalgam of individual and world history. . . . Using the devices of Stalin-
> ist indoctrination, they have attempted to demonstrate the similarity of
> this myth to those of both the present and the past in order to reconstruct
> the single mythological network in which the modern consciousness func-
> tions. (Groys 1992: 93, 95)

The avant-garde claim to express the inexpressible, to realize the utopian
project, to overcome the power of tradition is inverted by the return of that
very avant-garde project to the context of world mythologies and eternal
archetypes, that is, a return to the most traditional of traditions. According
to Groys, the result of this turnabout is "to regard with indifference such
questions as whether or not the thinking of the individual can be completely
manipulated . . . whether this thinking is authentic, whether there is any
distinction between a simulacrum and reality, and so on" (ibid., 110). This
state he characterizes as "postutopian."

Yevgeny Dobrenko has a different conception of Sots-Art. He suggests
that it be understood as the artificial mythologizing of the Socialist Realist
myth, the revelation of the device that liberates consciousness from the
power of the primary myth and allows one to see in it only language; it is not
a universal and monopolistic incarnation of truth but one of many systems of
signs: "[T]he removal of the second, mythical, meaning is possible only by
mythologizing the myth itself . . . the target of this *other* culture is not so
much the myths and mirages as the entire myth-producing system itself"
(Dobrenko 1990: 181, 183). Vyacheslav Kuritsyn disagrees, arguing that

Sots-Art does not produce a new myth . . . but reveals what stood behind the sign, before the sign: in concrete terms, it reveals the schemes of thought, the models of world creation, the matrices of existence that we cannot reasonably judge "from inside" Socialist Realism. Sots-Art remains in the process and is itself a process for realizing these schemes and models. It looks at them from the outside and reveals their mechanism. (Kuritsyn 1992b: 80)

According to Kuritsyn, Sots-Art is characterized by a dual modality—"there are those who speak the text 'from the text' and those who observe from the sidelines and write the text 'from the outside' "—which determines the most important aesthetic effect of Sots-Art: "the rush of assimilation [*kaif o-svoeniia*] of the foreign, the other . . . the overcoming, the removal of the very category of otherness" (ibid., 83–84).

This diversity of opinion is in itself very revealing: Despite their divergent interpretations of Sots-Art (the apophatic confirmation of an inexpressible absolute or the achievement of a state of postutopian indifference, liberation from the power of ideology or the rush of the assimilation of the consciousness of the Other), all the critics approach the task of defining Sots-Art in a similar manner, combining the terminology of theories of myth with the Russian formalist notion of art as a device. Both of these discourses are closely connected with the avant-garde and, more generally, with the aesthetics of high modernism. Their combination is apparently characteristic of a decidedly postmodern game plan.

Furthermore, the use of these particular categories in relation to Sots-Art seems to make perfect sense. After all, Sots-Art really does work with the categories of Socialist Realism, playing with their hidden semantics, which are distinctly mythological in nature. However, unlike other types of games with cultural mythologies, Sots-Art works with a mythology that from its inception possessed a *dual* semantic system. Komar, Melamid, Kabakov, Prigov, Rubinshtein, Sorokin, Popov, and many other authors involved in this movement belong to a generation (or generations) that was psychologically and culturally formed after the start of the Thaw, which was marked by the total (though ultimately temporary) collapse of the legitimacy of Socialist Realist discourse. Therefore Socialist Realism for them is not an object to be overthrown, as it would be for those of the sixties. They perceive Socialist Realism not only in its direct, legitimate meaning as the aesthetic code of the "ideology in power" but also in its delegitimized form, as a special kind of *world of the absurd*. "Sots-Art does not destroy abstractions. It receives them already in the form of ruins," notes Dobrenko (1990: 183). And therefore the attempt to speak in the language of Socialist Realism constitutes their effort to engage in a dialogue with the absurd, a dialogue with chaos.

Thus Dmitri Prigov, the godfather of Russian literary conceptualism, describes the conceptualist fiction of Vladimir Sorokin in terms of the relationship between chaos and culture:[1]

> When speaking of Sorokin, I cannot help but bring up Anton Pavlovich Chekhov.
> It is in his work that this entire thread of sweet, delicate, and touching relations attempts to cover up the eerie, subcutaneous chaos (from Chekhov's point of view—eerie and destructive), striving to climb out and breathe, to cleanse away the fine, dominating thread of culture with its breath. . . . Without dealing with the cultural-historical and artistic-value parameters of such cultural threads but only with the fact of their appearance before the gaze of the artist, we note that the thread that Sorokin is dealing with is very different from Chekhov's, not only in its concrete, historical *realia* but, more important, in its intention. That is, it no longer attempts to cover up chaos but to approach man and envelope him; indeed, it attempts to become him, to become his way of thinking and feeling. In approaching man, it also brings him face to face with chaos. . . . Sorokin chooses . . . a position of recognition and contemplation of the co-existence of this thread and chaos. (Prigov 1992: 117)

Of course, the references to Chekhov sound rather dubious (the name of more or less any "classic" writer could be dropped here), but it is obvious that it is precisely in the context of Socialist Realism that the aesthetic identification of culture ("thread") and chaos gets its explicit expression. The philosophical hypothesis of the metafiction of the 1920s and 1930s (Vaginov, Mandelstam, Krzhizhanovsky, Kharms) and the consciousness that was spontaneously born in the process of artistic play in Bitov's *Pushkin House,* Venedikt Erofeev's *Moscow to the End of the Line,* and Sokolov's *A School for Fools* now acquires the significance of an understanding of the world, a predetermining *plan,* the *original intention* of the creative act.

# Yevgeny Popov: The Jester's Work

The works of Yevgeny Popov are founded on ambivalent interpretations of "Soviet" culture and the "Soviet" mentality; Popov portrays these phenomena as simultaneously wonderful and absurd, "literary" and barbaric, highly significant and meaningless. His style, despite its apparent carelessness and eclecticism, is actually highly controlled. It is a style based primarily on parody, constantly transforming the standard phrases, clichés, and plots of both Soviet literature and social everyday reality into something bizarre and striking. It is difficult to speak of "reality" when discussing Popov's fiction:

The "realistic" situation in his work constantly imitates the texts of newspapers and paraliterature. The writer's parodic style merely exaggerates the simulation that already "exists." His book *The Beauty of Life: A Novel with a Newspaper, Which Will Never Be Begun or Completed* (1990) is emblematic of Popov's techniques: Here, stories Popov has written over the years are combined with humorous (and ominous) quotes from the Soviet press. Moreover, the stories are all directly or indirectly related to newspaper slogans, entering into a dialogue with them through either their tone or their subject matter, usually as a parody of the Socialist Realist epic and its heroes' gallant attempts *to live in accordance with the logic of Socialist Realist Discourse.* Alternately, they show that the rebellious attempts to break the boundaries of ideological standards result in a return to those very same standards, only from the other direction. Popov himself says of his work that "it is both a story and a parody of that sort of story. Moralizing reduced to idiocy" (Popov 1989: 6).

Popov creates this parodic multivoicedness of depersonalized versions of Socialist Realist discourse within the fairy-tale logic of the play. As Anatoly Vishevsky argues,

[T]he epic elements in the stories are subordinated to the author's concept of creating a contemporary fairy tale (*skazka*)—a single fairy tale, since the totality of Popov's stories constitute a single meta–fairy tale conveying the author's conception of the world. . . . Popov's metatale contains all the necessary elements of the fairy tale: all its functions, main characters, and narrative formulas are present. The dispersal of these elements over a number of stories, the unequal weight of a given element in a given story, the absence of one element in one instance and its duplication in another do not by any means confuse the overall picture; quite the contrary, all this reinforces the reader's conviction that he is engaged in a single long and occasionally repetitious tale (but repetitions are characteristic of fairy tales). (1993: 120)

This fairy-tale pattern apparently allows Popov to combine the reproduction of the structures of the Socialist Realist epic with their unabashed parodies; after all, this is how the fairy tale itself treated the classical myths of initiation in the early stages of the genre's development (for example, while re-creating the structure of the ritual, the fairy tale turned the initiating magus into Baba-Yaga, who is burned in the stove rather than the proposed sacrificial victim). For these very reasons, eclecticism in style and content is typical for the fairy-tale tradition; as Propp writes, "The old continues to co-exist with the new . . . , creating hybrids that are impossible in both nature and history. Though they give the impression of pure fantasy, they nonetheless arise completely independently of each other in all places where the historical shifts that called them to life took place" (Propp 1976: 86). In such an atmosphere, any plot developments, no matter how "true to life" they might seem, immediately reveal their dependence on the discourse of Socialist Realism (which Popov understands first and foremost as an example of epic discourse); at the same time, they are immediately turned inside out. We can see how this process works by examining the story "The Electronic Accordion" (Popov 1997: 24–32). From the very beginning, the story's protagonist is a personified parody of the Socialist Realist model of the "simple Soviet man" and his simple Soviet happiness:

> "Jesus! How come a simple man like me can have such happiness? Little Vitya will grab me round the knees, shouting: 'Dad! Dad! Let's get the building bricks and make a moon buggy to go to the moon!' He's growing up, the clever little devil, but he won't get spoilt for all that he's got. When we were his age we didn't live like him at all, no way. Never enough grub . . . just a bit of bread and salt to eat. . . . Jesus! How come I've got all this happiness? All this just for me, just for a simple man like me!"
>
> Such, roughly speaking, were the thoughts of one Pyotr Matveevich Palchikov, an honest man, a good, middle-ranking specialist, thirty-seven years old and, as you see, a family man, as he wended his way home after a stressful day at work. (Ibid., 24)

Even the very first paragraphs of the story lay bare the central narrative devices. Here both the narrator and the protagonist are self-consciously simulative, since each is utterly without the slightest original individual features. The hero consciously identifies himself with an ideological stereotype, while the narrator never goes beyond clichés. In addition, we are immediately faced with the stratified discourse of the other: The same Socialist Realist semantics are expressed in the pseudo-folksy style of Pyotr Matveevich ("the clever little devil" [umnyi chertenok]; "never enough grub" [vechno ne zhramshi] "just a bit of bread and salt to eat" [podshamaesh ] ibid., 24) and the official language of the narrator. The transitions from one level of Socialist Realist discourse only seem significant; in actuality, they are tautological.

This thesis is developed quite literally on the level of the story's plot. The "meeting with Music" that shocks the "honest man, [the] good, middle-ranking specialist" only initially clashes with the grandeur of the system of Socialist Realist stereotypes presented in the beginning of the story. This very situation is a quotation from another model in the literature of the sixties generation, that of "Socialist Realism with a human face," with its disdain for "bourgeois comfort." And this is why the scene in which Pyotr Matveevich "has his eyes opened" is drawn with such a distinctly parodic brush, when he hurls accusations at his wife: "'Drinking! Drinking!' he yelled. 'I'll give you "drink"! All you can think of is drinking and stuffing yourself! You haven't got a thought in your head! You live like a carp under the ice! Are you going to drag me into the grave with you?'" (ibid., 30). The tautological transitions within one and the same discourse are emphasized by the ease with which the narration returns to its point of departure: "Then Pyotr Matveevich more or less came to his senses, more or less returned to his old self. He looked slowly around. The house was still a house. The flat still a flat. The furniture still furniture. The people were still people" (ibid.). Nothing has happened, because nothing can happen: The stylistic tautologies of Socialist Realist discourse become metonymic for existential emptiness and senselessness—total "havoc" (*razor*), to use the title of one of Popov's stories.[2] In the end of "The Electronic Accordion," this "havoc" is for one brief moment depicted through the perceptions of a child, Pyotr Matveevich's son: "Pyotr Matveevich laughed as well. They both laughed and slapped each other on their fleshy backs. And only their little son Vitya looked on like a wolf cub. The tears on his cheeks had dried, but his lips were pressed tightly together" (ibid., 31).

This everyday "havoc," which is a metonymic substitute for the tautologies of Socialist Realist discourse, becomes the constant world model of all of Popov's fiction. Against this backdrop, we can clearly see the simulative character of all categories of reality of the heroes, the narrator, and, in a number of Popov's works, even the "author" who has created this given text. On the level of content, this quality is expressed in the ease with which happiness and misfortune, farce and tragedy, drama and vaudeville, spite and tenderness flow from one to the other. Everything can be explained by the condition of complete existential lightness that forms the subject of so many of Popov's stories, including "No, That's Not It," "Five Tales about Vodka" (1997: 1–18), "The Mistakes of Youth" (ibid., 126–29), "Laughing and Smiling" (ibid., 177–80), "Ruin" (ibid., 71–76), "The Drummer and the Drummer's Wife" (ibid., 181–83), "Uncle Lyova and Aunt Musya," "The Green Massif," "How They Ate the Cock." The abrupt shifts from one category to its polar opposite are dictated not by dialectics but by the absurd, since there is no motivation for these shifts; everything occurs incoherently and for no apparent purpose. Vergasov the happy metalworker sits on his balcony eating his favorite blintzes, when suddenly, without any reason, he leans backward and starts to fall down. And his wife falls after him. From the thirteenth floor ("The Green Massif," Popov 1990: 345–48). A husband and wife who truly hate each other (she scalds him with boiling water, he knifes her) are inseparable, living their entire lives together in three square meters ("How They Ate a Cock," Erofeyev 1995: 270–77). The horror sparked by the cruel order of 1920, which has been reverentially preserved in the historical museum, is immediately transformed in the consciousness of the narrator-protagonist into patriotic ecstasy and even gratitude for the fact that they are not being shot like those "deserters" in 1920 ("No, That's Not It," Popov 1990: 104–10).

On the level of expression, the world model of "havoc," which is hidden behind the language of Socialist Realist discourse, forms a unique type of metafictional poetics. Popov's work abounds with such devices as the inclusion of doubles and namesakes for the biographical author, Yevgeny Anatolievich Popov, in the stories themselves ("The Eschatological Mood of a Certain Segment of the Former Youth," "The Unattainability of the Shining Ideal," "A Thoroughly Shameful Incident," "No Shooting at the Musician"), the demonstration of the very process of writing ("A Slanderous Sketch," "A Bed of Flowers," "Fyodor's Local Motherland"), self-quotations in combination with parodic slips of the tongue, and self-commentary that reveals the artifice and destroys the illusion of verisimilitude ("The Send-off for the So-Called Russian Winter, or Mirzlikin's Broken Head," "Deadly Head Cheese"). However, the sum effect of these devices is different from that of similar elements in the works of Andrei Bitov and Venedikt Erofeev. If these writers interpret the open interconnectedness of creativity and simulation, and hence creativity and death, *tragically,* Popov renders all these devices unabashedly *comically.* And the fairy-tale "genre memory" that deprives the author of the right to be taken seriously (in the denouement of the magic tale, the narrator undermines the veracity of his story, even demonstratively becoming like a jester) only strengthens this effect. In Popov's hands, the holy foolishness of Kharms's narrators or of Venichka Erofeev turns into the voice of an unabashed *jester.* For instance, the "Motherflickers" ("Udaki"—this is Popov's euphemism for the Russian obscenity *mudak*) cycle includes the following dialogue: "VOICE OF THE INVALID: Are you a motherflicker, Author? AUTHOR: Why should I be any worse than everybody else?" (Popov 1992: 22). In metafiction, the author is tortured by his inability to merge with the world of chaos, and attempts to resolve this conflict through a dialogue that is paid for tragically by being drawn into chaos. The author-figure created by Popov has no such troubles—he is no worse than anyone else; his existence is just as simulative as the world around him, if not more so.

Why does this happen? Probably because both in Sots-Art and in Popov's work the artistic conception of *death* is radically different from that in metafiction. Here we should note that Popov's stories constantly play with the motif of the threshold of death. This is one of the most enduring chronotopes of his seemingly disorganized and hardly everyday prose: It predominates in such works as *The Soul of a Patriot, or The Various Epis-*

*tles to Ferfichkin* (the state mourning for Brezhnev), "The Circumstances Surrounding the Death of Andrei Stepanovich," "Uncle Lyova and Aunt Musya" (the death of Aunt Musya), "The Singing of the Brass," "The Green Massif" (the death of Vergasov and the conversations at the cemetery), "Deadly Head Cheese," and "No, That's Not It" (the lethal devastation resulting from the catastrophes of Soviet history).[3] In metafiction, death is the last, tragic reality in the chaos of simulacra. Not so for Popov: In his work, death turns out to be an *imaginary* threshold, since it is confined *within* the total "havoc" that creates the simulacrum of being. This is why it lacks a serious, let alone triumphant, aura and why any attempts to heighten the narrative tone inevitably turn into parody (hence the style of *The Soul of a Patriot, or The Various Epistles to Ferfichkin*). A man's death is overshadowed by everyday things and relationships: a funeral is reduced to the body and its coffin falling off the truck into a stream ("The Circumstances Surrounding the Death of Andrei Stepanovich"), while an urn full of ashes is handed out like dry-cleaning, and mixed-up, no less ("Uncle Lyova and Aunt Musya").

It is completely natural that when the story "The Eschatological Mood of a Certain Segment of the Former Youth" presents the image of the end of the world foretold for August 5, 1984, the prophecy fails to spark any reaction in the narrator, no matter how hard he tries. Far more important (and more frightening) for him than the end of the world is the way in which he is customarily pushed out of one hospital and into another, writhing in pain as green pus oozes from his ear: "And that was such a night, that after that no August 4, 1984, can scare me" (Popov 1990: 37). In addition, the way to this picture has been paved by copious quotations from *Pravda* and by the atmosphere of May Day, as well as conversations about the classic Soviet writer L. (probably Leonov), who "already has all the medals a country has to offer, except for that last one, which he now also has" (ibid., 34). Indeed, the world of Socialist Realist simulacra plus the constant headache, the apparently inevitable result of everyday chaos—all of this combines to create an image of everyday existence after the end of the world, when "eschatological moods" easily become a part of everyday life, not as metaphysical premonitions but as statements of fact. Yet Popov ends his story with a refrain about the "wonder of life": "[H]ere my suffering practically comes to an end, dear friends, which once against proves that life is wonderful and that no temporary difficulties can shatter my patriotic opinion about it" (ibid., 38). Of course, this obtrusive exaltation of the beauty of life parodically recapitulates the demands of Socialist Realism: For the narrator/protagonist, the return to the norm (already located on the threshold of being) is the same as a return to the embrace of Socialist

Realist discourse. But this is not the most important thing. What passes for Popov's philosophical credo can be found in "No, That's Not It," a story about irretrievable loss as a constant of social and personal history, about life as an endless process that crushes and destroys everything of value:

> CONCLUSION AND MORAL: If you've lost a shoe, if they've stolen a fox or even stolen everything you own, it's too late to torture yourself wondering who's to blame and what to do. You're better off either looking for a shoe, working up a sweat and running around with your hair standing on end, or, better yet, going to the Bolshoi, to the Little Theater, the Conservatory, the Tretyakov Gallery, anywhere, as long as you aren't late to where you're going. Because the absence of a shoe, the theft of a fox or of everything you own only means that you don't have a shoe, a fox, or everything you owned, just the way it was before you were given all that by a good person. *You've got nothing, but life goes on, because it can't do anything else.* (1990: 110; emphasis added)

If Bitov discovers in *Pushkin House* that everything that seems like life in Soviet reality is the afterlife of being and culture, Popov, and all of Sots-Art, proposes a different point of view: Even the tautological desert burned out by the Socialist Realist consciousness is also a *form of life,* and it also has some subverted beauty, although it continues in emptiness and ends with havoc, "because it can't do anything else." Life is too broad and unprincipled to be understood tragically; it goes on after death and after tragedy, thereby depriving death (and itself) of all value. The fact that the difference between life and death proves insignificant explains Popov's comic interpretation of that which metafiction can only find tragic.

If we look for a tradition to which Popov's prose hearkens back, it is probably the tradition of Russian jesting. Dmitri S. Likhachev writes:

> "jesting work" has its inertia, too. He who is laughing is not disposed to stop in his laughter. Particularly revealing in this regard is the typically Russian form of laughter—jesting [*balagurstvo*]. . . . Jesting destroys the meaning of words and mangles their outer form. The jester exposes the absurdity in the structure of the words, giving a false etymology or inappropriately emphasizing the etymological meaning of the word, linking words that superficially sound alike, and so forth. . . . The author builds his own work as an unending toppling of everything real into the world of laughter, like an uninterrupted humorous doubling of what is happening, what is being described or related. (Likhachev, Panchenko, and Ponyrko 1984: 21, 36, 37)

Of course, Popov transforms this tradition profoundly: In his stories, the inertia of "laugh work" is displayed precisely in the exposure of the simulation not only of the socialist mind or in history but also of death, of creative work, and of the reality of writing. Due to the continuity of the laughing process, Popov's narrator simultaneously passes off (or tries to pass off) something simulated as something real, genuine, and seriously tragic. And if, as Likhachev suggests, the stylistic play of jesting forms the poetics of the "antiworks" of the medieval culture of laughing (with antiprayers, anti-doctors, antijudges), then Popov uses jesting as the foundation for his "anti-literature," which uses its own substance to fashion not only the "destruction" of culture but also its transformation into the habitual, every-day habitat, "the wheel of life" (to use the title of one of Popov's stories). Naturally, this form of stylistic playfulness is fraught with repetitions: The "laughter relay race" follows a closed circuit, inevitably kicking over its own traces. But in Popov's best works, the paraliterary style and endless repetitions are the structural components of an entire model of the world.

Such is the case, for example, in *The Soul of a Patriot* (written in 1982, first published in 1989). The novella's central paradox is linked to the cate-gory of time. On the one hand, we have the search for historicity, for per-sonal contact between the autobiographical "I" and history, at first through the description of his pedigree and the fates of his relatives, who personally experienced many troubles of the Soviet epoch, then through a detailed account of the funeral of Brezhnev ("HE WHO ONCE WAS" [Popov 1994: 69 and passim]) and of the "historical wanderings" of E.A. Popov and D.A. Prigov in the environs of this funeral. But history in the lives of grandmoth-ers and grandfathers—with all its changes—represents an alien, destructive primordial force. Thus the narrative about ancestors is felt as a sort of double illogicality: First, historical reality itself is illogical, and, second, the percep-tion of the descendant, E.A. Popov, constantly striving to make bad, irrele-vant jokes on someone's grave, is also illogical. The death of "HE WHO ONCE WAS" is the culmination of this absurd story. Telling about the state mourning and accompanying rumors, trying to preserve the solemn and his-toric tone, yet constantly striking farcical notes, taking great pains over meaningless trifles, mocking, chuckling, mimicking, Popov re-creates the stream of consciousness of his autobiographical hero as a "historical phe-nomenon"—as a snapshot of the history of the absurd, which paused at 1982 and then proceeded; of the absurd in which everything is nonsense, every-thing is unimportant, including life, death, and blood.

On the other hand, the novella's poetics affirms the possibility of only one type of time—extrahistorical time, the eternal present, haphazardly taken down in shorthand by a jesting author. His slogan is sly: "[D]on't waste any TIME on it, describe instead what there IS FOR THE TIME BEING" (ibid., 130). But what IS THERE FOR THE TIME BEING? The very process of writing exists, but—unlike in the metafiction of Mandelstam ("The

Egyptian Stamp," *The Noise of Time,* "Fourth Prose") or Nabokov (*The Gift, The Real Life of Sebastian Knight*)—this process is actually concentrated on the absence of any serious justification for itself aside from a personal "planned economy" with a "premium" from God and comic calculations of proposed honoraria in case of publication and republication of the present composition in *Novel-Newspaper (Roman-gazeta).* What Julia Kristeva called the geno-text—the metatext, describing its own birth—in Popov looks roughly like this:

> Look, Ferfichkin, I'm producing all this self-duplicating rubbish for you, producing it mechanically, but do I know myself if I've got enough honesty and courage (impudence and cynicism) to describe the next detail of our social being, destroying as it does the lyricism of the narrative. (Ibid., 66)

> . . . I'll carry on interrupting myself. . . . I, as one of God's vibrant creatures, perhaps HAVE THE RIGHT to write badly and just anyhow . . . after all they DINNA pay monEE for rIting, just the opposite even, they insult you, like the nihilists used to insult the God's fool, yet still you want, you want to read mEE . . . See, you've read this far, Ferfichkin, so some other person would too. (Ibid., 94–95)

> However, the fact is, the New Year is just around the corner, but I still can't get past the frontier of 14 November 1982! Perhaps, I should decrease the volume of epistles? Break them off right now, at this very line, at this word, at this lett . . ." (Ibid., 143–44)

The very process of writing, of the self-expression of the potential "I" that is unrealizable in social and historical reality, is devalued, and what devalues it is precisely the absence of time, the emptiness in which the writing takes place and by which it is dictated. Popov's refrain is basically "no, the wrong thing, I am always talking about the wrong thing" (ibid., 29)—and it points to this gaping emptiness of absolute timelessness beyond the written text.

In this context, the absence of any time other than the ephemeral and discredited blathering of the present moment turns out to be an extremely historical condition: While the protagonists of the story feel that "we were involved in History, and were rejoicing the distinct realization that none of our friends, acquaintances or relatives would be so close," this feeling leads to the feeling of a vacuum. Thus, let us say, the Miracle resulting from their "historical wanderings" (ibid., 160) is represented by a policeman who

> "DID NOT LET US THROUGH, AS THOUGH HE WERE LETTING US THROUGH. It seemed as if he was on the point of letting us through. But in actual fact, really, he didn't let us through, as though he were letting us

through, that is, politely, almost condescendingly. Wonders will never cease!" (Ibid., 157–58)

The absurdity of the narrator's consciousness is specifically rooted in Soviet history and culture: The narrator's main complex is the desire for community, for community with the reader (hence the familiar, ingratiating dialogue with the faceless Ferfichkin), with social ideology, with "the demands of time," and with Great History, as it allegedly unfolds beyond the circle of police cordons. But Popov's stylistic games allow this absurdity to pass unnoticed into the realm of metaphysics, becoming a metaphor for *world chaos*, of which the Soviet absurd is only one particular example. Hence the open discussions of chaos that appear twice in *The Soul of a Patriot:*

> The new MAT [Moscow Art Theater]. A citadel . . . There is everything, but there is nothing. It is cold in these huge halls, where the smart set whoops it up and the waitress bangs open bottles of beer and mineral water. . . . But would it be better in a barn? Or in a Nissen hut? But how does one achieve harmony? How does one defeat chaos? I have no idea. Who does know? Does anyone know? Maybe someone does know, but he died a long time ago, and there's still no harmony, none at all. But there's still chaos, and plenty of it. And death, there's still plenty of that. However, there is also life as well, I admit, though it's an unequally matched line-up—life, death, harmony, chaos. . . . The line-up is unequally matched, but is that my fault? (Ibid., 127)

> [S]ometimes it seems to me that this—that is, the struggle against chaos and lack of discipline—is exactly what I have been occupied with all my life, suffering one defeat after another and retreating from positions that have been prepared in advance." (Ibid., 116)

These declarations are all the more important in that they are linked with the reinterpretation of classical notions on the "role of the poet" and the purpose of art in general. On the one hand, Alexander Blok's proud belief that the poet is the "son of harmony" (in his Pushkin speech [Blok 1968: 161]) is replaced by the experience of defeats by chaos. On the other hand, this experience is significant nonetheless, if for no other reason than that chaos allows one to make contact with that unequal line-up that includes life, death, and harmony. Chaos does not contrast with these universals; rather, it is placed on the same level. Is there a breakthrough in the chaos of the Soviet consciousness that leads toward anything even remotely resembling meaning and harmony?

In his afterword to the first publication of *The Soul of a Patriot* in a Russian journal, Sergei Chuprinin writes,

What about the wanderings of two friends around a chilled and depopulated Moscow? . . . Isn't this another reminder of the short sprints from one set of relatives' house to another, almost as though bullets were whistling overhead? These houses contain no mysteries for the narrator/protagonist. But look closely: the usually sharp-tongued and mercilessly frank narrator becomes surprisingly reserved and reticent about details when he speaks of his own friends and, more generally, of people from his circle." (1989: 80)

If we take this observation further, we must note that it is these very images of friends that the novel presents as reminiscent of the ideal of the poet as the son of harmony. Take, for example, this brief portrait of "A., a great poet of contemporaneity (female gender)" (Popov 1994: 32): "Her pure voice, a voice for writing poetry, the music of explosion and breaking which seeks out a head-spinning harmony at a conjunction of mysterious vocabulary and the simplest objects of the surrounding realism" (ibid., 99). Typically, the narrator's exaggeratedly tongue-tied manner turns into a stylistic parody of the irrational syntax of the poetry of Bella Akhmadulina, one of the foremost poets of the sixties generation. But these images, like the image of the gay writer Yevgeny Kharitonov, who "throughout his entire life . . . was unable to publish a single line of his own work" (ibid., 101), is not placed on the same level as Soviet absurdity; it lived, and continues to live, above it.

The narrator is another matter. He creates his text within the Soviet consciousness, accentuating rather than masking its chaotic logic. The absence of time as a form of history; the fictitious nature of death's threshold, of government mourning; emptiness as the meaning of literary writing—all these are not only the oxymorons of chaos but carnivalesque *mésalliances* that become a source of special carnivalesque freedom for the narrator.

In Popov, the narrator's "I" with all its "Soviet-ness" possesses a truly carnivalesque consciousness, dethroning everything that is superficial, stable, and firm. This consciousness perceives the world as a multitude of equivalent theatrical masks, a consciousness that proves to be perfectly appropriate for those conditions of culture "when previous forms of life, moral principles and beliefs were being turned into 'rotten cords' and the previously concealed, ambivalent, and unfinalized nature of man and human *thought* was being nakedly exposed" (Bakhtin 1984: 166–67).

This type of merciless jesting, which even reveals the emptiness of the creative process itself—this form of carnivalesque consciousness and ambivalent freedom is debased and comic but is also the expression of the "unfinalized nature of man and human *thought*." The Soviet, unfree consciousness, made neurotic by the thirst for community with something suprapersonal, turns out to be simultaneously an absurd, chaotic consciousness; but chaos also acts as a condition for freedom and thus paradoxically undermines its own premises. This is Yevgeny Popov's central artistic discovery, his version of Sots-Art. This is the fertile dialogue with chaos, where carnivalesque freedom is the living and tangible result of the dialogic conflict that is at the heart of Sots-Art: the conflict between Socialist Realist discourse and the metaphysical world model of chaos, which breaks through the discourse's stereotypes.

The connection between Socialist Realist discourse and carnivalesque freedom is played out differently by the various authors who are close to Sots-Art. Thus in Zufar Gareev's *Park* and *Multifiction,* the emphasis is on the simulative nature of the characters from the Soviet world: They are the resurrected metaphors of Socialist Realist literature. And the carnivalesque, farcical relations turn the fear and violence hidden within the depths of Soviet consciousness into pure theater of the absurd ("Fedoskina ate half of Chanskaya's head, and the number of thoughts in her own head grew; her inner world became more complicated. And this is what she then shouted with satisfaction: 'Look at me! I got lucky! Me, and I look so ordinary on the outside, sort of homely, I get to live two lives!' " [Gareev 1992: 133]). Anatoly Gavrilov uses a similar strategy (in the stories from his collection *On the Doorstep of the New Life*), as does Alexander Khurgin ("The Country of Australia").

By contrast, in *Omon Ra* (1992), and particularly in *The Life of Insects* (1994),[4] Viktor Pelevin tries to bring back the human dimension (pain, suffering, the desire for meaning) to the impersonal formulas of Socialist Realism. He portrays the Soviet world as a universal, existential metaphor for postmodern existence, with its total relativism of values, its destruction of stable orders of existence, its metaphors combining contradictory states of live and categorical oppositions of consciousness. Starting with the early stories and novellas contained in his collection *The Blue Lantern*[5] (which won the Small Booker Prize in 1992), Pelevin quite clearly defines his central theme, which he has yet to change to this very day, somehow avoiding the trap of repeating himself. Pelevin's characters desperately try to answer the question "What is reality?" Moreover, if the classical postmodernism of the sixties through the eighties was concerned with revealing the simulative character of that which seemed to be reality, for the young heroes of Pelevin (born in 1962, he is the youngest of the most famous postmodernists), the realization that everything around them is a simulative illusion is only the starting point for further meditation. Yes, life turns out to be a dream ("The Blue Lantern"), a computer game ("The Prince of Gosplan"), the movement of freshly hatched chicks along an incubator's conveyer belt ("Hermit and Six-Toes"), and even the senseless "buzzing of insects ("The Life of Insects"). Pelevin masterfully plays out the imperceptible metamorphoses of an impressive boss into a tank driver from a computer game or of a beach whore into a dragonfly. But his purpose is not satirical: By mixing up human passions with an insect's instincts, he tries to see beyond the shell of this crushing comparison of the senselessness of human existence with the blindness of moths flying toward a flame. Pelevin is interested not in the transformation of reality into simulacra but rather in the reverse process: the birth of reality out of simulacra. This strategy is the polar opposite of the major postulates of postmodernist philosophy. As a character in his early novella "The Prince of Gosplan" says: Even if the goal of the quest on which one spends one's whole life turns out to be a trivial, deceptive, cardboard fiction, "when a man spends so much time and energy on the road and finally arrives, he no longer can see everything as it really is. . . . Although that's not exactly right. There is no 'really,' really. Let's say that he can't allow himself to see" (Pelevin 1996a: 23). That's why the eponymous hero of Pelevin's *Omon Ra,* who discovers that the space flight for which he has lost his legs and for which his friends have died is nothing but a secret theatrical fraud played out somewhere under the Moscow metro, does not cease to be a hero of space, like the Egyptian deity who has overcome death: It does not matter how real his flight is, for Omon Ra it represents completion, like an archaic rite of passage, a crossing through the zone of horrible tests, a temporary death. And Pelevin's scarabs, for whom the entire universe is concentrated on a piece of manure, are not a mockery of human quests for the meaning of life; on the contrary, Pelevin's dung beetle accords such quests a grotesque seriousness: Even the manure ceases to be simply manure if it is connected with the drama of consciousness, with pain, hope, desperation, and stubbornness.

In his latest and best novel, *Chapaev and Void* (1996b), Pelevin irrevocably blurs the boundary between dream and reality. The very heroes of these interconnected phantasmagorias do not know which of the plots in which they live is the waking world and which is a dream. The young Pyotr Pustota ("Void") meets the Red Commander Vasily Ivanovich Chapaev. Chapaev is a legendary civil-war hero who became extremely popular in the 1930s, after the release of the movie by the Vasiliev brothers; this movie also led to an endless series of jokes about Chapaev and his comrades, including Petka. Chapaev in Pelevin's novel is very different from his "prototype," although many scenes from the book directly refer to the famous movie and no less famous jokes. Chapaev is presented as a teacher of Buddhist wisdom; under his direction, Pyotr (Petka from the movie and jokes) gradually comes to realize that the question as to where illusion ends and reality begins has no meaning, since everything is the void and the product of the void. But if "any form is the void," then "the void is any form" (Pelevin 1996b: 367). Therefore, the one who realizes his freedom from the authority of both simulacra and "realities" gains the power to create the world anew, infinitely expanding the boundaries of his self and his "inner Mongolia"—Pelevin's metaphor for the realm of the hidden and true self. Without a doubt, this novel has a Zen-Buddhist feel about it, but I would not call the novel itself "Buddhist." In *Chapaev and Void,* Buddhist philosophy is reproduced with distinct irony, as one of the possible illusions—otherwise, why would Pelevin transform Chapaev, who has been lifted almost in his entirety from the popular Socialist Realist film bearing his name, into one of the incarnations of the Buddha, and why would he interpret the folkloric jokes about Petka and Chapaev as ancient Japanese koans and mysterious parables with numerous possible answers (see Genis 1997b: 232–33)? Pelevin has written a paradoxical Bildungsroman about the transformation of simulacra and illusions into the only indisputable reality, which in turn easily exposes its simulative character and its insignificance to anyone but the protagonist. Strictly speaking, Pelevin's hero seeks utopia but is entirely aware of the impossibility and danger of the utopianism that has been achieved.

In all these works, as in those of Popov, Socialist Realist discourse opens up from within, becoming an image of everyday chaos; total "havoc" becomes an absurdist game, a carnivalesque consciousness. This large, playful context deprives Socialist Realist mythology of the absurdity of absolute meaning, relativizes it, opening it up for dialogic relations. But there is also another path: to go deeper into Socialist Realist discourse, into the depths of the mechanisms that give rise to the mythology of the absurd. This path is followed to its logical conclusions by Vladimir Sorokin, who lays the devices as bare as possible.

# Vladimir Sorokin: Narrative Theater of Cruelty

*The disappearance of the individual subject, along with its formal consequence, the increasing unavailability of the personal style, engender the well-nigh universal practice today of what may be called pastiche. . . . Pastiche is, like parody, the imitation of a peculiar or unique, idiosyncratic style, the wearing of a linguistic mask, speech in a dead language. But it is a neutral practice of such mimicry, without any of parody's ulterior motives, amputated of the satiric impulse, devoid of laughter and of any conviction that alongside the abnormal tongue you have momentarily borrowed, some healthy linguistic normality still exists. Pastiche is thus blank parody, a statue with blind eyeballs.*

—Fredric Jameson (1991: 16, 17)

When reading Sorokin's works, one is immediately struck by the duality of their very construction. Few who have written on Sorokin have failed to note his sharp transitions from a smooth Socialist Realist style to a bloody and nauseating sort of horror story or to a stream of nonsense—at times, the text is reduced to nothing more than a set of letters. Is there a connection between the construction of the Sots-Art narrative and the dual meaning of the myth (which is sacred to official discourse and absurd to its unofficial counterpart) with which this narrative works? And if so, then how does it work?

Let us examine this effect using Sorokin's stories as an example. Rather than playing with truly Socialist Realist forms, many of them function on the principle of combining absolutely incompatible stylistic strata—for example, criminal slang and bookish preciousness ("Memorial"); the stylistic gibberish of the quasi-folk language of "village prose" and poetic exercises in a Symbolist vein ("The Competition"); a style consciously imitative of Bunin, interrupted, strangely enough, by echoes of Aksyonov's *The Island of Crimea* in combination with the "school tale," which is suddenly transformed into a Kafkaesque episode that could have come from "In the Penal Colony," which in turn is replaced by the confession and Freudian self-analysis of the narrator's childhood experiences ("Incident on the Road"). Those stories that lack distinctly Socialist Realist elements are indeed Sorokin's weakest. They usually come across as an imitation of surrealist "automatic writing"; the transitions from one style to another are as arbitrary as possible, with the author seemingly demonstrating the full freedom of the narrative flow, as well as his lack of adherence to any of the possible discourses that he nonetheless skillfully manipulates. But freedom is attained too easily. Sorokin himself acknowledges the important role in his work played by Foucault's notion of the totalitarian nature of any discourse; any discourse "claims power over the person. . . . It hypnotizes, and sometimes simply paralyzes" (Sorokin 1992: 121). The appeal to Socialist Realist discourse is thus dictated by the extreme complication of the task of disengagement from the power of the discourse. First, the semantics of power—in the literal, political-ideological sense—of the Socialist Realist style is still absolutely fresh and modern; it has not yet gone into the realm of cultural legend and can still be easily revived in the reader's consciousness. Second, there is no other style like this in Russian culture that by its very nature could symbolize the concepts of totalitarian power as a whole in such a pure, refined form.[6]

This supposition is supported by the fact that Sorokin's Socialist Realist stories most often contain a conflict that in one way or another reverses the relationship between the teacher (mentor, older comrade, leader) and the pupil (novice, younger successor). This conflict—which produces a motif of essentially *discursive* power (as opposed to, say political, physical, sexual, or any other power)—lies at the heart of such vivid stories as "Sergei Andreevich," "The Free Lesson," "The Eulogy," and "The First Subbotnik"; it is also present, if not quite as obvious, in stories such as "Passing Through," "The Opening of the Season," "The Geologists," and "Acorn Valley" (this is half of all Sorokin's collected works to date). This conflict is directly connected with one of the central myths of Socialist Realist culture.

Katerina Clark argues that the "prototypical subject" of Socialist Realism is based on the transformed structures of transitional, consecrating myths, and above all myths (and corresponding rituals) of initiation:

> The Stalinist novel usually depicts modern institutions and hierarchies, yet the motivating structure that brings all conflicts to their resolution harks back to the traditional world. This can be seen in the main plot elements of the typical Socialist Realist novel. A hero sets out consciously to achieve his goal, which involves *social integration* and *collective* rather than *individual* identity for himself. . . . The hero is assisted in his quest by an older and more "conscious" figure who has made just such a successful quest before him. (1981: 167; emphasis in original).

> The novel culminates in a scene marking the moment of passage itself, the rite of incorporation. The elder presides and confers his own status as a tribal elder on the initiate. Very commonly the elder will give the initiate some advice or "instruction." Since this is a rite of incorporation, the elder also often hands the initiate some object or token that symbolizes belonging to the "tribe"—e.g. a banner, badge, or Party card. Alternatively, the two may be linked temporarily when both touch the same object (as when Peter briefly touches Lefort's coffin in A. Tolstoy's *Peter the First*). (Ibid., 172–73)

How does Sorokin transform this mythologeme? The example of "Sergei Andreevich," a story that is quite clearly oriented toward this ritual-mythological model in its Socialist Realist medium, is particularly instructive. The graduates of a school go on a field trip with their teacher for the last time. This field trip, as well as the end of the school year, corresponds to the first

phase of initiation—the separation of the neophyte from his familiar surroundings. The essential content of the rite of "transition" is transmitted by
the teacher's lessons to the pupils. His precepts signify the standard Socialist Realist hierarchy of values, which is emphasized by a bland narrative
style absolutely devoid of any individuality (Sorokin, by the way, speaks of
his orientation toward "middle-of-the-road" Socialist Realism, from "some
[provincial] publisher or other"):

> "Yes, boys, the forest is an amazing phenomenon of nature. The eighth
> wonder of the world, as Mamin-Sibiryak said. One never tires of the forest, it
> never gets boring. How many riches there are in the forest! Oxygen, lumber,
> cellulose." (1992: 50)

> "Well, you know, Vitya, technology has certainly given man a great deal.
> But I think the main thing is that it has not replaced man himself, not pushed
> him into the background." (Ibid., 51)

The top girl pupil reports that she will go to an

> "ordinary textile factory rather than an institute. In order to really get a feel for
> production. . . . Then it'll be easier for me to study and I'll learn a bit more about
> life. All the women in our family have been weavers for generations." . . . [The
> teacher] looked Lebedeva knowingly in the eye: "Good for you. Then you'll
> study even better at the institute. A year at the factory is very good for you. In my
> time I also worked for a year as a simple lab technician at an observatory before
> entering Moscow State. Because of that I knew what I was doing in the practical
> classes more than the others." (Ibid., 54)

To any pupil's enthusiastic acknowledgment of the teacher as a "great
man," Sergei Andreevich, according to etiquette, would modestly respond:
"Great men, Misha, are few and far between. I am not a great man, but
rather a simple high school teacher. If I have truly helped you in any way,
then I'm happy. Thank you for your warm words" (ibid., 56).

Clearly set forth here are all the main points of reference of Socialist
Realist discourse: the ontological (nature–technology–man), the social
(school–institute–factory), and the individual (the greatness of the simple
man). At the same time a "test of magical knowledge" is being conducted,
which is also integral to the ritual of initiation. The ordeal looks like a simple
quiz about the knowledge of the heavens, but in the semiotics of Socialist
Realism the stars clearly correspond to the height of romantic aspirations. It
is revealing that only one pupil, Misha, passes this ordeal. As Clark notes, in
order to embody the Socialist Realist "quest" in its most concentrated form,
"the number of characters who assume either of these functions [the hero

who conducts the quest and the elder who assists him] is limited to the smallest possible number. Usually only two are selected from among all the positive characters" (Clark 1981: 168). The ritual incorporation that completes the "quest" logically becomes the culmination of the story:

> A small pile of [the teacher's] feces lay in the grass, gleaming greasily. Sokolov [the pupil] lowered his face to it. The feces had a strong smell. He picked up one of the little sausage-like pieces that were stuck together. It was warm and soft. He kissed it and began eating quickly, taking greedy bites, smearing his lips and fingers. (Sorokin 1992: 59)

The structure of the protosubject of the Socialist Realist quest has remained the same. But the banner or Party card is replaced by feces, which is ecstatically eaten by the character who has successfully completed his initiation. Semantically, such a substitution does not contradict the goal of the quest: the rejection of the individual in favor of the collective. Furthermore, it is the self-abasement in particular that is strengthened as much as possible here. The mechanism of "incorporation" through tactile contact, the passing of a material object from hand to hand, is also preserved. The main distinction is in the change of code—the symbolic code is forced out by a naturalistic code, conditional signals are replaced by unconditional ones, "culture" by "nature" (or by that which is perceived as extracultural, wild, primeval).

An analogous ritual gesture can be found in the climaxes of other Sorokin stories. In "Passing Through," the Regional Party Committee Leader (teacher) defecates on the hands of the District Party Committee Leader (pupil) as a sign of supreme approval of the design of the album in honor of the fiftieth anniversary of the training center, and this gesture is included in the context of the signs of discursive power (a speech before subordinates, a resolution—"an honest Party document"). "The Geologists" deals with the problem of how to connect with a lost group ("incorporation")—at the end an old geologist ("twenty years in the expeditions") suggests "simply to *pomuchmarit' fonku*" (an absolutely meaningless expression). Chanting more nonsense words ("*Myst', myst', myst', uchkarnoe soplenie*") all the geologists cup their outstretched palms, and Ivan Timofeevich "put two fingers in his mouth and hiccoughed, shuddering. He quickly threw up in the cupped palms" (ibid., 96). In the story called "The Free Lesson," erotic contact (which in the United States would legally be considered child molesting) forms the essence of the content of the lesson that the teacher gives the pupil:

> Chernyshev touched her swollen labia.
> "Touch some more . . . more . . . what are you afraid of . . . you're not a little girl . . . you're already a Young Pioneer, after all." (Ibid., 90)

This lesson is also surrounded by numerous signs of discursive power, such as:

"You, a pioneer, lifted someone's skirt?! . . . What, you don't have the guts to admit it? A future Komsomol member!" (Ibid., 85)

"What a shame that you can't tell me the truth!" (Ibid., 86)

"Don't ever try to find something out by dishonest means. This knowledge will only ruin you." (Ibid., 87)

"Don't lie! We're speaking candidly here! You want to [look at female genitalia]? Do it like a pioneer! Honestly! You want to?!" (Ibid., 89)

"Word of Party honor, don't tell anyone! Word of Party honor! You know what that is—word of Party honor!" (Ibid., 89)

A whole cascade of ritual gestures like this can be found in one of Sorokin's best works, "The Eulogy," and every one of these gestures specifically violates the initially created discursive expectations. The funeral that the characters are attending ("the first beats of Chopin's funeral march resounded through the rain-washed cemetery" [ibid., 107]) is turned upside down by the business-like execution of the person to be buried before the eyes of all his friends and relatives. In other words, they are "saying their last farewells" to a person who is still alive, and they call the firing squad "grave-diggers." A substitution is taking place here, but one that is the polar opposite of what we saw in "Sergei Andreevich" and other stories by Sorokin: A natural death is replaced by a violent death, unambiguously identified as a sign of power belonging to the cultural world of Socialist Realism. However, the framework of funeral rituals—also, by the way, one of the rituals of "transition"—is elastic enough to absorb this substitution without undergoing any fundamental changes. Indeed, this immutability of style, setting, behavior, words, and characters' reactions is the most aesthetically expressive element of this episode. Every ritual or custom involves an incarnation of the mythological order, which places the person within some universal scale. Here a flagrant violation of the order (the execution of a living person instead of the burial of a dead person) is written into ritual and, consequently, into the presumed mythological order. The clash of two types of rituals—the universal and archaic (the funeral) and the distinctly totalitarian and contemporary (the execution)— does not cause any contradictions on the level of discourse. The discourse is recognized only by the reader.

The next stage is the funeral banquet, traditionally symbolizing the return to life (the metaphors of eating and drinking) and the resurrection of the deceased (remembrance). The first two "eulogies" delivered by the brother and a geophysicist colleague reveal the clichés at the heart of the traditionally Socialist Realist interpretation of these archetypes: The deceased is resurrected as a "real warrior, a real man" with "the character of a true friend," who "always lived for others, . . . cared about others and not about himself" (ibid., 111–12). The third "eulogy," Seryozha's, violates these clichés in that it represents the description of another ritual: initiation, whereby the deceased appears in the role of the "elder" ("He was a great man" [ibid., 112]) who administers the ritual trials, without which the "adult," that is, married, life of the neophyte cannot begin. Here, too, initiation signifies attaining the right to marriage and sexual activity. The "deficiency" that the neophyte must overcome is of an emphatically natural character: "the underdeveloped sexual organ," on account of which the young man "can't even properly deflower his bride" (ibid., 113). However, the trials that Seryozha must endure under the leadership of his mentor are formulated in an emphatically social language, that of criminal slang, which once again is directly connected to the code of power realized through violence: Seryozha must "STRING UP A DUDE" [*PRISHMOTAT' CHUVAKA*] and "GET HIS ASS REAMED" [*PROSIFONIT' VERZOKHU*] (capitalized in the original), that is, he must hang a young man his own age and must be raped by his mentor. The incomprehensibility of the secret language and the internal logic of these trials is very important—it puts the reader on an equal footing with the neophyte.

Furthermore, this logic appears in the context of the preceding episode: Just as before, we have an archaic ritual forming the transition to the next phase of the natural order, fitting smoothly into the social-cultural code of violence. Initiation into manhood (the ritual phrases of the mentor emphasize the sacred significance of the ordeals: "good boy, almost a man," "good boy, now a man!" [ibid., 115]) thus requires the neophyte to play the role of both executioner and victim, thereby experiencing both sides of the power of violence. The executioner and victim were already present in the "funeral" episode, but this also fits right in with the mythological logic, since the initiation often represents a "temporary death" after which the neophyte is "reborn." The "object" that the initiate accepts from the mentor is the sexual organ. Here again bodily contact appears as the culmination of the "initiation."

The end of the story constitutes the third and last frustration of expectations and also reveals the profound logic of the discourse. It simultaneously caps off the two "transitions"—the initiation and the funeral ceremony:

". . . from that point on everything really went fine between me and Olya, everything fell into place. I mean, not in terms of sex and all that, but just . . .

well, everything really . . . That's it. And now, comrades, eight years have gone by, and we're together. But the main thing is, my penis was still the same after all this, so that's not really the point. Here, take a look . . ."

Seryozha put the piece of paper that he had been holding in his hands all through the story on the table. He quickly unfastened his pants, pulled his shorts down a bit, lifted his shirt slightly and showed everyone his naked groin, which was sparsely covered with white hairs. Over his tiny testicles protruded his erect white nine-centimeter penis, which was about as thick as a finger. On his pink oval glans was tattooed the letter "Ye."

Amid the total silence Seryozha raised his glass of vodka with a trembling hand and proclaimed:

"To your memory, Nikolai Fyodorovich Yermilov . . ." (Ibid., 115)

The expectation of a magical transformation as a result of the initiation is frustrated. The natural "deficiency" is not removed, but nevertheless "everything fell into place": Harmony has been restored. At the same time the "erect . . . nine-centimeter penis"—a clear manifestation of the mythological metaphor of fertility—with the "mentor's" initial tattooed on it is a symbol of the return to life, the resurrection of the deceased.[7] Moreover, all of these mythological symbols are parodied by the clinical nature of the description. The symbolic "succession," the "life in memory," the "passing of the baton from one generation to the next" here become almost dishearteningly literal. What Clark designates as the "modal schizophrenia of Socialist Realism," manifested in the constant "sudden, unmotivated transitions from realistic discourse to the mythic or utopian" (ibid., 36–37), Sorokin transforms into the absolute indistinguishability of the code of the mythological and the exaggeratedly mimetic, symbolic, and literal. On the level of the story as a whole, this indistinguishability is realized in categories: order and violations of order, the "natural" and the "cultural," the eternal and the socially determined, and even life and death. But when all is said and done, in the final scene it is harmony ("everything fell into place") and absurdity that turn out to be indistinguishable. The scene in which a memorial toast is proposed with pants down, penis protruding, and glasses of vodka in hand vividly embodies the absurdity of the whole story.

Moreover, the naturalism of the final description rends the narrative fabric, breaching the distance between the reader and the story's characters. While in the first episode the reader notices a breach that passes unnoticed by the characters, at the end the reader and the characters find themselves in the same position: The absence in the text of any reaction on the part of the characters to Seryozha's confession is particularly telling. The significance of this transformation becomes clear in the general composition of the story. Its three episodes correspond to the three stages of the initiation rite (temporary death, trials, and resurrection for a new life), but the original object of and participant in the ritual is the reader himself, and he is the one to whom the symbol of resurrection, Seryozha's erect penis, is "handed."

If we attempt to determine Sorokin's strategy for the transformation of Socialist Realism, we find that it combines several contradictory elements. First, Sorokin elucidates the implicit mythologism of Socialist Realist discourse, gives it a "plot," and makes it "graphically visible" by translating the hidden mechanisms forming the text into a direct depiction of ritual actions. Here, too, one may agree with Groys. Sorokin truly remythologizes Socialist Realism, or, more accurately, re-ritualizes it, but not through contact with other, ancient and contemporary, mythologies. Sorokin appeals not to the external but to the internal context of Socialist Realism. The mythologism is drawn entirely from the structure of the Socialist Realist tradition; Socialist Realism returns, as it were, to its structural nucleus. Second, with such a transformation, all discursive elements are dispersed as widely as possible, whereupon the "cultural" turns into the "natural" and vice versa. In accordance with this logic, discursive power is transformed into violent, physical, sexual power, whereupon the images expressing this power invariably elicit a direct emotional reaction—usually revulsion. Third, and perhaps most important, this "deconstruction" not only uses ancient rituals to render Socialist Realist clichés transparent; it also does the opposite—it illuminates the hidden mythological meaning of Socialist Realist patterns. On the one hand, the values of the Socialist Realist worldview are sharply parodied: The search for social integration literally leads to excrement, degradation, and sadistic violence. But, on the other hand, these are the very points that violate the mimetic inertia of Socialist Realist discourse and mark the final transition into myth. The revelation of the discourse's absurdity coincides with the triumph of the mythological order. And this is the source of the ambivalence of Sots-Art: The disgusting and absurd illustrates the mythological harmony, while the harmony thus achieved elicits nausea. This is what Fredric Jameson defines as "pastiche" (see epigraph).

The "modal schizophrenia" (Katerina Clark) of Socialist Realism is the main source of Sots-Art; here the mimetic dimension becomes naturalistic pastiche, and utopian discourse is transformed into a direct model of ritual. And while the first level is connected with the perception of Socialist Realism as a world of the absurd, the second is perceived as a world of the language of power and order. But the main characteristic of Sots-Art in general, and of Sorokin's poetics in particular, lies in the fact that, as in Socialist Realism, both of these dimensions exist simultaneously, constantly shifting back and forth without any motivation. It is the *moment of transition* that constitutes the main artistic problem of Sots-Art. It is through this transition that the interactions of the models of order and chaos take place. Furthermore, this element of the text represents a micromodel of the ritual "transition" taking place in the plot of Socialist Realism and, correspondingly, of Sots-Art.

Sorokin's repertoire contains a wide range of variations on such a transition. His book *The Norm* is a kind of "encyclopedia" of this type of device. It begins with a cycle of stylized novellas, stylization being one of Sorokin's favorite narrative strategies; in this case, the novellas are patterned after typical Soviet "urban" prose. As a rule, all these novellas include as a recurring motif something referred to as a "norm," which the characters are obliged to eat, willingly or unwillingly. It is gradually revealed that the "norm" is briquettes of children's excrement, which the true Soviet man is required to ingest. The narrative of these novellas is unshakably uniform; indeed, the word "norm" does not look disturbing in any of the texts and situations taken separately. The shift in the discourse occurs in the context of all the novellas as a whole—noticed by the reader but not by the characters. At the heart of this motif is a realized metaphor that is all the more compelling for having been left unstated: "to gorge oneself on shit" [*govna nazhrat'sia*]). With Sorokin it acquires the meaning of a pathological ritual upon which the unity of Soviet society depends: the accepted and observed *social order*.

The metaphor is also realized in the cycle of novellas that bring *The Norm* to a close: here the characters themselves literalize quotes from Socialist Realist texts (usually popular songs and poems) through their own actions. Moreover, in such cases the style always changes, although the unity of the discourse is still preserved. Thus, for example, the style of children's Socialist Realism becomes that of Soviet officialdom (in its "journalistic" and police variations):

"The boy who lives in Apartment 5 has a golden pair of hands, Comrade Colonel," reported the tanned Lieutenant, paging through Case #3541/128. "They come to this little handyman by word-of-mouth to have a key made or a coffee-pot soldered."

"Golden hands covered with calluses?" asked the Colonel, lighting up a cigarette.

"Exactly. With scratches and ink spots. Yesterday he glued a globe back together at the school, fixed a radio for his neighbor . . . His mother is proud of his hands, Comrade Colonel, even though the kid's only ten years old . . ."

The Colonel laughed: "How could she not be proud, the Bukharinite scum. She's raised herself such a cub."

Four days later the boy from Apartment 5's melted-down hands went for the purchase of rotary equipment, produced at a branch of the Ford factory in Holland, for regulating the hourly position of Lenin's head on the 80-meter statue at the Palace of Soviets. (Sorokin 1994: 224–25)

Of course, these are the simplest forms of transition. They are completed within the boundaries of a single discourse, that of Socialist Realism, demonstrating its almost limitless "elasticity" and exposing its internal contradictions. Sorokin brings together various possibilities of discourse, invariably creating the effect of absurdity. And since this transition is completed within the boundaries of one and the same discourse, it can be characterized as a transformation of the *power of discourse into the power of the absurd.* Sorokin is inventive enough to extend this device into other types of discourse besides Socialist Realism; absurdity is also revealed in Socialist Realism's ostensible opposite, the discourse of "dissidence" ("Marina's Thirtieth Love"), and in the classical tradition (the quasi-Turgenevesque novel *The Novel*). Indeed, one can easily imagine Sorokin's interpretation of the Bible or *The Divine Comedy.* After all, for him any authoritative discourse is potentially absurd, for the very goal of power over consciousness is itself absurd.

This type of transition can exist in Sorokin independently, for its own sake, but it can also serve as the first step in another, more complex type of transition: the transition from one discourse to another. Here we must note that Sorokin's project is thoroughly deconstructive: Another discourse is revealed *within* the Socialist Realist context. To borrow Eric Naiman's and Ann Nesbet's terminology, a kind of "poetics of interrogation" (see Naiman and Nesbet 1996: 52–68) is at work. Caught in absurd contradictions, the discourse blurts out its "secret of secrets": It admits its lack of identity—what is first perceived as a parody of Socialist Realism proves to be a quite serious reproduction either of ancient, ritualistic, and mythological discourses or an imitation of preconscious, prediscursive, precultural practices.

Thus, for example, the fifth part of *The Norm* takes on the style of "Village Prose"—the highly traditionalist movement in Soviet literature of the 1960s–70s that opposed the revolutionary utopia of Socialist Realism with the nationalist utopia of "the radiant past" (to use Kathleen Parthé's expression) and "a nostalgia generated by the loss of traditional rural life" (Parthé 1992: 3). The country relative's letters to the city at first represent a "pantheistic" narrative about the yearly concerns with the decaying barn, the gardens, and so forth. But gradually all the motifs familiar from the earlier part of the book are transformed into a stream of verbal abuse directed at the relatives in the city and the owner of the plot of land, to whom these letters are actually addressed. The foul language is in turn quickly transmuted into trans-sense chanting and nonsense syllables:

> We ain't a bunch of fucking kulaks either and you ain't gonna shit on me period. I'll be a son-of-a-bitch shit and I fucked you so you don't plow and us

scumbags fucked you. I fucked you scumbag . . . I sucked you fumbag . . . I bagged you scumfuck. I scagged fou yumfuck. I yag gou fumyuck . . . . (Sorokin 1994: 181)

Sorokin gives cursing, which is excluded from the language of Socialist Realism, the meaning of an absurd language, a more adequate illiterate "pantheistic idyll" than the traditional stylistic forms of "Village Prose." It is not coincidental that cursing arises in the most ideologically saturated places to form the image of the urban enemy:

> I won't let myself be shit on I'll fuck all of you so you can't shit any more. I'll get the public all worked up and you won't get a house, because the kulaks have to be liquidated. Because you don't work and you exploit me like this. And for this you'll get destroyed as a class. You're a bad element you tell your fucking little jokes and act like you're so educated and all. Educated my ass. And you got no right to have a house because you're not educated you're a fucking prick. educated types like you should be liquidated and shown to everybody so there won't any more of that! You're not educated you're shit that's what you are. I'm as educated as you are and you damn well better not tell me how to live. I know life a lot better than your kind. (Ibid., 179)

But the main thing is that cursing, which is intended as an embodiment of the absurdity of "village" discourse, here becomes a bridge into the realm of the unconscious, of aggression no longer expressed by means of words. Furthermore, the generalized nature of this style allows one to speak not of the individual but rather of the collective unconscious—a collective unconscious that differs from Jung's in that it is not described in archetypal categories but rather represents the fabric of chaotic nonsense.

Such a transition can be found in the third part of *The Norm*. A pseudo-Buninesque novella about the return of an aristocrat to his home is interrupted by the narrator's indecent sentence (which he immediately attempts to apologize for: "Well, it was just by chance. I just took off . . . you know, I had a lot of problems there, no money, a wife, kids"), and concludes with a "poetic" description of the protagonist masturbating. He has discovered that he is directly related to Tyutchev and proves in his own way the poet's famous dictum that "Russia cannot be with the mind": "when Anton's hot semen gushed onto the Russian Earth, the bell of the deserted church came to life. There you have it" (ibid., 121). This text is already constructed as a dialogue. The "Soviet" consciousness attempts to speak in a language foreign to it, hence the breaks and absurd inconsistencies. But Sorokin complicates the structure even more, offering a different variant of the text in which the protagonist digs up the story "The Cattle Plague," dated 1948, instead of Tyutchev's letter. Not only does this text, with its Socialist Realist orientation, enter into such a contradiction with the pseudo-Buninesque nostalgia of the previous text that the protagonist buries the manuscript (along with the author and the listener-advisor) back in the ground, but "The Cattle Plague" itself represents a rather complex form of transition from one discourse to another.

First of all, the central episode of the story is constructed as a transition within the same discourse. It is revealed that the cattle plague taking place at the collective farm concerns the "wreckers" [*vrediteli*—a word referring to both agricultural pests and political saboteurs—Trans.] who are kept in a cattle-like state. The naturalistic description of the corpses is combined with a stylistically bureaucratic capsule description of each of them, provided from memory by the chairman of the collective farm:

> "Rostovtsev, Nikolai Lvovich, 37 years old, son of an unrepentant wrecker, grandson of an émigré, great-grandson of a district doctor, yes a doctor . . . joined two years ago from the Maloyaroslavl State Cattle-Breeding Factory."
> "Relatives!"—Kedrin again shook the doors.
> "Sister—Rostovtseva, Irina Lvovna, used as living fertilizer in the planting of the Park of Glory in the city of Gorky." (Ibid., 137)

The self-revelation of the discourse in this case is strengthened by the naturalistic description, which is similar to the structure of Sorokin's short stories discussed above: The view from within Socialist Realism is combined with the view from without.

Second, the plot of the tale is constructed as a dialogic paraphrase of the canonical model of Socialist Realist narrative. The "elder mentors" (the secretary of the Regional Committee and the head of the KGB) turn into "tricksters" and "devils" who systematically destroy the entire operation of the collective farm.[8] In addition, the tale presents a graphic model of the Socialist Realist canon as a whole. A real village is doubled by its idealized model carefully constructed by a negligent chairman, and everything that decays and falls apart in "real life" shines like brand new in the model. This is the literal incarnation of the "modal schizophrenia" of Socialist Realism. In classical Socialist Realism, the utopian program eventually merges with "reality." The same effect is achieved by the characters in "The Cattle Plague," only they solve the equation not by creating a new order but by destroying the old one. Burning everything in their path, they carefully duplicate the operation on the model. When everything possible is destroyed and unity between the "model" and "reality" is achieved, the style of the text changes, signaling the transition to yet another discourse. The last pages of the story are constructed as a conversation between a coryphaeus and a choir, a pagan priest and the people, and each side pronounces and repeats phrases in which direct meaning is completely replaced by symbolic meaning. In accordance with this mythological logic, gasoline is splashed from a bucket labeled "water" onto the dirty and beaten Chairman Tishchenko—this is the water with which they water the "cattle":

"What does it say on the bucket?"
"Waaaater!"
"Does water burn?"
"Noooo!"
"Who was given water from this bucket?"
"Caaaattle!"
"These cattle, are they shitty and bloated?"
"Yeeees!"
"Does water burn?"
"Noooo!"
"Is this one shitty?"—the secretary pointed to Tishchenko.
"Yeeees!"
"Bloated?"
"Yeeees!"
"Who is given water from the bucket?"
"Caaaattle!"
"Cattle—are they shitty and bloated?"
"Yeeees!"
"Does water burn?"
"Noooo!" . . .
"Who is given water from the bucket?"
"Caaaattle!"
"So, this one?"
"Yeeees!" . . .
"Give water?"
"Give waaaater!"
"Yes?"
"Yeeeees!"

The secretary grabbed the bucket and splashed burning gasoline on the chairman. Within moments a swirling flame had engulfed Tishchenko. He screamed and took off running from the foundation, tearing though the quickly parting crowd.

The wind whipped the flame and pulled it into a gusty tail.

With amazing speed the chairman, completely engulfed in flames, crossed the plowed soccer field, flashed between the decrepit huts and trampled willow bushes and disappeared behind a knoll. (Ibid., 146)

The dialogic relations in this story do not amount to simply turning the Socialist Realist master plot on its head. Once again, we are dealing with a rite of passage, only this time it is social rather than individual: The renewal of life is paid for by the sacrifice of the "old tsar." Within the context of sacrifice, it makes sense that the chairman is consumed by flames and burnt to ashes, dissolving into the landscape of the collective farm—this is how his "social integration" takes place. Furthermore, the destructive activity of the "mentors" can also be explained by the nature of the rite of passage. As Mircea Eliade observes, the traditional rite of passage contains a "symbolic retrogression to Chaos. In order to be created anew, the old world must first be annihilated" (1958: xii). Expanding on Eliade's model, Katerina Clark argues that in the traditional Socialist Realist novel "[t]he majority of ordeals represented symbolic encounters with 'chaos.' . . . 'Ordeals' involve not only suffering but the transcendence of suffering." There is a "period of psychic chaos through which the initiate must pass before he can achieve psychic stasis" (1981: 178, 185).

Sorokin reinterprets this "transcendence of suffering." For him it is the stage of chaos that corresponds to the "new order," to "physical stasis." The end of the story embodies the final stage of the ritual. There can be nothing further, for there is already nothing. In essence the quality of the "new order" established by ritual only renders explicit that which is implicitly concealed in the "old order": The Socialist Realist world with its dead cattle, decaying buildings, a bell without a clapper, and precise plan—this world, which is associated with the mythology of Sholokhov's *Virgin Soil Upturned*—is already based on the principles of the absurd. Chaos is only the next logical step in the development of the absurd. Absurdity arises as a result of regular contradictions within a given discourse. Chaos testifies to the total mutual destruction of these elements. The transition to another, ritualistic discourse arises as a result of the void that emerges in place of the Socialist Realist world.

Many of Sorokin's other texts are constructed on this same structural basis, in particular his novel *Four Stout Hearts*.[9] Aleksandr Genis appears to be correct in concluding that in this novel

> Sorokin deconstructs the opposition of Man/Machine that lies at the basis of the genre of the "Socialist Realist industrial novel," demonstrating the falseness of both avant-garde and Socialist Realist interpretations. In Sorokin's world, no distinction whatsoever is made between animate and inanimate matter. Intensive industrial processes are carried out in the book, and its objects are equally likely to be people or machines. Therefore the text can be read as sadistic if one considers the characters to be living or as comic if one considers the characters to be nonliving. Sorokin's characters are "nonmachines" and "nonpeople." . . . At the end of the book, an incomprehensible technological process transforming the bodies of the characters into "compressed cubes and frozen hearts" seems to complete a closed circuit. The industrial production around which the entire novel revolves does not actually produce anything. It exists without any additional, external goal, and it is precisely in this respect that it is indistinguishable from life. (1994a: 248)

Furthermore, one can also see in this novel the "naturalization" of the Socialist Realist mythology of the "great family." On the one hand, the four main characters of the novel—a man, a young woman, an old man, and a boy—form something like a family unit, fulfilling "family" roles. However, as in Socialist Realism, the social family is formed on the basis of a "common cause," which often conflicts with actual genetic relations. That is why for Sorokin an indispensable element of the "ordeal" leading to the success of the "common cause" is the murder and dismemberment of Seryozha's parents (whereupon the glans of Seryozha's father's penis, which the "four" pass along to each other from mouth to mouth, serves as a material symbol of incorporation) and the grinding up of Rebrov's mother in a meat grinder ("liquid mother"). In the logic of Socialist Realism, the "great family" constantly increases in scope, transforming from a metaphor of society to its metonym. The same thing happens in Sorokin's novel, but with one important difference: "Family ties" are created with the help of murder, violence, sexual perversion, degradation, and the eating of excrement. Scenes like the "branding" of old man Staube by Rebrov and Olga in response to Seryozha's denunciation, and the degrading torture that Olga must endure in a military bunker (along with many other similar scenes) are related—degradation only strengthens family trust. It is also typical that the final scenes of the novel, consisting of a veritable avalanche of murders and torture that are totally unclear in purpose, are capped off by the appearance of the head of a baby in the perineum of a woman who has been tortured to death. And although the meaning of the "common cause" remains a mystery throughout the entire novel (a transcendental life that is theoretically incomprehensible), its ending is determined by the principle of the growth of the great family, the principle that unites arbitrariness (any person at all can join this family) with the necessity of violence (or, taken to its logical extreme, murder) as a necessary condition for family ties:

> Faceted pivots went into their [the four's] heads, shoulders, stomachs, and legs. The chisels began to turn, the pneumobatteries were lowered, the liquid freon began to flow, the heads of the presses covered the lower plates. After twenty-eight minutes the hearts of the four, pressed into cubes and frozen, dropped into a roller, where they were marked like dice. Three minutes later, the roller tossed them out onto an ice field covered with liquid mother. The hearts of the four came to a stop:
>
> 6, 2, 5, 5. (Sorokin 1994b: 116)

This is not merely a technological process; it is the total absorption of the human body by the substance of fate. Always guessing about the likelihood of various events with the help of a mysterious "apportionment" [*raskladka*], the characters eventually find the maximum possible unity with fate when their hearts are transformed into dice. The ritualization and naturalization of Socialist Realist mythology once again leads to the effect of *repulsive harmony with the universe.*

Similarly, in his play *Trust,* the syntax of a standard industrial play, slightly updated for the perestroika era, is filled with phrases uttered like common idioms that are in fact reminiscent of nothing other than Futurist "trans-sense," as in the words of the progressive Party organizer Pavlenko:

> Tamara Sergeevna: Do you feel this trust?
> Pavlenko: I feel it like ancestral branches, like sulfurous tin. This trust is like ribbedness to me. Perhaps I whistle in the corner only because they trust me. You know, Tomka, when they really trust you it's . . . it's like a salivary majority. When there are lilac notches behind your back, then there are also lines on one another. This is what I work for. (Sorokin 1991: 105)

And here is the speech of the honest head of the OTK (Department of Technical Control) at a special Party meeting concerning urgent restructuring (*perestroika*):

> "And now, when there is no point in deceiving ourselves—the tank and the baby are all in the milk as the workers say—now it is clear why we are fingernails and why it is possible to tug on us. And I'm not saying this because I eat dirt, I eat, over there, any old slop, but because that's enough already, covering up our own lack of discipline, enough wiping our glasses and fussing with foxes." (Ibid., 113)

In industrial drama, the characters' speeches always carried tremendous weight; it was through such speeches that new ideological directives were expressed. For Sorokin, the mere act of speaking, which is essentially nonsensical, is sufficient. The ritualistic nature of this speaking is highlighted by the fact that this factory produces Russian Orthodox crosses, and the climactic Party meeting that takes place in the workshop is gradually *drowned out* by the din of a huge cross rotating on its axis:

> The cross is rotating so quickly that its contours are hard to distinguish. The applause, the voices of the speakers—everything is drowned out by the monotonous hollow roar. San Sanych is saying, or rather, screaming something and gesticulating wildly. . . . Then Pavlenko makes a long speech. (Ibid., 116)

In *The Queue,* the linear structure of the social order is graphically depicted by columns in the text, which consists entirely of phrases uttered by the numerous "queues"; yet this structure turns out to be devoid of any particular purpose. The choice of the line is, of course, no accident: In Soviet culture, standing in line for merchandise or groceries became, in the final analysis, a social ritual unto itself. The presence of the line as the sole testimony to the value of the merchandise was the stuff of satire by numerous authors in the seventies and eighties (Grigory Gorin, Mikhail Zhvanetsky, and Mikhail Zadornov, just to name three). Sorokin gives this ritual a frankly mythological, rather than comic, cast. What the characters are waiting for is completely unclear—the vague outlines of the long-sought goal grow even murkier (first jeans, then furniture, then boots, then all of these together). But for the protagonist, this senseless standing is itself an act of initiation, which is completed by a chance meeting with a "sorceress" who, on the morning after they have spent the night together, promises to take the young protagonist directly to the warehouse for the goods. The longed-for goods are, of course, appropriate as a symbolic object, the touching of which signifies "the social integration of the protagonist."

These are the same motifs of utopian discourse that had not lost their charm in Aksyonov's ironic *Surplussed Barrelware*: There, the barrelware was the symbolic object around which the chance traveling companions miraculously attained a sense of utopian brotherhood. Twenty years separate Sorokin from Aksyonov, enough to strip utopianism of any possible charm. In Sorokin's work, anything that bears the mark of utopianism inevitably becomes absurd. This is why in "The Queue" the protagonist's search both is subject to the logic of ritual and devalues the ritual order of the line: He stands in line in order to get something without standing in line. The essentially mythological process of the search and the search's result cancel each other out, although they do not violate the unity of the ritual plot of initiation. Finally, the mythological structure embraces the emptiness left behind after the annihilation of meaning.

If we return to the question of Sorokin's (and, more generally, Sots-Art's) method for the transition from stylization under mimetic discourse to another dimension (whether it be absurdist–"trans-sense" or ritual/mythological), then we must acknowledge that its ideal form is the blank space on the page tearing the text in two (as in such stories as "Love" and "Night Guests"). In all of Sorokin's works we have examined so far, two parallel processes occur simultaneously: The *remythologization of the discourse,* the reconstruction of its ritual semantics, is combined with the consequent revelation of the discourse's contradictions—in a word, with the *deconstruction of the discourse,* which brings it into a state of absurdity or complete chaos. But since both of these parallel processes take place simultaneously, the result of any text by Sorokin is the *mythology of the absurd,* the *ritual of incorporation into chaos.* Due to its mythological structure, the absurd is constructed as the universal, initial, and final state of being and consciousness. Chaos, in the form of the rite of passage, is interpreted as a state equalizing all possible linguistic forms and any activity at all, as the point of man's complete convergence with his social milieu, discourse and the universe. But the basis for these universals, their common denominator, is the emptiness that remains when all possible meanings have been wiped away. And a tangible emotional shading is imparted to this entire ritual/mythological complex by the naturalistic motifs of violence, dismemberment, degradation, excrement, death—the processes of the deconstruction of the discourse are reified in the plot.

If in Daniil Kharms's "Cases" (Sluchai) the equation of creativity with activity directed toward death is based on an understanding of death as the only possible reality among simulacra, for Sorokin death and violence are included in the space of discourse; they merely translate discursive power into "natural" language, which, not coincidentally, coincides with the climax of the plot and the reconstructed ritual. Daniil Kharms's "cruelty" in his stories of the thirties embodies the utopian faith in the idea that writing, which encompasses the terrible authenticity of death, is capable of emerging into an "independent existence," into unsimulated culture and life. For Sorokin, there is nowhere to go beyond the limits of discourse. Only by immersing oneself in discourses can one arrive at the mythological state of chaos, which is by nature not subject to articulation, thus leaving the page blank.

More parallels can be found between Sorokin's poetics and Antonin Artaud's "theater of cruelty." Susan Sontag argues that Artaud's entire "theater of cruelty" project was based, first of all, on the identity of body and consciousness: "In his struggle against all hierarchical or merely dualistic notions of consciousness, Artaud constantly treats his mind as if it *were* a kind of body—a body that he could not 'possess'. . . and also a mystical body by whose disorder he was 'possessed' " (1976: xxiv). Second, the entire project represents a modernist interpretation of Gnostic philosophy, bringing the following tenets to the fore:

> To be free of "the world," one must break the moral (or social) law. To transcend the body, one must pass through a period of physical debauchery and verbal blasphemy, on the principle that only when morality has been deliberately flouted is the individual capable of a radical transformation: entering into a state of grace that leaves all moral categories behind. . . . The theater Artaud wants to create enacts a secularized Gnostic rite. It is not an expiation. It is not a sacrifice, or, if it is, the sacrifices are all metaphors. It is a rite of transformation—the communal performance of a violent act of spiritual alchemy. . . . The Gnostic passage through the stages of transcendence

implies a move from the conventionally intelligible to what is conventionally unintelligible. Gnostic thinking characteristically reaches for an ecstatic speech that dispenses with distinguishable words. . . . The Gnostic project is a search for wisdom that cancels itself out in unintelligibility, loquacity, and silence. (Sontag 1976: xlvi, lii–liii)

All of these characteristics correspond quite closely to Sorokin's poetics, with one reservation: Following the logic of the postmodern condition, he identifies both individual consciousness and morality with particular discourses and their power. But like Artaud, Sorokin gives discourse a physical dimension: He transforms the implicit mythologism of discourse into ritual action carried out with the body or over the body, describing it with as much medical detail as possible. Sorokin's deconstruction of discourse can be understood as a Gnostic violation of laws in the name of a transcendent escape from the limits of the body/discourse/consciousness. His streams of unintelligible speech or completely absurd babbling correspond to the ecstatic speech through which the inexpressible wisdom found in ritual expresses itself, the paradise beyond good and evil.

This structure corresponds to the general semantic construction of Sorokin's texts. Moreover, in Sorokin, as in Artaud (not to mention Kharms), the act of cruelty, re-created with naturalistic obviousness, violates the boundary between text and reader inherent in traditional discourses, including that of Socialist Realism. Writing about Artaud, Jacques Derrida asserts that they are aimed at nothing less than the destruction of representation, the cancellation of Aristotelian mimesis:

> The stage, certainly, *will no longer represent,* since it will not operate as an addition, as the sensory illustration of a text already written. . . . The stage will no longer operate as the repetition of a *present,* will no longer *re-*present a present that would exist elsewhere and prior to it. . . . Nor will the stage be a representation, if representation means the surface of a spectacle displayed for spectators. It will not even offer the presentation of a present, if present signifies that which is maintained *in front* of me. Cruel representation must permeate me. And nonrepresentation is, thus, original representation, if representation signifies, also, the unfolding of a volume, a multidimensional milieu, an experience which produces it own space. (1978: 237; italics in the original)

As a result, in Sorokin the object of the Gnostic metaritual played out in the text is no longer the characters but rather the reader. An indication of this transformation of the communicative function of Sorokin's texts is their "visualization." Certainly, this refers to the graphic video images of the text (e.g., in *The Queue*); but Vladimir Potapov makes an observation about "The Cattle Plague" that could be applied to almost any of Sorokin's works:

"Vladimir Sorokin's story is clearly 'cinematographic,' and it appeals to our visual (spectator's) memory no less than to our literary memory. . . . One may say that Vladimir Sorokin *films* 'The Cattle Plague' " (1991: 30; emphasis in the original).

However, while recognizing how much Sorokin's fiction has in common with Artaud's "theater of cruelty," one cannot help but also see a most profound distinction in the semantic function of these artistic systems as a whole. Artaud's "theater of cruelty" is, of course, utopian. The immersion of the viewer in a chaotic state presupposes the attainment of the archetypal Truth hidden beneath routine civilization. As Sontag writes, for Artaud, "to show the truth means to show archetypes rather than individual psychology; this makes the theater a place of risk, for the 'archetypal reality' is 'dangerous' " (1976: xxxiv). Sorokin worked with Socialist Realism and was intimately acquainted with the utopian projects for human transformation, especially on a collective basis (including even on the basis of the "collective unconscious"); he makes chaos both the signifier and the signified of the ritual that is being modeled: Nothing is attained by immersion in chaos other than chaos. It is absurdity and chaos that turn out to be the final signified object of any possible discourse.

Like many other Russian postmodernists (indeed, like Russian postmodernism as a whole), Sorokin unites specifically avant-garde *approaches* with deeply postmodern *outcomes*. In building a completely avant-garde construction of the text as ritual, Sorokin cuts off its utopian aspirations and closes off both ritual and text. The resulting *short circuit* is expressed not only in the shocking moments in the plot; the shock effect itself arises as a result of the visual, but not at all philosophical, compatibility of the ritual-mythological structures for producing order with the semantics of the total elimination of meaning (*obessmyslivanie*), that is, with a world model of chaos. In Sorokin, the mythology of chaos signifies that any structures of discursive power are based on the absurd, and any hierarchy of meaning or system of values is only an external cover for the total chaos of ontological absurdity. But does he see any order born out of chaos or formed inside of chaos *without devaluing* it, as he devalues any discursive order?

This kind of order, born out of chaos and coexisting with it, could be *freedom*—the freedom toward which the cruelty of the Gnostic search that breaks all possible laws is aimed. Dmitrii Prigov constantly speaks of freedom as the "center of values" not only of Sorokin's fiction but of Sots-Art culture as a whole: "It seems to me that Sorokin's position (as well as the whole direction in which he is drawn)—an understanding of freedom as the fundamental inspiration of the culture of this moment—is truly, if not solely, humanistic" (Prigov 1992: 118). And elsewhere, in reference to his own position, Prigov writes:

> I understood that the main task of art, its purpose in this world, is to show some sort of freedom, absolute freedom, with all its dangers. In the example of art a person can see that there is absolute freedom that cannot necessarily be fully realized in life. I took Soviet language as the most functional, clearest, and most accessible language of the time, the one that was representative of the ideology and that presented itself as the absolute, heaven-sent truth. Man was oppressed by this language not from the outside but from within. Any ideology that lays total claim to you, any such language, has totalitarian ambitions to seize the entire world, cover it with its own terminology, and show that it is the absolute truth. I wanted to show that there is freedom. Language is only language and not the absolute truth, and once we understand this we will obtain freedom. (Gandlevsky and Prigov 1993: 5)

But the problem is that the freedom toward which Sots-Art strives through remythologizing and deconstructing the power of discourse(s) is like Gnostic freedom: It has nothing in common with humanism. As Susan Sontag writes in reference to Artaud, "theater serves an 'inhuman' individuality, an 'inhuman' freedom, as Artaud calls it in *The Theater and Its Double*—the very opposite of the liberal, sociable idea of freedom" (Sontag 1976: xlvii). In Sorokin's case, freedom is stripped of its humanity primarily because *there is no one who can make use of it.* It cannot, of course, be used by an individual. Unlike the existentialists, who place the individual at the center of the "myth of the absurd," Sorokin transforms the individual into a simulacrum, into a pure function of discourse, and nothing more.

But even the impersonal author-creator can neither use nor express this freedom: For the author-creator the mythology of chaos turns into muteness. The mythology is universal, it has no exceptions, and if every discourse can be reduced to the power of the absurd and the emptiness of chaos, then the author-creator simply has *no language* to express the freedom that he may have found. But does the artistic world contain anything that cannot be aesthetically (or discursively) expressed? Apparently not. In Bakhtinian terms, this situation can be considered a particular type of dialogic paradox. Sots-Art, after all, represents an extreme form of dialogic writing: It contains absolutely *no word that is not the word of another,* and, moreover, this "otherness" is clearly recognized by both the author and the reader. But who is responsible for this word? The character? No, for he himself is openly simulative. The author? No, he only assembles the "foreign" discourses. It turns out that the responsible party is only an impersonal, "no one's" discourse—but then freedom from the deconstructed discourse also belongs to no one. Such freedom, which is not earned through responsibility, is hollow, empty; it is like a pastiche, like the mythology of the chaos of mutually destructive discursive meanings (after all, where are nondiscursive meanings to be found?).

The transformation of the mechanism of representation turns the ritual in the text back not only onto the reader but, to a much greater degree, onto the author-creator. It is the author-creator who must ultimately dissolve in chaos, renouncing his original position of "outsideness" in relation to the absurdity of discourse.

This is an ontological dead end. Both Sorokin's prose and Sots-Art as a whole merely expose it, taking the hidden contradictions of their own postmodern discourse to their logical extremes. In short, the reason for this dead end is the contradiction between, on the one hand, an "understanding of freedom as the fundamental inspiration of the culture of this moment" (Prigov) and, on the other hand, the "death of the author" (Barthes) and the "disappearance of the writing subject" (Foucault) thanks to which this freedom is obtained.

The semantic reduction of dialogism, the transformation of the strategy of dialogue with chaos into a monological acceptance of chaos, the self-destruction of philosophical freedom and the final transformation of artistic play into the basis of a new (or perhaps actually old and ultramodern) mythology—all this testifies to the growing crisis of Russian postmodernism in the eighties and, particularly, the nineties. A number of features of Sokolov's *Astrophobia* can be traced through many of the works of this period, such as Viktor Erofeyev's *Russian Beauty,* Mikhail Berg's "Ros and I," Tatyana Shcherbina's "The Mansion," Egor Radov's "The Snake-Sucker," Vladimir Zuev's "Black Box," Dmitrii Galkovsky's *Endless Dead End,* and the fiction of Valeria Narbikova, Andrei Levkin, Boris Kudriakov, and Vyacheslav Kuritsyn. Here we find a clear movement backward from postmodernism to thoroughly avant-garde solutions; in particular, these texts attempt to create narcissistic mythological utopias that are hermetic both philosophically and linguistically. Moreover, this return is accompanied by the noticeable loss of the feature that was the avant-garde's source of life: the sense of startling, even scandalous novelty. If early twentieth-century Russian avant-garde writers were preoccupied with their attempts to "resurrect the word," to return direct, primordial emotional meaning to turns of phrases and even the "naked" phoneme itself, the latter-day authors of "abstract fiction" often struggle with the opposite problem: They create a conflict between literary, cultural, and other contexts in order for these contexts to annihilate each other, leaving in their wake nothing but the effect of aesthetic silence.[10]

# 10

# Famous Last Words

> . . . *nothing conclusive has yet taken place in the world, the*
> *ultimate word of the world and about the world has not yet*
> *been spoken, the world is open and free, everything is still in*
> *the future and will always be in the future.*
> But this is, after all, also the *purifying sense* of ambivalent
> *laughter.*

> —Mikhail Bakhtin (1984: 166; emphasis in the original)

The paradoxical interweaving of text and context constitutes one of the mechanisms working within the postmodernist model of artistic unity. This is why comprehension of the principles behind the playful relations between the text and certain cultural and aesthetic contexts is so important for determining the generic and stylistic features of postmodernist fiction. Certainly, no single literary text of any artistic significance can exist outside the complicated network of relations with the cultural context, often including alienation from one set of traditions and attraction to another. The postmodernist play with context is different primarily because the same traditions spark both attraction and alienation simultaneously, with the natural result that they cancel each other out.

This terminology of *alienation/attraction* is not applicable to any description of Aksyonov's and Aleshkovsky's relations with utopian discourse, Tolstaya's and Sokolov's (in *Between Dog and Wolf*) connection to modernist and Romantic mythologies of creativity, Pietsukh's and Viktor Erofeyev's ties to various types of mythologization of history, as well as Sorokin's and Popov's appeals to Socialist Realist discourse. In all the texts discussed here in Part III, the demythologization of the context is inseparable from the remythologization of its ruins. The result is rather peculiar: the *defamiliarization of the entire cultural language*. But what is most interesting about this effect is that it is created *from within* the given cultural language, from within the intertextual material out of which the text is built; perhaps it would best be called "auto-defamiliarization." Mikhail Epstein argues that "culturology," the Russian equivalent of cultural studies developed throughout the seventies and eighties, was an important part of the postmodernist cultural consciousness of this period. Culturology was opposed to one-dimensional "Soviet culture": "For many decades, Soviet civilization assumed the right to judge and not to be judged. . . . It did not need culturology but rather 'culture-apology,' and so it lost the true attributes of culture, which needs a zone of distancing, nonparticipatory, or alienative thought" (1995a: 285). Culturology possessed an explosive liberating potential, since it represented the "culture's self-determination, including its ability for self-criticism, self-denial, and the formation of various countercultures. . . . In the process of self-reflection and self-estrangement, culture becomes an object of its own intellectual activities, and culturology is the locus of this activity" (ibid., 286–87).

The postmodernist author plays a culturological role as well. He or she writes a text by using an "alien" context, transforming any image or real-life situation into a *culturological formula*. The culturological meaning of this particular pattern is emphasized in the text's plot development, obscuring or even entirely replacing the "everyday-life" meaning of characters and events. One can find such passages from "everyday life" to culturology in the denouements of Tolstaya's short stories or in the climaxes of Sorokin's. The combination of "culturological" and "mimetic" approaches can explain the ambivalence of characters and chronotopes in the writings of Sokolov, Pietsukh, and Viktor Erofeyev. In postmodernist writing, any cultural context is represented as a myth, that is, as a universal and self-sufficient hierarchical construction. Each image is burdened with culturological associations, functioning as a *synecdoche* of the mythological discourse. Hence, postmodernist writing needs the specific stylistic forms that could serve double duty: On the one hand, they should be able to mythologize contextual signifiers; on the other hand, they must be strong enough to break the mythological spell surrounding those signifiers in order to deprive them of their mythological self-sufficiency, to destroy hierarchical orders, transforming them into material for play. In its search for such stylistic forms, the Russian postmodernist fiction of the eighties and nineties appealed to the fairy-tale and carnival traditions, both of which simultaneously recapitulate and destroy the logic of mythological binary oppositions. The fairy tale plays with myth from outside; as narrator, the fairy-tale jester performs a theatrical deconsecration of mythological symbols, transforming them into the elements of a totally fictional plot of fantastic adventures. Carnivalization is mythological by nature, disclosing the playfulness at the very core of the sacred discourse. The fairy tale lends subjectivity to play; a playful attitude is shown to be integral to creativity. Carnivalization is oriented toward the comprehension of the playful nature of being, the playful logic of eternity.

A strong fairy-tale style is characteristic of Aksyonov, Tolstaya, Sokolov, and Pietsukh, while carnivalization is the main model for Aleshkovsky, Viktor Erofeyev, and Vladimir Sorokin. Yevgeny Popov eclectically combines both fairy-tale and carnivalesque stylistic models. Moreover, each of these writers has found his or her own version of the traditional discourse. For Tolstaya, fairy-tale patterns correspond to the aestheticization of reality through fantasy, while the most important thing for Sokolov is the fairy tale's potential autonomy from "real" time and space. As for Pietsukh and Popov, their orientation toward fairy-tale discourse is expressed primarily through the stance of their narrators on the border between life and literary conventions as they demonstrate the mutual simulation of "truth" and "fiction."

Similarly, for Aleshkovsky carnivalization is a way to mock the oppressive ideology and to praise the organic philosophy of the "collective ancestral body of all people" (Bakhtin 1968: 19), while Viktor Erofeyev transforms the principle of carnivalesque *mésalliances* into narrative and stylistic oxymorons. Yevgeny Popov's style enacts the carnivalesque freedom through laughter, while carnivalization in Sorokin unfolds in the continuous (albeit gloomy) transfigurations of "high" sociocultural meanings into "low" biological and bodily ones, and vice versa. Carnivalesque and fairy-tale discursive patterns both exalt and subordinate such stylistic features as theatricality (in Aksyonov), irony (in Tolstaya and Viktor Erofeyev), parody (in Pietsukh and Popov, as well as in Sokolov's *Astrophobia*), and pastiche (in Sorokin). But all versions of those two stylistic trends serve as a weapon for uncovering the cultural myth-making process, the process that forms the basis of the postmodernist model of artistic wholeness.

As stylistic principles, the carnivalesque and fairy-tale paradigms lead to an *external* playful interpretation of mythologized cultural contexts, by setting them against a demythologizing and relativistic backdrop and surrounding them with a halo of ambivalent aesthetic connotations. But there is a deeper level to this artistic play, one at which the cultural mythology is reconstructed from within. This is the level of *metagenre*. Metagenre, according to Naum Leiderman, is "the structural principle for the creation of a world model" (Leiderman 1982: 221). This principle is embodied in the primary genre of a given literary period or movement. This genre's distinctive principle of world modeling is taken up by other genres, resulting in the transformation of old generic forms in the new artistic paradigm; this is how the genre system of a given movement forms its core. For example, "dramatization" became a metageneric principle in Neo-Classicism, spreading from tragedy and comedy to rhetorical genres (the ode, the satire) and didactic prose. In Romanticism, "lyricization" penetrated both prose and dramatic genres. "Novelization," as Bakhtin has shown, represents the constructive principle common to all genres connected to Realism (see Leiderman 1988: 4–17).

In postmodernism, the world model is structurally based on the concept of simulation as a constructive principle and on the concept of death as a major philosophic requirement for the discourse. Dialogism acts as a formal device, although it mutates in the direction of the total erasure of boundaries between author and character, as well as toward the maximum expansion of the "creative chronotope" zone. A similar conceptual combination of *death, simulation, and dialogism* can be found only in the generic tradition of Menippean satire. Simulation corresponds to the Menippean atmosphere of *"joyful relativity* of all structure and order, of all authority and all (hierarchical) positions" (Bakhtin 1984: 121) regarding all values and philosophies; dialogism corresponds to the Menippean concept of the dialogical nature of truth. As for death, "the menippea accorded great importance to the *nether world:* here was born that special genre of 'dialogues of the dead,' widespread in European literature of the Renaissance, and in the seventeenth and eighteenth century" (Bakhtin 1984:117). "[E]xtraordinary freedom of plot and philosophical invention" (ibid., 114)—especially regarding legendary and historical characters (as one can see in the writings of Pietsukh, and in Sokolov's *Astrophobia);* "slum naturalism" (ibid., 115) coupled with philosophical dialogue (as in Aleshkovsky, Sorokin, and both Erofe(y)evs; "sharp contrasts and oxymoronic combinations" (ibid., 118) in the presentation of characters (as in Sokolov, Viktor Erofeyev, and Tolstaya); "wide use of inserted genres" (ibid., 118), which are almost always parodic (as in Aksyonov, Sokolov, Popov, and Sorokin); "an active dialogic approach to one's own self, destroying . . . the outer shell of the self's image" (ibid., 120) (which is analogous to Tolstaya's and Sokolov's confessional dialogism); "a devaluation of all external positions that a person might hold in life, into *roles* played out on the stageboards of the theater of the world in accordance with the wishes of blind fate" (ibid., 119) (Tolstaya, Sokolov, Viktor Erofeyev, Pietsukh, Popov)—all these famous Bakhtinian characteristics of menippea correspond perfectly to the Russian "new-wave" fiction of the late eighties and nineties. And such features of Menippean satire as "extraordinary philosophical universalism and a capacity to contemplate the world on the broadest possible scale" and "the deliberate multistyled and hetero-voiced nature" directly correspond to the permanent play with the "culturological formulae" and stylistic intertextuality of Russian postmodernism. But the relation of postmodernist poetics to the Menippean tradition in genre and style cannot be limited to a mere enumeration of relatively easily indicated external features. The connection is actually much deeper.

One contemporary scholar of ancient Menippean satire, Joel Relihan, defines the genre as a first in the history of culture parody: the self-criticism of "philosophic thought and forms of writing, a parody of the habits of civilized discourse in general." He argues "that it ultimately turns into the parody of the author who has dared to write in such an orthodox way" (1993: 10). Menippea, according to Relihan, "opposes the word-centered view of the universe, and is a genre that, in words, denies the possibility of expressing the truth in words" (ibid., 11). It is based on the "assumption that no world can be understood, that language is inadequate to express or confine reality, and that the act of analysis is the work of a fool" (ibid., 24).

This role of Menippean satire is embodied in the following principles of the genre poetics:

- the special function of fantasy, which "serves not only to undermine other forms of cultural and literary authority, but also to undermine the importance of the particular Menippean satire itself" (ibid., 22). This effect is achieved through the author's self-parody, the use of an unreliable narrator, and the conventional Menippean ending "in which the lessons preached and learned in the body of the text are negated" (ibid., 22);
- a particular stylistics directed toward "making a joke at the expense of literature with all the means available to it: authorship, unity, genre, and style. . . . Vocabulary and grammar are allowed to be as fantastic as the action that they describe. . . . The lack of taste and artistic unity is an integral part of a genre whose essence is the shocking juxtaposition of irreconcilable opposites" (ibid., 26). The genre of Menippean satire presents a burlesque "battle of form and content, where all claims to perception, knowledge, and truth are negated by fantasy, form, style, language, and self-parody" (ibid., 28);
- the decentralization of artistic representation: the interpretation of the hero's search as aimless and absurd, the presentation of the world as irrational and incomprehensible; the author's identification of himself with his unreliable narrator, which in its turn results in the discreditation of the author's perspective, and the "rejection of the author's ability to preach, or even to understand" (ibid., 35).

This set of Menippean generic principles distinctively corresponds to the important characteristics of postmodernist poetics, even if the connection is indirect. For instance, the special role of fantasy is comparable to the function of *absurdity* in "new-wave" fiction. In these texts, the absurd is presented as the invariably *positive basis* of the plot and the artistic conception.

In Aksyonov's fiction, the absurdity of the characters and situations of Socialist Realist discourse is transformed into the main condition for transforming these characters and situations into the elements of a fairy-tale worldview and the establishment of a fairy-tale freedom from the power of social discourses. The absurdity of Filin's tall tales in Tolstaya's "Fakir" is interpreted as a sign of the "creative chronotope," based on the playful transformation of the mythological "truth." Pietsukh considers absurdity as a major expression of "the fullness of life," and therefore as the foundation of history in general and the Russian national mentality in particular. In Viktor Erofeyev's and Yevgeny Popov's fiction, absurdity serves as a major principle of unity, combining the "rhizomes" of history and contemporary time. In Sorokin's work, the realm of the absurd is where all the discourses meet, from the discourses of ancient times to those of present day, from obscenity to the high classics.

The special stylistics of Menippean satire corresponds not only to Russian postmodernism's carnivalesque and fairy-tale style; it is also related to postmodernism's interplay of *several different discourses* at once. Usually, all these discourses are equally subverted; the rigid opposition between, say, utopian and carnival discourses in Aleshkovsky's fiction leads to the monologism of the epic metagenre rather than to Menippean satire. Fragments of subverted discourses are very often combined within a single paragraph or even a single phrase. Moreover, discursive multiplicity can be created either quantitatively or qualitatively. For example, in our discussion of Pietsukh's "The Central–Ermolaevo War," we noted the absurdist effect resulting from the juxtaposition of three distinct discourses: The discursive models of Socialist Realism, Neo-Classicism, and ancient Russian heroic monumentalism clash in amusing and unpredictable combinations. A similar effect is achieved in Sokolov's *Astrophobia* through the interplay of modernist linguistic experimentation, the memoir tradition, and heroic discourses. If Sorokin brings together only two major discourses, those of Socialist Realism and mythology, he more than compensates for this relative simplicity with the wide variety of polyvalent forms he uses to express the mutual transformations and metamorphoses of the discourses he targets. Postmodernism's "antiliterary" slant also makes itself known to the extent that each of the works we have discussed demonstrates the impossibility of the very class of utterance to which it itself belongs. Thus we are faced with the last utopia (Aksyonov), the last Romantic and Modernist myths of the artist's "life-creation" (Tolstaya, Sokolov), the last historic fables and legends (Pietsukh, Viktor Erofeyev), the last memoirs (*Astrophobia*), and, finally, the last examples of Socialist Realism (Popov, Sorokin). If anything unites this motley postmodernist crew, it is that all of them want to get the last word.

As for the decentralization of the artistic (self-)representation, it expresses itself most strongly in the transformations of the image of the author. The author abdicates his traditional god-like control of his own text, becoming a participant in the very same game that his characters are playing (or, more often, losing). As noted earlier, the postmodernist text takes on the significance of an ontological gesture on the part of the author, who, in the course of the plot, comes to realize his dependence on the created world by metonymic analogy to the "life" of his characters, who are hostages in a playful reality created by the author. In modernism, the author creates something akin to a stained-glass window, insisting that genuine world harmony can be pieced together from the disparate elements of individual perception; in postmodernism, this stained-glass window has broken into pieces, but these pieces have been assembled into a kaleidoscope that extracts an aesthetic effect from random, continually moving splinters that reflect each other in a system of hidden mirrors. The author's "creative chronotope" is that system of mirrors: It does not have self-sufficient meaning, but its "reflective ability" produces the mutual projections of the characters' kaleidoscopic "creative chronotopes."

There is no contradiction here with Bakhtin's theory of "genre memory." While citing the "genre memory" of Menippean satire as an explanation for Dostoevsky's polyphony, Bakhtin stressed that "Dostoevsky linked up with the chain of a given generic tradition at that point where it passed through his own time" (1984: 121). Polyphony revived one side of Menippean genre memory, while postmodernism addresses itself to other, less obvious layers of genre memory: the "antiliterary" contents of the Menippean satire. To paraphrase Bakhtin, this is the point where a "given generic tradition" passes through postmodern time and texts.

Menippean "genre memory" represents a destructive, or perhaps deconstructive, pattern within postmodernist poetics, using philosophical and aesthetic nihilism against the text itself as well as its author. In its postmodernist reinterpretation, Menippean tradition equalizes inner orders of diametrically opposed cultural languages by appealing to absurdity, nonsense, and images of the comic unattainability of truth and the inadequacy of any language. All these transformations eventually form the concept of *culture as chaos.*

In addition, the Menippean "*testing* [of] the idea and the man of the idea" (Bakhtin 1984: 105) in postmodernist texts applies not only to "ideas" involved in the plot development but also to the philosophy of freedom immanent in the position of the author who laughs disrespectfully at all possible types of cultural and philosophic limitations. In the literature of the Russian "new wave," this situation results in two different types of artistic design. On the one hand, the equalization of writing with self-destruction, and, ultimately, with death, transforms the author's freedom of self-expression into his ontological dependence on his own text, as often happens in Tolstaya. In the works of Pietsukh and Viktor Erofeyev, this ontological dependence becomes explicit in the narrative structure, where different cultural meanings are annihilated, which paradoxically provides the narrator contact with the chaos of history.

On the other hand, the dismantling of authoritative discourses in Russian postmodernist fiction of the eighties and nineties is often understood as a condition of carnivalesque freedom and, consequently, as the devalorization of death as a fake threshold. In Sorokin's work, this tendency achieves its clearest expression: Death and violence are presented as discursive devices, as "letters on paper," which can only be overcome with other discursive devices, particularly defamiliarization. The "creative chronotope" that is so crucial for Russian postmodernism becomes vague and indistinct; the subject of consciousness is replaced by the figure of emptiness, by the "zero" sign. The author's almost absolute freedom (which in any case is thoroughly negative, based as it is on the total negation of any form of discursive control) is deprived not only of its humanistic dimension but of any other conceivable dimension as well. Freedom is transformed into pure abstraction.

However, Russian postmodernism combines the demythologization of cultural languages (including the concept of the author as an essential principle for cultural mythmaking) with the remythologization of cultural fragments and ruins on a totally different, nonhierarchical basis. If the Menippean metagenre is "responsible" for demythologization and deconstruction, what is the source of the opposite—remythologizing, re-constructive—tendency?

In all the texts that were analyzed in this chapter, the object for Menippean play is inevitably one of the "older" genres that have already given birth to an entire branch of generic descendants: utopia and the fairy tale in the novels of Aksyonov and Aleshkovsky, the Romantic fairy tale in Tolstaya's stories, the medieval chronicle or historical legend in Pietsukh, hagiography in Viktor Erofeyev, *Bildungsroman* in Sorokin and Pelevin, the idyll in Sokolov's *Astrophobia*. All these authoritative traditions, along with their corresponding hierarchies of values, are decentralized, turned upside down, and transformed into the material for postmodernism's Menippean presentation of culture as chaos.

And yet we know that chaotic systems can lead to the so-called "holographic" effect, which is based on a new, nontraditional relationship between part and whole: Here, the part is not determined by the whole but may still adequately represent the whole; the best-known example is the fractal.[1] Something similar seems to be at work in postmodern fiction. In any case, the Menippean deconstruction of the hierarchical structures of canonical cultural forms is combined in "new-wave" Russian fiction with the necessary activity of such fragments (or fractals?) of the "old" world model, which possess tremendous symbolic, world-making potential. These images usually express the concept of *eternity* distinct to the given discourse. Examples of this type of image might include the road in Aksyonov's novels; the fertile body in Aleshkovsky's; the magician and the wheel of fortune in Tolstaya's stories; the River and the Beggars' Parade in Sokolov's *Between Dog and Wolf;* timelessness and *déjà vu* in *Astrophobia;* the battle and the solar eclipse in "The Central–Ermolaevo War"; the child-martyr in "The Parakeet"; and the trial and initiation in Sorokin's stories. The meaning of these images rarely remains unchanged; more often than not, *they* are reproduced upside down. But even in the postmodernist context, they still function as symbols of eternity: Their humiliation and discreditation directly express the transformation of eternity itself into a large-scale simulacrum, annihilation of something significant, a yawning void.

These images cannot be divided into levels and subsystems. But, like a hologram, they keep the integrity of the given genre's "memory" in a concentrated form (one that cannot be unfolded in a simple way). These "holograms" offer an associative key to the genre concept of artistic harmony. It is important that these images, because of their concentrated form, correspond to the metageneric world-modeling principle rather than to the genre itself. In other words, this or that type of model of eternity is typical for an entire group of inter-related genres; it contains the "formula" for the specific transformation of the plot, which is local and limited in time and space, into an essential fragment of infinity. Aksyonov and Sorokin are prime examples: Aksyonov's road refers to the fairy tale, the chivalric romance, and other subsequent transformations of the fairy-tale generic archetype, while Sorokin's trials and initiations are typical not only of the *Bildungsroman* but of many adventure and didactic genres as well (from the parable to the children's adventure novel).

In any case, the internal structure of the postmodernist world model is created on the basis of a *combination* of the Menippean metagenre and "holograms" of other, rather traditional and often canonical metagenres. This combination is truly dialogical in its nature: Menippean structures expose the conventional and illusory character of any cultural order, undermining any claim for possession of truth. But the universality and artistic persuasiveness of the self-destructive postmodernist text is provided with the intermittent presence of metageneric signs of eternity located amidst the ruins of cultural languages. With their direct participation, the Menippean Babylon of scattered discourses acquires ontological meaning: It represents the specific model of eternity itself. This model is paradoxical: Chaos, which contains powerful modes of harmony within itself, provides *visual* proof that chaos and harmony are not opposed to each other, that without an understanding of chaos, the encounter with harmony and eternity is empty, that any, even the most authoritative order is local and temporary and always open to the uncompletable disorder of chaos. Such transitions from Menippean nihilism to reconstruction can explain such Russian postmodernist puzzles as the philosophical irony of Tatyana Tolstaya, which is based on the assignment of one and the same phenomenon to both chaos and cosmos simultaneously, or the odd, inverted epic synthesis in Pietsukh and Viktor Erofeyev, which is due to the erasure of boundaries between ontological oppositions, the norm and absurdity, torture and lessons of wisdom, death, and play. As for Sorokin, such transitions in his works are emphasized in the plot construction, directed strictly toward the final *catharsis:* the reader's nauseated involvement in repulsive harmony, the sacred and ironic incorporation into chaos. In Sokolov's *Astrophobia* one can find the ultimate result of such transitions: the formation of an almost motionless mythological world, where eternity is equal to death, time to timelessness, and the author's stylistic virtuosity to entropic chaos.

Eventually, this kind of dialogue between metagenres creates the artistic equivalent of *chaosmos* as the basic model of the Russian postmodernist artistic consciousness.

# IV.
## Conclusion

# 11

# On the Nature of Russian Postmodernism

*Is there a writing that founds the world and is not the Book?*
*. . . Rearranging the letters of the Book means rearranging*
*the world. There's no getting away from it.*

—Umberto Eco, *Foucault's Pendulum* (1988: 466)

Why should the controversy over what would seem to be such an academic subject as postmodernism be so tempestuous, if not to say scandalous? Russian critics have not engaged in such heated arguments since the time of the Thaw: the gamut runs from hosannas to anathema, from proclaiming postmodernism to be "progressive and relevant" to warding off the devil with an Orthodox cross. Even Solzhenitsyn has found it impossible to resist cursing this new temptation.[1] It would be too facile to dismiss these debates as the thinly veiled generational conflict between the "men of the sixties" and their hungry offspring, for the fault line runs within a single generation: Such famous younger critics as, for example, Aleksandr Arkhangel'skii, Andrei Nemzer, or Pavel Basinskii can in no way be considered apologists for postmodernism. It is quite possible that their indignation is aroused by the arrogance of the postmodernists, a group of hardly starving artists who have adopted the best habits of the literary avant-garde, from unrestrained bragging to a caste-like intolerance in their evaluation of other people's work.

Nonetheless, one would like to believe that the problem is not merely a matter of conflicting ambitions. The question of Russian postmodernism is clearly more significant than the perfectly normal historical phenomenon of a literary trend elbowing its predecessors and its more traditional contemporaries aside. It is, first and foremost, a question of Russian culture's identity.

In *The Total Art of Stalinism,* Boris Groys asserts that Russian postmodernism arises as a result of two successive culture shocks: first, the discovery that the "totality of the ideological horizon" has not simply obscured reality, as had been previously thought, but rather has swallowed it whole; second, that "utopia is immanent to history," and therefore the attempt to return "*homo sovieticus*" to world history has collapsed precisely because of the "end of history" brought on by the collapse of the Soviet (final) utopia. Groys sees the meaning of Russian postmodernism in the achievement of blissful ignorance:

> The moment we realize that Borges' Library of Babel is not unique, but there also exists, say, a library approved by Stalin, we will no longer care which of them holds what we have written or what place it occupies there. So what if my text is merely a move in the endless play of language; even language, after all, is merely a move in my narration. It is possible to say anything in a given language, but one can also invent a new one. This language need not be comprehensible in order for something to be said in it; but it is not necessarily incomprehensible, either. (1992: 110–11)

Strangely similar to this project are the stubborn assurances of Mikhail Iampol'skii, who argues that "our art differs from postmodernism in that is lacks aesthetic" (Iampol'skii and Solntseva 1992: 50). This, perhaps, is that very language in which one can speak "without agitation": art without an aesthetic (and, after all, as Iampol'skii surely knows, the hideous also constitutes an aesthetic) is just as much a pseudotheoretical abstraction as, say, "scientific communism" (the obligatory course in Soviet universities).

Nonetheless, all these elegant constructs do little to explain Russian postmodernism in practice. It is telling that these theoreticians strictly limit Russian postmodernism to conceptualism and Sots-Art: All generalizations come from the works of Prigov, Rubinshtein, Sorokin, Kabakov, Bulatov, and . . . no one else. Sokolov's *Astrophobia* also makes the list, but never his *School for Fools* or *Between Dog and Wolf*. Bitov, Venedikt Erofeev, Tolstaya, Pietsukh, Yevgeny Popov, and many others apparently do not exist. Why? Because all these models are attempts to translate the logic of Western (European and American) postmodernism into Russian culture. In the West, postmodernism arises from the deconstruction of the monolithic, hierarchical culture of modernism and the canonized avant-garde. The only equivalent to such a monolith in Russian culture is Socialist Realism; therefore, postmodernism is restricted to the art of reflection on the ruins of Socialist Realism, that is, Conceptualism and Sots-Art.

But even if we approach Socialist Realism as the "official" avant-garde, it is still impossible to prove that the role and place of Socialist Realism in Russian culture is equal to the role and place of modernism in Western culture. For the sovereignty of the modernist value system in the West was the result of an organic process, while in Russia the institution of the Socialist Realist canon came at the price of the destruction of the organic culture. Today it is crystal clear that Soviet culture was never monolithic. Along with the Socialist Realist paradigm (which included not only official art but also "Socialist Realism with a human face" in both its published and its *samizdat* versions), the tradition of the Silver Age was never broken, despite all the efforts of the authorities—in fact, it is this tradition that is constantly invoked in connection with the Russian geniuses of the twentieth century. The culture of the avant-garde was preserved, passing from Mayakovsky and Kruchenykh to Vladimir Kazakov and Gennady Aigi in literature, and from Shostakovich and Prokofiev to Shnittke and Gubaidullina in music. Finally, it is in the Soviet era that one finds a paradoxical relapse of a certain populist, provincial variant of the "natural school" of the previous century, in the figures of Seifulina, Neverova, to a large extent Sholokhov, then the sketches of *Novyi mir,* and, finally, the "Village Prose" of the sixties and seventies. If there were not such variety, where would we get such fascinating cultural hybrids as Andrei Platonov, Ilya Ehrenburg, Mikhail Sholokhov himself, or the later Valentin Kataev?

The fundamental issues for Western postmodernism are the blurring of the boundaries between center and periphery, the decentralization of consciousness (expressed in the concept of the "death of the author"), and the fragmentation of the modernist model based on the integrity of the creative subject and his or her absolute freedom. Yet Russian postmodernism arises from the search for an answer to a diametrically opposed problem: cultural fragmentation and disintegration, as well as the literal (rather than metaphysical) "death of the author"; even within the bounds of a single text, Russian postmodernism attempts to restore and reanimate organic culture by involving diverse cultural languages in dialogue:

> [W]riters have come to the paradoxical conclusion that language is their only reality, although, at the same time, the reality is illusory. . . . The result is a baroque intermingling of forms of discourse, a literary language that is simultaneously local and cosmopolitan, a reflection of specific times and a stylization.

The validity of this diagnosis of Russian postmodernism is patently obvious; one need only recall the relevant declarations of Nabokov, Brodsky, or Bitov; one might not even bother to put it into words, if only . . . If only this quote were not a description of Latin American postmodernism (McAdam and Shimanovich 1985: 158). And the main reason for this resemblance is that Latin American literature, just like Russian literature, has long been infected by a "longing for world culture" (Mandelstam):

> The fear of incurring these involuntary parodies has always made Latin American writers sensitive to the difference between the cultures in which they live and the "other" culture, that of the metropolitan centers, real or imagined, of the Western world. In this they are different from their counter-

parts in the U.S., at least in the twentieth century, who imagined the Anglo-American tradition to be self-sufficient. Latin American culture constantly reminds itself of its own insufficiency. (Ibid., 254)

As, we might add, does Russian culture, whose "inferiority complex" is expressed equally in Westernizing and nationalism, and the Soviet ideological campaigns against the "corrupted" and "wicked" Western influence only exacerbate the sense of cultural isolation.

But the cultural isolation of Latin America provided fertile soil for Borges, Cortazar, Garcia Marquez, Carpentier, and other contemporary classics who have shaped a self-sufficient postmodern cosmos of incredible power and beauty. Cultural insufficiency has coincided with the crisis of cultural identity, resulting in an incredible discharge of artistic energy. But perhaps the same thing has happened in Russian postmodernism?

Both Latin American and Russian postmodernisms can be approached according to the model of "border writing," which is characterized by "its emphasis upon the multiplicity of languages within any single language; by choosing a strategy of translation rather than representation, border writers ultimately undermine the distinction between original and alien culture" (Hicks 1988: 51). The classic example of border writing is the works of Kafka, a Jew who lived in Prague and wrote in German. If Latin American postmodernism plays with *spatial* isolation, and thus with the spatial boundary between the cultures of old Europe, the new North American civilization and a completely different but equally old pre-Columbian South America, Russian culture, especially in the twentieth century and particularly in the past thirty years, experiences isolation as *isolation in time,* and the "borderness" takes shape within a special mythology of *backwardness.* In each case a key role is played by the category Deleuze and Guatarri call "deterritorialization"; that is, every cultural phenomenon sees itself as transplanted to alien soil from outside and rejects the immediate surrounding context, anxiously reaching out to make connections that lead to a different, native context: to a far-off time (for Russians) or a far-off place (for Latin Americans). Moreover, "deterritorialization" is interpreted by the creators of schizoanalysis not as a state but as a production process, which "pushes the simulacra to a point where they cease being artificial images to become indices of the new world. That is what the completion of the process is: not a promised and a pre-existing land, but a world created in the process of its tendency, its coming undone, its deterritorialization" (Deleuze and Guattari 1992: 322). It other words, the return to a lost context nonetheless remains a utopian ideal, but the critique of the surrounding, contemporary contexts proves to be productive because it creates its own cultural space, a postmodern space of *language,* a "creative chronotope," in which simulacra, the imaginary, and fictions replacing a lost reality take on a *new status of authenticity.* Such is the path of both Russian and Latin American postmodernisms.

This model truly does explain a great deal about Russian postmodernism. It explains why the experience of Nabokov proved so valuable: Before all others (and practically at the same time as Borges), Nabokov transformed modernism into postmodernism. Indeed, his modernism is inextricably linked with the drama of exile—in other words, with deterritorialization; his flight from Europe to America, and hence from one language to another, forced him to compensate for his lost context with his text, with its semitransparent structure, its riddles and mysteries, its characters who are wholly rooted only in the text (such as Sebastian Knight's brother, or Humbert Humbert, or Kinbote [*Pale Fire*], or Van [*Ada*]). We can understand why such ambiguous games are played so intensely not only with Socialist Realism but with the tradition of the Silver Age (at last, the nearest native context!); moreover, the range is much wider than that of Sots-Art: from the metafictional "culturology" of Bitov to the holy-foolish universalism of Venedikt Erofeev, from Tolstaya with her bitterly ironic aestheticism to the historical-philosophical fantasies of Aksyonov, Aleshkovsky, Pietsukh, and Viktor Erofeyev. Why is the apparently modernist mythology of creation and life creation so anxiously understood in terms of aesthetic logic? This is a theme not only for Nabokov but for all the works of Sokolov (who solved this problem with alacrity in *Between Dog and Wolf*) and once again for Tolstaya, Rubinshtein, and even, as travesty, for Yevgeny Popov; more to the point, this is the theme of all of Russian postmodernism, which, unlike its Western counterpart, does not fight with context but rather tries to produce context from the text, from the process of writing. It is clear why Russian postmodernism is so enamored with the archetype of the holy fool: On the one hand, this is a classic variant on the "border subject" (who floats between two diametrically opposed cultural codes), and, on the other—once again, a version of context, a link to the mighty branch of cultural archaism, stretching across Rozanov or Kharms to today. Why do Russian postmodernists strive so doggedly to reduce any plot, even one that is developed over a long period of time (as in *Astrophobia,* for example), to the *present time* of the text and, in its most extreme manifestation, to the surface of the page (as Sorokin often does)? This is how the present, which had collapsed under the burden of utopianism, is restored, how the gap between the present and the future is filled; this is how exile is softened in time.

Theoretically, the Russian version of postmodernist aesthetics creates a *field* where the value contexts of various cultural systems can meet, including those which, it would seem, have long ago been irrevocably lost, killed, forgotten, and those that were never successfully established on Russian soil (such as the Renaissance, Surrealism, or Existentialism). But the particularity of this encounter is that, in the resulting polylogue, the artist does not have his "own" word: *Everything is quotation.* Some contexts act as the cursed space-time of cultural isolation, others as objects of nostalgia. But in each case, there is no contact without alienation: The tortoise of cultural history runs ahead of the postmodern Achilles. Epstein connects this situation with the hope for the birth of a "transculture" that would release man from the dictates of a single culture and would place him at the point of "outsideness," where that which unites all cultures at their heart is opened to him:

> The transcultural world lies not apart from, but within all existing cultures, like a multidimensional space that appears gradually over the course of historical time. It is a continuous space in which unrealized, potential elements are no less meaningful than "real" ones. As the site of interaction among all existing and potential cultures, transculture is even richer than the totality of all known cultural traditions and practices. (1995a: 229)

As a graphic model of "transculture," Epstein himself cites Borges's famous story "The Aleph," which describes "one of the points in space that contains all other points":

> In that single gigantic instant I saw millions of acts both delightful and awful; not one of them amazed me more than the fact that all of them occupied the same point in space, without overlapping or transparency. What my eyes beheld was simultaneous." (Borges 1978: 23, 36)

This, in all likelihood, is the *intracultural myth* of Russian and Latin American postmodernisms; this is their utopian vision of inner wholeness attained upon leaving behind the state of exile or "deterritorialization." Moreover, we must note that this myth is clearly opposed to the myth of the "end of ends," "the impossibility of the Apocalypse" (Derrida), "the end of history" (Fukuyama), which are at the heart of West European and North American postmodernism. What Epstein calls "transculture" signifies a new level of fullness and historical universality, a new scale of history's dramas and potential; by no means is it history's annihilation, by no means is it the bad infinity of self-repetition.

But the artistic practice of Russian postmodernism offers a substantial corrective to this utopian myth. As an analysis of many works of the "new wave" shows, the culturological poetics of Russian postmodernism, which draws upon the metafiction of the 1920s and 1930s (from "The Egyptian Stamp," *Zoo,* and Kharms's "Cases" to Nabokov's *The Gift* and *Lolita*), allowed various cultural systems to meet and intermingle, not so much on the ideological level as through the clash of various generic traditions, plot structures, styles, and the most minute stylistic elements. But of all the most significant phenomena of Russian postmodernism, the common denominator (itself born in this dialogue), the point of "outsideness" in which the author, the protagonist, and the reader are found has invariably turned out to be *death as a world-modeling meta-image.*

Bitov understands the everyday, unnoticed afterlife of culture as a necessary condition for the encounter between the conserved classical tradition, the simulated existence of the contemporary hero, and the author's failed attempts to create a "present tense of the novel," "so that its ugly and tiresome present tense ... would disappear." After suffering a martyr's death, Venichka Erofeev narrates his life, a life that is otherworldly from the start. Death becomes a space for metamorphoses, uniting the chaos of poetic consciousness with the chaos of totalitarian madness in Sokolov's *A School for Fools;* though it is also true that subsequently in *Astrophobia* it becomes the main condition ("post-mortem") for blurring all possible boundaries of meaning and hence of meanings themselves. After the death of the dream, of all the heroes' hopes for life, one hears a conciliatory authorial voice in the prose of Tolstaya. In the best stories of Viktor Erofeev and Vyacheslav Pietsukh, the self-destruction of the human, the absurd deconstruction of all possible meanings, acts as the harsh precondition for a continuous and indestructible history. In the stories of Yevgeny Popov, the sardonic "paraliterary" mumblings and parodic style embody the devalorization of the very process of writing itself. This devalorization corresponds to the concept of timeliness, the universal neglect of being, which is so characteristic of Popov. But it also gives rise to the carnivalesque freedom expressed by Popov's narrator and provides a clue to his poetics as a whole. And in Sorokin, the naturalization of the mechanisms of the Socialist Realist text (indeed, any text) leads to bloody death rituals, structurally and semantically approaching prehistorical culture.

Thus death becomes the integral symbol of Russian postmodernism. If this is "transculture," then it is one in which death acts as the universal strategy for translating from one cultural language to another, for connecting the archaic and the contemporary, the avant-garde and the traditional, the classical and the paraliterary, Socialist Realism and high modernism, in their mutual *weakness in the face of ontological chaos, in the powerlessness of their attempts to bring order to life and overcome death.* "Transculture" itself in such an interpretation takes on the features of a rhizome, that is, of a system of regular ruptures and breaks of all kinds of structural links. Nonetheless, this is not the fragments of something smashed to bits but rather a special, particularly postmodern type of wholeness, one that can be found on the level of the artistic work's interior organization.

From time immemorial, from rites of passage and their attendant myths, one general semiotic model has been rooted in different cultures in order to then repeat itself again and again in artistic texts, religious rituals, and calendar holidays: *a temporary death that one must undergo in order to be born again or to obtain a new quality.* Temporary death is connected with liminal states, with the incursion of the forces of chaos, which can no longer be held back by any social restrictions (see Van Gennep 1960; Melentinskii 1976: 250–30). Moreover, isolation, exile, the removal from one's "normal" surroundings—these are the essential conditions of a rite of passage.

All of this bears a strong resemblance to the function of postmodernism in the history of world culture. Born of an extremely profound recognition of cultural crisis (and, in Russia, of the constant awareness of the dead end of Soviet civilization), postmodernism, as it were, consciously brings about the *temporary death of culture;* through a strategy of dialogue with chaos during the process of this global rite of passage, postmodernism models a liminal liberation from all versions of structural order. According to chaos theorists, in an unbalanced (that is, chaotic) dynamic, a self-organizing system is not subject to disintegration into the sum of its component parts: Every element is inseparable from the whole, and every element influences the entire system (see Deleuze and Guattari 1992: 42–43; Hayles 1991: 72–74). An analogous effect is noted by investigators of the boundary states of culture, who emphasize that in these situations a special type of *holographic effect* is possible, in which a fragment torn from its context is capable of recreating the entire volume of the whole. But does a similar effect not arise in postmodernism as well? After all, this transitory, boundary cultural state acts as the intersection of an organic, unsegmented, antistructural unity of all previous cultural experience (potential as well as actual) and all impulses and promises of the future. This is the unity that is born within "boundary writing" and that most closely corresponds to the internal drama of Russian culture's isolation in time. In other words, postmodernism translates the alienation from world culture, common to Russian, Soviet, and post-Soviet culture, onto a global scale but by doing so achieves the opposite effect: *the complete synchronization of Russian culture with world culture.* This synchronization is accomplished through temporary death, which is possible only on the scale of what Bakhtin calls culture's "great time," in turn understood as an organic, living, dying wholeness that has the potential for rebirth.

In one of his last works, Iurii Lotman wrote that a phenomenon can "become a language . . . only at the expense of immediate reality and of translation into a purely formal, 'empty' sphere that is therefore ready for any content" (Lotman 1994: 22). Does this not mean that postmodernism, which enacts the temporary death of culture with obsessive reflexivity, thereby empties and formalizes death itself, renders it obsolete, a process that inevitably consigns postmodernism itself to obsolescence at the same time?

Other questions inevitably arise: What is born from postmodern chaos? Does temporary death become a new characteristic of cultural reality? Can the postmodern rite of passage ever be completed? Only from a great historical distance can these questions be answered with any certainty. Nonetheless, we will hazard some hypotheses.

In the beginning of the 1990s, Russian literary postmodernism began to show signs of crisis. Two main symptoms are readily apparent, the first of which is external: the leading authors of Russian postmodernism (such as Tolstaya, Viktor Erofeyev, Popov, Pietsukh) either begin to repeat themselves or fall silent.[2] Most likely, a unique "automatization of the device" is at work. But why has this happened so quickly? It seems that a special role has been played by the particular harshness and inflexibility of postmodern poetics. A particular given image of chaos gives rise to (and assumes) a particular form of dialogue with it. And since the conception of chaos is too wide an artistic-philosophical category to change from one work to another (it is instead more likely rooted in the organic worldview of the artist), the problem of repeating oneself takes on special significance; in any case, this is a common feature of any transitional system (as was the case with Hellenism or sentimentalism).

Another symptom is more deeply rooted in the artistic philosophy of postmodernism and is connected to the instability of the very position of the dialogue with chaos, an instability that is a matter of principle. The author's involvement in the dissonance of cultural languages allows him to enter into a dialogue with ontological chaos. But the discrediting of all cultural languages as a mask for chaos in turn cannot help but undercut the position of the author as the subject of this dialogue. For no matter how many narrative masks he may don, the author-creator is nonetheless connected to one or several cultural languages. The logical development of postmodern semantics includes all cultural languages without exception in the macroimage of chaos, which in turn leads to the replacement of the dialogue with chaos by the dissolution of the dialogue's subject within cultural-ontological chaos.

We gave this problem closest attention during our analysis of the prose of Vladimir Sorokin and of Sasha Sokolov's *Astrophobia*. We also noted the rather wide dissemination of neo–avant-garde tendencies within Russian postmodernism.

And yet American and Russian postmodernisms, which developed in opposite directions from the 1960s on (the former from a monolith to diversity; the latter from disintegration to paradoxical versions of wholeness), came together at the end of the eighties and the beginning of the nineties; moreover, it is telling that the processes of postmodernism's poetic and aesthetic self-destruction are symmetrical. Thus in recent years a wide range of studies have appeared in America, such as, for example, Alan Wilde's *Middle Grounds* (1987), Robert Begibing's *Towards a New Synthesis* (1989), John Kuehl's *Alternate Worlds* (1989), and, especially, Susan Strehle's *Fiction in the Quantum Universe* (1992), which argue that the anglophone postmodernism of such writers as Norman Mailer and John Fowles (in their later works), Raymond Carver, Donald Barthelme, Margaret Atwood, Toni Morrison, Don DeLillo, and Max Apple leads to a peculiar rebirth of the realistic impulse, or, more precisely, to a sort of compromise between postmodernism and realism. To these names should be added Milan Kundera and the South African author J.M. Coetzee; the more recent novels of Garcia Marquez (most frequently *Love in the Time of Cholera*) are often mentioned as well. Strehle calls this phenomenon "actualism," explaining that all these authors

> affirm *both* art (self-consciously aware of its processes and of aesthetic traditions) *and* the real world (specifically, the postmodern world, with a detailed awareness of its nature and history). Their fiction admits both the garden and the glass. . . . Breaking off the false and restrictive duality between realism and antirealism, these postmodern authors manage an original fusion that transforms both strands of their literary heritage. (1992: 5–6)

For his part, Wilde, who is known for his work on postmodern theory, connects the future of American postmodern literature with the movement that he defines as the literature of interrogation or "midfiction." Midfiction is

> the kind of fiction that rejects equally the oppositional extremes of realism on the one hand and a world-denying reflexivity on the other, and that invites to perceive the moral, as well as epistemological, perplexities of inhabiting and coming to terms with a world that is itself ontologically contingent and problematic. (1987: 4)

This type of fiction shares a number of features with postmodernism, such as parody, an impulse toward playfulness, an emphasis on the relativity of time and space, and a hypertrophied dialogism that brings into conflict various versions of events and their interpretations, all the while juxtaposing genres, styles, and the voices of both the characters as well as the equally empowered voice author. But this new fiction returns to a *humanistic conception of reality,* making common human *fate* the center of attention, thus undercutting the postmodernist axiom that reality is merely the sum total of simulacra. According to these Anglo-American critics, it is the palpable lack of humanism and the disappearance of a reality that is "shared" with the reader that lies at the heart of the crisis of postmodernist metafiction, a kind of writing that, as Kuehl has noted, will never reach a wide audience.

It is important to emphasize that this is not simply a return to realism; the drama of human fate is played out in the chaotically multilayered and polyvalent world of postmodernism. Strehle says that many works of "actualism" are modeled on the *Bildungsroman,* the novel of individual fate, but the "education" of the hero, which unfolds in the "quantum universe" of the postmodern conception of the world, inevitably acquires the traits of an "absurd quest": none of the heroes comes to "self-identical harmony, nor does their education suggest the proper order in the world. None of these protagonists is truly 'educable,' nor does their environment provide the series of clear 'lessons' that would lead to 'illumination' and alignment with 'truth' " (Strehle 1992: 231). However, the very context of the *Bildungsroman* deprives these failures of any sense of inevitability: Meaning, including the meaning of human life, is not given in a ready-made form; rather, it is continually being born in the dialogue of individual quests, each of which is only a single move in the game of the world.

A survey of Russian literature of the late eighties and early nineties reveals an analogous phenomenon: Just as the crisis of postmodernism identifies, another kind of fiction is gaining ground, a movement that is clearly rooted in the realistic tradition but that just as clearly has learned from the experience of postmodern art. In works by Vladimir Makanin (*Escape Hatch, Qusai,* "Surrealism in a Proletarian Neighborhood," "Prisoner of the Caucasus"), Ludmilla Petrushevskaya (her novellas, *The Time: Night*), Mark Kharitonov *(Lines of Fate),* and Sergei Dovlatov, as well as in the fiction of such young authors as Mikhail Shishkin *(One Night Awaits All),* Pyotr Aleshkovsky *(Skunk: A Life),* Marina Palei *(Cabiria from the Bypass),* Andrei Dmitriev *(Voskoboev and Elizabeth),* Aleksandr Ivanchenko *(Monogram),* Alexei Slapovsky *(The First Second Coming),* and Oleg Yermakov *(The Number of the Beast),* the dialogue with chaos is also at center stage, but everyday chaos is presented here not as cultural multivoicedness but as the weaving together of social, everyday, historical, psychological, *and also* cultural circumstances. The subject of the dialogue is not the all-powerful author but the private person with limited options, who searches within the surrounding workaday madness for an existential apology for his life.[3] It becomes readily apparent, for example, that practically all Russian "postrealists," along with American "actualists," give new life to the generic archetype of the novel of education, from straightforward versions of the genre, such as Aleksandr Ivanchenko's *Monogram,* Pyotr Aleshkovsky's *Skunk: A Life,* or Oleg Yermakov's *The Number of the Beast* to the dialogization of the Master-Disciple relationship in Sharov's *Rehearsals,* Mark Kharitonov's *Lines of Fate,* Alexei Slapovsky's *The First Second Coming,* or the paradoxical didacticism of the parables of Sergei Dovlatov, Ludmilla Petrushevskaya, and Vladimir Makanin. Here, too, the novel of education becomes so entangled with the absurd quest that the hero rarely discovers the truth in the end: His failures are what turn out to be significant, and not only for the author or reader but, first and foremost, for the hero himself, for it is his failures that fill his life with personal and inalienable meaning. This meaning is acquired not in spite of but *within* the surrounding ontological chaos that attempts to engulf the individual, a chaos that is perceived and portrayed with the help of the artistic optics of postmodernism. Scientific chaos theory places great importance on the idea of the accidental irritant, the grain of sand around which a chaotic system will suddenly begin to form a funnel, giving birth to a new organic order *within itself.* In art, thanks to the power of the anthropocentric nature of the aesthetic, such an irritant, such a grain of sand, could only be the human character, only human fate, but a fate that is understood in turn as both ineluctable destiny and a cascade of absurd accidents that are not subject to any order. The individual and subjective experience of the *meaning of life* (which is also accidental, momentary, local, extremely fragile and conscious of its fragility, sometimes even absurd from an outside point of view) acquires the designation *chaosmos.*[4] The co-evolution of Russian postmodernism and American "actualism" demonstrates to a certain extent that, first, the particular character of Russian postmodernism simultaneously not only broke but also expressed the general trajectory of postmodernism as a whole and, second, that, as a state of world culture, postmodernism has by and large entered into a period of crisis and "semicollapse."

In postmodernism (and in this instance, Russian postmodernism is no exception), the cultural-philosophical paradigm that covers the entire literary evolution of the period of modernity undergoes a rupture. To put it schematically, at the basis of this paradigm lies a dialectical struggle between the ideals of Order and World Harmony on the one hand and the notion of freedom of self-expression on the other. If Neo-Classicism, the

Enlightenment, and realism subordinate individual freedom to a higher order of government, nature, or society, the Renaissance, Romanticism, and modernism find world harmony in the attainment of total freedom. Modernist culture sees a token of harmony with the world in the maximal freedom of the individual consciousness that creates its world in spite of an illogical, senseless reality. "My staff is my freedom, the heartbeat of being," exclaimed the young Mandelstam in 1914. And here is the aesthetic credo of contemporary writer Fazil Iskander:

> When I consider what lies at the heart of creative talent and what lies at the heart of the pleasure we get from it, I come to the simple conclusion that art has no other content but freedom. Whatever a writer writes about, it seems to me that the result is art when the final goal within his writing is freedom.[5]

In the modernism of the Silver Age, in the avant-garde of the 1920s, in the literature of moral resistance, in the masterpieces of Mikhail Bulgakov, Anna Akhmatova, Marina Tsvetaeva, Boris Pasternak, and Varlam Shalamov, in the entire spectrum of unofficial literature from Alexander Solzhenitsyn and Andrei Sinyavsky to the young underground of the eighties, and even in that part of the officially sanctioned literature of the sixties and seventies that was penned by war veterans and the sixties generation—freedom has everywhere been understood as the highest spiritual value. Postmodernism continues this tendency, turning the very process of the construction of the text into the formation of a nondogmatic consciousness, imparting the significance of spiritually liberating art to the very poetics of verbal artistry.

Unlike Western postmodernism, which considers the modernist myth of the freedom of the creative consciousness to be one of the "totalities" that is subject to stratification and atomization, Russian postmodernism, which continues rather than rejects modernist tradition, understands the very search for an alienated "native context" as the search for a cultural space of freedom. The paradoxical discovery of such a context in death has, on the one hand, truly liberated postmodern writers from the pressure of all discourses. We can see the most radical version of such liberation in the fiction of Vladimir Sorokin: Having developed a technique for subverting any authoritative discourse, beginning with Socialist Realism, he then uses the same means to expose the same repressiveness in any tradition, from Turgenev to Shakespeare. As already noted, this freedom *belongs to no one*. It cannot be used by the author, who recognizes the threat of totalitarianism in all cultural languages without exception; the author is thus left without a language, dooming himself to aesthetic muteness. Nor can the hero avail himself of this freedom: Led into a state of temporary death, he turns into a shadow, *the shadow of the sign;* his being is simulative from the very start, and as a result his freedom can only be a fictional self-parody (as, say, the freedom of Sokolov's Palisander Dalberg). Hence even the most confirmed partisans of postmodernism today now admit to an increasing sense of this freedom's dehumanization and emptiness. Mikhail Iampol'skii's acknowledgment of the limits of Sots-Art is extremely revealing:

> When the talk is constantly about emptiness and senselessness, it is difficult to make this talk truly interesting. . . . For me culture and art are a disinterested, perhaps even absurd subject to which I dedicate my time, receiving nothing from it but the sense that I am human; the disappearance of the human dimension is, for me, fatal. (Iampol'skii and Solntseva 1991: 52)

On the other hand, look how often the Russian fiction corresponding to "actualism" features scenes of departure from the underworld, of existence on the edge of the "next world." This motif is, of course, most distinctly embodied in Makanin's *Escape Hatch,* where the very chronotope of the escape hatch, the transitional space that unites the underground world with the world above, becomes the knot of the tale's artistic philosophy. But this same motif completes Viktor Pelevin's *Omon Ra* and Marina Palei's *Cabiria from the Bypass,* as well as providing the metaphysical map of Aleshkovsky's *Skunk: A Life.*[6] Is it also crucial that the modernist conception of the meaning of life as a direct *result* of freedom is transformed into a conception of meaning as an essential *condition* of freedom, a condition without which freedom itself becomes a trifle, a toy, the "unbearable lightness of being," as Milan Kundera would have it. In the works of Petrushevskaia, Kharitonov, and Dovlatov, human self-awareness always presupposes not only unfreedom but even the quest for dependence. In their works, the problem of freedom and meaning comes to a paradoxical solution: Only by attaining an existential understanding of unfreedom can man endure the burden of freedom of choice and elevate himself to moral responsibility for that solitary point of being in time and space that is occupied by his unique human personality and fate.

All of this can be interpreted as signs of the culmination of the temporary death of culture, experienced by and reflected in postmodernism.

The relativist map of the world created by physics at the turn of the century made common cause with the culture of modernism and the avant-garde, which drastically changed the entire system of conceptions of man, history, and being. Historians of science and specialists in cultural studies come together in their common understanding of the fact that contemporary scientific chaos theories and the postmodern cultural consciousness are related, in that they both lead humanity toward a new paradigm through which to view the world: the paradigm of chaos. Russian literary postmodernism—with its bitter skepticism regarding any attempts by culture to bring order to the world, with its attempts to unfetter the chaos within which it distinguished the multivoicedness of culture—has fashioned a rite of passage: At the price of temporary death, Russian postmodernism has shifted culture from a paradigm based on freedom's constant struggle with order and harmony to a paradigm of chaos. What is happening today in Russian and world culture can be viewed as an attempt to *reconstruct the edifice of humanism in the space of chaos*. Not because the testing of culture by death has proven the infallibility of humanism; on the contrary, the weakness and even absurdity of any belief in man is taken as an axiom. Rather, the attempt at reconstruction is made because any alternative to humanism reeks of potential bloodshed. And everything begins once again with the most elementary ideas: pity, sentimentality, tenderness toward humanity, the search for a sincere tone. Let us not argue about the terminology—call it the "new autobiography" (Chaikovskaia, Bykov), "neosentimentalism" (Zolotonosov, Ivanov, Kuznetsov), the "new sincerity" (Epstein), actualism, or postrealism. Let us only understand that against the backdrop of chaos and in the context of chaos all these simple feelings and states truly *cannot fail to be reinterpreted,* for the experience of death has deprived them of their right to monological imperatives. They have been saturated with explosive dialogic energy, rooted not only in age-old ties and traditions but in their ruptures, breaks, voids. And the ideal of the new humanism will probably not be man's harmony with the universe for a very long time to come but rather chaosmos, "dissipative orders," born within the chaos of being and culture.

# Notes

## Notes to Chapter 1

1. The period known as the "Thaw," which takes its name from the title of Ilya Ehrenburg's 1954 novel, lasted from 1956 through 1968. The roots of the Thaw can be found in the Twentieth Communist Party Congress in 1956, when Nikita Khrushchev read his famous "secret speech," which signaled the beginning of the so-called "struggle with Stalin's cult of personality." The Thaw constituted a series of attempts to liberalize the Soviet system inherited from Stalin, and it ended in 1968 with the Soviet invasion of Czechoslovakia and the suppression of the "Prague Spring," a far more thorough and radical reform program than the Soviet Thaw. The Thaw was a period of great contradictions: liberal reforms were combined with an aggressive propaganda campaign for communist ideology and with the persecution of freethinkers. Nonetheless, the liberal atmosphere of the period allowed for the formation of a new generation of the Soviet intelligentsia, one that espoused antitotalitarian ideals. The spiritual leaders of this generation were Alexander Solzhenitsyn and Andrei Sakharov (both of whom actually belonged to an older generation, but who only became known during the Thaw), Andrei Sinyavsky (Abram Tertz), and Joseph Brodsky. When the reforms of the Thaw came to an end under Brezhnev (1964–82), this same generation would become the core of the political opposition (the dissidents) and the third wave of emigration. In literature and art, this generation was represented by such poets as Joseph Brodsky, Vladimir Vysotsky, Yevgeny Yevtushenko, Andrei Voznesensky, Bella Akhmadulina, and Bulat Okudzhava; by such prose writers as Chingiz Aitmatov, Vasily Aksyonov, Yuz Aleshkovsky, Bulat Okudzhava, Andrei Bitov, Vladimir Voinovich, Georgy Vladimov, Anatoly Gladilin, Sergei Dovlatov, Venedikt Erofeev, and Fazil Iskander; and in film and theater by such directors as Andrei Tarkovsky, Yuri Lyubimov, Marlen Khutsiev, Larisa Shepitko, Nikita Mikhalkov, Andrei Konchalovsky, and Tengiz Abuladze. Despite the fact that the aesthetics of the "sixties generation" was oriented primarily toward the traditions of Russian realism, this generation played a crucial role in the history of Russian postmodernism (see Chapters 6, 10, and 11). For more on the culture of the Thaw, see Vail' and Genis 1996.

2. See, for example, Groys 1992 and Dobrenko 1993.

3. For a detailed analysis of this process, see Hosking 1992.

4. In one of the earliest manifestos of American postmodernism, John Barth's "The Literature of Exhaustion" (1967), Nabokov, along with Borges and Beckett, is named as one of the main forerunners of the new, postmodernist understanding of literature (Barth 1984: 62–79). On the significance of Nabokov's works for American postmodernism, see also Courturier 1993 and Medarić 1991.

5. On Russian metafiction, see Shepherd 1992. Shepherd's examples of metafiction include Leonid Leonov's *The Thief,* Konstantin Fedin's *Brothers,* Veniamin Kaverin's *Troublemaker,* and Mikhail Prishvin's *Homeland of the Cranes.* One could also add much of the work of Viktor Shklovsky and Daniil Kharms, Abram Tertz's *Strolls with*

*Pushkin* and *In the Shadow of Gogol,* and some of the later works of Valentin Kataev, such as *The Holy Well* and *My Golden Wreath.*

6. Mimesis can certainly be understood far more broadly than as the mere "imitation of life," but for the purposes of the present study, mimesis is used to describe a concept that sets aside a special role for art as the specific "reflected likeness" of some objective reality.

7. The terms "modernism" and "avant-garde" are often used interchangeably. We are following a different terminological tradition, one that interprets modernism as a broad cultural movement encompassing Decadence, Symbolism, various avant-garde trends (Expressionism, Surrealism, Dada, Futurism, Absurdism, etc.), as well as the so-called "high modernism" of Kafka, Proust, Joyce, Beckett, and Thomas Mann. For example, in Russian literature Futurism certainly belongs to the avant-garde, while Acmeism would constitute "high modernism"; nonetheless, both movements are part of Russian modernism.

8. See also Dering-Smirnova and Smirnov 1980.

9. See Paperno and Grossman 1994 and Gunther 1986.

10. See also Calinescu 1983.

11. Iurii Levin provides an extremely telling illustration of this thesis when he discusses the theme of creativity in Borges:

This theme is expressed most baldly in that this story appears to be composing itself before our very eyes (or not even the story itself but only its plot): What is shown is not the result of creativity but creativity itself as an activity, moreover in its first, liveliest stage. And the very process of setting down the plot that is being born before our very eyes becomes a complete story (while it is paradoxically asserted that this story "may someday be written"). Here we are dealing with creativity in all its open-endedness. . . . The profound theme that arises represents some kind of concreate, unfinished (or unfinalizable) problem, a paradox. And this very unresolvable and paradoxical character, which gives rise to intellectual unease and dizziness on the part of the reader (in its purest form, completely independent of the contents) forms the metalevel of the dimension of contents and is the metatheme or "metaproblem" common to the majority of Borges's stories. (Levin 1981: 54, 56)

12. The resemblance between the Baroque and postmodern aesthetics is examined by Bornhofen (1995).

13. Raymond Federman, the compiler and coauthor of a collection of manifestos of American postmodernism, has this to say about postmodern characters: "[T]he people of fiction, the fictitious beings, will also no longer be well-made characters who carry with them a fixed identity, a stable set of social and psychological attributes—a name, a situation, a profession, a condition, etc. The creatures of new fiction will be as changeable, as unstable, as illusory, as nameless, as unnameable, as fraudulent, as unpredictable as the discourse that makes them. This does not mean, however, that they will be mere puppets. On the contrary, their being will be more genuine, more complex, more true to life in fact, because they will not appear to be simply what they are; they will be what they are: word-beings" (Federman 1975: 12–13).

14. Similar transformations of dialogism have been noted by Viola Eidinova, using the prose of the Russian Absurdism of the twenties and thirties (Leonid Dobychin, Daniil Kharms) as examples (Eidinova 1994).

15. More on the concept of "strange attractors" and other recent theories of chaos in relation to contemporary philosophical and literary movements can be found in Hayles 1990, Briggs and Peat 1989, and Paulson 1988.

16. On chaos and cosmos as the most universal models of the world in culture, see Meletinksii 1994 and Leiderman 1996.

17. In his *O literaturnykh arkhetipkah,* Meletinskii shows that the struggle between the forces of chaos and cosmos in the novels of Dostoevsky is transferred to the framework of a single human soul; moreover, the "low" end of consciousness is defined as chaos (Meletinskii 1994: 89).

18. In Socialist Realism, the avant-garde imperative for freedom is implemented "accurately and inversely." Using Erich Fromm's idea of "escape from freedom," Yevgeny Dobrenko finds in Socialist Realism "a complex of unconscious fear of individual integrity and freedom." He notes that

The totalitarian cult relates to the type of cultural formations where the process of individuation is turned around: life is reduced to the minimum ("you can't make an omelet without breaking a few eggs"), but there is no death in this culture, for the deed and the idea in which a man is dissolved are immortal; equally immortal is the transpersonal value that man serves (hence the cult of youth, of the deathless heroic deed, and of the teleology of life— "so that it would not be so terribly painful for the years lived *without a goal*"); there is no death because the phenomenon of individual death has died along with individuality itself. Meanwhile, fear cannot be eradicated. The "conquest of death" in totalitarian culture stems from the radical nihilism of revolutionary culture, from the "death of God" and the "victory over the Sun" in the avant-garde. (Dobrenko 1993; 51)

19. A rhizome is a "rootlike subterranean stem, commonly horizontal in position, that usually produces roots below and sends up shoots progressively from the upper surface" (*Random House Webster Dictionary,* 2nd ed. [New York: Random House, 1987], 1651). More broadly, rhizomes include various types of molds, virus colonies, ants, wasps, and rats.

## Notes to Chapter 2

1. See also Genis 1994a and 1997a.

2. Of course, the situation is complicated by the fact that Bitov's reliance on modernist tradition, and even more so on contemporary postmodernist experiments, often appears to be the product of "ambient influences." Bitov's admission of the connection between *Pushkin House* and Nabokov's fiction is particularly telling: "For better or for worse, there would never have been a *Pushkin House* if I had read Nabokov earlier; what there would have been instead, I can't imagine. When I first opened *The Gift,* my novel had been completely written up to page 337 [that is, up to the end of the plot— M.L.], and the rest had been written in chunks and sketches. I read *The Gift* and *Invitation to a Beheading* one after the other and—I shut up, and for half a year I couldn't recover from not the impression so much as the blow; only then did I finish the finale. From that time on I no longer have the right to deny not only an ambient influence but even a direct one, although I have tried to get back into the groove of what I had written before I was disarmed by what I had read. I tried to banish any phrase that

seemed to point toward Nabokov, with two exceptions that I left on purpose in order to be scolded, since they had already been written in those chunks" (Bitov 1989: 397–98).

3. One can easily recall similar scenes in the works of Trifonov, Aksyonov, Bond-arev, Yevtushenko, and others.

4. This aesthetic program found its clearest expression in Mandelstam's famous essay "The Word and Culture" (1921):

> Culture has become the Church. A separation of Church–Culture and the State has taken place. . . . But I say: yesterday has not yet been born. It has not really existed. I want Ovid, Pushkin, and Catullus to live once more, and I am not satisfied with the historical Ovid, Pushkin, and Catullus. . . . Thus, not a single poet has yet appeared. We are free from the burden of memories. On the other hand, we have so many rare presentiments: Pushkin, Ovid, Homer. . . . Thus the poet has no fear of recurrence and is easily intoxicated on Classical wine. . . . Today a kind of speaking in tongues is taking place. In sacred frenzy a poet speaks the language of all times, all cultures. Nothing is impossible. As the room of a dying man is open to everyone, so the door of the old world is flung wide open before the crowd. Suddenly everything becomes public property. Come and take your pick. Everything is accessible: all labyrinths, all secret recesses, all forbidden paths. The word has become not a seven-stop, but a thousand-stop flute, brought to life all at once by the breathes of the ages. The most striking thing about speaking in tongues is that the speaker does not know the language he is speaking. He talks in com-pletely unknown language. . . . It is something like a complete reversal of erudition. (Mandelstam 1979: 112, 113–14, 116)

T.S. Eliot argued a similar point, albeit in more rational terms, in his article "Tradition and the Individual Talent" (1919). On Mandelstam and Western modernism, see Cav-anagh 1995.

5. The effect of the self-destruction of the novelistic form is so convincing that even a critic as sensitive as Iurii Karabchievskii takes it at face value. In his essay on *Pushkin House,* he writes: "The conditional character of the narration, which has been reinforced through hundreds of pages of joint effort by the author and reader, cannot withstand such insistent shaking of its own foundations. The powerful literary self-criticism also fails to strengthen the novel's structure; on the contrary, it brings all its unconditional weight down onto the conditional flesh of the novel and at times seems to take the novel's place completely" (Karabchievskii 1989: 82). The fragments of this essay pub-lished after Karabchievskii's death contain a rather harsh assessment of the novel's finale: "Some kind of orgy of self-destruction is played out. . . . As if some external force is making him [Bitov] write not just anything but a novel; and in accordance with the manner in which this external force understands the word 'novel.' Or as if some sort of enchanted accordion were playing, and we are dancing an endless *gopak,* while our faces show grief and exhaustion" (Karabchievskii 1993: 233).

If one ignores the essay's negative emotional coloring. this is a brilliant description of the postmodern effect planned by Bitov.

6. Sven Spieker compares the narrative strategy of Bitov's novel with that of Cicero's and Quintilian's accounts on the invention of mnemotechnics by Greek lyric poet Simonides Melicus: "The point of departure for systematic remembering is the domestic catastrophe, the impossibility of recognizing the former order of things and people. The house of memory is littered with corpses which have been thrown off their

seats. Semiotically speaking, the domestic disaster implies a system of signs which have become opaque or undecipherable. This catastrophe is heralded by forgetting, a forgetting which calls for remembering" (Spieker 1996: 123–24).

7. In addition to all the various literary subtexts, Lyova's article also contains clear references to the biography of the characters, as well as to that of Bitov himself, since, according to Ellen Chances, "at twenty-seven, Leva reads a piece his grandfather had written when *he* was twenty-seven. The date Bitov writes at the end of his novel is the twenty-seventh day of the month. Bitov was born on May 27, and he began writing *Pushkin House* when he was 27" (1993: 206).

8. Chances feels that Tynianov's theory of literary evolution has, to a large extent, formed Bitov's principles of artistic modeling. "It seems to me that what Bitov does in *Pushkin House* is to take Tynianov's ideas concerning the study of literary text, and to apply them to the 'real world' life that he, as author, creates in *Pushkin House*" (1993: 234). Of course, the illustration of this fruitful thesis with the assertion that Stalin is Tynianov's leitmotif that sets "the tone for the entire system of Soviet life" (ibid., 234) in the novel seems a rather straightforward oversimplification of *Pushkin House*.

9. Indeed, Part Two of *Pushkin House* was even published separately in a collection of Bitov's short stories in 1976 (*Dni cheloveka* [Moscow: Sovremennik]), which can be explained after the fact not only by tactical considerations but by the weak links between this part and the novel as a whole.

## Notes to Chapter 3

1. The sentences "Oh, to be carefree! Oh heavenly birds, who neither sow nor reap. Oh, the lilies of the field are dressed more beautifully than Solomon!" are omitted in the translation by H.W. Tjalsma.

2. Olga Sedakova recalls: "It was even harder for me to understand the other side of this humanism: hatred of heroes and heroic deeds. The champion of his hatred became poor Zoia Kosmodemianskaia [the famous heroic martyr of World War II, a young Komsomol girl who was tortured and executed by the Nazis; after her death, she would become an icon of Soviet patriotic propaganda—M.L.]. . . . He often spoke not only of the excusability but also of the normalcy and even the praiseworthiness of faintheartedness, about the fact that man should not be subjected to extreme trials. Was this a revolt against communist stoicism, against the courage and "madness of the bold"? . . . Or would unadulterated courage and sacrifice be intolerable for Venya? I don't know" (Frolova et al. 1991: 91).

3. Apparently, this philosophy of freedom was near to Venedikt Erofeev's heart; Vladimir Murav'ev writes: "The most important thing in Erofeev was freedom. . . . Of course, he destroyed himself. Well, that's what he thought: life is self-destruction, self-immolation. That's the price of freedom" (Frolova et al. 1991: 94).

4. For a detailed and illuminating analysis of the motif of grief in Erofeev's poem, see Ryan Hayes ("Erofeev's Grief" 1997) and Kustanovich 1997.

5. On the tradition of "holy foolishness" in Kharms's works, see Roberts 1992 and Anemone 1991.

6. Vladimir Murav'ev also recalls that Erofeev "was a great admirer of reason (hence his attraction to the absurd). . . . Erofeev lived and thought according to the laws of the rational, and not because his right heel itched. His obvious anarchism only means that he did not live under reason's command. . . . Like any reasonable person, if he is not also a fool (which sometimes happens), he was drawn to clearly-defined structures rather than vague ones, to analysis" (Frolova et al. 1991: 93). I should also point out that

Erofeev's play *Walpurgisnacht, or The Steps of the Commander* was written with a clear orientation to classical tragedy—a kind of example of aesthetic rationalism.

7. Erofeev's treatment of "travelogue" topics is analyzed by Eduard Vlasov (1997).

## Notes to Chapter 4

1. On the role of cyclical models in the poetics of *A School for Fools,* see Karriker 1987: 287–99 and Boguslawski 1987: 231–46.

2. Compare Sokolov's and Eliade's interpretations of time:

Eliade—"the need of archaic societies to regenerate themselves periodically through the annulment of time" (Eliade 1954: 85); an archaic man "does not bear the burden of time, does not record time's irreversibility; in other words, completely ignores what is especially characteristic and decisive in a consciousness of time" (ibid., 86); "In the 'lunar perspective,' the death of the individual and the *periodic* death of humanity are necessary, even as the three days of darkness preceding the 'rebirth' of the moon are necessary. The death of the individual and the death of humanity are alike necessary for their regeneration" (ibid., 88); "Everything begins over again at its commencement every instant. The past is but a prefiguration of the future. No event is irreversible and no transformation is final" (ibid., 89).

Sokolov—"I cannot be precise and make definite judgments about anything that is in the slightest degree connected with the concept of *time.* It would appear to me that we have some sort of misunderstanding and confusion about it, about time, not everything is what it should be. Our calendars are too arbitrary: the numbers that are written there do not signify anything and are not guaranteed by anything, like counterfeit money. . . . There is no line, the days come whenever one of them feels like it, and sometimes several come all at once. And sometimes a day doesn't come for a long time. Then you live in emptiness, not understanding anything, quite sick. . . . [T]omorrow is just another word for today, as if it had been granted us to comprehend even a small portion of what happens to us here in the closed space of an explicable grain of sand, as if everything that happens here is, exists,—really, in fact *is, exists*" (Sokolov 1977: 33–34).

3. The Japanese classical *tanka* quoted in the text is a textbook example of the cyclical space–time model of the world: "Flowers in the spring, a cuckoo in the summer. And in the autumn—the moon. Cold clean snow in the winter" (Sokolov 1977: 54).

4. *Vetrogon,* as has already been noted in the criticism, anagramatically coincides with Pavl/Savl's last name, Norvegov (Johnson 1980: 226).

5. D. Barton Johnson is correct to emphasize that "one should be extremely cautious about setting Sokolov's novel in a theological context." See Johnson 1980: 227.

6. See, for example, "This someone, polyped, like a prehistoric dinosaur, and as unending as medieval torture, kept walking and walking, knowing neither weariness nor peace, and still couldn't get all the way past, because it could never get all the way past" (Sokolov 1977: 171–72). See also the description of the "inexorable polyped street" as a part of the school for fools' absurdity (ibid., 208).

# Notes to Chapter 6

1. See Belaia 1992. The postmodernist potential of "Youth Prose" is analyzed by Sven Spieker (1996).

2. The term *samizdat* literally means "self-published." It actually refers to unpublished texts that would be repeatedly typed and retyped by the authors and/or readers (an activity that could lead to prosecution for "anti-Soviet propaganda"). Correspondingly, *tamizdat*—literally, "published over there"—are the books of "anti-Soviet" authors (including Nabokov, Bulgakov, Platonov, Gumilev, Galich, Brodsky, Orwell) printed abroad and illegally distributed in the USSR, usually in the form of barely legible photocopies.

3. The plot of Aksyonov's novella, including its very artlessness, is a parody of the novella *Alyonka* by Sergei Antonov, a very popular realist writer in the sixties.

4. Note that after *Surplussed Barrelware,* Aksyonov would write two fairy-tale novellas for children ("My Grandfather Is a Monument" [1970] and "The Little Trunk with Something Knocking Inside It" [1976]), based on a fairy-tale interpretation of the stereotypes of Soviet mass culture. For more on these works, see Kogan 1994.

5. "The barrelware is a magical object similar to the magical caps or carpets found in fairytales," write Aksyonov's translators, Joel Wilkinson and Slava Yastremski (Aksyonov 1985: 11).

6. For more on fairy-tale patterns and "genre memory" in literature, see Lipovetskii 1992: 11–40, 153–63.

7. About *Surplussed Barrelware,* Laura Beraha writes: "What fires the text instead is a poetics of spontaneous and mutual implication, not the hierarchical exchange of direct and ironic discourse that underwrite the decade's obsession with Aesopianism, but a merely barreling over all levels, such that everything implies and implicates everything and anything else. The spirit of playfulness, the intoxicating range of allusions was rare for its time and intended to break new grounds" (1997: 213).

8. Not long before Aksyonov, Abram Tertz performed a fairy-tale deconstruction of socialist utopianism in his 1963 short novel *The Makepeace Experiment.*

9. Propp writes that "many wondertale motifs derive from social institutions, among which the rite of initiation occupies a special place. We also observe many ideas about the world beyond the grave and journeys to the other world. . . . Combination of these two sequences yields *nearly* all the basic items of the wondertale. It is impossible to draw the line between the two, for the entire initiation rite was experienced as a visit to the land of death, and conversely, the deceased went through everything experienced by the initiate—he received a helper, encountered a swallower, and so forth" (Propp 1984: 116–17). See also Propp 1946.

10. For a more detailed analysis of these novels, see Dalgard 1982, Nemzer 1991, Kustanovich 1992, and Svitel'skii 1994.

11. According to Bakhtin, many elements of carnival culture "express a peculiar utopian strain, the brotherhood of fellow-drinkers and of all men, the triumph of affluence, and the victory of reason" (1968: 90). He also comments on the "utopian radicalism" of carnival freedom (ibid., 89, 92).

12. Allen Thiher, for example, asserts that "Derrida's work, however, is not exactly another theoretical activity. His essays are closer to the literary form of contestation and questioning; . . . they act like distorting mirrors that reflect back toward theory a deformed image that demonstrates what was latent in that thought. . . . It is no exaggeration to state that increasingly Derrida has been as much a poet—a maker of words—as a philosopher" (Thiher 1984: 82).

13. Here we should recall the story of the 1979 *Metropol'* collection, the unofficial almanac edited by Aksyonov and Viktor Erofeyev that would be harshly attacked by the Union of Soviet Writers. As a result of this campaign, Aksyonov and Friedrich Gorenshtein emigrated, Viktor Erofeyev and Yevgeny Popov were expelled from the Writers' Union, and the poet Semyon Lipkin and his wife Nina Lisnyanskaya gave up their membership. Other writers, such as Fazil Iskander, Andrei Bitov, and Bella Akhmadulina, found that it was not possible to publish their works in the USSR for the next several years. It was on the pages of *Metropol'* that Aleshkovsky, Aksyonov, Iskander, and Bitov first met with the postmodernists of the new generation, particularly Viktor Erofeyev and Yevgeny Popov. Without going into a detailed analysis of *Metropol'*, we note only that, despite the collection's obvious eclecticism, one senses the attempt to declare a postmodernist alternative not only to the canon of Socialist Realism but also to the aesthetics of traditional realism dating back to the classics of the nineteenth century. The *Metropol'* affair and its significance for Russian contemporary literary history are examined by Robert Porter in his book *Russia's Alternative Prose* (1994: 26–30).

## Notes to Chapter 7

1. Tatyana Tolstaya places her own work in the context of the modernism of the twenties: "The fiction of the twenties gives the impression of a half-empty auditorium. This is a thoroughly new type of fiction—in style, lexicon, metaphors, syntax, plot, construction. Everything is different, everything is changing, hundreds of new possibilities appear, only a small part of which are actually implemented. My heart is with this literature, with this tradition that had only just begun to develop. . . . It is very easy to imagine that there had been a writer at that time whom no one knows, who never published a single line, and who died, and everyone who knew him also died, and his work remains unfinished. So you can consider that I am doing it for him" (Tolstaya 1986: 7).

2. Among Russian and émigré scholars to write about Tolstaya are Leonid Bakhnov, Alexander Genis, Andrei Vasilevsky, Mikhail Zolotonosov, Irina Muravieva, Elena Nevzglyadova, Vladimir Piskunov and Svetlana Piskunova, and Peter Vail; the most prominent Western critic of Tolstaya's work is Helena Goscilo, who has published the first monograph on Tolstaya (Goscilo 1996).

3. I cannot entirely agree with Peter Vail and Alexander Genis, who write that "Tolstaya's metaphors, each of which is a tightly knit fairy tale in the Andersen manner" (1989: 350), primarily surround the world of objects, embodying an inanimate eternity that resists time's destructive influence on human lives. The fairy-tale patterns of Tolstaya's work express the joyous aestheticism of everything that enters the orbit of human existence, including objects.

4. This observation was originally made by Goscilo in "Paradise, Purgatory, and Post-Mortems in the World of Tat'jana Tolstaja," *Indiana Slavic Studies*. 1990, no. 5: 97–114. See also Goscilo 1996: 11–28.

5. Helena Goscilo finds a particularly apt link to Lermontov's poem "So the abandoned temple is still a temple, The fallen idol is still God!" (Goscilo 1996: 110, 196). Whether or not Tolstaya deliberately truncated this phrase, it nonetheless expresses the internal strategy of "The Fakir."

6. Mikhail Zolotonosov develops this idea more thoroughly in his essay "Tatianin den' " (1988).

7. See, for example, "Mama Was Washing the Frame," written in 1987: "Galya

Fomina studied at the pedagogical institute. When I asked her why it rained, she would start to explain, 'Our country has many seas and rivers. . .' I forgot the rest. 63. Sasha Smirnov was in the habit of farting indoors. 64. You could hear it, but it didn't stink" (Rubinshtein 1995: 61).

## Notes to Chapter 8

1. Subsequently, in his novel *ROMMAT* (Romantic Materialism), Pietsukh places this hypothesis at the foundation of an artistic idea; the Decembrist Uprising of 1825 is described as a prank played by young Russians hungry for life, in the spirit of "The Central–Ermolaevo War."

2. A number of motifs common to Viktor Erofeyev's works are without a doubt rooted in the culture of high modernism. Thus the treatment of murder in "Death and the Maiden" clearly echoes André Gide's novel *Les Caves du Vatican* (I am grateful to Anita Mozhaeva for this observation).

3. Curiously, Brodsky described this very same strategy in 1975: "Carrion!" he exhaled, grabbing his belly/but he will prove farther away/than the earth from the birds,/because carrion is freedom/ from cells, from/the whole: an apotheosis of particles" (Brodsky 1994: 12). Quoted from the translation by Marian Schwartz in *Russian Studies in Literature* 30, no. 1 (Winter 1993–94): 51.

4. Note that the classmates' names are clear anagrams of the names of members of the Moscow Union of Writers who played an active role in the attack on the independent almanac *Metropol'* (1979), whose editors included Aksyonov and Viktor Erofeyev. Balkazhanov is an obvious distortion of Grigory Baklanov, Mukhanov is Ivan Ukhanov, Klyshko is Nikolai Klychko, and Trunina is Iuliia Drunina. Some of the names are left unchanged: the black marketeer Verchenko is named after Iurii Verchenko, who was then the organizational secretary of the Union of Soviet Writers (i.e., the KGB representative).

5. James Klinkowitz traces the development of a similar artistic concept of history in American postmodernist fiction (Klinkowitz 1992).

## Notes to Chapter 9

1. If we keep in mind the programmatic character of all of Prigov's nonpoetic statements, then even his afterword to one of Sorokin's books can be understood as a manifesto of conceptualism.

2. Robert Porter translates this title as "Ruin" (Popov 1997: 171–76).

3. Some of these stories are published in English translations in Popov 1997.

4. See the translations by Andrew Bromfield: Pelevin 1996c, 1997a.

5. See, in translation, Pelevin 1997b.

6. The interpretation of Socialist Realism as a discursive "metaphor of power" is expounded in detail in Dobrenko's research on the literature of the Stalin era (1993).

7. The teacher's full name combines two diametrically opposed associations, one pointing to Nikolai Fedorovich Fedorov, whose philosophy of the common cause was devoted to the project of resurrecting the dead, and that classic writer of Socialist Realist denunciations, Vladimir Ermilov.

8. The devilish features of the characters in "The Cattle Plague" are analyzed by Vladimir Potapov (1991).

9. The title of this novel repeats the title of the popular Soviet comedy of the 1930s,

which in its turn refers to the novel *Hearts of Three* by Jack London, a work that was extremely popular among Soviet readers.

10. This series of problems, which are closely connected with the crisis of post-modern art, is examined in Lipovetsky 1993–94 and Leiderman and Lipovetsky 1993.

## Notes to Chapter 10

1. Theoreticians of "chaos" have learned that "the evolution of a complex dynamic system can't be followed in causal details because such systems are holistic. Everything affects everything else. To understand them it's necessary to see into their complexity. . . . David Bohm proposed another scientific image to convey a new holistic view of nature, the hologram: 'Cutting a piece from the hologram and sending the laser beam through the fragment also produces an image of the whole object, although this image may not be quite as sharp. The holistic effect is analogous to the self-similarity of a fractal, repeating the shape of the whole at different scales' " (Briggs and Peat 1984: 110–11).

## Notes to Chapter 11

1. In his acceptance remarks for the medal of honor for literature of the National Arts Club, Solzhenitsyn wrote:

> [W]e witness, through history's various thresholds, a recurrence of one and the same perilous anti-cultural phenomenon, with its rejection of and con-tempt for all foregoing tradition, and with its mandatory hostility toward whatever is universally accepted. Before, it burst in upon us with the fanfares and gaudy flags of "futurism"; today the term "post-modernism" is applied. . . . For a post-modernist the world does not possess values that have reality. He even has an expression for this: "the world as text," as something secondary, as the text of an author's work. . . . A denial of any and all ideals is consid-ered courageous. And in this voluntary self-delusion, "post-modernism" sees itself as the crowning achievement of all previous culture, the final link in its chain. . . . There is no God, there is no truth, the universe is chaotic, all is relative, "the world as text," a text any post-modernist is willing to compose. How clamorous it is all, but also—how helpless. (Solzhenitsyn 1993: 3, 17)

2. For more on this phenomenon, see Lipovetsky 1994.

3. For more on the contemporary transformations of realism, see Leiderman and Lipovetsky 1993 and Stepanian 1994. For a working definition of this new type of realism, Naum Leiderman and I have proposed the term "postrealism," by analogy with "postmodernism." The typological character of the relationship between postmodernism and what we call postrealism is suggested by the observations made by Iurii Lotman in his article "Asymmetry and Dialogue." In this work, Lotman describes two main types of cultures that replace each other: a culture that Lotman calls "left-brained," which is noteworthy for its elevated "semiotic-ness," its tendency to shut itself off within an isolated semiotic world; this culture opens freedom to the game, develops comparatively subtler instruments of extrasemiotic analysis; it is inevitably replaced by a culture of a different sort ("right-brained'), in which semiosis is directed toward a content-oriented interpretation of the semiotic models received from the culture of the first type in the

context of an extratextual reality, which fills these models with the "blood of real interests" and lends them a real existence alongside other objects. See Lotman 1983: 14–30.

4. In her autobiographical sketch "The Children of Utopia," Dora Shturman, having sensed within the aesthetic experience of "postrealism" something that resonated with her own life experience, said:

We did not know the terms used then or especially now. But we felt (and I reread the accounts of this) that neither avant-gardism (of any sort) nor a certain *hyperrealism* (in our time either "impressionistic" or "subjective" or simply "new"; according to today's critics, "postrealism") *gives art the chance to survive*. Both by itself and among people. And it is this very realism, however it is called, that fumbles in the chaos for life-saving *spiritual-everyday coordinates,* which the capitulation to chaos attempts to dissolve in its fear and masochism. Our "subjective realists," first of all, feel the enormity of the world as a consolation (apparently, of an appropriate size) and not as a source of self-destruction or oppression. Second, through the absurdity of life they feel the *harmony* of this enormity. Third, they do not identify the horror of history with the horror of being. Fourth, it has not only not convinced them of the senselessness of higher imperatives but, on the contrary, has proved to them that one can escape the horror and not dissolve in chaos only by keeping their eyes on these landmarks. *Or they may not escape*; but they will still follow *their* law. . . . And it is no accident that the most colorful of those who are called "postmodernists" have chosen the path of "postrealists": talent feels out the true proportions of meaning and chaos in being; sharp vision detects the flickering of eternal landmarks; the hand, led by a healthy instinct, unconsciously searches for the guiderails of compassion (not only for "oneself alone") and of the search. (Shturman 1994: 192; emphasis in the original)

5. Quoted from Piskunova and Piskunov 1992: 172.

6. In the realist literature of the previous era, the motif of immersion in death appeared just as frequently: "exhuming graves" in Iurii Trifonov's *Another Life* and *The Old Man;* the return to the ruined cemetery in "Village Prose"; Chingiz Aitmatov (*And the Day Lasts Longer Than an Age);* and even Vladimir Makanin ("The Tale of the Old Village," "Loss"), and Varlam Shalamov's metaphorical comparison of the writer and bearer of camp knowledge not to Orpheus but to Pluto (Shalamov 1989: 54).

# References

Aksyonov, Vasily. 1991. *Pravo na ostrov.* Moscow: Moskovskii rabochii.

Aksyonov, Vassily. 1985. *Surplussed Barrelware.* Edited and translated by Joel Wilkinson and Slava Yastremski. Ann Arbor: Ardis.

Aleshkovsky, Yuz. 1986. *Kangaroo.* Translated by Tamara Glenny. New York: Farrar, Straus & Giroux.

———. 1993. *Izbrannoe: Ruka, Nikolai Nikolaevich, Maskirovka, Sinen'kii skromnyi platochek.* St. Petersburg: Vega.

Altshuller, Mark G. 1982. "*Moskva-Petushki* Venedikta Erofeeva i traditsii klassicheskoi poemy." *Novyi zhurnal* (New York) 142: 75–85.

Anemone, Anthony. 1991. "The Anti-World of Daniil Kharms." In *Daniil Kharms and the Poetics of the Absurd,* edited by Neil Cornell. New York: St. Martin's Press, 77–78.

Anikin, Vladimir. 1991. *Russkaia narodnaia skazka.* Moscow: Prosveshchenie.

Arkhangel'skii, Aleksandr. 1991. Foreword to Yuz Aleshkovsky's "Plain Blue Scarf." *Druzhba narodov* 7: 6–8.

Bakhtin, Mikhail. 1968. *Rabelais and His World.* Translated by Helene Iswolsky. Boston: MIT Press.

———. 1981. *The Dialogic Imagination: Four Essays.* Edited by Michael Holquist. Translated from the Russian by Caryl Emerson and Michael Holquist. Austin: University of Texas Press.

———. 1984. *Problems of Dostoevsky's Poetics.* Edited and translated by Caryl Emerson. Introduction by Wayne C. Booth. Minneapolis: University of Minnesota Press.

———. 1990. *Art and Answerability: Early Philosophical Essays.* Edited by Michael Holquist and Vadim Liapunov. Translation and notes by Vadim Liapunov. Austin: University of Texas Press.

Barth, John. 1984. *The Friday Book: Essays and Other Nonfiction.* New York: Putnam.

Barthes, Roland. 1989. *The Rustle of Language.* Translated by Richard Howard. Berkeley and Los Angeles: University of California Press.

Baudrillard, Jean. 1983. "The Ecstasy of Communication." In *The Anti-Aesthetic: Essays on Postmodern Culture,* edited by Hal Foster. Washington, DC: Bay Press, 126–34.

———. 1991. "Simulacra and Simulation." In *Postmodernism: An International Anthology,* edited by Wook-Dong Kim. Seoul: 446–92.

———. 1993. "The Precession of Simulacra." In Natoli and Hutcheon 1993: 342–75.

Bauman, Zygmunt. 1993. "Postmodernity, or Living with Ambivalence." In Natoli and Hutcheon 1993: 9–24.

Begiebing, Robert J. 1989. *Toward a New Synthesis: John Fowler, John Gardner, Norman Mailer.* Ann Arbor, London: UMI Research Press.

Belaia, Galina. 1992. "The Crisis of Soviet Artistic Mentality in 1960s and 1970s." In *New Directions in Soviet Literature,* edited by Sheelagh D. Graham. New York: St. Martin's Press.

Beraha, Laura. 1997. "Roll Out the Barrels: Emptiness, Fullness, and the Picaresque-Idyllic Dynamic in Vasilii Aksenov's 'Zatovarennaia bochkotara.'" *Slavic Review* 56, no. 2 (Summer): 212–32.

Berkovskii, Naum. 1989. "O proze Mandel'shtama." In *Mir, sozdavaemyi literaturoi.* Moscow: Sovetskii pisatel', 286–304.

Berry, Ellen E., and Anesa Miller-Pogacar, eds. 1995. *Re-Entering the Sign: Articulating New Russian Culture.* Ann Arbor: Ardis.

Bethea, David. 1989. *The Shape of the Apocalyplse in Modern Russian Fiction.* Princeton: Princeton University Press.

Bibler, Vladimir S. 1991. *Nravstvennost'. Kul'tura. Sovermennost'.* Moscow: Znanie.

Bitov, Andrei. 1987. *Pushkin House.* Translated by Susan Brownsberger. New York: Farrar, Straus & Giroux.

———. 1989. "Blizkoe retro, ili Kommentarii k obshcheizvestnomu." *Pushkinskii dom.* Moscow: Sovremennik, 397–98.

———. 1991. "Povtorenie neproidennogo." *Znamia* 6: 194–206. [On the works of Yuz Aleshkovsky]

Blok, Aleksander. 1968. *Sobranie sochinenii.* V 8–mitt. T.8. Moscow: Khudozhestvennaia literatura.

Boguslawski, Alexander. 1987. "Death in the Works of Sasha Sokolov." *Canadian-American Slavic Studies* 21: 231–46.

Borges, Jorge Luis. 1978. *The Aleph and Other Stories, 1933–69.* Translated by Norman Thomas di Giovanni in collaboration with the author. New York: E.P. Dutton.

Bornhofen, Patricia. 1995. *Cosmography and Chaography: Baroque to Neobaroque. A Study in Poetics and Cultural Logic.* Ph.D. diss., University of Wisconsin–Madison.

Briggs, John and F. David Peat. 1984. *Looking Glass Universe: The Emerging Science of Wholeness.* New York: Simon and Schuster.

———. 1989. *Turbulent Mirror: An Illustrated Guide to Chaos Theory and the Science of Wholeness.* New York: Harper & Row Publishers.

Briker, Boris. 1986. *"In Search of a Genre:* The Meaning of the Title and the Idea of a 'Genre.'" In *Vasily Pavlovich Aksënov: A Writer in Quest of Himself.* Mozeiko, Briker, Dalgard eds.: 148–64.

Brodsky, Joseph. 1994. *Sochineniia Iosifa Brodskogo.* Sankt-Peterburg: "Pushkinskii Fond." Vol. 3.

Calinescu, Matei. 1980. "Ways of Looking and Fiction." In *Romanticism, Modernism, Postmodernism,* edited by Harry R. Garvin. Lewisburgh: Bucknell University Press, 155–70.

———. 1983. "From One to the Many: Pluralism in Today's Thought." In *Innovation/Renovation: New Perspectives on the Humanities,* edited by Ihab Hassan and Sally Hassan. Madison: University of Wisconsin Press, 263–87.

Cavanagh, Clare. 1995. *Osip Mandelstam and the Modernist Creation of Tradition.* Princeton: Princeton University Press.

Chances, Ellen. 1993. *Andrei Bitov: The Ecology of Inspiration.* Cambridge: Cambridge University Press.

Chudakova, Marietta O. 1991. "Pasternak i Bulgakov: rubezh dvukh literaturnykh tsiklov." *Literaturnoe obozrenie* 5: 11–17.

Chuprinin, Sergei I. 1989. "Prochitannomu verit'!" *Volga* (Saratov) 2: 77–81.

Clark, Katerina. 1981. *The Soviet Novel: History as Ritual.* Chicago and London: University of Chicago Press.

Clowes, Edith W. 1993. *Russian Experimental Fiction: Resisting Ideology After Utopia.* Princeton: Princeton University Press.

Condee, Nancy, and Vladimir Padunov. 1994. "Pair-a-dice Lost: The Socialist Gamble,

Market Determinism, and Compulsory Postmodernism." *New Formations* 22 (Spring): 72–94.

Connor, Steven. 1989. *Postmodernist Culture: An Introduction to Theories of the Contemporary.* Oxford, Cambridge, MA: Blackwell.

Courturier, Maurice. 1993. "Nabokov in Postmodernist Land." *Critique* 34, no. 4 (Summer): 247–60.

Dalgard, P. 1982. *The Function of the Grotesque in Vasilij Aksenov.* Minneapolis: Aarhus.

Deleuze, Gilles. 1992. "Rhizome Versus Trees." In *The Deleuze Reader,* edited by Constantin V. Boundas. New York: Columbia University Press, 3–38.

Deleuze, Gilles, and Felix Guattari. 1992. *Anti-Oedipus: Capitalism and Schizophrenia.* Translated by R. Hurley, M. Seem, and H.R. Lane. Minneapolis: University of Minnesota Press.

Dering-Smirnova, Renata, and Igor P. Smirnov. 1980. "Istoricheskii avangard s tochki zreniia evoliutsii khudozhestvennykh sistem." *Russian Literature* 8, no. 5: 403–68.

Derrida, Jacques. 1991. *A Derrida Reader: Between the Blinds.* Edited with an introduction and notes by Peggy Kamuf. New York: Columbia University Press.

———. 1978. "The Theater of Cruelty and the Closure of Representation." In *Writing and Difference,* translated by Alan Bass. Chicago: University of Chicago Press: 232–50

Dobrenko, Yevgeny. 1990. "Preodolenie ideologii." *Volga* 11: 168–88.

———. 1993. *Metafora vlasti: Literatura stalinskoi epokhi v istoricheskom osveshchenii.* Munich: Verlag Otto Sagner, 1–74.

Eco, Umberto. 1984. Postcript to *The Name of the Rose.* Translated from the Italian by William Weaver. San Diego, New York, London: Harcourt Brace Jovanovich.

———. 1988. *Foucault's Pendulum.* Translated by William Weaver. New York: Ballantine.

Eidinova, Viola. 1994. "Antidialogizm kak stilevoi printsip russkoi literatury absurda 1920–kh–nachala 1930–kh godov (k probleme literaturnoi dinamiki)." *XX vek. Literatura. Stil': Stilevye zakonomernosti russkoi literatury XX veka (1900–1930 gg.).* Vol. 1. Ekaterinburg: Ural'skii Pedagogicheskii universitet, 7–23.

Eliade, Mircea. 1954. *The Myth of Eternal Return.* Translated by Willard R. Trask. New York: Pantheon Books.

———. 1958. *Birth and Rebirth: The Religious Meaning of Initiation in Human Culture.* Translated by Willard R. Trask. New York: Harper & Row.

———. 1975. *Rites and Symbols of Initiation.* San Francisco: Harper Torchbooks.

Eliot, T.S. 1932. "Tradition and the Individual Talent." In *Selected Essays.* London: Harcourt, Brace & Co., 3–21.

Epstein, Mikhail. 1995a. *After the Future: The Paradoxes of Postmodernism and Contemporary Russian Culture.* Translated with an introduction by Anesa Miller-Pogacar. Amherst: University of Massachusetts Press.

———. 1995b. "Posle karnavala, ili Vechnyi Venichka." In Venedict Erofeev 1995: 3–30.

———. 1996. "Istoki i smysl russkogo postmodernizma." *Zvezda* 8: 166–88.

———. 1997. "Demonicheskoe, apofaticheskoe i sekuliarnoe v russkoi kul'ture. Perekhod ot dvoichnoi modeli k troichnoi." Unpublished manuscript. Presented at the Second Nevada Conference on Russian Culture, University of Nevada, Las Vegas, November 1997.

Erofeev, Venedikt. 1994. *Moscow to the End of the Line.* Translated by H. William Tjalsma. Evanston: Northwestern University Press.

———. 1995. *Ostav'te moiu dushu v pokoe: Pochti vse.* Moscow: Izd. Kh.G.S

Erofeev, Viktor. 1988. "Pamiatnik proshedshemu vremeni." *Oktiabr'* 6: 202–4.
———. 1993. *Izbrannoe, ili Karmannyi apokalipsis*. Moscow, Paris, New York: The Third Wave.
Erofeyev, Victor. 1990. "The Parakeet." Translated by Leonard J. Stanton. In *Glasnost: An Anthology of Russian Literature Under Gorbachev*, edited by Helena Goscilo and Byron Lindsey. Ann Arbor: Ardis, 367–77.
———. 1991. "Russia's *Fleurs du Mal*," In *New Russian Writing: Russia's Fleurs du Mal*, edited by Victor Erofeyev and Andrew Reynolds. London: Farrar, Straus & Giroux, ix–xxx.
Federman, Raymond. 1975. "Surfiction—Four Propositions in the Form of an Introduction." In *Surfiction: Fiction Now . . . and Tomorrow*, edited by Raymond Federman. Chicago: Swallow Press, 11–23.
Fiedler, Leslie. 1975. "Cross the Border—Close that Gap: Postmodernism." In *American Literature Since 1900*, edited by M. Cunliffe. London: Barrie and Jenkins, 344–66. Orig. publ. 1968.
Foucault, Michel. 1977. *Language, Counter-memory, Practice: Selected Essays and Interviews*. Ithaca, NY: Cornell University Press.
Freedman, John. 1987. "Memory, Imagination and the Liberating Force of Literature in Sasha Sokolov's *A School for Fools*." *Canadian-American Slavic Studies* 21: 265–78.
Freidberg, Maurice. 1962. *Russian Classics in Soviet Jackets*. New York: Columbia University Press.
Freidenberg, Olga M. 1936. *Poetika siuzheta i zhanra: period antichnoi literatury*. Leningrad: Izd. Akademii Nauk.
Frolova, Nina, et al. 1991. "Neskol'ko monologov o Venedikte Erofeeve." *Teatr* 9: 74–22.
Fukuyama, Francis. 1992. *The End of History and the Last Man*. New York: Free Press.
Gaiser-Shnitman, Svetlana. 1984. *Venedikt Erofeev's Moskva-Petushki, ili "The Rest Is Silence."* Bern, Frankfurt am Main, New York, Paris: Peter Lang.
Gandlevsky, Sergei, and Dmitrii Aleksandrovich Prigov. 1993. "Mezhdu imenem i imidzhem." *Literaturnaia gazeta*, no. 19 (May 12): 5.
Gareev, Zufar. 1992. *Mul'tiproza: povesti*. Moscow: Soiuz Teatral'nykh Deiatelei.
Genis, Aleksandr. 1994a. "Treugol'nik: Avangard, sotsrealizm, postmodernizm." *Inostrannaia literatura* 10: 245–56.
———. 1994b. "Luk i kapusta: Paradigmy sovremennoi kul'tury." *Znamia* 8: 188–200.
———. 1997a. *Vavilonsakaia bashnia: Iskusstvo nastoiashchego vremeni*. Moscow: Nezavisimaia gazeta.
———. 1997b. "Beseda desiataia: Pole chudes. Viktor Pelevin." *Zvezda* 12: 230–33.
Gleick, James. 1987. *Chaos: Making a New Science*. New York: Viking.
Golosovker, Iakov. 1987. *Logika mifa*. Moscow: Nauka.
Goscilo, Helena. 1996. *The Explosive World of Tatyana N. Tolstaya's Fiction*. Armonk, NY: M.E. Sharpe.
Groys, Boris. 1992. *The Total Art of Stalinism: Avant-Garde, Aesthetic Dictatorship, and Beyond*. Translated by Charles Rougle. Princeton: Princeton University Press.
Groys, Boris, and Ilya Kabakov. 1996. "Dialog o musore." *Novoe literaturnoe obozrenie* (Moscow) 20: 319–30.
Gunter, Hans. 1992. "Zheleznaia garmoniia: Gosudarstvo kak total'noe proizvedenie iskusstva." *Voprosy literatury* 1: 27–41.
———. 1986. "Zhiznestroenie." *Russian Literature* 20: 41–48.
Hayles, N. Katherina. 1990. *Chaos Bound: Orderly Disorder in Contemporary Literature and Science*. Ithaca and London: Cornell University Press.

Hayles, N. Katherine, ed. 1991. *Chaos and Order: Complex Dynamics in Literature and Science*. Chicago and London: University of Chicago Press.

Heim, Michael, and Olga Matich, eds. 1984. *The Third Wave: Russian Literature in Emigration*. Ann Arbor: Ardis.

Hellebust, Rolf. 1991. "Fiction and Unreality in Bitov's *Pushkin House*." *Style* 25, no. 2 (Summer): 265–79.

Hicks, Emily D. 1988. "Deterritorialization and Border Writing." In *Ethics/Aesthetics: Post-Modern Positions*, edited by Robert Merrill. Washington, DC: Maisonneuve Press, 47–58.

Holquist, Michael. 1990. *Dialogism: Bakhtin and His World*. New York and London: Routledge.

Hosking, Geoffrey. 1992. *History of the Soviet Union: 1917–1991*. Final edition. London: Fontana.

Huizinga, Johan. 1980. *Homo Ludens: A Study of the Play-Element in Culture*. London, Boston, and Henley: Routledge & Kegan Paul.

Hutcheon, Linda. 1981. *Narcissitic Narrative: Metafictional Paradox*. Ontario: Willford University Press.

Hutcheon, Linda. 1988. *A Poetics of Postmodernism: History, Theory, Fiction*. New York and London: Routledge.

Huyssen, Andreas. 1984. "Mapping the Postmodern." *New German Critique* 33: 5–52.

Iampol'skii, Mikhail, and Alena Solntseva. 1991. "Postmodernizm po-sovetski." *Teatr* 8: 48–60.

Ivanova, Natalia. 1988. "Sud'ba i rol' (Andrei Bitov)." In *Tochka zreniia*. Moscow: Sovetskii pisatel', 182–83.

Jameson, Fredric. 1991. *Postmodernism, or the Cultural Logic of Late Capitalism*. Durham: Duke University Press.

Johnson, D. Barton. 1980. "A Structural Analysis of Sasha Sokolov's *School for Fools*: A Paradigmatic Novel." In *Fiction and Drama in Eastern and Southeastern Europe: Evolution and Experiment in the Postwar Period*, edited by Henrik Birnbaum and Thomas Eekman. Columbus, Ohio: Slavica, 207–38.

———. 1987. "Sasha Sokolov: A Literary Biography." *Canadian-American Slavic Studies* 21, nos. 3–4. (Fall-Winter): 203–30.

Karabchievskii, Iurii. 1989. "Tochka boli: O romane Andreia Bitova 'Pushkinskii dom'." In *Ulitsa Mandel'shtama*. Orange, CT: Antiquary, 67–103.

———. 1993 "Filologicheskaia proza." *Novyi mir* 10: 219–36.

Karriker, Alexandra Heidi. 1979. "Double Vision: Sasha Sokolov's *School for Fools*." *World Literature Today* 53, no. 4 (Autumn): 610–13.

———. 1987. "Narrative Shifts and Cyclic Patterns in *A School for Fools*." *Canadian-American Slavic Studies* 21: 287–99.

Klinkowitz, Jerome. 1992. *Structuring the Void: The Struggle for Subject in Contemporary American Fiction*. Durham: Duke University Press.

Kogan, Igor. 1994. "Parodiinye elementy v povesti Vasiliia Aksenova *Moi dedushka— pamiatnik*." In *Vasily Aksenov: Literaturnaia sud'ba*. Saratov: Izd-vo Saratovskogo universiteta, 97–106.

Kuberski, Philip. 1994. *Chaosmos: Literature, Science, and Theory*. New York: State University of New York Press.

Kuehl, John. 1989. *Alternate Worlds: A Study of Postmodern Antirealistic Fiction*. New York and London: New York University Press.

Küng, Hans. 1990. "Religiia na perelome epokh: Trinadtsat' tezisov." *Inostrannaia literatura* 11: 223–29.

Kuritsyn, Viacheslav. 1992a. "My poedem s toboiu na 'A' i na 'Iu.' " *Novoe literaturnoe obozrenie* 1: 296–304.

———. 1992b. *Kniga o postmodernizme*. Ekaterinburg.

Kustanovich, Konstantin. 1992. *The Artist and the Tyrant: Vassily Aksenov's Works in the Brezhnev Era*. Columbus: Slavica.

———. 1997. "Venichka Erofeev's Grief and Solitude: Existential Motifs in the Poema." In Ryan-Hayes 1997: 123–52.

Leiderman, Naum. 1982. *Dvizhenie vremeni i zakony zhanra*. Sverdlovsk: Sredne-Uralskoe Knizhnoe izd.

———. 1988. "Zhanrovye sistemy literaturnykh napravlenii i techenii." In *Vzaimodeistvie metoda, stilia i znara v sovetskoi literature*, edited by Naum Leiderman. Sverdlovsk: Sverdlovskii pedagogicheskii institut, 4–17.

———. 1996. "Kosmos i khaos kak metamodeli mira (K otnosheniiu klassicheskogo i modernistskogo tipov kul'tury)." *Russkaia literatura XX veka: napravleniia i techeniia*. Vyp. 3. Ekaterinburg: Ural'skii Pedagogicheskii universitet, 4–11,

Leiderman, Naum, and Mark Lipovetskii. 1993. "Zhizn' posle smerti, ili Novye svedeniia o realizme." *Novy mir* 7: 233–52.

Lettsev, Vladimir. 1989. "Kontseptualizm: chtenie i ponimanie." *Daugava* (Riga) 8: 107–13.

Levin, Iurii. 1990. "Bispatsial'nost' kak invariant poeticheskogo mira Nabokova." *Russian Literature* 28, no. 1: 45–124.

———. 1981. "Povestvovatel'naia struktura kak generator smysla: Tekst v tekste u Kh.-L. Borkhesa." *Trudy po znakovym sistemam. Tekst v tekste*. Vol. 14. Tartu: Tartuskii universitet: 45–64.

Levin, Iurii I. 1992. "Klassicheskie traditsii v 'drugoi' literature: Venedikt Erofeev i Fedor Dostoevskii." *Literaturnoe obozrenie* 2: 45–50.

Likhachev, Dmitrii; A. Panchenko; and N.V. Ponyrko. 1984. *Smekh v Drevnei Rusi*. Leningrad: Nauka.

Lipovetskii, Mark. 1992. *Poetika literaturnoi skazki: Na materiale russkoi literatury 1920–80 godov*. Sverdlovsk: Izd. Ural'skogo universiteta.

———. 1993–94. "The Law of Steepness." *Russian Studies in Literature* 30, no. 1 (Winter): 5–39.

———. 1994. "Thanks for the Holiday! The Old Age of the 'New Wave.' " *Russian Studies in Literature* 30, no. 2 (Spring): 75–82.

Lotman, Iurii. 1994. *Iu.M. Lotman i tartusko-moskovskaia semioticheskaia shkola*. Moscow: Gnosis.

Lotman, Iurii M. 1983. "Assimetriia i dialog." *Trudy po znakovym sistemam: Tekst i kul'tura*. Vol. 16. Tartu: Tartuskii universitet, 14–30.

Lotman, Iurii M., and Boris A. Uspenskii. 1985. "Binary Models in the Dynamics of Russian Culture (to the End of the Eighteenth Century)." Translated from the Russian by Robert Sorenson. In *The Semiotics of Russian Cultural History*. Essays by Iurii M. Lotman, Lidiia Ia. Ginsburg, Boris A. Uspenskii, edited by Alexander D. Nakhimovsky and Alice Stone Nakhimovsky. Ithaca: Cornell University Press, 30–68.

Lupanova, Irina P. 1979. " 'Smekhovoi mir' russkoi volshebnoi skazki." *Russkii fol'klor*. Leningrad: Nauka, 66–79.

Lyotard, Jean-Francois. 1984. *The Postmodern Condition: A Report on Knowledge*. Translated from the French by Geoff Bennington and Brian Massumi. Minneapolis: University of Minnesota Press.

Mandelstam, Osip. 1979. *The Complete Critical Prose and Letters*. Edited by Jane Gary Harris. Translated by Jane Gary Harris and Contance Link. Ann Arbor: Ardis.

Maravall, Josè Antonio. 1986. *Culture of the Baroque: Analysis of a Historical Structure.* Translated by Terry Cochran. Minneapolis: University of Minnesota Press.

McAdam, Alfred J., and Flora H. Shimanovich. 1985. "Latin American Literature in the Postmodern Era." In *The Postmodern Moment: A Handbook of Contemporary Innovation in the Arts,* edited by Stanley Trachtenberg. London: Greenwood Press, 251–62.

McHale, Brian. 1987. *Postmodernist Fiction.* New York and London: Methuen.

Medarić, Magdalena. 1991. "Nabokov i roman XX stoletiia." *Russian Literature* 29: 79–100.

Meletinskii, Eleazar M. 1994. *O literaturnykh arkhetipakh.* Moscow: Izd. RGGU.

———. 1976. *Poetika mifa.* Moscow: Nauka.

Moody, Fred. 1979. "Madness and the Patterns of Freedom in Sasha Sokolov's *A School for Fools.*" *Russian Literature Triquarterly* 16: 7–32.

Morin, Edgar. 1984. "The Fourth Vision: On the Place of the Observer." In *Disorder and Order: Proceedings of the Stanford International Symposium,* edited by Paisley Levingston. Stanford Literature Studies. Stanford: Anma Libri, 98–108.

Morson, Gary Saul. 1992. "Bakhtin i nashe nastoiashchee." *Bakhtinskii sbornik 2.* Edited by D. Kuindzhich and L. Makhlin. Moscow: Izd. RGGU, 5–31.

Morson, Gary Saul, and Caryl Emerson. 1990. *Mikhail Bakhtin: Creation of a Prosaics.* Stanford: Stanford University Press.

Mozejko, E.; Boris Briker; and Per Dalgard, eds. 1986. *Vasily Pavlovich Aksënov: A Writer in Quest of Himself.* Columbus: Slavica.

Naiman, Eric, and Ann Nesbit. 1996. "Documentary Discipline: Three Interrogations of Stanislav Govorukhin." In *Soviet Heorogliphics: Visual Culture in Late Twentieth Century Russia,* edited by Nancy Condee. Bloomington: Indiana University Press, 52–68.

Nakhimovsky, Alice Stone. 1988. "Looking Back at Paradise Lost: The Russian Nineteenth Century in Andrei Bitov's *Pushkin House.*" *Russian Literature Triquarterly* 22 (Winter): 195–204.

Natoli, Joseph, and Linda Hutcheon, eds. 1993. *A Postmodern Reader.* New York: State University of New York Press.

Nemzer, Andrei. 1991. "Strannaia veshch', neponiatnaia vesch'." *Novyi mir* 11: 243–49.

Nevzgliadova, Elena. 1986. "Eta prekrasnaia zhizn': O rasskazakh Tat'iany Tolstoi." *Avrora* 10: 111–20.

Newman, Charles. 1985. *The Post-Modern Aura.* Evanston: Northwestern University Press.

Novikov, Vladimir. 1988. "Tainaia svoboda." *Znamia* 3: 230–31.

Oraić, Dubravka Tolic. 1994. "Avangard i postmodern." *Russian Literature* 36, no. 1: 95–114.

———. 1988. "Tsitatnost'." *Russian Literature* 24, no. 8: 121–35.

Paperno, I.A., and B.M. Gasparov. 1981. "Vstan' i idi." *Slavica Hierosolymitana* 5–6: 387–400.

Paperno, Irina, and Joan Delaway Grossman, eds. 1994. *Creating Life: The Aesthetic Utopia of Russian Modernism.* Stanford: Stanford University Press.

Parshchikov, Alexei. 1995. "Sobytiinaia kanva." *Kommentarii* 7: 3–42.

Parthé, Kathleen F. 1992. *Russian Village Prose: The Radiant Past.* Princeton: Princeton University Press,

Paulson, William. 1988. *The Noise of Culture: Literary Text in a World of Information.* Ithaca and London: Cornell University Press.

Pelevin, Viktor. 1996a. *Buben nizhnego mira.* Moscow: Terra.

———. 1996b. *Chapaev i Pustota.* Moscow: Vagrius.

———. 1996c. *The Life of Insects.* Translated from the Russian by Andrew Bromfield. London: Harbor.

———. 1997a. *Omon Ra.* Translated from the Russian by Andrew Bromfield. New York: New Directions.

———. 1997b. *The Blue Lantern and Other Stories.* Translated by Andrew Bromfield. New York: New Directions.

Perloff, Marjorie. 1993. "Russian Postmodernism: An Oxymoron?" In *Postmodern Culture: An Electronic Journal of Interdisciplinary Criticism (PMC).* Cary, NC. Vol. 3, no. 2 (January).

Pietsukh, Viacheslav. 1990. *Ia i prochee.* Moscow: Khudozhestvennaia literatura.

———. 1995. "The Central–Ermolaevo War." Translated by Arch Tait. In *The Penguin Book of New Russian Writing: Russia's Fleurs du Mal,* edited by Victor Erefeyev and Andrew Reynolds. London: Penguin Books.

Piskunova, Svetlana, and Vladimir Piskunov. 1992. "Estetika svobody." *Zvezda* 1: 172–80.

Popov, Yevgeny. 1989. "Prekrasnost' zhizni, ili Poiski smysla prochnosti." *Literaturnaia gazeta,* 20 April: 6

———. 1990. *Prekrasnost' zhizni, Roman s gazetoi, kotoryi nikogda ne budet nachat i zakonchen.* Moscow: Moskovskii rabochii.

———. 1992. "Udaki: Neskol'ko istorii o k sozhaleniiu vse eshche vstrechaiushchikhsia v nashei zhizni vremenami vsegda otdel'nykh nedostatkakh." *Druzhba narodov* 1: 5–24.

———. 1994. *The Soul of a Patriot, or Various Epistles to Ferfichkin.* Translated from the Russian by Robert Porter. Evanston: Northwestern University Press.

———. 1997. *Merry-Making in Old Russia, and Other Stories.* Translated from the Russian by Robert Porter. Evanston: Northwestern University Press.

Porter, Robert. 1994. *Russia's Alternative Prose.* Oxford, Providence: Berg.

Potapov, Vladimir. 1989. "Na vykhode iz 'undergrounda.' " *Novyi mir* 10: 251–55.

———. 1991. "Begushchie ot dyma: Sots-art kak zerkalo i posledniaia stadiia sotsrealizma." *Volga* 9: 29–34.

Prigogine, Ilya. 1984. "Order out of Chaos." In *Disorder and Order: Proceedings of the Stanford International Symposium,* edited by Paisley Livingston. *Stanford Literature Studies.* Stanford: Anma Libri, 41–60.

———. 1989. "Pereotkrytie vremeni." *Voprosy filosofii* 3: 3–19.

Prigogine, Ilya, and Isabelle Stengers. 1984. *Order out of Chaos: Man's New Dialogue with Nature.* Boulder and London: New Science Library.

Prigov, Dmitrii A. 1992. "A im kazalos': v Moskvu, v Moskvu!" In Sorokin 1992: 114–20.

Propp, Vladimir. 1946. *Istoricheskie korni volshebnoi skazki.* Leningrad: Leningrad University.

———. 1976. *Fol'klor i deistvitel'nost'.* Moscow: Nauka.

———. 1984. *Theory and History of Folklore.* Translated by Ariadna Y. Martin and Richard P. Martin et al. Edited with an introduction and notes by Anatoly Liberman. Minneapolis: University of Minnesota Press.

Pushkin, Alexander. 1963. *Eugene Onegin: A Novel in Verse.* Translated from the Russian with an introduction and notes by Walter Arndt. New York: E.P. Dutton & Co.

Relihan, Joel C. 1993. *Ancient Menippean Satire.* Baltimore and London: Johns Hopkins University Press.

Rich, Elisabeth. 1995. *Russian Literature After Perestroika.* Special Issue of *South Central Review* 12, nos. 3–4 (Fall–Winter).

Roberts, Graham. 1992. "A Matter of (Dis)course: Metafiction in the Works of Daniil

Kharms." In *New Directions in Sovet Literature,* edited by Sheelagh D. Graham. New York: St. Martin's Press, 145–46.

Roll, Serafima. N.d. "Re-surfacing: The Shades of Violence in Viktor Erofeev's Short Stories." Unpublished manuscript.

Rubinshtein, Lev. 1995. *Vse dal'she i dal'she (Iz "Bol'shoi kartoteki").* Moscow: Obscuri Viri.

———. 1996. "Nevozmozhno okhvatit' vse sushchestvuiushchee: Eto—ia." *Novyi mir* 1: 69–76.

———. 1991. "Chto tut mozhno skazat'?" *Indeks* (Moscow): 112–15.

Rubinshtein, Lev, and Zara Abdullaeva. 1997. "Voprosy literatury." *Druzhba narodov* 9: 180–85.

Ryan-Hayes, Karen, ed. 1997a. *Venedikt Erofeev's Moskva-Petushki: Critical Perspective.* New York: Peter Lang.

———. 1997b. "Erofeev's Grief: Inconsolable and Otherwise." In Ryan-Hayes 1997a: 101–22.

Sedakova, Ol'ga. 1991. "Neskazannaia rech' na vechere Venedikta Erofeeva." *Druzhba narodov* 12: 264–65.

Segal, Dmitrii. 1979. "Literatura kak vtorichnaia modeliruiushchaia sistema." *Slavica Hierosolymitana* 4: 1–35.

———. 1981. "Literatura kak okhrannaia gramota." *Slavica Hierosolymitana* 5–6: 151–244.

Serres, Michel. 1984. "Dream." In *Disorder and Order: Proceedings of the Stanford International Symposium,* edited by Paisley Livingston. Stanford Literature Studies. Stanford: Anma Libri, 25–39.

Shalamov, Varlam. 1989. "O moei proze." *Novyi mir* 12: 59–62.

Shepherd, David. 1992. *Beyond Metafiction: Self-Consciousness in Soviet Literature.* Oxford: Clarendon Press.

Shneidman, N.N. 1995. *Russian Literature, 1988–1994: The End of an Era.* Toronto, Buffalo, London: University of Toronto Press.

Shturman, Dora. 1994. "Deti utopii: Fragmenty ideologicheskoi avtobiografii." *Novyi mir* 10: 161–213.

Siniavskii, Andrei. 1982. *"Opavshie list'ia" V.V. Rozanova.* Paris: Syntaxis.

Smirnova, Elena A. 1990. "Venedikt Erofeev glazami gogoleveda." *Russkaia literatura* 3: 58–66.

Smyth, Edmund. 1991. "Introduction." In *Postmodernism and Contemporary Fiction,* edited by Edmund Smyth. London: B.T. Batsford.

Solzhenitsyn, Aleksandr. 1993. "The Relentless Cult of Novelty and How It Wrecked the Century." Translated by Ignat Solzhenitsyn and Stephan Sozhenitsyn. *New York Times Book Review.* February 7: 3, 17.

Sokolov, Sasha. 1977. *A School for Fools.* Translated from the Russian by Carl R. Proffer. Ann Arbor: Ardis.

———. 1980. *Meshdu sobakoi i volkom.* Ann Arbor: Ardis.

———. 1989. *Astrophobia.* Translated from the Russian by Michael Henry Heim. New York: Grove Weidenfeld.

———. 1992. "Palissander—c'est moi?" In *Palisandriia.* Moscow: Glagol, 264–69.

Sokolov, Sasha, and Viktor Erofeyev. 1989. "Vremia dlia chastnykh besed." *Oktiabr'* 8: 195–202.

Sontag, Susan. 1976. "Artaud." In *Antonin Artaud: Selected Writings.* New York: Farrar, Straus & Giroux, i–lxxiii.

Sorokin, Vladimir. 1991. "Doverie: p'esa v piati aktakh." *Iazyk i deistvie (p'esy).* Moscow: Ruslan Elinin, 76–116.

————. 1992. [*Stories.*] Moscow: Russlit.

————. 1994a. *Norma.* Moscow: Obscuri Viri and Izdatel'stvo "Tri Kita."

————. 1994b. "Serdtsa chetyrekh." *Konets veka.*

Spieker, Sven. 1996. *Figures of Memory and Forgetting in Andrej Bitov's Prose: Postmodernism and the Quest for History.* Frankfurt am Main, Berlin, Bern, New York, Paris, Vienna: Peter Lang.

Stepanian, Karen. 1994. "Realism as the Concluding Stage of Postmodernism." *Russian Studies in Literature* 30, no. 2 (Spring): 58–74.

Strehle, Susan. 1992. *Fiction in the Quantum Universe.* Chapel Hill: University of North Carolina Press.

Svitel'skii, Vladislav. 1994. "Dinamika izobrazheniia v romane Vasiliia Aksenova *Ostrov Krym.*" In *Vasilii Aksenov: Literaturnaia sud'ba.* Samara: Samarskii universitet: 125–34.

Thiher, Allen. 1984. *Worlds in Reflection: Modern Language Theory and Postmodern Fiction.* Chicago and London: University of Chicago Press.

Toffler, Alvin. 1984. "Science and Change." In Prigogine and Stengers 1984: xi–xxvi.

Toker, Leona. 1987. "Gamesman's Sketches (Found in a Bottle): A Reading of Sasha Sokolov's *Between Dog and Wolf.*" *Canadian-American Slavic Studies* 21, nos. 3–4: 345–67.

Tolstaya, Tatyana. 1986. "Ten' na zakate." *Literaturnaia gazeta* 30 (July 23): 7.

————. 1990. *On the Golden Porch.* Translated by Antonina W. Bouis. New York: Vintage.

Tumanov, Vladimir. 1996. "The End in V. Erofeev's *Moskva-Petushki.*" *Russian Literature* 39: 95–114.

Ugrešić, Dubravka. 1990. "Avangard i sovremennost': Vaginov i Kabakov: Tipologicheskaia parallel.'" *Russian Literature* 27, no. 1: 83–96.

Vail', Petr, and Aleksandr Genis. 1996. *60-e: Mir sovetskogo cheloveka.* Moscow: Novoe literaturnoe obozrenie.

————. 1989. "Printsip matreshki." *Novyi mir* 10: 247–50.

Van Baak, J.J. 1987. "Avangardistskii obraz mira i postroenie konflikta." *Russian Literature* (Amsterdam) 21, no. 1: 1–9.

Van Eenwyk, John R. 1997. *Archetypes and Strange Attractors: The Chaotic World of Symbols.* Toronto: Inner City Books.

Van Gennep A. 1960. *The Rites of Passage.* Chicago: University of Chicago Press.

Vishevsky, Anatoly. 1993. "Creating a Shattered World: Toward the Poetics of Yevgeny Popov." *World Literature Today: Russian Literature at a Crossroad* 67, no. 1 (Winter): 119–24.

Vlasov, Eduard. 1997. "Zagranitsa glazami ekstsentrika: k analizu 'zagranichnykh' glav." In Ryan-Hayes 1997a: 197–220.

Waugh, Patricia. 1984. *Metafiction: The Theory and Practice of Self-Conscious Fiction.* London and New York: Methuen.

Wilde, Alan. 1981. *Horizons of Assent: Modernism, Postmodernism, and the Ironic Imagination.* Baltimore and London: John Hopkins University Press.

————. 1987. *Middle Grounds: Studies in Contemporary American Fiction.* Philadelphia: University of Pennsylvania Press.

Williams, Garnett P. 1997. *Chaos Theory Tamed.* Washington, DC: Joseph Henry Press.

Zholkovsky, Alexander. 1987. "The Stylistic Roots of *Palisandriia.*" *Canadian-American Slavic Studies* 21, no. 3–4 (Fall–Winter): 369–400.

————. 1994a. *Text Counter Text: Rereadings in Russian Literary History.* Stanford: Stanford University Press.

————. 1994b. *Bluzhdaiushchie sny: Iz istorii russkogo modernizma.* Moscow: Sovetskii pisatel'.

Zolotonosov, Mikhail. 1988. "Tatianin den'." In *Molodye o molodykh.* Moscow: Molodaia gvardiia, 105–18.

Zorin, Andrei. 1989. "Stikhi na kartochkakh: poeticheskii iazyk L'va Rubinshteina." *Daugava* (Riga) 8: 100–101.

————. 1991. "Opoznavatel'nyi znak." *Teatr* 9: 119–22.

# Appendix

## Biographical and Bibliographical Notes

The biographical and bibliographical information provided here may be helpful to readers who wish to familiarize themselves further with the writers discussed in *Russian Postmodernist Fiction*.

AKSYONOV, VASILY PAVLOVICH (b.1932, in Kazan). One of the leaders of the literary generation of the Thaw (1956–64). His first stories and novels (*Colleagues* [1959], *A Starry Ticket* [1961], *Oranges from Morocco* [1963], *Surplussed Barrelware* [1968]) were published in the journal *Iunost'* (Youth) in the early sixties. Although his works were harshly condemned by official critics, his use of irony and the grotesque helped make him very popular with the Soviet readership. In the sixties and seventies, the "realist" approach of his early works gave way to an idiosyncratic mixture of modernism and Socialist Realist parody, resulting in something quite close to the aesthetics of postmodernism; in addition to *Surplussed Barrelware,* the best examples of Aksyonov's works of this period are his parodic novels for children and adults, *Jean Green Untouchable* (written with Ovidy Gorchakov and Grigory Pozhenyain under the collective pen-name Grivady Gorpozhaks), and *My Grandpa Is a Monument* (1972). His later experimental novels *The Burn* (1980) and *The Island of Crimea* (1981) were rejected by the Soviet censors. The only postmodernist fiction Aksyonov published in Russia after *Surplussed Barrelware* (1968) was *In Search of a Genre* (1978). In 1980 after the scandal with the unofficial almanac *Metropol'* edited by Aksyonov, he emigrated to the United States and now teaches literature at George Mason University in Fairfax, VA. Free from the strictures of Soviet literary controls, Aksyonov's fiction is, strangely enough, marked by a nostalgia for traditional realism, for family sagas—albeit more in the tradition of Hollywood than of Russia (*The Moscow Saga* [1993–96], *The New Sweet Style* [1997]). His latest attempts to adjust his original style to the standards of the Russian "new wave" of the 1990s (in his collection of short stories) apparently failed. Although his works are published widely in post-Soviet Russia (a five-volume "collected works" edition, numerous individual works, articles, and stories in journals, and interviews with the press), he has not become the "father" of the postmodernist generation; this role was already occupied by the late Venedikt Erofeev. Aksyonov now lives in Washington, DC.

## Works

*Negativ polozhitel'nogo geroia: rasskazy.* Moscow: Vagrius, 1996.
*Novyi sladostnyi stil': roman.* Moscow: Izd-vo "Izograf," 1997.
*Sobranie sochinenii.* Vol. 1. Ann Arbor: Ardis, 1987.
*Sobranie sochinenii. V 4–kh tomakh.* Moscow: Izdatel'skii Dom "Iunost'," 1994.

## Translations

*The Burn: A Novel in Three Books (Late Sixties–Early Seventies).* Translated from the Russian by Michael Glenny. New York: Vintage Books, 1985.
*Colleagues.* London: Putnam, 1962.
*The Destruction of Pompeii: Stories.* Ann Arbor: Ardis, 1991.
*Generations of Winter.* Translated from the Russian by John Glad and Christopher Morris. New York: Vintage Books, 1995.
*In Search of Melancholy Baby.* New York: Vintage Books, 1987, 1989.
*The Island of Crimea.* New York: Random House, 1983; London: Abacus, 1986; London: Hutchinson, 1983, 1985.
*It's Time, My Friend, It's Time.* London: Macmillan, 1969.
*Our Golden Ironburg: A Novel with Formulas.* Ann Arbor: Ardis, 1989.
*The Papercase: A View from the Flag Tower of the Smithsonian Institution Building.* Washington: Kennan Institute for Advanced Russian Studies, 1982.
*Quest for an Island.* New York: PAJ, 1987.
*Say Cheese!* New York: Random House, 1989; London: Bodley Head, 1990.
*A Starry Ticket.* London: Puthan, 1962.
*The Steel Bird, and Other Stories.* Ann Arbor: Ardis, 1979.
*Surplussed Barrelware.* Edited and translated by Joel Wilkinson and Slava Yastremski. Ann Arbor: Ardis, 1985.
*The Winter's Hero.* Translated by John Glad. New York: Random House, 1996.

## Secondary Literature

Anninskii, Lev. "Zhanr-to naidetsia!" *Literaturnoe obozrenie* 7 (1978): 44–46.
Basinskii, Pavel. "O chem napisal Aksenov? Opyt retsenzii v manere pereskaza." *Literaturnaia gazeta,* 10 August 1994: 4.
Berhara, Laura. "Roll Out the Barrels: Emptiness, Fullness, and the Picaresque-Idyllic Dynamic in Vasilii Aksenov's 'Zatovarennaia bochkotara'." *Slavic Review* 56, no. 2 (Summer 1997): 212–32.
Dalgard, Per. *The Function of the Grotesque in Vasilij Aksenov.* Arizona: Aarhus, 1982.
Efimova, N.A. *Intertekst v religioznykh i demonicheskikh motivakh Aksenova.* Moscow: Izd. MGU, 1993.

Evtushenko, Evgenii. "Neobkhodimost' chudes." *Literaturnoe obozrenie* 7 (1978): 42–44.
Gimpelevich, Zina. "The Intelligentsia: What It Used to Be and What It Is in Aksenov's Skazhi izium!" *Canadian Slavonic Papers/Revue Canadienne des Slavistes* 37, no. 1–2 (1995): 201–17.
Johnson, J.J. "V.P. Aksenov: A Literary Biography." In *Vasily Pavlovich Aksenov: A Writer in Quest of Himself,* edited by Edward Mozejko, Boris Briker, and Per Dalgard. Columbus: Slavica, 1986.
Kustanovich, Konstantin. *The Artist and the Tyrant: Vassily Aksenov's Works in the Brezhnev Era.* Columbus: Slavica, 1992.
Kuznetsov, Sergei. "Obretenie stilia: Doemigrantskaia proza Vasiliia Aksenova." *Znamia* 8 (1995): 206–12.
———. "Vassily Aksyonov's Parody of V." *Pynchon Notes,* 32–33 (Spring–Fall 1993): 181–85.
Linetskii, Vadim. "Aksenov v novom svete: Fenomen dvoinichestva kak faktor literaturnogo protsessa." *Neva* 8 (1992): 246–51.
McMillin, Arnold. "Vasilii Aksenov's Writing in the USSR and the USA." *Irish Slavonic Studies* 10 (1989): 1–16.
———. "Western Life as Reflected in Aksenov's Work before and after Exile." In *Under Eastern Eyes: The West as Reflected in Recent Russian Emigre Writings,* edited by Arnold McMillin. New York: St. Martin's Press, 1992: 212–32.
Meyer, Priscilla. "Aksenov and Stalinism: Political, Moral and Literary Power." *Slavic and East European Journal* 30 (Winter 1986): 509–25.
Mozejko, Edward, ed. *Vasiliy Pavlovich Aksenov: A Writer in Quest of Himself.* Columbus: Slavica, 1986.
Rassadin, St. "Shestero v kuzove, ne schitaia bochkotary." *Voprosy literatury* 10 (1968): 93–115.
Schmidt, Herta. "Postmodernism in Russian Drama: Vampilov, Amalrik, Aksenov." In *Approaching Postmodernism,* edited by Douwe Wessel Fokkema and Hans Willem Bertens. Amsterdam: Benjamins, 1986: 157–84.
Simmons, Cynthia. *Their Father's Voice: Vassily Aksyonov, Venedikt Erofeev, Eduard Limonov and Sasha Sokolov.* New York: Peter Lang, 1993: 15–55.
Simmons, Cynthia. "The Poetic Autobiographies of Vasilij Aksenov." *Slavic and East European Journal* 40, no. 2 (Summer 1996): 309–23.
Skobelev, Vladislav, and Lev Fink, eds. *Vasilii Aksenov: Literaturnaia sud'ba.* Samara: Samarskii universitet, 1994.
Zverev, Aleksei. "Bliuzy chetvertogo pokoleniia." *Literaturnoe obozrenie* 11–12 (1992): 9–17.

ALESHKOVSKY, YUZ (IOSIF EFIMOVCH) (b.1929, in Krasnoiarsk). Raised in Moscow, Aleshkovsky was forced to interrupt his high-school education when he was drafted during World War II. Aleshkovsky was imprisoned for four years in the labor camps (1950–53) for breach of military discipline. He returned to Moscow and started publishing children's fiction in the mid-1950s, while his "prison" songs and "obscene" novels (especially *Nikolai Nikolaevich* [1968]) were widely circulating on tapes and in *samizdat.* He took part in the almanac *Metropol',* and then emigrated to the United States. Since then, he has published such novels as *The Mask* (1980), *The Hand* (1980), *The Plain Little Blue Scarf* (1982), *A Book of Last*

*Words* (1984), *Kangaroo* (1985), *Death in Moscow* (1985), *Flea Tango* (1986), and *Ring in a Case* (1995). After perestroika, most of his works were republished in Russia. In his early works, the carnivalesque poetics of the "lower bodily stratum" serves the purposes of political satire, but its significance extends beyond merely mocking Soviet ideology; Aleshkovsky's emphasis on gross physicality is the basis of the omnipresent postmodernist irony that characterizes Aleshkovsky's style. In his later works, the author/narrator's unmediated moral invectives against the Soviet regime leave no room for any playfulness or carnivalesque freedom. He lives in Middletown, Connecticut.

## Works

*Dva bileta na elektrichku. Rasskazy dlia detei.* Moscow: Detskaia literatura, 1965.
*Kysh, dva portfelia i tselaia nedelia.* Moscow: Detskaia literatura, 1970.
*Sobranie sochinenii v 3–kh tomakh.* Moscow: "NNN," 1996.

## Translations

*The Hand, or, Confession of an Executioner.* Translated by Susan Brownsberger. London: Halban, 1989.
*Kangaroo.* Translated by Tamara Glenny. New York: Farrar, Straus & Giroux, 1986.
*A Ring in a Case.* Translated by Jane Ann Miller. Evanston: Northwestern University Press, 1995.

## Secondary Literature

Arkhangel'skii, A. Introduction to "Sinen'kii skromnyi platochek: Skorbnaia povest'." *Druzhba narodov* 7 (1991): 7–8.
Bitov, Andrei. "Povtorenie neproidennogo." *Znamia* 6 (1991): 194–206.
Brodsky, Iosif. "Predislovie." In *Sobranie sochinenii. V 3–kh tomakh,* by Iuz. Aleshkovskii. Vol. 1. Moscow: NNN, 1996: 3–11.
Bocharov, Sergei. "Ne unyvai, zimoi dadut svidanie . . ." *Novyi mir* 12 (1988): 121–24.
Brown, Edward J. "Zinoviev, Aleshkovsky, Rabelais, Sorrentino, Possibly Pynchon, Maybe James Joyce, and Certainly Tristam Shandy: A Comparative Study of a Satirical Mode." *Stanford Slavic Studies* 1 (1987): 307–25.
Meyer, Priscilla. " 'Skaz' in the Work of Juz Aleškovskij." *Slavic and East European Journal* 28, no. 4 (1984): 455–61.
Vasilevskii, Andrei. "Dar pristoinogo stilia." *Novyi mir* 3 (1994): 239–40.
Zhukhovitskii, Leonid. "Bomzh vo frake: V Moskve vyshel trekhtomnik Iuza Aleshkovskogo." *Literaturnaia gazeta,* 31 July 1996: 6.

## BITOV, ANDREI GEORGIEVICH (b.1937, in Leningrad). Before embarking on his career as an author, Bitov studied at the Leningrad Mining Institute, served in the army, took part in geological expeditions, and

attended advanced screenwriting courses at the Moscow Film Institute. His first short stories, which had some affinities with the Youth Prose movement, were published in the late 1950s. They were collected in the book *The Big Balloon* (1963). He was acclaimed by critics as a profound and innovative psychological writer who provided a refined cultural and intellectual analysis of his generation. The place of the Thaw generation in the vast context of the Russian cultural legacy became the theme of his masterwork, *Pushkin House*. Before 1988, the novel was published in the USSR only in fragments; the first full edition of *Pushkin House* appeared in the United States in 1971 (Ann Arbor: Ardis). His other books, such as *Countryside* (1967), *Way of Life* (1972), *The Choice of Nature* (1974), *Seven Journeys* (1976), *Life in Windy Weather* (1986, 1991), and the novel *The Monkey Link* (1995, consisting of the novels *Birds, A Man in the Landscape,* and *Waiting for Monkeys*), earned him a reputation for his profound grasp of psychology and for his sophisticated style. Using the self-referential poetics of metafiction, he offers a sarcastic and mournful portrait of the Soviet intelligentsia's conformity and moral degradation. His psychological analysis is often based on vast intertextual references to the Russian nineteenth-century tradition. He considers the Russian intelligentsia to be an inseparable part of the Russian/Soviet empire: the intelligentsia can play its sacred role of moral judge of the authorities only when the empire is strong and pitiless; but the decline and collapse of the Russian/Soviet empire meant, according to Bitov, the death of the Russian intelligentsia. Many of Bitov's works, such as "Close Retro" (1987—the author's commentary on *Pushkin House*), "The Teacher of Symmetry" (1987), and "Pushkin's Photography (1799–2099)" (1987), indulge in postmodernist narrative games similar to those of Italo Calvino or Milorad Pavić. In 1979 he participated in the almanac *Metropol'*, after which his works were not published in the Soviet Union for seven years. He was the first chairperson of the Russian Pen Club. He lives in Moscow.

## Works

*Imperiia v chetyrekh izmereniiakh. Sobranie sochinenii v 4–kh tomakh.* Kharkov: Folio; Moscow: TKO ACT, 1996.
*Nachatki astrologii russkoi literatury.* Moscow: Mir kul'tury, 1993.
*Novyi Gulliver: aine klaine arifmetika russkoi literatury.* Tenafly, NJ: Hermitage, 1997.
*Pervaia kniga avtora: Aptekarskii prospekt, 6.* St. Petersburg: Izd-vo Ivana Limbakha,1996.
*Sobranie sochinenii v trekh tomakh.* Moscow: Molodaia gvardiia, 1991.
*Trudoliubivyi Pushkin.* Moscow: Aiurveda, 1991.

## Translations

*A Captive of the Caucasus: Journeys in Armenia and Georgia.* Translated by Susan Brownsberger. New York: Farrar, Straus & Giroux, 1992.
*Life in Windy Weather: Short Stories.* Translated by Priscilla Meyer. Ann Arbor: Ardis, 1986.
*Pushkin House.* Translated by Susan Brownsberger. New York: Farrar, Straus & Giroux, 1987.
"Pushkin's Photograph (1799–2099)." Translated by Priscilla Meyer. In *The New Soviet Fiction: Sixteen Short Stories.* Compiled by Sergei Zalygin. New York: Abbeville Press, 1989, 15–60.
*Selected Short Stories.* Translated by Priscilla Meyer. Ann Arbor: Ardis, 1983.
*Ten Short Stories.* Translated by E. Nesterova. Moscow: Raduga, 1991.
*The Monkey Link.* Translated by Susan Brownsberger. New York: Farrar, Straus & Giroux, 1995.

## Secondary Literature

Bakich, Olga Hassanoff. "A New Type of Character in the Soviet Literature of the 1960s: The Early Works of Andrei Bitov." *Canadian Slavonic Papers/Revue Canadienne des Slavistes* 23, no. 2 (1981): 125–33.
Chances, Ellen. *Andrei Bitov: The Ecology of Inspiration.* Cambridge: Cambridge University Press, 1993.
Drozda, Miroslav. "Roman Andreja Bitova *Puskinskij Dom.*" *Sbornik Praci Filosoficke Fakulty Brnenske University: Rada Literarnevedna* 38 (1991): 109–14.
Erofeyev, Viktor. "Pamiatnik proshedshemu vremeni." *Oktiabr'* 6 (1988): 203–4.
Fridman, John. "Vetru net ukaza: Razmyshleniia nad tekstami romanov 'Pushkinskii dom' A. Bitova i 'Shkola dlia durakov' S. Solokova." *Literaturnoe obozrenie* 12 (1989): 14–16.
Hellebust, Rolf. "Fiction and Unreality in Bitov's *Pushkin House.*" *Style* (DeKalb, IL) 25, no. 2 (Summer 1991): 265–79.
Ivanova, Natal'ia. "Sud'ba i rol'." *Druzhba narodov* 3 (1988): 244–55.
Karabchievskii, Iurii. "Tochka boli: O romane Andreia Bitova 'Pushkinskii dom.' " *Grani* 106 (1977): 141–203.
Krasevec, Borut. "*Puskinov dom* Andreja Bitova in problemi ruskega postmodernizma." *Slavisticna Revija* 44, no. 3 (1996): 279–94.
Ksepma, V.O. [Peskov, A.V]. " 'Po tu storonu lobnoi stenki': Konspekt neproiznesennogo dialoga po povodu nekotorykh sochinenii pisatelia A.G. Bitova." *Literaturnoe obozrenie* 3 (1989): 24–27.
Latynina, Alla. "Duel' na muzeinykh pistoletakh: Zametki o romane Andreia Bitova 'Pushkinskii dom'." *Literaturnaia gazeta,* 27 January 1988: 4.
Lavrov, Vladimir. "Tri romana Andreia Bitova, ili Vospominaniia o sovremennike." *Neva* 5 (1997): 185–95.
Mondry, Henrietta. "Literaturnost' as a Key to Andrey Bitov's *Pushkin House.*" In *The Waking Sphinx: South African Essays on Russian Culture,* edited by Henrietta Monday. Johannesburg: Lib. University of the Witwatersrand, 1989, 3–19.
Nakhimovsky, Alice Stone. "Looking Back at Paradise Lost: The Russian Nineteenth Century in Andrei Bitov's *Pushkin House.*" *Russian Literature Triquarterly* 22 (1989): 195–204.
Novikov, Vladimir. "Tainaia svoboda." *Znamia* 3 (1988): 229–31.

Pesonen, Pekka. "Bitov's Text as Text: The Petersburg Text as Context in Andrey Bitov's Prose." In *Literary Tradition and Practice in Russian Culture*, edited by Valentine Polukhina, Joe Andrew, and Robert Reid. Amsterdam: Rodopi, 1993, 325–41.

Piskunov, V. "Uroki zazerkal'ia." *Oktiabr'* 8 (1988): 188–98.

Rich, Elisabeth, and Adam Perri, trans. "Andrei Bitov." *South Central Review* 12, no. 3–4 (Fall–Winter 1995): 28–35.

Schmid, Wolf. "Nachtrag zur Bitov-Bibliographie." *Wiener Slawistischer Almanach* 5 (1980): 327–34.

———. "Verfremdung bei Andrej Bitov." *Wiener Slawistischer Almanach* 5 (1980): 25–53.

Shklovskii, Evgenii. "V poiskakh real'nosti." *Literaturnoe obozrenie* 5 (1988): 32–38.

Spieker, Sven. *Figures of Memory and Forgetting in Andrej Bitov's Prose: Postmodernism and the Quest for History*. Frankfurt am Main, Berlin, Bern, New York, Paris, Vienna: Peter Lang, 1996.

Updike, John, and V. Abarinov, trans. "Razmyshleniia o dvukh romanakh." *Literaturnaia gazeta*, 5 July 1989: 4.

## BRODSKY, JOSEPH (IOSIF ALEKSANDROVICH) (1940 [Leningrad]–1996 [New York]).

This poet and essayist started writing verse in the sixties, when he was part of Anna Akhmatova's circle of Leningrad poets. In 1964, Brodsky was arrested and sentenced to five years of forced labor for "parasitism" (lack of officially recognized employment). His trial prompted letters of protest from prominent figures in Soviet arts and literature, contributing substantially to the rise of the dissident movement in the USSR. After one and a half years, he was released, and in 1972, he emigrated to the United States. Only a handful of his poems and translations were published while he was in the Soviet Union, although large collections of his poetry circulated in *samizdat*. (The writer Vladimir Maramzin compiled a five-volume *samizdat* collection of Brodsky's poetry in 1972–74.) In the United States, Brodsky taught at a variety of colleges and universities. Numerous collections of his poetry were published in America and throughout the world, but his reputation also rested on his highly intellectual and ironic essays (collected in *Less Than One* and *On Grief and Reason*). Brodsky is also the author of two plays, *Democracy* and *The Marble*. After perestroika, most of his works were republished in Russia. In 1992–94, a four-volume collection of his poetry appeared in St. Petersburg. Brodsky became a cult figure for Russian postmodernists, although many critics consider his works to be a return to the tradition of Russian modernism, especially in its Neo-Classical (Acmeist) version. Brodsky constantly insisted that the poet is an instrument of language, whose metaphysical power is the only guarantee of the poet's freedom. Brodsky is a metaphysical poet *sui generis,* and his poetry and essays demonstrate how modernist conceptions of such categories as death, eternity, time, empire, solicitude, and language are transformed in the postmodernist context. His works are arguably the most convincing link between Russian modernism and postmodernism. Brodsky won the Nobel Prize for literature of 1987 and was the American poet laureate in 1991.

## Works (Russian)

*Forma vremeni: stikhotvoreniia, esse, p'esy v dvukh tomakh.* Compiled by V.I. Ufliand; illustrated by S.V. Balenok. Minsk: Eridan, 1992.
*Stikhotvoreniia i poemy.* Washington, DC: Inter-Lang Lit. Associates, 1965.
*Sobranie sochineni v 4kh tomakh.* St. Petersburg: Pushkinskii Fond, 1993–94.
*Iosif Brodskii: Trudy i dni.* Edited by Lev Losev and Petr Vail'. Moscow: "Nezavisimaia gazeta," 1998.

## Works (English)

Brodsky, Joseph; Seamus Heaney; and Derek Walcott. *Homage to Robert Frost.* New York: Farrar, Straus & Giroux, 1996, 1997.
Proffer, Carl R., and Joseph Brodsky. *Modern Russian Poets on Poetry.* Ann Arbor: Ardis, 1976.
*Less Than One: Essays.* New York: Farrar, Straus & Giroux, 1986.
"Nobel Prize Speech." *Index on Censorship* 17, no. 2 (1988): 12–15.
*On Grief and Reason: Essays.* New York: Farrar, Straus & Giroux, 1995, 1997.
*Two Addresses.* New York: Farrar, Straus & Giroux, 1988.
*Watermark.* New York: Farrar, Straus & Giroux, 1992, 1993.

## Translations

*Joseph Brodsky: Selected Poems.* Translated from the Russian by George L. Kline. Foreword by W.H. Auden. New York: Harper & Row, 1973.
*The Funeral of Bobo.* Translated by Richard Wilbur. Ann Arbor: Ardis, 1974.
*A Part of Speech.* New York: Farrar, Straus & Giroux, 1980.
*To Urania.* New York: Farrar, Straus & Giroux, 1988.
*Marbles: A Play in Three Acts.* Translated by Alan Myers, with the author. New York: Farrar, Straus & Giroux, 1989
*So Forth: Poems.* New York: Farrar, Straus & Giroux, 1996

## Secondary Literature (Books Only)

Batkin, Leonid M. *Tridtsat' tretia bukva: zametki chitatelia na poliakh stikhov Iosifa Brodskogo.* Moscow: Rossiiskii gos. gumanitarnyi univ., 1997
Bethea, David M. *Joseph Brodsky and the Creation of Exile.* Princeton: Princeton University Press, 1994.
*Brodskii o Tsvetaevoi: interviu s Solomonom Volkovym, esse.* Moscow: "Nezavisimaia gazeta," 1997.

Kreps, Mikhail. *O poezii Iosifa Brodskogo*. Ann Arbor: Ardis, 1984.

Lapidus, A.Ia. *Iosif Brodskii: ukazatel' literatury na russkom iazyke za 1962–1995 gg.* St. Petersburg: Rossiiskaia natsional'naia biblioteka, 1997.

Lemkin, Mikhail. *Joseph Brodsky, Leningrad: Fragments*. Foreword by Czeslaw Milosz; afterword by Susan Sontag. New York: Farrar, Straus & Giroux, 1998.

Loseff, Lev, and Valentina Polukhina, eds. *Brodsky's Poetics and Aesthetics*. New York: St. Martin's Press, 1990.

Losev, Lev V., ed. *Poetika Brodskogo*. Tenafly, NJ: Hermitage, 1986.

Polukhina, Valentina. *Brodsky Through the Eyes of His Contemporaries*. New York: St. Martin's Press, 1992.

———. *Slovar' tropov Brodskogo: na materiale sbornika "Chast' rechi."* Tartu: Tip. izd-va Tartuskogo universiteta, 1995.

———. *Brodskii glazami sovremennikov*. St. Petersburg: Zhurnal "Zvezda," 1997.

Polukhina, Valentina, ed. *The Myth of the Poet and the Poet of the Myth: Russian Poets on Brodsky*. Oxford: Berg, 1994.

———. *Joseph Brodsky*. Special Issue of the Journal *Russian Literature* 37, no. 2–3 (1995).

Strizhevskaia, Natal'ia. *Pismena, perspektivy: o poezii Iosifa Brodskogo*. Moscow: Graal, 1997.

Volkov, Solomon. *Conversations with Joseph Brodsky: A Poet's Journey Through the Twentieth Century*. Translated by Marian Schwartz; with photographs by Marianna Volkov. New York: Free Press, 1998.

Volkov, Solomon, and Marianna Volkov. *Iosif Brodskii v Niu-Iorke: fotoportrety i besedy s poetom*. New York: Slovo, 1990.

*Vspominaia Akhmatovu: Iosif Brodskii–Solomon Volkov, dialogi*. Moscow: "Nezavisimaia gazeta," 1992.

CONCEPTUALISM. See Sots-Art.

DOVLATOV, SERGEI DONATOVICH (1941 [Ufa]–1990 [New York]). Dovlatov lived in Leningrad and Tallinn (Estonia) and studied at Leningrad State University, first in the Philology (Languages and Literatures) School, then in the School of Journalism. He was expelled from the university and drafted into the army, where he served as a guard in the northern labor camps. This experience would provide the basis of his book *The Zone*. In the seventies he worked as a journalist in various Leningrad and Estonian newspapers and magazines. He belonged to a group of Leningrad nonconformist writers known as "*Gorozhane*" ("City-People"). Some of his works were published in Soviet journals, but his major collections of short stories were rejected by a variety of publishing houses. In 1979 Dovlatov left the Soviet Union for the United States, where he became one of the most popular writers of emigration. His works were widely published in Russian and in translations (after Nabokov, he was the first Russian author whose works were published in *The New Yorker*). Dovlatov's short stories were highly praised by American writers such as Kurt Vonnegut and Joseph Heller. Perestroika brought Dovlatov fame and popularity in Russia; a four-volume collection of his works, letters, and memoirs was republished twice in St. Petersburg. Dovlatov's fiction seems to consist largely of "slice-of-life" comic stories with strong autobiographical underpinnings. But in reality, Dovlatov used the facts of his own life as the material for his "absurd quest," proving the paradoxical role of absurdity and chaos as the foundations of human existence, as the only valid sources of personal freedom, and as the forces uniting a person with other people and history. The combination of realistic representation with the postmodernist message of his "absurd quest" results in an artistic philosophy based on the dialogic relations between traditions of Russian realism and the postmodernist approach to chaos.

## Works

Dovlatov, Sergei, and Marianna Volkova. *Ne tol'ko Brodskii: russkaia kul'tura v portretakh i anekdotakh.* Moscow: RIK "Kul'tura," 1992.
*Iz neopublikovannogo.* St. Petersburg: Dovlatovskii fond: TOO "Iarus," 1994.
*Inostranka: A Russian Reader.* Ann Arbor: Ardis, 1995.
*Maloizvestnyi Dovlatov.* St. Petersburg: Zhurnal "Zvezda,"1996.
*Sobranie prozy v trekh tomakh.* St. Petersburg: Limbus-Press, 1993, 1995.

## Translations

*The Compromise.* Translated from the Russian by Anne Frydman. London: Chatto & Windus, 1983; New York: Alfred A. Knopf, 1983; Chicago: Academy Chicago Publishers, 1990.
*A Foreign Woman.* Translated from the Russian by Antonina W. Bouis. New York: Grove Weidenfeld, 1991.
*The Invisible Book: (Epilogue).* Translated from the Russian by Katherine O'Connor and Diana L. Burgin. Ann Arbor: Ardis, 1979.
*Not Just Brodsky: Russian Culture in Portraits and Anecdotes.* Photos by Marianna Volkov. Text by Sergei Dovlatov. Translated from the Russian by Brian J. Baer. New York: Slovo, 1988.
*Ours: Scenes from Russian Family Life.* Translated from the Russian by Anne Frydman. New York: Weidenfeld & Nicolson, 1989.
*The Suitcase.* Translated from the Russian by Antonina W. Bouis. New York: Grove Weidenfeld, 1990.
*The Zone: A Prison Camp Guard's Story.* Translated from the Russian by Anne Frydman. New York: A.A. Knopf, 1985.

## Secondary Literature

Eliseev, Nikita. "Chelovecheskii golos." *Novyi mir* 11 (1994): 212–25.
Genis, Aleksandr. "Korova bez vymeni, ili Metafizika oshibki." *Literaturnaia gazeta,* 24 December 1997: 11.

————. "Sad kamnei: Sergei Dovlatov." *Zvezda* 7 (1997): 235–38.

Kamianov, Viktor. "Svoboden ot postoia." *Novyi mir* 2 (1992): 242–44.

Lipovetskii, Mark. " 'Uchites', tvari, kak zhit' ': paranoia, zona i literaturnyi kontest." *Znamia* 5 (1997): 199–212.

Sokolova, Nadia. "Snova o lagernoi teme: Zona Sergeia Dovlatova." *Australian Slavonic & East European Studies* 10, no. 2 (1996): 157–64.

Sukhikh, Igor' N. *Sergei Dovlatov: vremia, mesto, sud'ba.* St. Petersburg: Kult-Inform Press, 1996.

Tsiv'ian, T.V. "Veshchi iz chemodana Sergeia Dovlatova i byvshaia (?) sovetskaia model' mira." *Russian Literature* (Amsterdam) 37, no. 4 (1995): 647–58.

Zverev, Aleksei. "Zapiski sluchainogo postoial'tsa." *Literaturnoe obozrenie* 4 (1991): 65–73.

*Zvezda* 3 (1994). Special issue devoted to Dovlatov.

EROFEEV, VENEDIKT VASILIEVICH (1938 [Komi Peninsula]–1990 [Moscow]). One of the most influential authors of Russian postmodernism. Besides *Moscow to the End of the Line* (also translated as *Moscow Circles* and *Moscow Stations)* (1970), he wrote the play *Walpurgisnacht, or The Commander's Steps,* several essays ("Vasily Rozanov through the Eyes of an Eccentric," "My Little Lenininana"), the unfinished play "Fanny Kaplan," and notebooks. Although he never completed his university education (he was expelled from Moscow State University after three semesters and fared no better at Vladimir Pedagogical Institute), he was extraordinarily well read. Among his literary precursors he named Saltykov-Schedrin, Gogol, the early Dostoevsky, and Sasha Cherny. Erofeev was the spiritual heart of the intellectual circle that included the translator and philologist Vladimir Muraviev, the poet Olga Sedakova, and other noteworthy writers and scholars. Although he was never published in the Soviet Union under the Communist regime, he did not belong to the dissident movement. *Moscow to the End of the Line* was first published in the USSR only in 1988–89 by the newly formed journal called *Sobriety and Culture.* In an ironic twist of fate that the author himself might well have appreciated, Erofeev's "poem" would thus be artificially associated with Gorbachev's ill-fated anti-alcohol campaign. Publication of the poem (which had been previously known only thanks to foreign editions and *samizdat*) brought it tremendous popularity, especially among the younger generation. At the same time, postmodernism was just becoming the topic of heated debates in Russian criticism, and Erofeev was acknowledged as a postmodernist classic. A notoriously heavy drinker, Erofeev can be said to have predicted his premature death in the ending of his most famous work, although the cause of his demise was throat cancer rather than the brutal beating that would end the life of his fictional counterpart.

# Works

*Glazami ekstsentrika.* Foreword and afterword by P. Vail' and A. Genis. New York: Serebrianyi vek, 1982.

*Moskva-Petushki.* Paris: YMCA-Press, 1977, 1981; Moscow: Prometei, 1989, 1990; Moscow: Interbuk, 1990.

*Ostav'te moiu dushu v pokoe: Pochti vse.* Moscow: Izd. Kh.G.S., 1995, 1997.

"Valpurgieva noch', ili Shagi Kommandora." In *Kontinent* 45 (1985): 96–185; *Teatr* 4 (1989): 2–32.

# Translations

*Moscow Circles.* Translated from the Russian by J.R. Dorrell. London: Writers and Readers Publishing Cooperative, 1981.

*Moscow Stations: A Poem.* Translated by Stephen Mulrine. London: Faber and Faber, in association with Brian Brolly, 1997.

*Moscow to the End of the Line.* Translated by H. William Tjalsma. New York: Taplinger, 1980; Evanston: Northwestern University Press. 1992, 1994.

"Through the Eyes of an Eccentric." Translated from the Russian by Stephen Murline. In *New Russian Writing: Russia's Fleurs du Mal,* edited by Victor Erofeyev and Andrew Reynolds. London: Penguin, 1995, 126–45.

"Vasily Rozanov Through the Eyes of an Eccentric." Translated by Arkady Yanishevsky. In *The Times of Turmoil: A Collection of Stories,* edited by Irina Broude. Tenafly: Hermitage, 1993, 154–69.

# Secondary Literature

Binova, Galina. "Sotsart kak preodolenie utopicheski-ideinoi traditsii: Prozaicheskii variant: V. Sorokin, V. Erofeev, Z. Gareev." *Sbornik Praci Filosoficke Fakulty Brnenske University: Rada Literarnevedna* 43, no. 41 (1994): 107–14.

Epstein, Mikhail. "Posle karnavala, ili Vechnyi Venichka." In Venedict Erofeev 1995: 3–30.

Gaiser-Shnitman, Svetlana. *Venedikt Erofeev's Moskva-Petushki, ili "The Rest Is Silence."* Bern, Frankfurt am Main, New York, Paris: Peter Lang, 1984.

Levin, Iurii. "Klassicheskie traditsii v 'drugoi' literature: Venedikt Erofeev i Fedor Dostoevskii." *Literaturnoe obozrenie* 2 (1992): 45–50.

———. *Kommentarii k poeme "Moskva-Petushki" V. Erofeeva.* Graz: Grazer Gesellschaft zur Forderung slawischer Kulturstudien, 1996.

Novikov, Vladimir. "Tri stakana tertsovki: Vydumannyi pistel' (O Venedikte Erofeeve)." *Stolitsa* 31 (1994): 55–57. The same in Novikov, Vladimir. *Zaskok.* Moscow: Knizhnyi sad, 1997, 103–12.

Orlova, E.I. "Posle skaza: Mikhail Zoshchenko—Venedikt Erofeev—Abram Terts." *Filologicheskie nauki* 6 (1996): 13–22.

Paperno, I.A., and B.M. Gasparov. "Vstan' i idi." *Slavica Hierosolymitana* 5–6 (1981): 387–400.

Ryan-Hayes, Karen. "Beyond Picaresque: Erofeev's *Moscow—Petushki.*" In *Contemporary Russian Satire. A Genre Study.* Cambridge: Cambrige University Press, 1995, 58–100.

Ryan-Hayes, Karen, ed. *Venedikt Erofeev's Moscow-Petushki: Critical Perspective.*

New York: Peter Lang, 1997 (detailed bibliography: 223–31).

Sedakova, Ol'ga. "Neskazannaia rech' na vechere Venedikta Erofeeva." *Druzhba narodov* 12 (1991): 264–65.

Simmons, Cynthia. "Moscow-Petushki: A Transcendental Commute." In *Their Father's Voice: Vassily Aksyonov, Venedikt Erofeev, Eduard Limonov and Sasha Sokolov.* New York: Peter Lang, 1993, 57–90.

Smirnova, E.A. "Mifologema stradaiushchego boga i strasti Venichki Erofeeva." *Sintaksis* 33 (1992): 96–107.

Tumanov, Vladimir. "The End in V. Erofeev's Moscow-Petushki." *Russian Literature* 39, no., 1 (1996): 95–114.

Vail', Petr, and Aleksandr Genis. "Strasti po Erofeevu." In *Sovremennaia russkaia a proza.* Ann Arbor: Hermitage, 1982, 41–50.

Waegemans, Emmanuel. "Roem en drek van het Brezjnev-tijdperk: Venedikt Jerofejevs cultroman Moskou op sterk water." In *De Cultroman,* edited by Erik Hertog. Antwerp: Vlaamse Vereniging voor Algemene en Vergelijkende Literatuurwetenschap, 1995, 88–97.

Zorin, Andrei. "Opoznavatel'nyi znak." *Teatr* 9 (1991): 119–22.

Zvonnikova, Livia. "Moskva-Petushki i pr. Popytka interpretatsii." *Znamia* 8 (1996): 214–20.

**EROFEYEV, VIKTOR VLADIMIROVICH** (b.1947, in Moscow). Essayist and prose writer. Erofeyev graduated from Moscow State University Philology (Languages and Literatures) School and completed his graduate study at the Moscow Institute of World Literature, where he defended his Ph.D. dissertation on Dostoevsky and French existentialism. He started his literary career as a critic, gaining notoriety for his essays on Lev Shestov, Sade, Céline, Camus, Rozanov, Nabokov, Sologub, and other authors who were either totally or partly prohibited in the USSR. In 1979, Erofeyev took part in the compilation of the almanac *Metropol'* (he was one of the co-editors). In *Metropol'*, Erofeyev published his fiction (a novella and short stories) for the first time. After the scandal around the publication of *Metropol'* in the United States, he was expelled from the Union of Soviet Writers. During perestroika, he became one of the most active propagandists of literary postmodernism. His own short stories were published in Russia and abroad. His article "The Funeral Feast for Soviet Literature" (1990) provided a provocative critique of all of Soviet literature from the position of the new (postmodernist) aesthetics, causing heated discussion in the Russian literary press. His erotic and mystical novel *The Russian Beauty* (first published in 1990, written in 1980–82) is narrated from the perspective of the Russian high-class prostitute Irina Tarakanova, who considers herself to be Russia's spiritual savior (since, according to Prince Myshkin, "beauty will save the world"). This novel was translated into many languages. He compiled a collection of the new Russian literature, *The Penguin Book of New Russian Writing: Russia's Fleurs du Mal* (1995). In

1993–95 he hosted a talk show on Russian television, introducing postmodernist authors and projects to a wider public. His short story "Life with an Idiot" became the libretto for Alfred Schnittke's opera of the same name. In 1994–95, a three-volume collection of his works was published in Moscow. His new novel, *Judgement Day* (1995), which was included in this collection, received very cold reviews in the Russian press. The critics wrote that Erofeyev intended to be rebellious and provocative but failed on both accounts due to a tedious plot and a style that was obviously dependent on the influence of various modernist and postmodernist luminaries. He lives in Moscow.

## Works

*Muzhschina.* Moscow: Podkova, 1997.
*Naiti v cheloveke cheloveka: Dostoevskii i ekzistentsializm.* Benson, VT: Chalidze Publications, 1991.
*Russkie tsvety zla.* Compiled by Viktor Erofeev. Moscow: Podkova, 1997.
*Sobranie sochinenii v 3–kh tomakh.* Moscow: "Soiuz fotokhudozhnikov Rossii, 1996.
*V labirinte prokliatykh voprosov.* Moscow: Sovetskii pisatel', 1990.

## Translations

Schnittke, Alfred. *Leben mit einem Idioten: Oper in zwei Akten (Prolog und 4 Bilder).* Libtetto (*sic*), Viktor Jerofejew; deutsche Adaptation, Jorg Morgener; auf der Grundlage der gleichnamigen Erzahlung von Viktor Jerofejew, ubersetzt von Beate Rausch. Hamburg: Hans Sikorski, 1993.
"The Parakeet," "Anna's Body." Translated by Leonard J. Stanton. In *Glasnost: An Anthology of Russian Literature Under Gorbachev,* edited by Helena Goscilo and Byron Lindsey. Ann Arbor: Ardis, 1990, 367–82.
*Russian Beauty.* Translated by Andrew Reynolds. London: H. Hamilton, 1992; New York: Viking, 1993; London: Penguin, 1993.
"Zhenka's A to Z." Translated from the Russian by Andrew Reynolds. In *New Russian Writing: Russia's Fleurs du Mal,* edited by Victor Erofeev and Andrew Reynolds. London: Penguin, 1995, 349–68.

## Secondary Literature

Fomina, V. "Metafizicheskii Erofeev i kak s nim borot'sia." *Druzhba narodov* 7 (1997): 212–16.
Lipovetskii, Mark. "Mir kak tekst." *Literaturnoe obozrenie* 6 (1990): 63–65.
Novikov, Vladimir. "Erofeev Viktor Vladimirovicih: Vse-taki pisatel'!" In *Zaskok: esse, parodii, razmyshleniia kritika.* Moscow: Knizhnyi sad, 1997, 260–63.
Rich, Elisabeth, and Charles Rougle, trans. "Viktor Erofeyev." *South Central Review: The Journal of the South Central Modern Language Association* (College Station, TX) 12, no. 3–4 (Fall–Winter 1995): 70–83.
Roll, Serafima. "Re-Surfacing: The Shades of Violence in Viktor Yerofeyev's Short

Stories." *Australian Slavonic & East European Studies* 9, no. 2 (1995): 27–46.
Sotnikova, Tatiana. "Tsvetok neschast´ia." *Znamia* 5 (1997): 213–19.
Zholkovskii, A.K. "V minus pervom i minus zerkale: Tat´iana Tolstaia, Viktor Erofeev—akhmatoviana i arkhetipy." *Literaturnoe obozrenie* 6 (1995): 25–41.

KABAKOV, ILYA IOSIFOVICH (b.1933, in Dnepropetrovsk). Famous Conceptualist artist and essayist. Kabakov graduated from the Surikov Art Institute in Moscow. For many years he worked as a children's book illustrator, while he was simultaneously one of the leaders of conceptualist underground art of Moscow. In the seventies and eighties, he created a series of albums presenting the unconscious of Soviet everyday life, its fundamental myths and archetypes. In 1989 he moved to Paris, and since 1992 he has been living in New York. He is the author of numerous installations. Most of his works combine everyday objects and artifacts with texts, often providing the philosophical clue to the entire project. His art has been exhibited in leading art museums, including the Pompidou Center for Modern Art in Paris, the Institute of Contemporary Art in London, and the Hirshhorn Museum in Washington, DC. His theoretical essays on the aesthetics of conceptual art and installations are collected in his course of lectures *On the Total Installation* (1995).

## Works

*Auf dem Dach/On the Roof: Installation.* Paleis voor Schone Kunsten Brussel, Palais des beaux-arts de Bruxelles, 1996. Dusseldorf: Richter Verlag, 1997.
*Illustrations As a Way to Survive: Exhibition Installation.* Curators, M. Catherine de Zegher and Joseph Bakstein. Kortrijk, Belgium: Kanaal-Art Foundation, 1992.
*Ilya Kabakov: Ausstellung eines Buches.* Berlin: Kunstlerprogramm des DAAD, 1989.
*Ilya Kabakov: das Leben der Fliegen. Ilia Kabakov: zhizn mukh.* Stuttgart: Edition Cantz, 1992.
*Ilya Kabakov: Incident at the Museum, or Water Music.* Chicago: Museum of Contemporary Art, 1993.
*Ilya Kabakov: Installations 1983–1995.* Francois Barre, ean-Hubert Martin, Robert Storr, et al. Paris: Editions du Centre national Georges Pompidou, 1995.
*Ilya Kabakov: Ten Characters.* London: ICA, in association with Ronald Feldman Fine Arts, New York, and Untitled II, New York, 1989.
*My navsegda uezzhaem otsiuda! [We are Leaving Here Forever!].* Installation, Carnegie Museum, Pittsburgh, 1991.
*Noma, ili, Moskovskii kontseptual´nyi krug: installiatsiia.* Cantz: Hamburger Kunsthalle, 1993.
*Okno/Das Fenster: der aus dem Fenster schauende Archipow [The Window: Arkhipov looking through the window].* Bern: Benteli, 1985.
"On Emptiness." Translated by Clark Troy. In *Re-Entering the Sign: Articulating New Russian Culture,* edited by Ellen E. Berry and Anesa Miller-Pogacar. Ann Arbor: University of Michigan Press, 1995, 91–99.

*Sumasshedshii dom, ili institut kreativnykh issledovanii/Mental Institution or Institute of Creative Research: Installation.* 1991.
*Uber die "totale" Installation = O "total'noi" installiatsii = On the "total" installation.* Bonn: Cantz, 1995.

## Secondary Literature

Epstein, Mikhail. "Pustota kak priem: slovo i izobrazhenie u Il'i Kabakova." In *Vera i obraz: Religioznoe bessoznatel'noe v russkoi kul'ture dvadtsatogo veka.* Tenafly: Hermitage, 1994, 140–69.
Ugrešić, Dubravka. "Avangard i sovremennost': Vaginov i Kabakov: Tipologicheskaia parallel'." *Russian Literature* (Amsterdam, Netherlands) no. 1 (1990): 83–96.
Wallach, Amei. *Ilya Kabakov: The Man Who Never Threw Anything Away.* With commentaries by Ilya Kabakov. New York: Harry N. Abrams, 1996.
Watten, Barrett. "Post-Soviet Subjectivity in Arkadii Dragomoshchenko and Ilya Kabakov." In *Essays in Postmodern Culture,* edited by Eyal Amiran and John Unworth. New York: Oxford University Press, 1993, 325–49.

**KHARMS, DANIIL IVANOVICH** (real surname—Yuvachev; 1905 [St. Petersburg]–1942? [Leningrad]). Classic of Russian absurdist literature, author of numerous poems, short stories, the novel *The Old Woman* (1939), and the drama *Elizaveta Bam* (1927). Together with Aleksandr Vvedensky and Nikolai Oleinikov, Kharms was the initiator and ideologist of the literary group OBERIU (an abbreviation for *Ob''edinenie real'nogo iskusstva,* or the "Association of Real Art," 1927–30), whose program combined the ideas of Futurism and Surrealism with declarations on the centrality of absurdity as an artistic principle. His works are predicated on total unpredictability: fantastic, illogical, and grotesque events and characters are presented as part of everyday life. Though his work is humorous and paradoxical, Kharms is actually a tragic writer. For him absurdity represents the process of the disintegration of the world under the onslaught of simulation, of words and signs that do not refer to anything real. His short, grotesque texts can also be read as metafictional reflections of the process of writing itself, a process that leads to death and the destruction of reality. This has led some contemporary critics (such as Graham Roberts) to consider Kharms one of the first postmodernist and post–avant-garde writers in Russian literature. During Kharms's life, only his works for children were published. He was arrested in 1941 and died in a psychiatric prison. His works for children started to be republished in the USSR during the Thaw. At the same time, his other works began to be circulated in *samizdat.* Kharms's absurdism influenced several generations of Russian unofficial writers. His stylistic and plot patterns can easily be recognized in the works of Venedikt Erofeev, Vasily Aksyonov, Vladimir Maramzin, Vladimir Uflyand, Yevgeny Popov, Valery Popov, Zufar Gareev, and many other writers.

## Works

*Polet v nebesa.* Introduction, compilation, preparation of text and notes by A.A. Aleksandrov. Leningrad: "Sovetskii pisate'l," Leningradskoe otd-nie, 1991.
*Polnoe sobranie sochinenii.* St. Petersburg: Gumanitarnoe Agentstvo "Akademicheskii Proekt," 1997.
*Sobranie proizvedenii.* Edited by Mikhail Meilakh and Vladimir Erlia. Bremen: K Presse, 1978.

## Translations

*First, Second.* Translated from the Russian by Richard Pevear. New York: Farrar, Straus & Giroux, 1996.
*Incidences.* Edited and translated by Neil Cornwell. London: Serpent's Tail, 1993.
*The Man with the Black Coat: Russia's Literature of the Absurd. Selected Works of Daniil Kharms and Alexander Vvedensky.* Edited and translated by George Gibian. Evanston: Northwestern University Press, 1997.
*The Plummeting Old Women.* Introduction and translation by Neil Cornwell. Dublin: Lilliput, 1989.
*Starukha [The Old Woman].* Edited with introduction, notes, and vocabulary by Robin Aizlewood. London: Bristol Classical, 1995.

## Secondary Literature

Cornwell, Neil (ed. & bibliog.); Robin Milner-Gulland (afterword); Julian Graffy (bibliog.). *Daniil Kharms and the Poetics of the Absurd.* Houndmills: Macmillan, 1991.
Discacciati, Ornella. "Aspetti teorici dell'opera di Daniil Charms." Acme: Annali della Facolta di Lettere e Filosofia dell'Universita degli Studi di Milano 48, no. 2 (1995): 103–28.
Jaccard, Jean-Philippe. "De la realite au texte l'absurde chez Daniil Harms." *Cahiers du Monde Russe* 26, no. 3–4 (1985): 269–312.
Makowiecka, Katarzyna. "Homo sovieticus jako homo ludens: O prozie Danila Charmsa." *Slavia Orientalis* 41, no. 1 (1992): 25–31.
Milner-Gulland, R.R. " 'Left Art' in Leningrad: The OBERIU Declaration." *Oxford Slavonic Papers* 3 (1970): 65–75.
Nakhimovsky, Alice Stone. "The Ordinary, the Sacred, and the Grotesque in Daniil Kharms's *The Old Woman.*" *Slavic Review* 37 (1978): 203–16.
Roberts, Graham. *The Last Soviet Avant-Garde: OBERIU—Fact, Fiction, Metafiction.* Cambridge, New York: Cambridge University Press, 1997.
Stelleman, Jenny. "The Transitional Position of *Elizaveta Bam* Between Avant-Garde and Neo–Avant-Garde." In *Avant-Garde: Interdisciplinary and International Review,* edited by Jan van der Eng and Willem Weststeijn. Amsterdam: Rodopi, 1991, 207–21.
Tokarev, D.V. "Daniil Kharms: Filosofiia i tvorchestvo." *Russkaia literatura: Istoriko-literaturnyi zhurnal* 4 (1995): 68–93.
Tumanov, Larissa, and Vladimir Tumanov. "The Child and the Child-Like in Daniil Charms." *Russian Literature* 34, no. 2 (1993): 241–70.
Zhakkar, Zhan-Filipp. *Daniil Kharms i konets russkogo avangarda.* St. Petersburg: Akademicheskii proekt, 1995.

MAKANIN, VLADIMIR SEMENOVICH (b.1937, Orsk, Orenburg region). Makanin graduated from the Moscow State University School of Mathematics. Later he attended advanced courses for screenwriters at the Moscow Film Institute. He worked as a researcher for the military project bureau. In 1967, his first novel *The Straight Line* was published in the USSR. This debut would make Makanin famous, possibly because of the fact that his novel was one of the last works of Youth Prose. In the seventies he worked as an editor at a prestigious publishing house and authored several short novels with action-packed plots and moderately satiric characters. In the late seventies and early eighties, he wrote several stories and novellas ("The Man from the Retinue," "Antileader," "Voices," "Safety-Valve," *The Precursor*) that provoked critical controversy. These works were opposed to the Socialist Realist mainstream because of the author's refusal to judge his characters: Makanin presents the plot as an ambivalent puzzle with several possible solutions. The transformation of concrete "real-life" situations into open-ended parables about the human search for identity became the major topic of his later works, such as *At the Place Where the Sky Met the Hills* (1984), *The Loss* (1987), "Left Behind" (1988), *Escape Hatch* (1991), and *The Prisoner of the Caucuses* (1995). In these and other texts, he elaborates an original strategy of narrative collage: a jazz-like combination of different stories and their intellectual interpretation from different points of view, providing the basis for an unstable "paralogical" compromise between opposite categories, such as freedom and dependence, individuality and the power of the social order, loss and redemption, love and hatred. Makanin's narrative practice is reminiscent of the works of such postmodernist authors as Milan Kundera and Peter Handke. And yet his works constantly hearken back to the Russian realistic classics (primarily, to Gogol and Leo Tolstoy), subjecting their moral didacticism to a critical reinterpretation. In 1998 he published his largest work—the novel *Underground, or The Hero of Our Time*. He is the winner of the Russian Booker Prize (1993) for the short novel *Baize-Covered Table with Decanter* and the German Pushkin Prize (1998). He lives in Moscow.

## Works

"Andergraund, ili Geroi nashego vremeni." *Znamia* 1–4 (1998).
*Gde skhodilos' nebo s kholmami.* Moscow: Sovremennik, 1984.
*Golosa: povesti, rasskazy.* Moscow: Sovetskaia Rossiia, 1982.
*Kavkazskii plennyi.* Moscow: Panorama,1997.
*Odin i odna: povesti.* Moscow: Sovremennik, 1988.
*Otstavshii: povesti i rasskazy.* (Afterword by A. Marchenko. Moscow: "Khudozhestvennaia literatura," 1988.

*Portret i vokrug; Odin i odna: romany.* Moscow: Sovetskii pisatel', 1991.
*Utrata: povesti i rasskazy.* Moscow: Molodaia gvardiia, 1989.

## Translations

"Antileader." Translated by Jamey Gambrell. In *The New Soviet Fiction: Sixteen Short Stories,* compiled by Sergei Zalygin. New York: Abbeville Press, 1989, 163–204.

"Left Behind." Translated by Nadezhda Peterson. In *Glasnost: Russian Prose Under Gorbachev,* edited by Helena Goscilo and Byron Lyndsey. Ann Arbor: Ardis, 1990, 196–270.

*Baize-Covered Table with Decanter.* Translated from the Russian by Arch Tait. Columbia: Readers International, 1995.

*Escape Hatch; &, The Long Road Ahead: Two Novellas.* Translated with an afterword by Mary Ann Szporluk. Dana Point, CA: Ardis, 1996.

## Secondary Literature

Ageev, Aleksandr. "Istina i svoboda: Vladimir Makanin: Vzgliad iz 1990 goda." *Literaturnoe obozrenie* 9 (1990): 25–33.

Anninskii, Lev. "Struktura labirinta: Vladimir Makanin i literatura seredinnogo cheloveka." *Znamia* 12 (1986): 218–26.

Basinskii, Pavel. "Igra v klassiki na chuzhoi krovi." *Literaturnaia gazeta,* 7 June 1995: 4.

Bocharov, Anatolii. "Na reke s bystrym techeniem." *Druzhba narodov* 1 (1984): 231–39.

Dowsett, Colin. "Postmodernist Allegory in Contemporary Soviet Literature: Vladimir Makanin's *Utrata.*" *Australian Slavonic & East European Studies* 4, no. 1–2 (1990): 21–35.

———. "The Writer and Writing in the Fiction of Vladimir Makanin." *Australian Slavonic & East European Studies* 10, no. 1 (1996): 29–36.

Gessen, Elena. "Vokrug Makanina, ili shtrikhi k portretu." *Grani* 44, no. 161 (1991): 144–59.

Ivanova, Natal'ia. "Sluchai Makanina." *Znamia* 4 (1997): 215–20.

Jankowski, Andrzej. "Iz nabliudenii za nekotorymi chertami sovremennoi prozy: Na materiale povesti Vladimira Makanina 'Odin i odna.' " In *Neueste Tendenzen in der Entwicklung der russischen Literatur und Sprache: Probleme in Forschung und Lehre,* edited by Erwin Wedel; assistant editors Reinhard Ibler, Hans-Jurgen Otte, and Kai Sieveking. Hamburg: Buske, 1992, 85–91.

Kireev, Ruslan. "Obretenie cherez utratu." *Literaturnaia gazeta,* 1 April 1987: 4.

Latynina, Alla. "Ne igra, a prognoz khudozhnika." *Literaturnaia gazeta,* 7 June 1995: 4.

Lipovetskii, Mark. "Iz plena 'samotechnosti.' " In *Svobody chernaia rabota.* Sverdlovsk: Sredne-Ural'skoe Knizhnoe izdatel'stvo, 1991, 95–128.

———. "Paradoks o gore i tunnele." *Literaturnaia gazeta,* 10 June 1992: 4.

Peterson, Nadya. "Vladimir Makanin's Solution to the Loss of the Past." *Studies in Comparative Communism* 21, no. 3/4 (1991): 349–56.

Piskunova, S., and V. Piskunov. "Vse prochee—literatura." *Voprosy literatury* 2 (1988): 38–77.

Rich, Elisabeth, and W.G. Fiedorow, trans. "Vladimir Makanin." *South Central Review* 12, no. 3–4 (Fall–Winter 1995): 92–107.

Rodnianskaia, Irina. "Neznakomye znakomtsy: K sporam o geroiakh Makanina." *Novyi mir* 8 (1986): 230–47.

———. "Siuzhety trevogi: Makanin pod znakom 'novoi zhestokosti,' " *Novyi mir* 4 (1997): 228–34.

Solov'eva, Inna. "Natiurmort s knigoi i zerkalom." *Literaturnoe obozrenie* 4 (1988): 46–49.

Swiezy, Janusz. "Tvorcheskii put' Vladimira Makanina." *Slavia Orientalis* 45, no. 3 (1996): 367–83.

Tolstaia, Tat'iana, and Karen Stepanian. ". . . Golos, letiashchii v kupol." *Voprosy literatury* 2 (1988): 78–105.

Vail', Petr, and Aleksandr Genis. "Laz Makanina: Vzgliad iz N'iu-Iorka." *Nezavisimaia gazeta,* 25 July 1991: 7.

Ventavoli, Bruno. "Il russo Makanin: La burocrazia e dentro di noi." *La Stampa: Tuttolibri* 14, no. 606 (18 June 1988): 5.

Zarnowski, Lila. "Makaninskii laz v dushu." *Australian Slavonic & East European Studies* 10, no. 2 (1996): 181–86.

Zolotonosov, Mikhail. "Makanin i VKR." *Ural* 8 (1988): 213–22.

METROPOL' (Metropole). An independent literary almanac compiled in Moscow by Vasily Aksyonov, Viktor Erofeyev, Yevgeny Popov, Fazil Iskander, and Andrei Bitov in 1979. Other contributors to the almanac include Yuz Aleshkovsky, Bella Akhmadulina, Vladimir Vysotsky, Fridrikh Gorenshtein, Inna Lisnianskaia, Semen Lipkin, Andrei Voznesensky, and Genrikh Sapgir. The texts collected in the almanac were opposed to Socialist Realism aesthetically rather than politically. Most of the works represented various antirealist literary movements, from expressionism and the grotesque to postmodernism. Despite its eclectic character, *Metropol'* was the first organized act that proved that modernist and avant-guarde traditions had been reborn in the Soviet Union after more than fifty years of the dictatorship of Socialist Realism. The almanac was published in eight copies and presented to the literary public in a Moscow cafe. Then it began to circulate in samizdat. Very soon, in 1979, it was brought out by Ardis Publishers in Ann Arbor, Michigan, whereupon the Union of Soviet Writers began to wage an all-out war against the co-editors and contributors to the almanac. As a result, Vasily Aksyonov and Fridrikh Gorenshtein emigrated from the USSR, Viktor Erofeyev and Yevgeny Popov were expelled from the Union of Soviet Writers (effectively banning their works from publication in the USSR), Semen Lipkin and Inna Lisnianskaia expressed their protest against the pursuit for the freedom of speech by quitting their membership in the Writers' Union, and most of the other participants (except Andrei Voznesensky) were forbidden to publish in the Soviet Union for several years. This affair provoked an international response: letters in support of *Metropol'* were signed by Kurt Vonnegut, John

Updike, William Styron, and other prominent American writers. *Metropol'* was finally published in Russia in 1992.

## Bibliography

Aksyonov, Vasily. "Prazdnik, kotoryi pytalis' ukrast'." *Ogonek* 10 (1991): 18–19.
Aksyonov, Vasily; Andrei Bitov; Viktor Erofeyev; Fazil Iskander; Yevgeny Popov, eds. *Metropol'* Ann Arbor: Ardis, 1979.
Erofeyev, Viktor. "Desiat' let spustia." *Ogonek* 37 (1990): 16–18.
Proffer, Carl. *A Metropole White Book.* Ann Arbor: Ardis, 1985.

NABOKOV, VLADIMIR VLADIMIROVICH (pseud. Sirin, 1899 [St.-Petersburg]–1977 [Montre, Switzerland]). Prominent Russian and American novelist, poet, essayist, translator. He was born to the family of a liberal Russian politician. His family emigrated to Berlin in 1919. Nabokov subsequently graduated from Cambridge University with a degree in Slavonic and Romance Literatures. He then moved back to Germany, where he lived until moving to France in 1933. In 1939 he left France for the United States, just before the Nazi occupation. Before emigration to the United States, he wrote his prose in Russian, but since 1939 he worked primarily in English. He taught at several American universities. In 1958, after the international success of Lolita, he returned to Europe and settled in Switzerland, where he lived until his death in 1977.

Nabokov's Russian novels (the most important of which are *Mary* [1926], *The Defense* [1930], *Glory* [1933], *The Gift* [1937–38], and *Invitation to a Beheading* [1938]) develop the tradition of the Russian symbolist novel (Andrei Bely) and elaborate the idiosyncratic form of modernist metafiction, in which the process of literary creation becomes the central metaphor for existence. This process is continued in his early English-language novels, such as *The Real Life of Sebastian Knight* (1941) and *Bend Sinister* (1945–46), although these novels demonstrated the impossibility for the modernist creator of imaginative order to resist social and existential chaos. The tragic discovery of the illusory nature of various attempts to provide order to a chaotic reality led Nabokov to the works that subsequently were recognized as the classics of American and world postmodernism—*Lolita* (1955, which the author translated into Russian in 1967) and *Ada or Ardor* (1969). Although Nabokov's works were not published in the USSR until 1986, they were widely circulated in *samizdat* and *tamizdat,* and in the seventies and eighties it was Nabokov who was almost unanimously recognized among the Russian intelligentsia as the most important Russian writer of the twentieth century. It is safe to say that Nabokov was the one who built the bridge between the Russian modernist Silver Age and Western (especially American) postmodernism, and that he was the one who brought postmodernist seeds to Russian soil.

## Works (Russian)

*Sobranie sochinenii.* Ann Arbor: Ardis, 1986. 15 volumes.
*Sobranie sochiinenii. V 4–kh tomakh.* Edited by Viktor Erofeyev. Moscow: Izvestiia, 1990.

## Translations

*(Note: Virtually all of Nabokov's translated works can be found in paperback editions published by Vintage Books.)*

*The Defense.* Translated by Michael Scammell in collaboration with the author. London: Weidenfield and Nicolson, 1964; New York: Vintage Books, 1990.
*Despair.* Translated by Dmitri Nabokov in collaboration with the author. New York: Putnam, 1979.
*The Enchanter.* Translated by Dmitri Nabokov. New York: Putnam, 1986.
*The Eye.* Translated by Dmitri Nabokov in collaboration with the author. London: Penguin, 1966, 1992.
*The Gift.* Translated by Michael Scammell in collaboration with the author. London: Penguin Books, 1963; New York: Putnam, 1963.
*Glory.* Translated by Dmitri Nabokov in collaboration with the author. London: Penguin Books, 1974.
*Invitation to a Beheading.* Translated by Dmitri Nabokov in collaboration with the author. New York: Putnam, 1959.
*King, Queen, Knave.* Translated by Dmitri Nabokov in collaboration with the author. New York, McGraw-Hill, 1968.
*Laughter in the Dark.* Translated by the author. Indianapolis, New York: Bobbs-Merrill, 1938.
*The Luzhin Defence.* Translated by Michael Scammell in collaboration with the author. London: Penguin, 1964, 1994. (See *The Defense.*)
*The Man from the USSR and Other Plays.* Introduction and translations by Dmitri Nabokov. San Diego: Harcourt Brace Jovanovich, 1985.
*Mary.* Translated by Michael Glenny in collaboration with the author. Greenwich: Fawcett, 1970, 1971.
*Nabokov's Dozen: Thirteen Stories.* Translated by Dmitri Nabokov in collaboration with the author. New York: Penguin, 1960, 1990.
*The Stories of Vladimir Nabokov.* New York: Knopf, 1996.

## Selected Bibliography

Alexandrov, Vladimir E. *Nabokov's Otherworld.* Princeton: Princeton University Press, 1991.
Aleksandrov, Vladimir, ed. *The Garland Companion to Vladimir Nabokov.* New York: Garland, 1995.

Appel, Alfred, Jr. *Nabokov's Dark Cinema.* New York: Oxford University Press, 1974.

Bader, Julia. *Crystal Land: Patterns of Artifice in Vladimir Nabokov.* Berkeley: University of California Press, 1973.

Bloom, Harold, ed. *Lolita.* New York: Chelsea House, 1987, 1993.

Boyd, Brian. *Vladimir Nabokov: The Russian Years.* Princeton: Princeton University Press, 1990.

———. *Vladimir Nabokov: The American Years.* Princeton: Princeton University Press, 1991.

Clark, Beverly Lyon. *Reflections of Fantasy: The Mirror-Worlds of Carroll, Nabokov, and Pynchon.* New York: Peter Lang, 1985.

Couturier, Maurice. "Nabokov in Postmodernist Land." *Critique: Studies in Contemporary Fiction* 34, no. 4 (Summer 1993): 247–60.

Dembo, L.S., ed. *Nabokov: The Man and His Work.* Madison: University of Wisconsin Press, 1967.

Field, Andrew. *Nabokov: A Bibliography.* New York: McGraw-Hill, 1973.

———. *Nabokov: His Life in Part.* New York: Viking, 1977.

———. *Nabokov: His Life in Art.* New York: Viking, 1978.

Foster, John Burt, Jr. *Nabokov's Art of Memory and European Modernism.* Princeton: Princeton University Press, 1993.

Fowler, Douglas. *Reading Nabokov.* Ithaca: Cornell University Press, 1974.

Green, Geoffrey. "Beyond Modernism and Postmodernism: Vladimir Nabokov's Fiction of Transcendent Perspective." *Cycnos* 12, no. 2 (1995): 159–64.

Linetskii, Vadim. *Anti-Bakhtin—Luchshaia kniga o Vladimire Nabokove.* St. Petersburg: Tipografiia im. I.E. Kotliakova, 1994.

McHale, Brian. "Change of Dominant from Modernist to Postmodernist Writing." In *Approaching Postmodernism,* edited by Douwe Wessel Fokkema and Hans Willem Bertens. Amsterdam: Benjamins, 1986, 53–79.

Nicol, Charles, ed. *Nabokov's Fifth Arc: Nabokov and Others on His Life's Work.* Austin: University of Texas Press, 1982.

Parker, Stephen Jan, ed. *The Achievement of Vladimir Nabokov: Essays, Studies, Reminiscences, and Stories from the Cornell Nabokov Festival.* Ithaca: Center for International Studies, Committee on Soviet Studies, Cornell University, 1984.

Pifer, Ellen. *Nabokov and the Novel.* Cambridge: Harvard University Press, 1980.

Proffer, Carl R. *Keys to Lolita.* Bloomington: Indiana University Press, 1968.

Proffer, Carl R. ed., *A Book of Things about Vladimir Nabokov.* Ann Arbor: Ardis, 1974.

Quennell, Peter. *Vladimir Nabokov: His Life, His Work, His World: A Tribute.* London: Weidenfeld & Nicolson, 1979.

Rampton, David. *Vladimir Nabokov.* New York: St. Martin's Press, 1993.

Roth, Phyllis A., ed. *Critical Essays on Vladimir Nabokov.* Boston: Hall, 1984.

Sharpe, Tony. *Vladimir Nabokov.* London: Arnold, 1991.

Stark, John O. *The Literature of Exhaustion: Borges, Nabokov, and Barth.* Durham: Duke University Press, 1974.

Stegner, S. *Escape into Aesthetics: The Art of Vladimir Nabokov.* New York: Dial, 1966.

Stuart, Dabney. *Nabokov: The Dimensions of Parody.* Baton Rouge: Louisiana State University Press, 1978.

Tammi, Pekka. *Problems of Nabokov's Poetics: A Narratological Approach.* Helsinki: Suomalainen Tiedeakatemia, 1985.

Toker, Leona. *Nabokov: The Mystery of Literary Structures.* Ithaca: Cornell University Press, 1989.

PELEVIN, VIKTOR OLEGOVICH (b.1962, in Moscow). One of the youngest and most popular Russian postmodernists. He is the author of four novels, *Omon Ra* (1993), *The Life of Insects* (1994), *The Yellow Arrow* (1995), and *Chapaev and Void* (1996), as well as the short-story collections *The Blue Lantern* (awarded the Little Russian Booker Prize in 1992), *The Tambourine of the Lower World*, and *The Tambourine of the Upper World* (both published in 1996). His works have already been translated into English, French, Dutch, German, and Japanese. Pelevin combines the traditions of Soviet science fiction and Zen Buddhist mysticism with the techniques of postmodernist metafiction, and the result is an ambiguous, absurd style that is uniquely Pelevin's. Yet despite this intellectual playfulness, his plots are always captivating and unpredictable. Pelevin's imagination is apparently equally inspired by computer games, dreams, and contemporary popular entertainment. He lives in Moscow.

## Works

*Chapaev i Pustota.* Moscow: Vagrius, 1996.
*Omon Ra.* Moscow: Tekst, 1992.
*Sinii fonar'.* Moscow: Tekst, 1991.
*Sochineniia. v 2–kh tomakh.* Moscow: Terra. 1996
*Zhizn' nasekomykh: romany.* Moscow: Vagrius, 1997.

## Translations

*The Blue Lantern and Other Stories.* Translated by Andrew Bromfield. New York: New Directions, 1997.
*The Life of Insects.* Translated from the Russian by Andrew Bromfield. London: Harbor. 1996; New York: Farrar, Straus & Giroux, 1998.
*Omon Ra.* Translated from the Russian by Andrew Bromfield. New York: New Directions, 1997.
*The Yellow Arrow.* Translated from the Russian by Andrew Bromfield. New York: New Directions, 1996.

## Secondary Literature

Arbitman, Roman. "Predvoditel' serebristykh sharikov: Al'ternativy Viktora Pelevina." *Literaturnaia gazeta,* 14 July 1993: 4.
Arkhangel'skii, Aleksandr. "Obstoiatel'stva mesta i vremeni: Pustota. I Chapaev." *Druzhba narodov* 5 (1997): 190–193.
Basinskii, Pavel. "Iz zhizni otechestvennykh kaktusov." *Literaturnaia gazeta,* 29 May 1996: 4.
———. "Noveishie belletristy: Viktor Pelevin i Aleksei Varlamov: Ne pravda li, krainosti skhodiatsia?" *Literaturnaia gazeta,* 4 June 1997: 11.
Brown, Dalton S. "Ludic Nonchalance or Ludicrous Despair? Viktor Pelevin and Rus-

sian Postmodernist Prose." *Slavonic and East European Review* 75, no. 2 (1997): 216–33.

Genis, Aleksandr. "Viktor Pelevin: Granitsy i metamorfozy." *Znamia* 12 (1995): 210–14.

———. "Pole chudes: Viktor Pelevin." *Zvezda* 12 (1997): 230–33.

Kornev, S. "Stolknovenie pustot: Mozhet li postmodernizm byt' russkim i klassicheskim? Ob odnoi avantiure Viktora Pelevina." *Novoe literaturnoe obozrenie* 28 (1997): 244–59.

Rodnianskaia, Irina. ". . . I k nei bezumnaia liubov' . . ." *Novyi mir* 9 (1996): 212–13.

Stepanian, Karen. "Realizm kak spasenie ot snov." *Znamia* 11 (1996): 194–200.

**PETRUSHEVSKAYA, LUDMILLA STEFANOVNA** (b.1938, in Moscow). Author of plays and fiction. Petrushevskaya graduated from Moscow University and began writing in the midsixties; however, her short stories were rejected by the major journals for their "dark content." In the seventies, she became famous as a playwright. Although in the Soviet period her plays were published very rarely (*Love* was published in 1979; *Three Girls in Blue,* in 1984), they were very popular among actors and directors and were staged by small theaters. In the early eighties, her plays were performed on the stages of such popular Moscow theaters as the Taganka (under the direction of Yuri Lyubimov), the Sovremennik (Roman Viktiuk), the Lenkom (Mark Zakharov), and the Moscow Art Theater (Oleg Efremov). Her favorite dramatic genre is the one-act play, which, in her hands, usually combines intense psychological dialogue with a grotesque plot (*Cinzano, A Glass of Water, Colombina's Apartment*). Since perestroika, her plays and stories have been published widely, but the cruel and bleak plots of her short stories of the past two decades caused a kind of aesthetic shock. Petrushevskaya is often considered to be the leader of the recent wave of neonaturalistic fiction *(chernukha),* and yet the goal of both her fiction and her drama is something more than merely revealing the dark and disgusting aspects of Soviet or post-Soviet reality. Most of Petrushevskaya's plots are focused on the tragedies of everyday life caused by poverty, housing problems, sicknesses, alcoholism, and love affairs. By depicting these situations from the inside, through the voices of unreliable narrators, she consistently unveils the hidden intertextuality of everyday life: Each of her short stories reveals the archetypal, mythological plots within the bleak banality of Soviet life. Petrushevskaya's combination of mythological references with gloomy naturalism situates her fiction on the border between realism, modernism, and postmodernism. Her most important works include "Our Crowd," "Immortal Love," "Across the Fields," "Observation Deck," "A Modern Family Robinson," "Hygiene," and the short novel *The Time: Night*. Recently, she has turned her attention to more fantastic genres, such as surrealistic parables (*Songs of the Eastern Slavs*), ironic fables (*Wild Animal Fables*), and fairy tales (*Fairy Tales for the Entire Family, The Doll Novel,* and others). This genre emphasizes the mythological aspect of her art, but the creative tension between the naturalistic and the mythological layers of the narrative tends to fall by the wayside. Her short novel *The Time: Night* (1992) was short-listed for the first Russian Booker Prize. She lives in Moscow.

## Works

*Sobranie sochinenii v piati tomakh.* Kharkov: Folio; Moscow: TKO ACT, 1996.

## Translations

"A Modern Family Robinson." Translated by George Bird. In *Dissonant Voices: The New Russian Fiction,* edited by Oleg Chukhontsev. London: Harvill, 1991, 414–24.
*Cinzano: Eleven Plays.* Translated by Stephen Mulrine. London: Nick Hern Books, 1991.
*Four by Lyudmila Petrushevskaia.* Translated by Alma H. Law. New York: Institute for Contemporary East European Drama and Theater of the Center for Advanced Studies in Theater Arts, 1984.
*Immortal Love.* Translated from the Russian by Sally Laird. New York: Pantheon Books, 1995, 1996.
"Nets and Traps." Translated by Alma H. Law. In *The Image of Women in Contemporary Soviet Fiction: Selected Short Stories from the USSR,* edited and translated by Sigrid McLaughlin. New York: St. Martin's Press, 1989, 100–112.
"Our Crowd." Translated by Helena Goscilo. In *Glasnost: An Anthology of Russian Literature Under Gorbachev,* edited by Helena Goscilo and Byron Lyndsey. Ann Arbor: Ardis, 1990: 3–24.
"The Overlook." Translated by Dobrochna Dyrcz-Freeman. In *Soviet Women Writing,* introduction by J. Grekova. New York, London, Paris: Abbeville Press, 1990.
*The Time: Night.* Translated from the Russian by Sally Laird. New York: Vintage Books, 1995.
"Through the Fields." Translated by Stefani Hoffman. In *The New Soviet Fiction: Sixteen Short Stories,* edited by Sergei Zalygin. New York: Abbeville Press, 1989: 235–38.

## Secondary Literature

Aiken, Susan Hardy. "Telling the Other('s) Story: Or, the Blues in Two Languages." In *Dialogues/Dialogi: Literary and Cultural Exchanges between (ex)Soviet and American Women,* edited by Susan Hardy Aiken, Adele Marie Barker, Maya Koreneva, and Ekaterina Stetsenko. Durham: Duke University Press, 1994, 206–23.
Autant-Mathieu, Marie-Christine. "Ljudmila Petrusevskaja dramaturge et la critique soviétique des années 70 et 80." *Cahiers du Monde Russe* 37, no. 4 (1996): 467–78.
Cheaure, Elisabeth. "Das Schicksal dreier Generationen: Oder, Von der Illusion zur Desillusionierung. Zu Alexandra Kollontajs 'Die Liebe der drei Generationen' und

Ljudmila Petruschewskajas' Meine Zeit ist die Nacht'." *Osteuropa: Zeitschrift fur Gegenwartsfragen des Ostens* 43, no. 10 (1993): 965–77.

Clowes, Edith W. "The Robinson Myth Reread in Postcolonial and Postcommunist Modes." *Critique: Studies in Contemporary Fiction* 36, no. 2 (Winter 1995): 145–59.

Condee, Nancy. "Liudmila Petrushevskaia: How the 'Lost People' Live." *Newsletter to the Institute of Current World Affairs,* 1986: 1–12.

Doktor, Raisa, and Aleksei Plavinskii. "Khronika odnoi dramy: Tri devushki v golubom: P'esa, spektakal', kritika." *Literaturnoe obozrenie* 12 (1986): 88–94.

Fast, L.V. "Osobennosti rechevogo standarta v iazyke sovremennoi dramaturgii." *Russkii iazyk za rubezhom* 5–6 (1992): 73–76.

Goscilo, Helena. "Mother as Mothra: Totalizing Narrative and Nurture in Petrushevskaia." In *A Plot of Her Own: The Female Protagonist in Russian Literature,* edited by Sona Stephan Hoisington. Evanston: Northwestern University Press, 1995: 102–13.

———. "Speaking Bodies: Erotic Zones Rhetorized." In *Fruits of Her Plume: Essays on Contemporary Russian Women's Culture,* edited by Helena Goscilo. Armonk, NY: M.E. Sharpe, 1993, 135–64.

Ivanova, Natalia. "Bakhtin's Concept of the Grotesque and the Art of Petrushevskaia and Tolstaia." In *Fruits of Her Plume: Essays on Contemporary Russian Women's Culture,* edited by Helena Goscilo. Armonk, NY: M.E. Sharpe, 1993: 21–32.

Johnson, Maya. "Women and Children First: Domestic Chaos and the Maternal Bond in the Drama of Liudmila Petrushevskaia." *Canadian Slavonic Papers/Revue Canadienne des Slavistes: An Interdisciplinary Journal Devoted to Central and Eastern Europe* 34, no. 1–2 (1992): 97–112.

Karriker, Alexandra Heidi. "Claustrophobic Interiors and Splintered Selves: Petrushevskaia's Prose in Context." *West Virginia University Philological Papers* 41 (1995): 124–31.

Kolesnikoff, Nina. "The Generic Structure of Liudmila Petrushevskaia's *Pesni vostochnykh slavian.*" *Slavic and East European Journal* 37, no. 2 (Summer 1993): 220–30.

Koreneva, Maya. "Children of the Sixties." In *Dialogues/Dialogi: Literary and Cultural Exchanges between (ex)Soviet and American Women,* edited by Susan Hardy Aiken, Adele Marie Barker, Maya Koreneva, and Ekaterina Stetsenko. Durham: Duke University Press, 1994, 191–205.

Kostiukov, Leonid. "Iskliuchitel'naia mera." *Literaturnaia gazeta,* 13 March 1996: 4.

Kuralekh, A. "Byt i bytie v proze Petrushevskoi." *Literaturnoe obozrenie* 5 (1993): 63–67.

Kustanovich, Konstantin. "The Naturalistic Tendency in Contemporary Soviet Fiction: Thematics, Poetics, Functions." In *New Directions in Soviet Literature,* edited by S. Duffin Graham. New York and London: St. Martin's Press, 1992, 77–88.

Lipovetskii, Mark. "Tragediia i malo li chto eshche." *Novyi mir* 10 (1994): 229–32.

Nevzgliadova, Elena. "Siuzhet dlia nebol'shogo rasskaza." *Novyi mir* 4 (1988): 256–60.

Remizova, Mariia. "Vychitanie liubvi: L. Petrushevskaia predlagaet chitateliu khleb, a on zhazhdet vzbitykh slivok . . ." *Literaturnaia gazeta,* 9 April 1997: 12.

Simmons, K. *Plays for the Period of Stagnation: Lyudmila Petrushevskaia and the Theatre of Absurd.* Birmingham Slavonic Monographs, No. 21. Birmingham, 1992.

Turovskaia, M. "Trudnye p'esy." *Novyi mir* 12 (1985): 247–52.

Vanchu, Anthony J. "Cross(-Dress)ing One's Way to Crisis: Yevgeny Popov and Lyudmila Petrushevskaia and the Crisis of Category in Contemporary Russian Culture." *World Literature Today: A Literary Quarterly of the University of Oklahoma* 67, no. 1 (Winter 1993): 107–18.

Woll, Josephine. "The Minotaur in the Maze: Remarks on Lyudmila Petrushevskaya." *World Literature Today: A Literary Quarterly of the University of Oklahoma* 67, no. 1 (Winter 1993): 125–30.

Zonina, M. "Bessmertnaia liubov'." *Literaturnaia gazeta,* 23 November 1983: 6.

PIETSUKH, VIACHESLAV ALEKSEEVICH (b.1946). Pietsukh graduated from the School of History of the Moscow State Pedagogical Institute and worked as a high-school history teacher for several years before becoming an editor for various Soviet journals. His first stories were published in the late seventies and early eighties. His fiction often consists of retellings of famous events in Russian history, usually ironically and often transposed into contemporary life. His major theme is the metaphysical paradoxes and puzzles of Russian history and the Russian national character. Unlike the writers of Village Prose, Pietsukh's search for metaphysical roots leads to the discovery that absurdity is a constant feature of the Russian mentality. Evidence for this argument can be found in his novels *The New Moscow Philosophy* (an ironic retelling of Dostoevsky's *Crime and Punishment*) and *Rommat [Romantic Materialism]* (a pastiche version of the 1825 Decembrist uprising) and in numerous short stories. Currently Pietsukh is editor-in-chief of the journal *Druzhba narodov* (Friendship of Peoples), one of the most significant Russian literary journals. He lives in Moscow.

## Works

*Alfavit: povesti i rasskazy.* Moscow: Sovetskii pisatel', 1983.

*Gosudartsvennoe ditia: povesti i rasskazy.* Moscow: Vagrius, 1997.

*Ia i prochee: tsikly, rasskazy, povesti, roman.* Moscow: Khudozhestvennaia literatura, 1990.

*Novaia moskovskaia filosofiia: khronika i rasskazy.* Moscow: Moskovskii rabochii, 1989.

*Rommat.* Moscow: SP "Vsia Moskva," 1990.

## Translations

"Anamnesis and Epicrisis." Translated by Andrew Reynolds. In *Dissonant Voices,* edited by Oleg Chukhontsev. London: Harvill. 1991, 389–413.

"Novyi Zavod." Translated by Jan Butler. In *The Wild Beach, and Other Stories,* edited by Helena Goscilo and Byron Lyndsey. Ann Arbor: Ardis, 1992, 277–82.

"The Central–Ermolaevo War." Translated by Arch Tait. In *The Penguin Book of New Russian Writing: Russia's Fleurs du Mal,* edited by Victor Erefeyev and Andrew Reynolds. London: Penguin Books, 1995: 237–56.

"The Pessimist's Comedy." Translated by Arkady Yanishevsky. In *The Times of Turmoil: A Collection of Stories,* edited by Irina Broude. Tenafly: Hermitage, 1993: 137–53.

"The Ticket." Translated by Byron Lyndsey. In *The Wild Beach, and Other Stories,* edited by Helena Goscilo and Byron Lyndsey. Ann Arbor: Ardis, 1992, 265–75.

## Secondary Literature

Gibian, George. "The Quest for Russian National Identity in Soviet Culture Today." In *The Search for Self-Definition in Russian Literature,* edited by Ewa M. Thompson. Houston: Rice University Press, 1991, 1–20.

Mil'shtein, Il'ia. "Viacheslav P'etsukh." *Literaturnoe obozrenie* 2 (1989): 69–70.

Nikolaeva, Ol'ga, and Aleksandr Nikolaev. "Russkii—eto ne tol'ko natsional'nost', no prezhde vsego nastroenie: Viacheslav P'etsukh v besede s Ol'goi i Aleksandrom Nikolaevymi." *Literaturnaia gazeta,* 16 April 1997: 10.

Polikovskaia, L. "Tragediia noveishego obraztsa." *Literaturnoe obozrenie* 3 (1990): 51–53.

Rich, Elisabeth, and Laura Weeks, trans. "Vyacheslav Pyetsukh." *South Central Review: The Journal of the South Central Modern Language Association* 12, no. 3–4 (Fall–Winter 1995): 135–47.

Taroshchina, S. "Moskva, Sankt-Peterburgskii variant." *Literaturnaia gazeta,* 17 May 1989: 7.

Ulyashov, Pavel. "Authors and Positions." *Soviet Literature* 1, no. 502 (1990): 107–11.

POPOV, YEVGENY ANATOLIEVICH (b.1946, in Krasnoyarsk). Popov graduated from the Krasnoiarsk Geological Institute and worked as a geologist for seven years. His stories began to appear in print in 1971, and a collection of them was published in 1974 in *Novyi mir* with a foreword by Vasily Shukshin, one of the most famous writers of Village Prose. In 1978 he was accepted into the Union of Soviet Writers. But in 1979, as a co-editor of the unofficial almanac *Metropol',* he was expelled from the Writers' Union and banned from publication in the USSR. In 1981, a collection of his stories was published in the United States (*Merry-Making in Old Russia*). Since 1986, his numerous short stories have been published widely in various Russian journals, and now he is considered one of the leaders of the "new wave" of postcommunist literature. In addition to his short stories, he is the author of several absurdist plays, the novel *The Soul of a Patriot, or Various Epistles to Ferfichkin,* and an idiosyncratic book entitled *The Beauty of Life, or Novel with a Newspaper,* which is a postmodernist collage of fictional sketches with copious citations from Soviet newspapers. He lives in Moscow.

## Works

*Dusha patriota, ili Razlichnye poslaniia k Ferfichkinu.* Moscow: Tekst, 1994.

*Prekrasnost' zhizni, Roman s gazetoi, kotoryi nikogda ne budet nachat i zakonchen.* Moscow: Moskovskii rabochii, 1990.

*Veselie Rusi.* Ann Arbor: Ardis, 1981.

*Zhdu liubvi ne verolomnoi: rasskazy.* Moscow: Sovetskii pisatel', 1989.

## Translations

*Merry-Making in Old Russia, and Other Stories.* Translated from the Russian by Robert Porter. London: Harvill, 1996; Evanston: Northwestern University Press, 1997.

*The Soul of a Patriot, or Various Epistles to Ferfichkin.* Translated from the Russian by Robert Porter. Evanston: Northwestern University Press, 1994.

"Three Tales." Translated by Joel and Monica Wilkinson. In *The Barsukov Triangle, The Two-Toned Blond, and Other Stories,* edited by Carl R. Proffer and Ellendea Proffer. Ann Arbor: Ardis, 1984, 217–27.

## Secondary Literature

Bershin, Efim. "Diktatura strakha." *Literaturnaia gazeta,* 28 August 1996: 3.

Engel, Christine. *"Tristram Shandy* und *Ulysses* in Moskau: Textstruktur und Bedeutungsaufbau in *Dusa patriota, ili Razlicnye poslanija K Ferfickinu* von Eugenij Popov." In *Georg Mayer zum 60. Geburtstag,* edited by Ursula Bieber and Alois Woldan. Munich: Sagner, 1991, 167–81.

Hosking, Geoffrey. "Profile: Evgeny Popov." *Index on Censorship,* 12, no. 6 (1983): 36–38.

Kustanovich, Konstantin. "The Naturalistic Tendency in Contemporary Soviet Fiction: Thematics, Poetics, Functions." In *New Directions in Soviet Literature,* edited by Sheelagh Duffy Graham. New York: St. Martin's Press, 1992, 75–88.

Taroshchina, S. "Prekrasnost' zhizni, ili poiski smysla prochnosti." *Literaturnaia gazeta,* 20 April 1988: 6.

Vanchu, Anthony J. "Cross(-Dress)ing One's Way to Crisis: Yevgeny Popov and Lyudmila Petrushevskaia and the Crisis of Category in Contemporary Russian Culture." *World Literature Today: A Literary Quarterly of the University of Oklahoma* 67, no. 1 (Winter 1993): 107–18.

Vishevsky, Anatoly. "Creating a Shattered World: Toward the Poetics of Yevgeny Popov." *World Literature Today: A Literary Quarterly of the University of Oklahoma* 67, no. 1 (Winter 1993): 119–24.

**PRIGOV, DMITRII ALEKSANDROVICH** (b.1940, in Moscow). Artist and poet, the leader and ideologue of Russian Conceptualism *(Sots-Art).* Prigov graduated from the Sculpture Department of the Moscow Art-Industrial Institute. As a Conceptualist artist, he has participated in many exhibitions; as a writer, he has published thousands of poems collected in various cycles. Before late 1980s, his works circulated in *samizdat.* Prigov's first book was published in the USSR in 1990. Each of Prigov's cycles is written from the point of view of a particular character, functioning as the personification of an authoritative discourse. His poems of the seventies and eighties were written from the point of view of the brainwashed (and unwashed) Soviet citizen *(sovok)* as a deconstruction of Soviet ideological language. The most famous among these cycles concerns a militiaman (the Soviet equivalent of a policeman) who becomes the symbol of omnipresent state power and the object of poetic admiration. By the same token, his more recent poems deconstruct a variety of discourses that are not necessarily influenced by Soviet ideology ("Women's Poems" or "A Collection of Forewords to Various Things"). In his essays, Prigov introduces the major ideas of Conceptualist art, the most important of which are the categories of the "borrowed perspective" and "new sincerity." Prigov emphasizes that he is not making fun of his narrator but is rather trying to embody him or her as sincerely as possible in order to deconstruct the narrator's language. Prigov was awarded the German Pushkin Prize in 1992. He lives in Moscow.

## Works

*Iavlenie stikha posle ego smerti.* Moscow: Tekst, 1995.
*Napisannoe s 1975 po 1989.* Moscow: Nov', 1996.
*Obrashcheniia Dmitriia Aleksandrovicha Prigova k narodu.* Moscow: "ITS-Garant," 1996.
*Piat'desiat kapelek krovi.* Moscow: Tekst, 1993.
*Podobrannyi Prigov.* Moscow: RGGU, 1997 (includes several critical articles on Prigov's work and includes bibliographical references).
*Russian Poet Dmitri Prigov Reading His Poetry.* Recording. 1 sound tape reel: analog, 7½ ips, full track, mono. Recorded for the Archive of World Literature on Tape. Production level cataloging. Recorded 9 January 1990, in the Library of Congress Recording Laboratory, studio B, Washington, DC. Archive of World Literature on Tape (Library of Congress).
*Sbornik preduvedomlenii k raznoobraznym veshcham.* Moscow: Ad Marginem, 1996.
*Slezy geral'dicheskoi dushi.* Moscow: Moskovskii rabochii, 1990.
*Sobranie stikhov.* Vol. 1. Vienna: Wiener Slawistischer Almanach, 1996.
*Sobranie stikhov.* Vol. 2. Vienna: Wiener Slawistischer Almanach, 1996.
*Sovetskie teksty, 1979–84.* St. Petersburg: Izdatel'st Ivana Limbakha, 1997.
*Stikhogrammy.* Paris: Izdatel'stvo zhurnala "A-IA," 1986.
*Texts of Our Life.* Keele: Essays in Poetics, 1995 (poems in Russian with parallel English translation).
*Zapredel'nye liubovniki: teksty.* Moscow: ARGO-RISK, 1995.

## Translations

"Come In, If You Can." Translated by Anesa Miller-Pogacar. In *Re-Entering the Sign: Articulating New Russian Culture,* edited by Ellen E. Berry and Anesa Miller-Pogacar. Ann Arbor: University of Michigan Press, 1995, 216–18.
"Description of Objects." Translated from the Russian by Mark Shuttleworth. In *The Penguin Book of New Russian Writing: Russia's Fleurs du Mal,* edited by Victor Erofeyev and Andrew Reynolds. London: Penguin, 1995, 292–99.
"Dmitrii Prigov." In *Contemporary Russian Poetry. A Bilingual Anthology,* selected, with an introduction, translations, and notes by Gerald S. Smith. Bloomington and Indianapolis: Indiana University Press, 1993, 212–22.
"Dmitrii Prigov." Translated by Albert C. Todd. In *Twentieth Century Russian Poetry: Silver and Steel, An Anthology,* edited by Albert C. Todd and Max Hayward (with Daniel Weiss); selected, with an introduction by Yevgeny Yevtushenko. New York: Doubleday, 1993, 978.

"What More Is There to Say? From Reagan's Image in Soviet Literature. Forty-ninth Alphabet Poem. Screaming Cantata (Who Killed Stalin)." Translated by Lyn Hejinian, Elena Balashova, Andrew Wachtel, and Gerald J. Janecek. In *Third Wave: The New Russian Poetry,* edited by Kent Johnson and Stephen M. Ashby. Ann Arbor: University of Michigan Press, 1992, 101–16.

## Secondary Literature

Hirt, Gunter, and Sasche Wonders. "Der Moskauer Dichter Dmitrij Alexandrowitsch Prigow." *Akzente: Zeitschrift fur Literatur* 38, no. 4 (1991): 382–83.
Kuritsyn, Viacheslav. "Poet–militsaner." *Oktiabr'* 6 (1996): 183–86.
Nicholas, Mary A. "Dmitrij Prigov and the Russian Avant-Garde, Then and Now." *Russian Literature* 39, no. 1 (1996): 13–34.
———. "Dmitrij Aleksandrovic Prigov: Selected Bibliography." *Russian Literature* 39, no. 1 (1996): 35–38.
Olskaia, Viktoria A. " 'Machrot' vseja Rusi' by Dmitrij Prigov as a Composition of Moscow Conceptualism." *Russian Literature* 39, no. 1 (1996): 39–64.

RUBINSHTEIN, LEV SEMENOVICH (b.1947) graduated from the Russian Language and Literature School of the Moscow State Pedagogical Institute. Perhaps influenced by his work as a librarian, Rubinshtein has invented a unique literary genre: a kind of prose poem in the form of a "card catalogue," a collection of often enigmatic fragments and citations that, when taken together, combine numerous styles and discourses within a single work. This literary form allowed Rubinshtein to develop his own, seemingly chaotic, version of the elegy ("The Six-Winged Serafim"), drama *(This Time),* poetic self-portrait ("That's Me"), dream interpretation ("Thursday Night–Friday Morning"), philosophic argument ("Life Is Everywhere," "Further and Further"), letters ("A Regular Letter"), lyrical memoirs ("Mama Was Washing the Frame"), and so on. His works are filled with existential paradoxes emphasizing the interplay between chaos and order. His first collections were published in Germany; in Russia, his first collections appeared only in 1994–96 *(Problems of Literature, Further and Further, A Regular Letter).* Since 1996, Rubinshtein has been working as a journalist for the Russian magazine *Itogi* (a joint venture with *Newsweek*). He lives in Moscow.

## Works

*Malen'kaia nochnaia serenada, 1986.* Moscow: "Renaissance," 1992.
*Mama myla ramu, 1987.* Moscow: "Renaissance," 1992.
*Poiavlenie geroia.* Moscow: "Renaissance," 1992.
*Reguliarnoe pis'mo.* St. Petersburg: Izdatal'st Ivana Limbakha, 1996.
*Voprosy literatury.* Moscow: ARGO-RISK, 1996.
*Vse dal'she i dal'she: iz "Bol'shoi kartoteki," 1975–1993.* Moscow: Obscuri viri, 1995.

## Translations

"The Six-Winged Seraph." Translated from the Russian by Andrew Reynolds. In *The Penguin Book of New Russian Writing: Russia's Fleurs du Mal,* edited by Victor Erofeyev and Andrew Reynolds. London: Penguin, 1995: 300–8.

"Statement. A Little Nighttime Serenade. From 'Thursday to Friday.'" Translated by Gerald J. Janecek. In *Third Wave: The New Russian Poetry,* edited by Kent Johnson and Stephen M. Ashby. Ann Arbor: University of Michigan Press, 1992, 137–50.

"What Can One Say?" Translated by Gerald J. Janecek. In *Re-Entering the Sign: Articulating New Russian Culture,* edited by Ellen E. Berry and Anesa Miller-Pogacar. Ann Arbor: University of Michigan Press, 1995, 212–16.

## Secondary Literature

Fleischer, Michael. "Das Fragment und die Bedeutung: Eine besondere Textsorte." In *Probleme der Textlinguistik/Problemy lingvistiki teksta: Gemeinschaftsarbeit von Wissenschaftlern der Partneruniversitaten Bochum und Minsk,* edited by Helmut Jachnow and Adam E. Suprun. Munich: Sagner, 1989, 141–72.

Khirt, Gunter, and Sasha Vonder. "Seriinoe proizvodstvo: Moskovskii avtor Lev Rubinshtein." In *Vse dal'she i dal'she: iz "Bol'shoi kartoteki," 1975–1993,* by Lev Rubinshtein. Moscow: Obscuri viri, 1995: 98–103.

Zorin, Andrei. "Stikhi na kartochkakh: Poeticheskii iazyk L'va Rubinshteina." *Daugava* 8 (1989): 100–102.

*SAMIZDAT* AND *TAMIZDAT.* The term *samizdat* literally means "self-published." It actually refers to unpublished texts distributed covertly by authors and/or readers (an activity that could lead to prosecution for "anti-Soviet propaganda"). The term was coined in the late 1960s, when the persecution of Solzhenitsyn and the trials of the writers Andrei Siniavskii (Abram Terts), Iulii Daniel (Nikolai Arzhak), and Iosif Brodsky prompted an increase in the distribution of "anti-Soviet" literary and journalistic writings. Because of the government ban on the private use of photocopiers, *samizdat* texts were typed and retyped or photographed in multiple copies. Among the most popular authors of *samizdat* were Osip Mandelstam, Nikolai Gumilev, Mikhail Bulgakov, Venedikt Erofeev, Lidiia Chukovskaia, Fazil Iskander, Vladimir Voinovich, and Georgy Vladimov. *Tamizdat*—literally, "published over there"—refers to works by "anti-Soviet" authors (including Nabokov, Bulgakov, Platonov, Gumilev, Galich, Brodsky, Bitov, and Sokolov) published abroad and illegally distributed in the USSR, usually in the form of barely legible photocopies. Collections of *samizdat* publications have been published by various European and American research institutes.

## Bibliography

Medvedev, Roy, ed. *The Samizdat Register.* London: Merlin Press, 1977.

Meerson-Aksenov, Michael, and Boris Shragin, eds. *The Political, Social and Religious*

*Thought of Russian Samizdat: An Anthology.* Translated by Nickolas Lupinin. Belmont, MA: Nordland, 1977.

Paskalova, M. *Samizdat i novaia politicheskaia pressa: Po materialam kollektsii Moskvy i Sankt-Peterburga.* Moscow, 1993.

*Samizdat: spravochnik: 576 izdanii, 125 gorodov.* Moscow: Informatsionnoe agentsvo SMOT, 1990.

Saunders, George. *Samizdat: Voices of the Soviet Opposition.* New York: Monad Press; distributed by Pathfinder Press, 1974.

Scammell, Michael. *Russia's Other Writers: Selections from Samizdat Literature.* Selected and introduced by Michael Scammell. Foreword by Max Hayward. New York: Praeger, 1971.

Suetnov, Aleksandr. *Samizdat.* Moscow: Tsentr obrazovatel'nykh programm in-ta Novykh tekhnologii obrazovaniia, 1992.

Woll, Josephine. *Soviet Unofficial Literature—Samizdat: An Annotated Bibliography of Works Published in the West.* Durham: Duke University Center for International Studies, 1978.

———. *Soviet Dissident Literature, A Critical Guide.* In collaboration with Vladimir G. Treml. Boston: G.K. Hall, 1983.

**SHAROV, VLADIMIR ALEKSANDROVICH** (b.1952, in Moscow). The son of Aleksandr Sharov, an author of cheerful romantic fairy tales for children, Vladimir Sharov graduated from the Voronezh State University School of History. Later he defended his dissertation on the Russian Time of Troubles (seventeenth century). He is the author of four quasi-historical novels: *Following in the Footsteps* (1989), *Rehearsals* (1991), *Before and During* (1993), and *Could I Not Feel Pity?* (1995). All his novels are constructed as complex networks of mythological narratives that transpose the events of seventeenth-century Russian history from the seventeenth century into Stalin's times, entailing a mystical— and very often absurd—search for God. Sharov makes extensive use of the fantastic and borrows his mystical imagery from a variety of religious and occult traditions, but his unbelievable stories are told in a pseudodocumentary manner, in a serious tone devoid of irony. Sharov's work deconstructs historical mythologies by creating a fictitious but nonetheless convincing mythology of history. The publication of his novel *Before and During* (1993) in the journal *Novyi mir* prompted heated polemics in the Russian press, when two members of the journal's editorial board expressed their protest against Sharov's "distortion and mockery" of Russian history. Sharov lives in Moscow.

Works

*Do i vo vremia.* Moscow: Nash Dom L'Ag d'Homme, 1995.
*Repetitsii. "Mne li ne pozhalet'."* Moscow: Nash Dom L'Ag d'Homme, 1997.
*Sled v sled.* Moscow: Nash Dom L'Age d'Homme, 1996.

Secondary Literature

Bavil'skii, Dmitrii. "Nishi Sharova." *Novoe literaturno obozrenie* 28 (1997): 269–84.
Sharov, Vladimir, and Vladimir Berezin. "Est' obraz mira, kotoryi ia khochu zapisat'."
   *Druzhba narodov* 8 (1996): 172–77.

SOCIALIST REALISM was the "fundamental method of Soviet litera-ture," as declared at the First Congress of the Union of Soviet Writers (1934). According to the bylaws of the Writers' Union, Socialist Realism "demands of the artist a truthful, historically concrete depiction of reality in its revolutionary development." Socialist Realism was directed against both the avant-garde and modernism, which presented a "distorted" image of reality through irony, the grotesque, and the absurd; it also ruled out any naturalistic depiction of the dark side of Soviet history and everyday life. The doctrine of Socialist Realism requires the total subordination of litera-ture and authors to the ideological leadership of the Communist Party. Deviation from the ideology of Socialist realism was a common pretext for official persecution of such authors as Yevgeny Zamyatin, Mikhail Bulgakov, Osip Mandelstam, Yuri Olesha, Il'f and Petrov, Anna Akhma-tova, Mikhail Zoshchenko, Alexander Solzhenitsyn, and Vasily Aksyonov. The major features of Socialist Realist art include "historical optimism," simplicity of form, one-dimensional characters, a propagandistic message, the priority of collectivist values, and the presentation of the individual as an instrument of the will of the Party. The principles of Socialist Realism were attacked in *samizdat* after the death of Stalin (1953); especially im-portant was the essay of Abram Terts (Andrei Siniavskii) "What Is Socialist Realism?" where the "fundamental method of Soviet literature" was defined as a kind of neoclassicism that pretends to be realistic. In the seventies, the official critics tried to make the doctrine more flexible by suggesting the concept of "Socialist Realism as an open system" that legitimized such forms of "modernist poetics" as the fantastic, the grotesque, myth, irony, Impressionism, and Expressionism, already widely used by Soviet writers of the 1960s and 1970s. In the literature of this period, it is actually difficult to find a writer whose works really follow the principles of So-cialist Realism. Even those authors who were highly esteemed by the authorities often broke the rules of Socialist Realism (Chingiz Aitmatov, Valentin Kataev, Konstantin Simonov, among others). Since the collapse of Socialist Realism as a living artistic system, there has been renewed interest in the doctrine among Russian, American, and European critics (Katerina Clark, Boris Groys, Hans Gunther, Thomas Lahusen, Yevgeny Dobrenko, among others).

# Bibliography

Banks, Miranda, ed. *The Aesthetic Arsenal: Socialist Realism under Stalin.* Long Island City: Institute for Contemporary Art, 1993.

Chung, Hilary, ed., with Michael Falchikov et al. *In the Party Spirit: Socialist Realism and Literary Practice in the Soviet Union, East Germany and China.* Amsterdam and Atlanta: Rodopi, 1996.

Clark, Katerina. *The Soviet Novel: History as Ritual.* Chicago: University of Chicago Press, 1980, 1985.

Dobrenko, E.A. *Formovka sovetskogo chitatelia: sotsial'nye i esteticheskie predposylki retseptsii sovetskoi literatury.* St. Petersburg: Gumanitarnoe agentstvo "Akademicheskii proekt," 1997.

————. *The Making of the State Reader: Social and Aesthetic Contexts of the Reception of Soviet Literature.* Stanford: Stanford University Press, 1997.

Ermolaev, Herman. *Soviet Literary Theories, 1917–1934: The Genesis of Socialist Realism.* New York: Octagon Books, 1977.

Groys, Boris. *The Total Art of Stalinism: Avant-Garde, Aesthetic Dictatorship, and Beyond.* Translated by Charles Rougle. Princeton: Princeton University Press, 1992.

*Izbavlenie ot mirazhei: sotsrealizm segodnia.* Edited by E.A. Dobrenko. Moscow: Sovetskii pisatel', 1990.

Kolesnikoff, Nina, and Walter Smyrniw, eds. *Socialist Realism Revisited: Selected Papers from the McMaster Conference.* Hamilton, Ontario, Canada: McMaster University, 1994.

Lahusen, Thomas. *How Life Writes the Book: Real Socialism and Socialist Realism in Stalin's Russia.* Ithaca: Cornell University Press, 1997.

Lahusen, Thomas, and Evgeny Dobrenko, eds. *Socialist Realism Without Shores.* Durham: Duke University Press, 1997.

Papernyi, Vladimir. *Kul'tura dva.* Ann Arbor: Ardis, 1985; Moscow: Novoe literaturnoe obozrenie, 1996.

Prokhorov, Gleb. *Art under Socialist Realism: Soviet Painting, 1930–1950.* New South Wales: Craftsman House: G + B Arts Int., 1995.

Robin, Regine. *Socialist Realism: An Impossible Aesthetic.* Stanford: Stanford University Press, 1992.

Terts, Abram. *The Trial Begins. On Socialist Realism.* New York: Random House, 1960.

*Znakomyi neznakomets: sotsialisticheskii realizm kak istoriko-kul'turnaia problema.* Edited by N.M. Kurennaia. Moscow: Institut slavianovedeniia i balkanistiki RAN, 1995.

**SOKOLOV, SASHA (ALEKSANDR VSEVOLODOVICH)** (b.1943, in Ottawa) is the son of a high-ranking Soviet diplomat in Canada (who was later expelled from the country for espionage). He studied at the Moscow Military Institute of Foreign Languages for two years and later at the Journalism School of Moscow State University. He was close to the avant-garde literary group SMOG (an acronym for "The Youngest Society of Geniuses," which, in Russian, sounds like a word meaning "I can" or "I did it"). Sokolov started publishing in provincial newspapers as a journalist, although some of his early articles were written in a manner reminiscent of the style of the Symbolist writer Andrei Bely. His first literary text was published in a Soviet journal for the blind. In the early seventies, Sokolov started working on *A School for Fools,* which was completed in 1973 while Sokolov was working as a game warden in a hunting preserve set aside for the Soviet elite (an experience he would use as the material for his second novel, *Between a Dog and a Wolf*). With the help of friends, Sokolov sent his manuscript abroad. The novel was rejected by several Russian émigré publishers (including Vladimir Maksimov of *Kontinent*) as politically vague. In 1974, Sokolov moved to Europe, his emigration facilitated by his claim to Canadian citizenship. The publication of *A School for Fools* in Russian by Ardis made Sokolov famous in Russian émigré circles, especially after the book was praised by Vladimir Nabokov. The novel was widely read by Russian readers not only in emigration but also in the USSR, where it had a cult following in *samizdat* and *tamizdat*. In 1977, Carl Proffer's English translation of *A School for Fools* appeared. The book was reviewed by the most prestigious British and American newspapers, which called it a complicated mixture of surrealism, profound psychological realism, and postmodernist irony. His second novel, *Between a Dog and a Wolf,* was finished in 1979 and published in 1980. Many of Sokolov's loyal readers (including Carl Proffer and Nina Berberova) were confused by the extreme complexity of the novel's style. This probably explains why *Between a Dog and a Wolf* has yet to be translated into English or into any other language. In 1981, the Leningrad *samizdat* journal *Chasy* (The Clock) awarded *Between a Dog and a Wolf* the Andrei Bely Prize. In 1979, Sokolov started working on *Astrophobia,* which marked a radical change in his approach: He moved from the tragic to the parodic, from metamorphosis as a major stylistic device to pastiche and grotesque. *Astrophobia* was finished in 1983, but it was published in Russian only in 1985 (by Ardis). The English translation appeared in 1987. Since perestroika, all of Sokolov's novels have been republished, both in major Russian journals and as separate volumes. His prose has become one of the models of highly sophisticated postmodernist style. In 1989 Sokolov decided to return to Moscow, but his stay there, despite the great popularity of his writings, was short. Since *Astrophobia,* he has published several short works, including poems, interviews, and essays. Some of his later essays are collected in the book *Waiting for Nobel* (1993). He lives in Canada.

## Works

*Mezhdu sobakoi i volkom.* Ann Arbor: Ardis, 1980.
*Palisandriia.* Ann Arbor: Ardis, 1985; Moscow: Glagol, 1992.

*Shkola dlia durakov.* Ann Arbor: Ardis, 1976, 1983, 1989; Moscow: Ogonek-Variant, 1990.
*V ozhidanii Nobelia, ili Obshchaia tetrad'?* St. Petersburg: 1993.

## Translations

"The Anxious Chrysalis." Translated by Olga Pobedinskaya and Andrew Reynolds. In *The Penguin Book of New Russian Writing: Russia's Fleurs du Mal,* edited by Victor Erefeyev and Andrew Reynolds. London: Penguin Books, 1995, 199–206.
*A School for Fools.* Translated from the Russian by Carl R. Proffer. Ann Arbor: Ardis, 1977 (with an introduction by D. Barton Johnson). New York: Four Walls Eight Windows, 1988.
*Astrophobia.* Translated from the Russian by Michael Henry Heim. New York: Grove Weidenfeld, 1989.

## Secondary Literature

Beraha, Laura. "The Last Rogue of History: Picaresque Elements in Sasha Sokolov's Palisandriia." *Canadian Slavonic Papers/Revue Canadienne des Slavistes* 35, no. 3–4 (September–December 1993): 201–20.
Boguslawski, Aleksandr. "Vremia Palisandra Dal'berga." *Russian Language Journal* 42, no. 141–43 (1988): 221–29.
Erofeev, Viktor. "Vremia dlia chastnykh besed . . ." *Oktiabr'* 8 (1989): 195–202.
Fridman, John. "Vetru net ukaza: Razmyshleniia nad tekstami romanov 'Pushkinskii dom' A. Bitova i 'Shkola dlia durakov' S. Solokova." *Literaturnoe obozrenie* 12 (1989): 14–16.
Johnson, D. Barton. "A Structural Analysis of Sasha Sokolov's *School for Fools:* A Paradigmatic Novel." In *Fiction and Drama in Eastern and Southeastern Europe: Evolution and Experiment in the Postwar Period,* edited by Henrik Birnbaum and Thomas Eekman. Columbus: Slavica, 1980, 207–37.
———. "Sasha Sokolov's Twilight Cosmos: Themes and Motifs." *Slavic Review* 45, no. 4 (Winter 1986): 639–49.
———. "A Selected Annotated Bibliography of Works by and about Sasha Sokolov." *Canadian-American Slavic Studies* 21, no. 3–4 (1987): 417–28.
———. "Sasha Sokolov: The New Russian Avant-Garde." *Critique: Studies in Contemporary Fiction* 30, no. 3 (Spring 1989): 163–78.
———. "Sasha Sokolov and Vladimir Nabokov." *Russian Language Journal* 41, no. 138–39 (1987): 153–62.
———. "The Galoshes Manifesto: A Motif in the Novels of Sasha Sokolov." *Oxford Slavonic Papers* 22 (1989): 155–79.
Johnson, D. Barton, ed. *Canadian-American Slavic Studies.* Special Issue Devoted to Sasha Sokolov, 2, no. 3–4 (Fall-Winter 1987).
Karriker, Alexandra H. "Double Vision: Sasha Sokolov's *School for Fools.*" *World Literature Today: A Literary Quarterly of the University of Oklahoma* 53 (1979): 610–14.
Kravchenko, Vladimir. "Uchitel' derzosti v shkole dlia durakov." *Literaturnaia gazeta,* 15 February 1995: 4.
Lipovetskii, Mark. "Mifologiia metamorfoz: Poetika 'Shkoly dlia durakov' Sashi Sokolova." *Oktiabr'* 7 (1995): 183–92.

Litus, Ludmilla L. "Sasha Sokolov's *Skola dlja durakov:* Aesopian Language and Intertextual Play." *Slavic and East European Journal* 41, no. 1 (Spring 1997): 114–34.

McMillin, Arnold. "Aberration or the Future: The Avant-Garde Novels of Sasha
Sokolov." In *From Pushkin to Palisandriia: Essays on the Russian Novel in Honor
of Richard Freeborn,* edited by Arnold McMillin. New York: St. Martin's Press,
1990: 229–43.

Moody, Fred. "Madness and the Pattern of Freedom in Sasha Sokolov's *A School for
Fools.*" *Russian Literature Triquarterly* 16 (1979): 7–32.

Simmons, Cynthia. *Their Father's Voice: Vassily Aksyonov, Venedikt Erofeev, Eduard
Limonov, and Sasha Sokolov.* New York: Peter Lang, 1993.

Smirnov, Igor P. "Geschichte der Nachgeschichte: Zur russisch-sprachigen Prosa der
Postmoderne." In *Modelle des literarischen Strukturwandels,* edited by Michael
Titzmann and George Jager. Tubingen: Niemeyer, 1991, 205–19.

Tumanov, Vladimir. "A Tale Told by Two Idiots: Krik idiota v 'Shkole dlia durakov' S.
Sokolova i v 'Shume i iarosti' U. Folknera." *Russian Language Journal* 48, no.
159–61 (Fall–Winter 1994): 137–54.

Vail', Petr, and Aleksandr Genis. "Uroki shkoly dlia durakov." *Literaturnoe obozrenie*
1–2 (1993): 13–16.

Zorin, Andrei. "Nasylaiushchii veter." *Novyi mir* 12 (1989): 250–53.

SOROKIN, VLADIMIR GEORGIEVICH (b.1955, in Bykovo [near Mos-
cow]) graduated from the Moscow Petroleum Institute and worked as a
graphic designer. Sorokin soon became known as a conceptual artist. In the
eighties, his literary texts, which developed the ideas of *Sots-Art* and *Conceptualism,* began to circulate in *samizdat.* Later they were published
abroad, mainly in Germany. Since perestroika, his works have been published in a variety of important journals, but it is worth noting that none of
the traditionally respected Russian literary "thick" journals *(Novyi mir, Znamia, Oktiabr', Druzhba narodov)* has ever published any of Sorokin's
works, although his leading role in Russian postmodernism is widely recognized. His destruction of the fundamental structures of literary communication, his games with the rhetoric of sex, cruelty, and physical pathology,
have made him unacceptable to the Russian literary establishment. Sorokin
is the author of numerous short stories, several plays, the generic hybrid
called *the Norm,* and the novels *The Queue, Marina's Thirtieth Love, Four
Stout Hearts, Roman* (this title can be translated as *A Novel* and as the name
of a protagonist, Roman), and *A Month in Dachau.* His novel *Four Stout
Hearts* was short-listed for the first Russian Booker Award in 1992. He
lives in Moscow.

## Works

"Doverie: p'esa v piati aktakh." In *Iazyk i deistvie (p'esy).* Moscow: Izd. R. Elinina,
1991.

*Norma.* Moscow: Obscuri Viri and Izdatel'stvo "Tri Kita," 1994.

*Ochered'*. Paris: Sintaksis, 1985.
*Roman*. Moscow: Obscuri Viri and Izdatel'stvo "Tri Kita," 1995.
"Serdtsa chetyrekh." *Konets veka*, Vol. 5. Moscow: 1994.
*Tridtsataia liubov' Mariny*. Moscow: Izd. R. Elinina, 1995.

## Translations

"A Business Proposition" (From *Four Stout Hearts*). Translated by Jamey Gambrell. In *Glas: New Russian Writing*, no. 2. Moscow, 1991: 23–45.
"Next Item on the Agenda." Translated from the Russian by Andrew Reynolds. In *The Penguin Book of New Russian Writing: Russia's Fleurs du Mal*, edited by Victor Erofeyev and Andrew Reynolds. London: Penguin, 1995, 321–44.
*The Queue*. Translated with an introduction by Sally Laird. New York: Readers International, 1988.
"Start of the Season." Translated by Sally Laird. In *Index on Censorship* 15, no. 9 (1985): 227–32.

## Secondary Literature

Binova, Galina. "Sotsart kak preodolenie utopicheski-ideinoi traditsii: Prozaicheskii variant: V. Sorokin, V. Erofeev, Z. Gareev." *Sbornik Praci Filosoficke Fakulty Brnenske University: Rada Literarnevedna* 43, no. 41 (1994): 107–14.
Gillespie, David. "Sex, Violence, and the Video Nasty: The Ferocious Prose of Vladimir Sorokin." *Essays in Poetics* 22 (Fall 1997): 158–75.
Kenzheev, Bakhyt. "Antisovetchik Vladimir Sorokin." *Znamia* 4 (1995): 202–5.
Kuritsyn, Viacheslav. "Svet netvarnyi." *Literaturnaia gazeta*, 1 February 1995: 4.
Lipovestkii, Mark. "Novyi 'moskovskii' stil': *Moskva* Vladimira Sorokina i Aleksandra Zel'dovicha i *Kul'tura dva* Vladimira Papernogo. Opyt parallel'nogo chteniia." *Iskusstvo kino* 2 (1998): 87–101.
Novikov, Vladmir. "Sorokin Vladimir Georgievich: I. Ditia sovetskogo veka; II. Topor Sorokina: Komu on strashen i komu net." In *Zaskok: esse, parodii, razmyshleniia kritika*. Moscow: Knizhnyi sad, 1997, 272–79.
Potapov, Vladimir. "Begushchie ot dyma: sots-art kak zerkalo i posledniaia stadiia sotsrealizma." *Volga* 9 (1991): 29–34.
Prigov, Dmitrii A. "A im kazalos': v Moskvu, v Moskvu!" In [*Stories*], by Vladimir Sorokin. Moscow: Ruslit, 1992, 114–20.
Roll, Serafima. "Stripping Socialist Realism of Its Seamless Dress: Vladimir Sorokin's Deconstruction of Soviet Utopia and the Art of Representation." *Russian Literature* 39, no. 1 (1996): 65–78.
Sokolov, Boris. "Dva litsa postsovetskoi literatury: O proze Iuriia Poliakova i Vladimira Sorokina." *Druzhba narodov* 6 (1997): 185–91.
Vail', Petr. "Konservator Sorokin v kontse veka." *Literaturnaia gazeta*, 1 February 1995: 4.

**SOTS-ART.** This idiosyncratic Russian version of Conceptualism is based on the whole-scale deconstruction of Soviet ideological language by presenting it as a language of a total metaphysical simulation. Sots-Art targets the hegemonic ambitions of Socialist Realism to substitute historical and everyday reality with its own symbolic discourse, reducing them to their logical extreme by creating a world where the characters actually live among the concrete manifestations of ideological language, where a communist slogan covers the actual horizon, and where Stalin is surrounded by the muses of antiquity. The term was invented by the artists Vitaly Komar and Alexander Melamid in the midseventies, but this kind of aesthetics had already developed in the art of Ilya Kabakov, Erik Bulatov, and Grisha Bruskin and in the poetry of Dmitri Prigov and Timur Kibirov; by contrast, its role in prose has been rather limited. In essence, the only true Sots-Art fiction writer is Vladimir Sorokin, although elements of Sots-Art play an important role in the works of Yevgeny Popov, Zufar Gareev *(Park)*, Anatoly Gavrilov, Arkady Bartov, Viktor Pelevin, and Sasha Sokolov's *Astrophobia.*

## Bibliography

Binova, Galina. "Sotsart kak preodolenie utopicheski-ideinoi traditsii: Prozaicheskii variant: V. Sorokin, V. Erofeev, Z. Gareev." *Sbornik Praci Filosoficke Fakulty Brnenske University: Rada Literarnevedna* 43, no. 41 (1994): 107–14.
Dobrenko, Evgeny. "Preodolenie ideologii." *Volga* 11 (1990): 168–88.
Epstein, Mikhail. *After the Future: The Paradoxes of Postmodernism and Contemporary Russian Culture.* Translated with an introduction by Anesa Miller-Pogacar. Amherst: University of Massachusetts Press, 1995.
Groys, Boris. *The Total Art of Stalinism: Avant-Garde, Aesthetic Dictatorship, and Beyond.* Translated by Charles Rougle. Princeton: Princeton University Press, 1992.
Kabakov, Ilia. "Kontseptualizm v Rossii." *Teatr* 4 (1990): 66–70.
Kholomogorova, O.V. *Sots-Art.* Moscow: Galart, 1994.
Letsev, Vladimir. "Kontseptualizm: chtenie i ponimanie." *Daugava* 8 (1989): 107–13.
Nekrasov, Vsevolod. "Kak eto bylo (i est′) s kontseptualizmom." *Literaturnaia gazeta* 31, 1990: 4.
Ratcliff, Carter. *Komar and Melamid.* New York: Abbeville Press, 1988.
*Russian New Wave.* 4 December 1981–28 February 1982. Contemporary Russian Art Center of America, New York. Mechanicsville, MD: Cremona Foundation, 1981.
*Sots Art: Russian Mock-Heroic Style: Semaphore Gallery.* New York, 4–28 January. The Gallery, 1984.
Tupitsyn, Margarita. *Sots Art: Eric Bulatov, Vitaly Komar and Alexander Melamid, Alexander Kosolapov, Leonid Lamm, Leonid Sokov, Kazimir Passion Group.* New York: New Museum of Contemporary Art, 1986.
———. "Sots-Art: The Russian Deconstructive Force." In *Sots-Art: The New Museum of Contemporary Art.* Catalogue of Exhibition, 1987, 4–15.
———. *Margins of Soviet Art: Socialist Realism to the Present.* Milan: Giancarlo Politi Editore, 1989.
Vasiliev, Igor′. "Russkii literaturnyi kontseptualizm." *Russkaia literatura XX veka: napravleniia i techeniia.* Ekaterinburg: Uralskii peduniversitet. Vyp. 3: 135–46.

TOLSTAYA, TATYANA NIKITICHNA (b.1951, in Leningrad) is the granddaughter of the prominent Soviet writer Alexei Tolstoy. She graduated from the School of Classical Philology at Leningrad State University and worked as an editor in an academic publishing house. Her first short stories were printed in 1983. From 1984 to 1991, she published over twenty stories, many of which were included in her collections *On the Golden Porch* (1987) and *Sleepwalker in a Fog* (1992) and have been recognized by many critics as the highest literary achievements of the perestroika period. Her stories are considered to be a return to the refined writing techniques characteristic of modernist metafiction, which had virtually disappeared in Socialist Realist culture. Starting in 1988, Tolstaya spent almost ten years as a professor of creative writing in various American colleges and universities. The publication of her works in the United States introduced her to the world's literary elite (*Partisan Review* proudly includes her name in the title list of their authors, along with such celebrities as Franz Kafka, Samuel Beckett, Albert Camus, William Faulkner, and Susan Sontag). In America, she also became known as a controversial publicist in *The New York Review of Books* and other newspapers, attacking feminism, American culture, and academia. She left the United States in 1997 and now spends most of her time in Moscow. Her essays are published in the leading Russian newspapers, especially *Russian Telegraph*. Known for her well-crafted short stories and essays, Tolstaya is said to have completed a large novel, which is being prepared for publication.

## Works

*Liubish'—ne liubish'.* Moscow: Olma-Press, 1997.
*"Na zolotom kryl'tse sideli . . .": rasskazy.* Moscow: Molodaia gvardiia, 1987.

## Translations

"Night." Translated by Mary F. Zirin. In *Glasnost: An Anthology of Literature under Gorbachev,* edited by Helena Goscilo and Byron Lindsey. Ann Arbor: Ardis, 1990, 187–94.
"Sonia." Translated by Nancy Condee. *Newsletter.* Institute of Current World Affairs, No. 17, 1988.
*On the Golden Porch.* Translated by Antonina Bouis. New York: Alfred A. Knopf, 1989; New York: Vintage International, 1990.
*Sleepwalker in a Fog.* Translated by Jamey Gambrell. New York: Alfred A. Knopf: distributed by Random House, 1992; New York: Vintage Books, 1993.
*Tri rasskaza/Three Stories.* Edited with introduction, bibliography, notes, and vocabulary by S. Dalton Brown. London: Bristol Classical Press; Newburyport: Available in United States and Canada from Focus Information Group, 1996.

## Secondary Literature

Alagova, Tamara; Nina Efimov; and Michael A. Aguirre, trans. "Interview with Tatyana Tolstaya." *World Literature Today* 67, no. 1 (Winter 1993): 49–53.

Givens, John. "Reflections, Crooked Mirrors, Magic Theatres. Tat'iana Tolstaia's 'Peters.'" In *Fruits of Her Plume: Essays in Contemporary Russian Women's Culture,* edited by Helena Goscilo. Armonk, NY: M.E. Sharpe, 1993, 251–70.

Goscilo, Helena. *The Explosive World of Tatyana N. Tolstaya's Fiction.* Armonk, NY: M.E. Sharpe, 1996.

Patrusheva, Elena. "Tatiana Tolstaya." *Soviet Literature* (Moscow) 2, no. 467 (1987): 169–174.

Piskunova, S., and V. Piskunov. "Uroki sozerkal'ia." *Oktiabr'* 8 (1988): 188–98.

Rich, Elisabeth. "Tatyana Tolstaya." *South Central Review* 12, no. 3–4 (Fall–Winter 1995): 84–91.

Vail', Petr, and Aleksandr Genis. "Gorodok v tabakerke: Proza Tat'iany Tolstoi." *Sintaksis* 24 (1988): 116–31.

Vasilevskii, Andrei. "Nochi kholodny." *Druzhba narodov* 7 (1988): 256–58.

Zolotonosov, Mikhail. "Mechty i fantomy." *Literaturnoe obozrenie* 4 (1987): 58–61.

THAW (*OTTEPEL'*). The period known as the "Thaw," which takes its name from Ilya Ehrenburg's 1954 novel of the same name, lasted from 1956 through 1968. The roots of the Thaw can be found in the Twentieth Communist Party Congress in 1956, when Nikita Khrushchev read his famous "secret speech" that signaled the beginning of the so-called "struggle with Stalin's cult of personality." The Thaw constituted a series of attempts to liberalize the Soviet system inherited from Stalin, and it ended in 1968 with the Soviet invasion of Czechoslovakia and the suppression of the "Prague Spring," a far more thorough and radical reform program than the Soviet Thaw. The Thaw was a period of great contradictions: Liberal reforms were combined with an aggressive propaganda campaign for Communist ideology and with the persecution of freethinkers. Nonetheless, the liberal atmosphere of the period allowed for the formation of a new generation of the Soviet intelligentsia, one that espoused anti-totalitarian ideals (*shestidesiatniki*—the generation of the sixties). The spiritual leaders of this generation were Alexander Solzhenitsyn, Andrei Sakharov (both of whom actually belonged to an older generation but only became known during the Thaw), and Andrei Siniavskii (Abram Tertz). When the reforms of the Thaw came to an end under Brezhnev (1964–82), this same generation would become the core of the political opposition (the dissidents) and the third wave of emigration. In literature and art, this generation was represented by such poets as Vladimir Vysotsky, Yevgeny Yevtushenko, Andrei Voznesensky, Bella Akhmadulina, and Bulat Okudzhava; by such prose writers as Vladimir Dudintsev, Vladimir Tendriakov, Chingiz Aitmatov, Vasily Aksyonov, Yuz Aleshkovsky, Andrei Bitov, Vladimir Voinovich, Georgy Vladimov, Anatoly Gladilin, and Fazil Iskander; and in film and theater, by such directors as Andrei Tarkovsky, Yuri Lyubimov, Marlen Khutsiev, Larisa Shepitko, Andrei Konchalovsky, and Tengiz Abuladze.

Despite the fact that the aesthetics of the "sixties generation" was oriented primarily toward the traditions of Russian realism, this generation played a crucial role in the history of Russian postmodernism—especially in the works of Aksyonov and Aleshkovsky. The Thaw generation is defined more by ideology than by demographics. For example, Joseph Brodsky or Sergei Dovlatov, who are the same age as Yevgeny Yevtushenko and Andrei Voznesensky, do not belong to the generation of the Thaw, because they never had any illusions about the possibility of "improving" socialism on the basis of humanist values and because they never shared the almost religious belief in the ideals of the revolution that was typical of Thaw culture on the whole.

## Bibliography

Alekseeva, Liudmila. *The Thaw Generation: Coming of Age in the Post-Stalin Era.* Pittsburgh: University of Pittsburgh Press, 1993.

Altshuller, Mark, and Elena Dryzhakova. *Put' otrecheniia.* Tenafly: Hermitage, 1985.

Apukhtina, Vera. *Molodoi geroi v sovetskoi proze: 60–e gody.* Moscow: Znanie, 1971.

Chuprinin, Sergei. "Non-Past Time: On the Traits of the 'Thaw' Period in the History of the Contemporary Literary Process." *Russian Studies in Literature* 28, no. 4 (Fall 1992): 4–21.

Elberg, Mariam Z. "Children as Portrayed by Soviet Prose Writers During the Period of the 'Thaw.' " Dissertation Abstracts International, Ann Arbor, vol. 33, 1972: 750A.

Gibian, George. "Soviet Literature during the Thaw." In *Literature and Revolution in Soviet Russia, 1917–62: A Symposium,* edited by Max Hayward and Leopold Labedz. London: Oxford University Press, 1963, 125–49.

*Ottepel': stranitsy russkoi sovetskoi literatury.* Compilation, introductory article, and "chronology" by S.I. Chuprinin. Vols. 1–3. Moscow: Moskovskii rabochii, 1989.

Rogers, Thomas F. *"Superfluous Men" and the Post-Stalin "Thaw": The Alienated Hero in Soviet Prose During the Decade 1953–1963.* The Hague: Mouton, 1972.

Sivokhina, T.A. *Apogei rezhima lichnoi vlasti, "Ottepel'," Povorot k neostalinizmu: obshchestvenno-politicheskaia zhizn' v SSSR v seredine 40-kh–60-e gody.* Moscow: Izdatel'stvo Moskovskogo universiteta, 1993.

Vail', Petr, and Aleksandr Genis. *60–e: Mir sovetskogo cheloveka.* Moscow: Novoe Literaturnoe Obozrenie, 1996.

**VAGINOV, KONSTANTIN KONSTANTINOVICH** (real last name: Vagingeim; 1899 [St. Petersburg]–1934 [Leningrad]). Poet and novelist. His novels *The Goat Song* (translated as *The Tower*) (1928), *Bambochada* (1931), and especially *The Works and Days of Svistonov* (1929) are examples of Russian modernist metafiction with a certain prepostmodernist twist. His recurring theme is the death of culture in postrevolutionary Russia. Consequently, the process of literary creation becomes for his characters a travelogue into the land of the dead, and the works of art become a manifestation of death itself. He was close to the absurdist OBERIU group (see

*Kharms*). Although his works were rejected by official Soviet criticism, they were published in the twenties and thirties at least once, thus allowing the writers of the postmodernist generation to get acquainted with his metafiction several decades before the large-scale republication of Vaginov's works in postcommunist Russia.

## Works

*Kozlinaia pesn'; Trudy i dni Svistonova; Bambochada. Garpagoniana.* Compiled by A.I. Vaginovoi; introduction by T.L. Nikolskoi; edited by T.L. Nikolskoi i V.I. Erlia. Moscow: "Khudozhestvennaia literatura," 1991.
*Opyty soedineniia slov posredstvom ritma.* Leningrad: Izdatel'stvo pisatelei v Leningrade, 1931; Moscow: Izdatel'stvo "Kniga," 1991.
*Puteshestvie v khaos.* Ann Arbor: Ardis, 1972.

## Translations

*Tower.* Translated by Benjamin Sher. In http://members. xoom.com/sher07/index.html.

## Secondary Literature

Bohnet, Christine. *Der metafiktionale Roman: Untersuchungen zur Prosa Konstantin Vaginos.* Munich: O. Sagner, 1998.
Gerasimova, A. "Trudy i dni Konstantina Vaginova." *Voprosy literatury* 12 (1989): 131–66.
Heyl, Daniela von. *Die Prosa Konstantin Vaginovs.* Munich: O. Sagner in Kommission, 1993.
Kibal'nik, Sergei. "Konstantin Vaginov i literaturnyi Petrograd. *Neva* 5 (1996): 197–201.
Marcialis, Nicoletta. "Il canto del capro." *Il Verri: Rivista di Letteratura (Verri)* 29–30 (1983): 139–43.
Mazur, Nataliia "Trudy i dni neizvestnogo literatora." *Literaturnoe obozrenie* 9 (1990): 56–58.
Purin, Aleksei. "Opyty Konstantina Vaginova." *Novyi mir* 8 (1993): 221–33.
Rippl, Daniela. "Die Erotik der Autor-Stadt: Zu Konstantin Vaginovs Kozlinaja Pesn'." In *Auto(r)erotik: Gegstandslose Liebe als literarisches Projekt,* edited by Annette Keck and Dietmar Schmidt; introduction by Sabine Kyora. Berlin: Schmidt, 1994, 69–84.
Silard, Lena. "Pushkin v zerkale avangardnykh travestii." In *The Contexts of Aleksandr Sergeevich Pushkin,* edited by Peter I. Barta and Ulrich Goebel. Lewiston, NY: Mellen, 1988, 11–24.
Ugrešić, Dubravka. "Avangard i sovremennost': Vaginov i Kabakov: Tipologicheskaia parallel'." *Russian Literature* (Amsterdam) 27, no. 1 (1990): 83–96.
Zavalishin, Viach. "Proza i stikhi Konstantina Vaginova." *Novyi Zhurnal/The New Review* 157 (1984): 283–90.

**VILLAGE PROSE.** An influential movement in post-Stalinist Soviet literature represented by such writers as Vasily Belov, Valentin Rasputin, Vasily Shukshin, Viktor Astafiev, Fyodor Abramov, and Boris Mozhaev. Early manifestations of Village Prose can be found in the fifties in works by Vladimir Soloukhin and Valentin Ovechkin, and especially in Alexander Solzhenitsyn's novella "Matryona's House" (1962). Village Prose opposed Socialist Realism with overt traditionalism, focusing on the ideals of patriarchal peasant Russia, an implicit critique of Stalinist collectivization, and the pursuit of religion. The philosophy of Village Prose is based on the search for metaphysical values, a concern for the environment, and a nostalgia generated by the loss of traditional rural life; these values are accompanied by a harsh criticism of urban life as immoral and corrupting, by a hatred for the Western, and by a form of nationalism that often verges on chauvinism. In the early eighties, the authors of Village Prose were highly esteemed by Soviet officials: The retrospective nationalistic utopia of Village Prose served as a complement to the decayed Communist utopianism of Soviet ideology. Since perestroika, leading representatives of Village Prose, such as Vasily Belov and Valentin Rasputin, have become spokesmen for radical right-wing, almost fascist ideological movements.

## Bibliography

Belaia, Galina. "The Crisis of Soviet Artistic Mentality in the 1960s and 1970s." Selected Papers from the Fourth World Congress for Soviet and East European Studies, Harrogate, 1990. In *New Directions in Soviet Literature,* edited by Sheelagh Duffy Graham. New York: St. Martin's Press, 1992, 1–17.

Clark, Katerina. "Zhdanovist Fiction and Village Prose." In *Russian Literature and Criticism,* edited by Evelyn Bristol. Berkeley: Berkeley Slavic Specialties, 1982, 36–48.

Dhingra, K.S. "Contemporary Soviet Prose about Village: Some Characteristics." In *Studies in Russian Literature,* edited by J.V. Paul. Hyderabad: Central Institute of English and Foreign Languages, 1984, 101–7.

Dunlop, John B. "Ruralist Prose Writers in the Russian Ethnic Movement." In *Ethnic Russia in the U.S.S.R.: The Dilemma of Dominance,* edited by Edward Allworth. New York: Pergamon, 1980, 80–87.

Gillespie, David C. *Valentin Rasputin and Soviet Russian Village Prose.* London: Modern Humanities Research Association, 1986.

———. "Apocalypse Now: Village Prose and the Death of Russia." *The Modern Language Review* 87, no. 2 (1992): 407–17.

Gizemann, Gerkhard. "'Proshchanie s Materoi' Valentina Rasputina i zapadnoevropeiskaia teologiia." In *Deutsch-russische Sprach-, Literatur- und Kulturbeziehungen im 20. Jahrhundert,* edited by Herbert Jelitte and Margot Sobieroj. Frankfurt: Peter Lang, 1996, 45–56.

Hosking, Geoffrey A. "The Russian Peasant Rediscovered: 'Village Prose' of the 1960s." *Slavic Review* 32 (1974): 705–24.

Nepomnyashchy, Catharine Theimer. "Our Contemporary and the Development of the Rural Prose Tradition." *Ulbandus Review: A Journal of Slavic Languages and Literatures* 1, no. 2 (Spring 1978): 58–73.

———. "The Search for Russian Identity in Contemporary Soviet Russian Literature."

In *Ethnic Russia in the U.S.S.R.: The Dilemma of Dominance*, edited by Edward Allworth. New York: Pergamon, 1980, 88–97.

Parthé, Kathleen F. *Russian Village Prose: The Radiant Past.* Princeton: Princeton University Press, 1992.

Petrik, A.P. " 'Derevenskaia proza': Itogi i perspektivy izucheniia." *Filologicheskie nauki* 1, no. 121 (1981): 65–68.

Starikova, Elizabeta. "The Sociological Aspect of Contemporary 'Village Prose.' " *Soviet Studies in Literature* 26, no. 1 (Winter 1989–90): 41–67.

Vil'chek L. "Vniz po techeniiu derevenskoi prozy." *Voprosy literatury* 6 (1985): 36–75.

YOUTH PROSE is a movement of young writers in the sixties (see *Thaw*), most of whom made their literary debut in the journal *Iunost'* (Youth), edited from 1955 to 1960 by Valentin Kataev. Youth Prose was represented by such authors as Vasily Aksyonov, Anatoly Kuznetsov, Anatoly Gladilin, Vladimir Voinovich, Fazil Iskander, Andrei Bitov, and Yurii Kazakov. They were greatly inspired by Western modernist writers (Hemingway and Salinger were the most influential). The major theme of the "youth" writers was the rebellion of young heroes who try to cleanse themselves of the bloody Stalinist past and win individual freedom. The ironic and playful language of Youth Prose was filled with colloquialisms and slang, which represented a breath of fresh air for Soviet literature at the time. Some critics define this movement as an attempt to resurrect the revolutionary utopia on the basis of humanism and freedom ("Socialist Realism with a human face"). Others retrospectively consider Youth Prose to be prepostmodernist: "Alienated from their parents and the traumatic past with which they identify them, youth prose characters are doomed to search for authentic experience and originality in the 'cool universe' where good and evil, the sacred and the profane, official culture and underground subculture appear perilously undifferentiated" (Spieker 1996: 35). The end of the Thaw caused profound disillusionment and despair for the writers of the Youth Prose movement (as documented most vividly in Aksyonov's novel *The Burn*), and many of the major figures in Youth Prose eventually emigrated to the West.

## Bibliography

Altshuller, Mark, and Elena Dryzhakova. *Put' otrecheniia.* Tenafly: Hermitage, 1985.

Apukhtina, Vera. *Molodoi geroi v sovetskoi proze: 60–e gody.* Moscow: Znanie, 1971.

Hassanoff, O. *The Style of Molodaja Malaja Proza.* Ph.D. dissertation, Alberta, 1978.

*Ottepel': stranitsy russkoi sovetskoi literatury.* Compilation, introduction, and "chronology" by S.I. Chuprinin. Vols. 1–3. Moscow: Moskovskii rabochii, 1989.

Rogers, Thomas F. *"Superfluous Men" and the Post-Stalin "Thaw": The Alienated Hero in Soviet Prose During the Decade 1953–1963.* The Hague: Mouton, 1972.

Spieker, Sven. *Figures of Memory and Forgetting in Andrej Bitov's Prose: Postmodernism and the Quest for History.* Frankfurt am Main, Berlin, Bern, New York, Vienna: Peter Lang, 1996.

# Index